P9-CMQ-761

THE FEDERAL SUBSIDY BEAST

The Federal Subsidy Beast

The Rise of a Supreme Power
in a Once Great Democracy

Brian J. Finegan

ALARY PRESS
2000

Copyright © 2000 by Brian J. Finegan

Published by Alary Press

All rights reserved. No part of this publication may be reproduced, stored in a retrieval system, or transmitted, in any form or by any means, electronic, mechanical, photocopying, recording, or otherwise, without prior permission except in the case of brief quotations embodied in critical articles and reviews. For information address Alary Press, P O Box 827, Sun Valley, ID 83353.

Printed in the United States of America

Cataloging-in-Publication Data

Finegan, Brian J.
    The federal subsidy beast : the rise of a
supreme power in a once great democracy / Brian J.
Finegan. – 1st ed.
        p. cm.
        Library of Congress Catalog Card Number: 99-96399
        ISBN: 0-9674445-1-9
        Includes bibliographical references and index

        1. Subsidies—United States   I. Title

HC79.S9F56 2000   338.973'02
                                        QBI99-1451

To my grandchildren . . . should I have any.

Contents

Acknowledgements

Over the nine years that this book was researched, I collected so many reports from the U.S. General Accounting Office that my office and an adjoining room took on a blue hue. Not once, during all that time, did my wife, Donna, say I was crazy—although I am quite sure that is what she was thinking. I am very grateful for her support and her excellent work in proof-reading.

John Carey, Ernest Fitzgerald, and Michael Tanner provided valuable input on the manuscript. I learned much from Lynn Kincannon and Shellie Hurrle, and my book is all the better for their editing.

Had I not come upon a General Accounting Office report in 1988, this book might not have happened. Nor would it have been possible without the thousands of GAO reports I have received since then. They were my primary source of information, and I have gained a deep respect for that agency's fine work. I am also very grateful that I was born in a country where an agency like the GAO is not only allowed to publish its frequently critical reports, but is also funded by the government it criticizes.

Selected Abbreviations

AFDC, Aid to Families With Dependant Children
AEC, Atomic Energy Commission
BOR, Bureau of Reclamation
BLM, Bureau of Land Management
BMD, Ballistic Missile Defense
BUR, Bottom-Up Review
CAFÉ, Corporate Average Fuel Efficiency
CBO, Congressional Budget Office
CFSA, Consolidated Farm Service Agency
COLA, Cost of Living Adjustment
CPI, Consumer Price Index
DI, Disability Insurance
DOD, Department of Defense
ESEA, Elementary and Secondary Education Act
EPA, Environmental Protection Agency
FAA, Federal Aviation Administration
FDIC, Federal Deposit Insurance Agency
FEMA, Federal Emergency Management Agency
FEO, Federal Energy Office
FHA, Federal Housing Administration
FHWA, Federal Highway Administration
FICA, Federal Insurance Contributions Act
FHLMC, Federal Home Loan Mortgage Corp.
FmHA, Farmers Home Loan Admin.
FNMA, Federal National Mortgage Assoc.
GAO, General Accounting Office
GDP, Gross Domestic Product
GNP, Gross National Product
GNMA, Government National Mortgage Association
GSE, Government Sponsored Enterprise
HCFA, Health Care Financing Admin.
HEW, Health, Education and Welfare
HFCS, High Fructose Corn Syrup
HHS, Health and Human Services
HI, Hospital Insurance
HTF, Highway Trust Fund
IG, Inspector General
ISTEA, Intermodal Surface Transportation Efficiency Act
IRS, Internal Revenue Service
ISS, International Space Station
ITC, International Trade Commission
MX, MX Missile

NASA, National Aeronautics and Space Administration
NEA, National Education Association
NHS, National Highway System
NPR, National Performance Review
NSC, National Security Council
NSLP, National School Lunch Program
NPPC, Northwest Power Planning Council
O&M, Operations and Maintenance
OEC, Organization for Economic Cooperation
OIG, Office of Inspector General
OMB, Office of Management and Budget
OPEC, Organization of Petroleum Exporting Countries
OTS, Office of Thrift Supervision
OVS, Offer Versus Serve
PAC, Political Action Committee
PBG, Pension Benefit Guarantee Corp.
PHA, Public Housing Authority
PMA, Power Marketing Administration
QDR, Quadrennial Review
R&D, Research and Development
REA, Rural Electrification Administration
RFG, Reformulated Gasoline
RTC, Resolution Trust Corporation
RUS, Rural Utilities Service
S&L, Savings and Loan
SBA, Small Business Administration
SBSP, State Based Subsidy Plan
SDI, Strategic Defense initiative
SO_2 Sulfur Dioxide
SS, Social Security
SSI, Supplemental Security Income
TANF, Temporary Assistance for Needy Families
TSM, Tax Systems Modernization
TVA, Tennessee Valley Authority
THAAD, Theater High-Altitude Defense
TSPIRS, Timber Sale Program Information Reporting System
TSSAM, TriService Standoff Attack Missile
USDA, U.S. Department of Agriculture
USFS, U.S. Forest Service
VA, Veterans Administration
VAT, Value Added Tax
WIC, Special Supplemental Food Program for Women, Infants, and Children

1

ICEBERG, DEAD AHEAD

Never in human history has so much been spent by so many for such a negative result. The cost of the lesson has been high, but we have learned that it is not only what we spend that matters; it is the way we spend it. Beyond this we confronted a collapse in confidence in government itself, a mounting distrust of all authority that stemmed in large measure from the increasing inability of government to deliver its services or to keep its promises.

That statement was from a speech by President Richard Nixon to the National Governor's Conference on September 1, 1969. However, it could have been made by any subsequent president; nearly all have made essentially the same statement. Therein lies the problem: for the past thirty years, federal politicians have been saying the same things over and over, but remarkably little has changed. During that period, Republicans and Democrats have each controlled Congress and held the Presidency. The post-Watergate and Con-tract-With-America revolutions sent large numbers of reformers to Congress, determined to change the way things were done in Washington. But what they found was what all those elected to federal office discover: you do not change Washington, it changes you. The federal government has a powerful immune system that protects it against agents of change. Those that persist have their political careers terminated. How did a nation founded on such noble principles, with such attention to insuring that real power remained in the hands of the people, end up with its elected representatives essentially powerless? There are two problems: subsidies and size, the second problem being largely due to the first.

In 1999, federal spending exceeded $1,700,000,000,000, that is $1.7 trillion.[1] To achieve that, millions of federal workers dispensed an average of $6.5 billion, five days per week, for the entire year. How many federal workers are there? According to calculations by Paul C. Light of the Brookings Institution, the federal government employs seventeen million people, almost equal to the population of Australia, directly and indirectly.[2] Perhaps the most vivid statistic is that the expenditures of the U.S. government exceed the entire national economy of every other nation in the world except China and Japan.[3]

Quite simply, it is a behemoth, the likes of which have never been seen before and likely will never be seen again.

It is difficult to imagine an area in which the federal government is not involved. It regulates and/or subsidizes what you eat and drink, what and where you may smoke, your clothing, what you sleep on (recall the "DO NOT REMOVE UNDER PENALTY OF FEDERAL LAW" tags on your pillows), where you live, what you live in, where you drive, what you drive, your employer and working conditions, labor unions, doctors, hospitals, schools and colleges, sports leagues, telecommunications, banks, financial markets, television and radio stations, trucks, buses, airlines, trains, air, water, farms, pigs, chickens, cattle, fish, birds, insects, guns, bombs, tanks, aircraft carriers, and the list goes on and on. The Herculean effort required to accomplish all that is reflected in the *Federal Register,* where all new regulations are recorded. It is estimated that between 1990 and 1999, over 613,000 pages were added to the *Federal Register* through the dedicated efforts of 125,000 federal regulators.[4] That is in addition to the 1,440,756 pages dating from 1940 to 1989.[5]

All the business and management experts at the nation's top universities do not have the capability to effectively manage the U.S. government. It simply cannot be done. The federal government is a tangle of millions of workers involved in tens of thousands of disparate tasks, operating with thousands of incompatible accounting and computer systems. Some very capable managers have attempted to straighten out individual agencies with precious little success. For example, over the past twenty years, we have had a succession of accomplished men serve as Secretary of Defense. They all knew that there were very serious problems and each went into the job determined to straighten things out. None of them succeeded. Government auditors have been reporting for decades that the Department of Defense (DOD) has tremendous inventory problems. But in 1997, the U.S. General Accounting Office (GAO) reported that the DOD still had $34 billion worth of unneeded supplies.[6]

The GAO reported in 1992, and again in 1995, that the $200 billion Medicare program was, "highly vulnerable to waste, fraud, abuse, and mismanagement;"[7] nonetheless, the Department of Health and Human Services Inspector General discovered in 1996 that there were $23.2 billion in overpayments.[8] Similarly, the $22 billion Supplemental Security Income program administered by the Social Security Administration was found to have $2.3 billion in overpayments outstanding in 1996.[9] The U.S. Department of Agriculture (USDA) operates a plethora of programs to assist farmers, one of which is a farm loan program. The GAO reported that at the end of 1996, 34% of the direct loans were delinquent.[10] That was good news—a year earlier, 41% were delinquent.[11] Unfortunately, much of the improvement was a result of the USDA writing off a significant number of delinquent loans.

Even small agencies have big problems. The Federal Aviation Administration (FAA) controls the air traffic in the U.S. In 1981, the agency initiated a plan to modernize and automate the Air Traffic Control System by the year 2000. The program has been a disaster, fraught with cost overruns, schedule delays, and performance shortfalls that now threaten the safety of air travel.

Through 1998, Congress had appropriated $23 billion of the program costs, which are now projected to exceed $42 billion.[12] The GAO has issued numerous reports on the program's problems over the years and in 1997 stated that the modernization effort

> . . . requires an effective organizational structure, disciplined investment management processes, reliable data upon which to base important decisions, a well defined architecture, or blueprint, to guide and constrain system development and evolution, and a healthy organizational culture.[13]

That seems a good, straightforward recommendation for any organization, but here is the distressing part: After many years, billions of dollars, and dozens of reports highlighting the problems, the GAO concluded that, "Our recent work shows that the FAA is not meeting any of the above cited requirements."[14]

These are just a few examples; you will find many more throughout the book. The question they suggest is: Are federal agencies staffed with incompetents? As in any organization, there are certainly some. Moreover, since federal employment places workers in a noncompetitive environment where tenure reigns supreme, there are unquestionably some government workers who could contribute considerably more than they do. However, it is unlikely that there is a significant difference in the capabilities of the average government worker and one employed in the private sector. It is clear that agencies often do not have sufficiently skilled people to achieve their missions, but that is a management problem, not a problem inherent in government workers.

Management is certainly a serious problem with federal agencies. Consider the statements of two Americans eminently qualified on the subject of federal management practices. The first was made by Donald R. Wurtz, Director of Financial Integrity Issues at the GAO, testifying before a House Ways and Means Subcommittee:

> Time and again over the past decade, our management reviews and audits in federal agencies have shown that the processes and systems fundamental to well run organizations are often not present. Most agencies have developed neither a strategic vision for the future nor good systems to collect and use financial and program information to gauge operational success and accountability. Many agencies do not have people with the skills needed to accomplish their missions.[15]

This statement was made by then Comptroller General of the United States, Charles A. Bowsher, before a Senate subcommittee:

> Over the years, our work has identified extensive management problems across the spectrum of federal activities: important program objectives are not being met, funds are wasted, major

*projects are over budget and behind schedule, and monies due
are not collected. These problems have existed for many years
and efforts to correct them have resulted in incremental improvements to the overall system of management, such as better
cash and debt management. But in too many cases, management
problems persist long after they have been brought to light and
long after agencies have agreed to correct them.*[16]

These pervasive and long-standing problems are not Democratic problems or Republican problems, and neither party has been able to make any significant progress toward resolving them. Over the last thirty years, both parties
have had their opportunities, although they have not exactly strained themselves—the House of Representatives scheduled only 89 days of legislative
work in 1998.[17] Certainly, as we will see later in this book, many of these
problems work to the benefit of politicians. As such, there has been no real
interest in Washington in resolving them, although serious, yet unsuccessful,
attempts have been made to resolve others. Compounding the questionable
resolve of federal politicians is the competence and tenure of the political appointees who run these ponderous federal departments and agencies. Even
when people with outstanding capabilities are chosen to head agencies, they
require considerable time to learn the intricacies of their new job directing the
spending of tens or hundreds of billions of taxpayer dollars. Then they leave.
The GAO has found that senior, federal political appointees spend an average
of 2.1 years on the job—hardly enough time to do much with a giant bureaucracy resistant to change. In addition, political appointees are most often chosen
for their politics rather than their management skills, and the results reflect the
selection criteria.

While it is likely that most the nation's best and brightest managers are
lured to private employment by the specter of making millions, many government managers would do quite well in the private sector. The government certainly spends enough trying to manage its workforce—$40 billion a year ac-
cording to the National Performance Review headed by Vice President Al
Gore.[18] (That review was the 500th such study since 1900.[19]) Unfortunately, it
is not the people, it is the system. Congress passes legislation regularly that
gives contradictory directives to federal agencies. It has created mind-boggling
procedures and reporting requirements. Moreover, politicians often make life
difficult for agency managers who crack down on waste or abuse that is benefiting favored constituents. The federal government has simply grown into an
entity too large, too complex, and with far too many perverse incentives to operate effectively.

The next question, then, is: How did we get into this mess? Without a
doubt, the answer is the relentless creation and expansion of federal subsidy
programs. We have a long history of subsidizing powerful interest groups. In
the early 1800s, the government began passing agricultural subsidies to protect
American farmers from foreign competition. Congress passed a sugar subsidy

in 1816, which raised the price Americans had to pay for sugar to double the world market price. That prompted Henry Lee to write in 1832:

> *Admit the principle, that a particular class of men or a particular state has a right to government aid, for the prosecution of a business, which could not be prosecuted without it, and there is no limit to the rightful claims of individuals and states.*[20]

Lee had observed over 150 years ago that opening the U.S. Treasury to those who claimed that the competition was too tough was to open it to all. History has proven him quite right. Subsidies now make up nearly 60 percent of the budget and have become *the* business of the federal government.

The debates among the nation's Founders clearly show that they were not only opposed to direct government subsidies (as opposed to tariffs, which cost the consumer, not the government), but considered the possibility of the federal government ever offering them to be so remote as to be laughable. As such, while they designed a number of constraints on federal power, they failed to limit its power to subsidize. That has proved to be a fatal flaw. If the Founders could see the extent of the federal government's involvement in every aspect of Americans' lives and the extraordinary amount of money it spends on those endeavors, they would surely roll over in their graves.

The Social Security Act of 1935 ushered in the modern subsidy era. In addition to Social Security, this act also created Aid to Families with Dependent Children (AFDC), which was replaced in 1997 by the Temporary Assistance for Needy Families program. Even with these programs, subsidies were still a relatively small proportion of federal spending until the Great Society programs of the 1960s, when subsidies became the primary business of the U.S. government. Social Security was greatly expanded, as was AFDC. Moreover, in 1965, two new programs, Medicare and Medicaid, were created. The Medicare program was the nation's first significant venture into health care subsidies, and it met with considerable opposition, with good reason. The program, which its proponents claimed would only cost a few billion each year, cost $208 billion in 1997.[21]

As the seventies and eighties unfolded, the federal dollars spent on subsidies skyrocketed. While Ronald Reagan represented himself as a fiscal conservative, subsidies flourished during his administration. Indeed, one of our largest subsidy programs, the defense budget, expanded dramatically under Reagan. Although we need a strong defense, one-third to one-half of all defense expenditures are nothing more than handouts to favored interests with no real military purpose; they are simply subsidies. Conservatives did not limit access to the U.S. Treasury to defense interests. Farm subsidies, without a doubt some of the most wasteful programs, reached all time highs while Ronald Reagan was president. Even worse was the explosion in the one federal expenditure that buys absolutely nothing—interest on the national debt.

The government receives no goods or services for the interest it pays. The payments largely transfer wealth from the middle class to American and foreign investors. In 1980 when Reagan took over the White House, interest payments amounted to $75 billion, or 12.7 percent of the federal budget. When Reagan left in 1988, that had jumped to $214 billion, or 20.1 percent. During the next four years under George Bush, interest payments rose further to $292 billion and comprised 21.1 percent of federal expenditures.[22] Of course, both presidents needed, and obtained, the approval of a solidly Democratic Congress for these dubious achievements. The point is that the self-proclaimed conservatives, the Republicans, should have been the party more likely to cut subsidies, but when they had the chance, they did just the opposite. Regardless of which party is in power, subsidies will continue to grow; it is only a question of which will grow the fastest.

In the late sixties and early seventies, when subsidy programs were growing by leaps and bounds, it became apparent to politicians, bureaucrats, and subsidy interests that there was no penalty whatsoever if a subsidy program turned out to cost far more than was projected. In short order, virtually all new programs resulted in costs far exceeding the modest amount projected by their sponsors. For example, the 1965 projection for 1990 Medicare hospital insurance expenditures was $9 billion—actual cost: $67 billion. In 1987, the projected annual cost for Medicaid special hospital subsidies was $100 million—actual 1993 cost: $11 billion.[23] B-1 bombers (a pure subsidy program) were projected to cost $37 million each—actual cost: $330 million and still climbing. For thirty years, everyone in Washington has known that once a subsidy program is passed, it will almost certainly be continued, regardless of cost.

If honest attempts were made to estimate program costs, one would expect the distribution of actual outlays to show some results higher, some lower, and some on target. Such a variation of results would be consistent with the imprecision inherent in predicting future outcomes. Even allowing for unforeseen growth, one might expect to see some programs exceed estimates by as much as fifty percent. However, it is a near certainty that any federal program will cost far more than projected and cost overruns of five hundred percent or more are not uncommon. This cannot be coincidental. Rather, it reflects the insidious strategy of greatly understating the projected costs and overstating the benefits of proposed programs to insure passage. The strategy has worked like a charm. However, it also introduced deception as a standard and acceptable practice in Congress, and that marked the beginning of the end of effective government.

The present system might have a chance if it were simply a matter of getting better people to run for federal office, but it is not. The people in Congress are largely intelligent and, at least initially, well intentioned. But things go downhill in a hurry. Once they are part of the system, they become infected by it, and power politics displaces ideology—regardless of the individual involved or the party. In discussions with several Senators and Congressmen who were retiring at the end of 1994, *U.S. News & World Report's* Gloria Borger found that, "Uniformly they express relief at leaving a system that works to misdirect or bury their own moral compass."[24]

It does not take most newly elected Congressmen or Senators long to realize the truth about their institutions. After they adjust to the shock of finding that they have very little say about anything, they quickly recognize that any notions they had about reforms or cutting spending were naive dreams. The federal system runs the show, and those who would get ahead join the system. Nearly all do, and then they get down to the real work of federal politicians: subsidies. They are the fuel that supplies the power to the federal system. The power to subsidize is a narcotic that few have been able resist, and once hooked, it is virtually impossible to break the habit.

Like most addicts, those in Congress have tried every conceivable scheme to hide the cost of their habit. The press has frequently used the euphemism "smoke and mirrors" to describe the budgetary actions of Congress, but the correct term is fraud. In 1990, Congress claimed credit for passing a budget that cut the federal deficit by $500 billion over five years. Then they claimed that the 1993 budget cut another $500 billion over five years. The truth is that the two budgets produced $2 trillion in *additional* federal spending.[25] The U.S. Congress annually passes legislation that would constitute criminal fraud if done by a public corporation. It is not an exaggeration to say that Congress lies and cheats; and they do it year after year, to the detriment of the nation. Mark Twain's reference to Congress as the only native American criminal class was only partly in jest.

In fairness, Congress has made some efforts to force discipline upon itself. The 1990 Budget Act put real limits on future spending. Nevertheless, as is always the case, the politicians simply found a way around them. Reductions in defense spending were diverted to increased domestic spending instead of deficit reduction, and again the politicians resorted to fraud. The law provided for exemptions from the spending caps for national emergencies, so Congress began calling all sorts of spending "emergencies" and, just like that, the spending limits no longer applied. Through 1996, Congress had declared almost $40 billion in spending to be emergencies, thereby making a mockery of the law.[26] In October 1998, anticipating a budget surplus for 1999, Congress passed a budget that included $20 billion worth of "emergency" spending—from the hypothetical surplus.[27] There was no emergency; it was simply another dishonest action to evade the spending caps. The deception that started by routinely understating the cost of subsidy programs has become institutionalized.

Until recently, the pace of creating new subsidy programs slowed because the runaway costs of existing programs already had the nation on a path to bankruptcy. Attempts have been made to reduce spending for existing programs, but they have hardly made a dent. Both Republicans and Democrats have made modest efforts, but the federal system, consisting of politicians, federal bureaucracies, and subsidy beneficiary groups, is a runaway train with no brakes. During the first Clinton Administration, Labor Secretary Robert Reich set out to consolidate the 154 frequently overlapping federal job training programs—a $25 billion bureaucratic jungle that the General Accounting Office found to be poorly managed.[28] However, all those redundant programs represent a gravy train for powerful politicians and federal bureaucrats, and Reich was set straight. There would be no consolidation. Bureaucrats and interest groups are pouring coal to the engine of the gravy train, and few politicians have any stomach for a heroic, and likely fatal, rescue. Rather, most find the ride exhilarating.

The Founders intended the voters to be the ultimate check on runaway government, but as each successive election has produced another batch of politicians and policies indiscernible from the last, increasing numbers of Americans have dropped out of the political system in disgust. A 1991 study by the Kettering Foundation found that Americans are not apathetic about politics as is widely believed. Rather, they are angry and frustrated; many no longer believe they live in a democracy.[29] While theoretically the public still has the ultimate power, in reality, the U.S. government is now beyond the control of the voters.

It is an axiom of American politics that to be elected or reelected, politicians have to support a broad array of subsidies, many of which are well known to serve no useful purpose beyond lining the pockets of political supporters. Political commentators matter-of-factly refer to opposing a major subsidy as "political suicide." They fully accept that a politician *should* vote for wasteful subsidies important to powerful (spelled M-O-N-E-Y) interests. It is one more indicator of our sorry state of affairs: trading federal dollars for power is widely accepted, even by the media—once a potent government watchdog. It is so acceptable, in fact, that the number of registered lobbyists and lawyers (unregistered lobbyists) in Washington more than tripled in the fifteen years prior to 1987.[30] Many of these lobbyists trade power for federal subsidies and then recycle a portion of the subsidies back to the politicians in the form of campaign contributions. All very neat, and no one has to commit political suicide.

The recycling of a portion of subsidy benefits back to supportive politicians is one of the most corrosive aspects of American politics. It is tantamount to paying politicians commissions on the subsidy benefits they produce, and it has provided subsidy interest groups with an ironclad grip on Congress. It is ironic that the groups most often associated with special interest politics, political action committees (PAC's), were created by campaign finance reform legislation in the wake of the bags-full-of-cash campaign fundraising scandal during the Nixon Administration. Now, we find that the creations of the last reform are possibly worse than that which was reformed. We need more reform, but it will not help; as long as subsidy programs control Congress, no reform will be effective.

Unfortunately, seats in Congress are won primarily based on how much money is spent campaigning, a testimony to the fact that Americans see little difference between Republicans and Democrats. When *Business Week* analyzed Federal Election Commission records for the 1996 House of Representatives races, they found that 83 percent of challengers who spent more than $1 million were successful, but only 3 percent of those spending less than $500,000 unseated the incumbent.[31] This sad state of affairs assures permanent control of Congress by subsidy interests. Raising a $1 million campaign war chest for a House seat is no easy feat and is virtually impossible without substantial contributions from subsidy interests. They are in a very good position to help friendly politicians—those that support their subsidy—because they have large amounts of subsidy dollars to work with. All they need do is recycle a small portion to buy an insurance policy for their unearned federal benefits. Should an incumbent become "unfriendly," a sufficient amount of funding for a friendly challenger will usually do the trick. The new congressman can then be put on commission to insure a long, friendly relationship. Perhaps to a somewhat slightly lesser extent, the same scenario applies to the Senate, only the numbers are considerably larger. The only role the voters play in this arrangement is to pay the taxes that fund the subsidy programs and to respond appropriately to the television campaign-advertising blitz.

One of the few differences between Democrats and Republicans is the subsidies they primarily support. Republicans tend to favor business while Democrats prefer social subsidies, but the issue is not if there should be more subsidies, but which ones. The compromise that is generally reached is to support all subsidies. It is a rare piece of legislation that does not include some subsidy provision, and subsidies are the primary purpose of most. Once passed, a subsidy very seldom ends, regardless of the perverse effects that the program produces. If unintended consequences result, it is likely that the politicians will create a new subsidy program to offset the negative results of the first—if one subsidy does not produce the desired result, pass another, but keep the first.

There is no power to be had from ending subsidies, and precious few campaign contributions, but plenty of both are associated with virtually any new subsidy. By discounting the people who will pay for the new subsidy, which politicians almost always do, they create a story in which all ends happily. The politician has more money and power, and another interest group has a brand new government handout. According to a study by the National Taxpayer's Union, during the first eight months of 1991, if all the bills proposed by the 435 members of the House were passed, government spending would have increased by $491 billion or 35 percent.[32] If all the bills introduced by the 100 Senators became laws, spending would have increased by $429 billion. The bills introduced in both houses would have spent an average of $43 for every dollar saved. Since very few new taxes were proposed, the vast majority of this new spending would have been additional deficit spending. Only one of the 535 members of Congress in 1991, Virginia congressman Herbert Bateman, proposed legislation that would have resulted in less government spending. It is clear that the business of Congress is subsidizing, not governing.

Politicians find it particularly easy to handout government money because, at least in appearance, subsidies help some deserving group. For example, a program that pays subsidies to cotton farmers ostensibly helps those farmers to raise their crops, and the smiling politicians take pride in lending a helping hand. By ignoring the fact that the vast majority of the money is given to a handful of very wealthy farmers to raise surplus cotton and that much of the money is taken from middle class taxpayers, the charitable image of the subsidy can be maintained. The question of why middle class Americans should be taxed to subsidize the wealthy is not asked. And should it be suggested that the large campaign contributions that those wealthy farmers make are little more than commissions paid to the politicians for the subsidies they deliver, it will be indignantly denied by all involved. Nevertheless, the connection could not be more direct; if the subsidies were to stop so would the contributions.

Is all this, as disquieting as it is, any real reason for concern? Very much so. The U.S. government is producing less and less public benefit from increasing amounts of money and that cannot continue indefinitely. It is only because of the extraordinary wealth of this land and the productivity of the American people, that the nation has performed as well as it has in recent decades. However, the wealth accumulated by past generations of Americans is being depleted. Trillions of dollars worth of roads, bridges, schools, parks, and other inherited public properties are being allowed to deteriorate as tax dollars are increasingly used to support bureaucracies, handouts, and consumption. At the same time, we have gone deeply into debt and are expending shameful amounts of tax revenues on interest. At $356 billion in 1997, interest on the national debt came within $6 billion of passing Social Security to become the single largest item in the federal budget.[33] In the not too distant future, our children and grandchildren will have to pay with a declining standard of living and it is doubtful whether our society will be able to withstand the pain.

At this point, even if we are just to provide our children with the quality of life that we enjoy today without a crushing tax load, our present system of government will have to change very soon. In June 1994, Robert Reischauer, Director of the Congressional Budget Office, testified that if present government policies continue, future generations will face an 80 percent net tax rate.[34] This heavy tax burden would not pay for benefits for themselves. Rather, it would be necessitated by the irresponsible spending of the present generation. However, no one can possibly believe that future generations will agree to pay anything remotely close to an 80 percent tax rate. Rather, they will throw off the yoke and make the very sensible decision to seek subsidies rather than working and having most of their wages taxed away. Naturally, we will demand the government benefits that we are "entitled to" and that the younger generation provide the taxes to pay for them. The inevitable result will be an intergenerational war that no one can win.

It is the very real prospect of just such a grandparent-against-grandchild conflict that demands we address our problems now. We do not have a great deal of time left. In August 1994, Senator Bob Kerrey, Chairman of the Bipartisan Commission on Entitlement and Tax Reform, flatly stated: "In 2012, when today's young children are just getting started in the labor force, there will not be one cent left over for education, children's programs, highways, national defense, or any other discretionary program."[35] Added Vice-chairman John Danforth: "We are on a course to national bankruptcy."[36] When the Commission disbanded, unable to come up with any plan to restrain subsidy spending, Senator Dale Bumpers commented, "We all know the problem is not unsolvable, it's just not politically palatable to do it."[37]

While the booming economy of the late 1990s has significantly brightened the deficit picture, it is only a temporary reprieve. We face the same problems, only a few years later. As we will see in Chapter Ten, the 1998 and 1999 budget "surpluses," which brought on a self-congratulatory orgy by federal politicians, were achieved through an accounting gimmick. In August 1998, the CBO issued a report showing that even with the projected budget surpluses, the national debt will skyrocket beginning around 2030.[38] Shortly thereafter, the national debt becomes unserviceable. In its January 1999 report, the agency suggested that if the much-ballyhooed surpluses do materialize—a very unlikely scenario—the nation's financial crisis could be postponed by twenty years.[39] Not solved, just postponed. In February 1999, David M. Walker, Comptroller General of the United States, in testimony before the House Ways and Means Committee stated,

Eventually, again assuming no program or financing changes, Social Security, health, and interest take nearly all the revenue the federal government takes in by 2050. This is true even if we assume that the entire surplus is saved and these continued surpluses reduce interest from current levels.[40]

With Democrats proposing to fund a plethora of new subsidy programs from the still hypothetical surpluses and Republicans pushing for major tax cuts, plan on the crisis arriving sooner rather than later.

We are intentionally passing on a huge debt and social welfare burden to our children because we simply refuse to deal with our own problems. Over two hundred years ago, Thomas Jefferson stated that, "we should consider ourselves unauthorized to saddle posterity with our debts, and morally bound to pay them ourselves," but we have chosen to ignore those tenets that are not self-serving. The plain truth is that we are selling our children into involuntary servitude so that we can shirk responsibility for the dysfunctional government that we have created and continue to consume more than we earn.

On a cold night in 1912, lookouts on the opulent and unsinkable ship, Titanic, spotted an iceberg when it was still more than a mile away. It takes a long time to change the course of a huge, fast-moving ship, and there was not enough time to avoid the tragic collision. Most of the wealthy survived, most of the rest did not. We are passengers on the largest ship of state ever, and like the Titanic, many are convinced they are aboard an unsinkable ship. However, there are no unsinkable ships, and there is a very large iceberg, dead ahead.

2

SUBSIDIES: THE BEST OF INTENTIONS

In 1816, Congress legislated a three-cent-per-pound tariff on imported sugar to protect several hundred southern sugar plantation owners from tough import competition.[1] The Merchant Marine Act of 1936 established subsidy programs to help maintain U.S. flag-ships as a naval auxiliary in time of war or national emergency.[2] The Mining Law of 1872, which allows free mining on federal lands, was enacted to promote the exploration and development of domestic mineral resources.[3] And the federal government has enacted over one hundred fifty job-training programs to assist adults and out-of-school youth.[4] Subsidies are almost always instituted with good intentions.

Nevertheless, few programs ever achieve their noble objective, and those that become somewhat successful, most often do so at an unjustifiable expense to American taxpayers and consumers. For over two hundred years, Congress has been subsidizing sugar growers, and rather than eliminating these senseless subsidies, Congress added a subsidy for maple sugar producers in the 1998 Supplemental Appropriations bill.[5] If the objective was to insure a long history of wealthy sugar producers, the program could be called a great success. However, between 1980 and 1988, the sugar subsidy program cost American consumers and taxpayers about $2 million for each domestic sugar grower.[6] The program that originated to protect wealthy, southern plantation owners still assures that sugar producers will be wealthy today by forcing Americans to pay about twice the world price for sugar. Between 1991 and 1995 the average world price of sugar was 11.5 cents per pound while the U.S. government forced American consumers to pay an average of 22.1 cents per pound.[7] The Commerce Department estimates that these generous subsidies cost American consumers about $3 billion each year.[8] Since 1816, Americans have had to pay tens of billions of dollars extra to obtain a readily available commodity, produced by 110 countries in the world, including 70 that export.[9] This great forced transfer of wealth has been largely from the poor and middle class to a small group of millionaires. Indeed, the GAO estimates that a single

Florida sugar producer, Flo-Sun, received $65 million in just one year due to the sugar subsidy program.[10]

The federal government has gone to great lengths to insure that American sugar producers have their cake and eat it, too. Sugar is used as a sweetening, preserving, and fermenting agent in a variety of processed food products. Because American manufacturers must pay twice the world price for sugar, their baked and confectionery goods are at a competitive disadvantage with foreign producers who buy sugar at half the price. To aid domestic producers, the government initiated the Sugar-Containing Products Re-Export Program in 1984.[11] This program allowed them to buy foreign sugar at world prices for use in products that would be re-exported within eighteen months. Thus, a cake baked at a given plant destined for sale in Chicago must use expensive, subsidized sugar, while an identical cake baked at the same plant for export can contain half-price foreign sugar. The U.S. government is forcing Americans to pay a higher price for an identical product so that only Americans, not foreigners, are charged to support wealthy American sugar growers.

Still not satisfied, and concerned that import restrictions alone might not result in a high enough price for domestic sugar producers, Congress enacted legislation in 1990 to insure that Americans continue paying the highest price in the world for sugar. The new law, which takes effect if domestic supply and demand come too close to being in balance, establishes marketing allotments.[12] It essentially gives the U.S. Department of Agriculture (USDA) the power to order growers to let a portion of their crop rot in the fields to contrive a supply-demand imbalance to inflate prices. In September 1994, the agency announced that it was establishing allotments for 1995, exposing processors to stiff penalties for selling more domestically produced sugar than that allowed by USDA bureaucrats. Violators were subject to civil penalties equal to three times the value of the "outlaw" sugar they sold.[13] The regulation authorized a fine to be imposed by the U.S. government on a U.S. company for selling a legal, harmless, and useful product, which was produced in the United States. Let there be no doubt about the extent to which the government is willing to go to guarantee the wealth of sugar producers, nor should there be any doubt about who is underwriting the multi-billion dollar annual cost. Meanwhile, Flo-Sun, the Florida sugar producer that has received hundreds of millions of dollars in sugar subsidies, has recycled at least $3 million of that back to politicians of both parties since 1979.[14] A commission by any other name is still a commission.

The second law passed by the U.S. Congress was the Tariff Act of 1789,[15] and one of its primary purposes was to subsidize American cargo ships by requiring that certain cargoes be carried on U.S.-flag ships. We have been subsidizing the U.S. merchant marine ever since, presently under the Merchant Marine Acts of 1920 (Jones Act) and 1936. The objective of these statutes was to ensure that an adequate and viable merchant marine is maintained (1) to serve as a naval auxiliary in time of war or national emergency, and (2) to carry a substantial portion of U.S. domestic and foreign waterborne commerce.[16] One is inclined to credit the legislators with sensible work, but a closer look reveals another program which failed miserably to achieve its objectives, but succeeded in channeling billions of dollars from American taxpayers and consumers into the pockets of wealthy ship owners.

In support of the effort to maintain a naval auxiliary as provided in the Merchant Marine Acts, American taxpayers spent an average of $710 million per year between 1989 and 1993 to subsidize foreign shipments on American ships.[17] However, the Department of Defense does not view the ships used as militarily useful.[18] And DOD has determined that it would only need 3,700 of the present 21,000 mariners in the merchant marine labor pool, so the 800 mariners associated with the subsidized, militarily useless ships are not needed either.[19] In short, the subsidy program contributes nothing to maintaining a naval auxiliary.

As for the second objective, U.S.-flag ships carry about four percent of the nation's ocean borne international trade, nowhere near a "substantial portion."[20] Rather than contributing to a "viable merchant marine," the GAO stated, "Thus, cargo preference laws make it possible for U.S. ship owners to maintain inefficient and commercially noncompetitive U.S.-flag ships . . . ." The Jones Act requires all shipping between American ports to be on U.S. ships, thereby eliminating foreign competition, but at a very heavy cost. The International Trade Commission (ITC), an agency of the U.S. government, calculated the subsidy cost of the Jones Act to be $3.09 billion per year to protect 11,905 jobs, a cost to American consumers of nearly $260,000 per job each year.[21] While eliminating the subsidies would cause the loss of those jobs, the increased volume of shipping resulting from the lower prices would create 12,709 new jobs.[22] The Jones Act is costing Americans over $3 billion per year and resulting in a net job loss, but over sixty years after its passage, it is still the law. The subsidies mandated by the Maritime Acts completely failed to achieve their objectives, indeed they were counterproductive, but they force Americans to pay $3.2 billion each year to wealthy ship owners.

In 1872, Congress was anxious to develop the mineral wealth of the west, and it passed one of this nation's most lucrative subsidies. If a miner found valuable minerals on the 688 million acres of federal lands,[23] he could take the minerals for free, and he could buy the land containing the strike for $2.50 to $7.50 per acre. It is possible that the law may have made sense in 1872, but over 125 years later, the same deal is still available. It is federally sanctioned grand larceny.

The GAO estimated that as of 1990, $65 billion worth of hard rock minerals (mostly gold and silver) had been found on federal lands, but was not yet mined.[24] The owners of that land and the minerals, the American people, will not receive one dime for the gold and silver taken from their property, just as they have not been paid for the tens of billions of dollars worth mined already. If the minerals were on private property, a miner would pay an 8-12 percent royalty, and that property could only be purchased at a price reflecting the surface and mineral values of the land. But mining companies, many of them foreign owned, are being given the minerals and the land—three million acres so far[25]—virtually free by the federal government, a multi-billion dollar subsidy.

In 1994, a Canadian company, American Barrick Resources Corporation, bought 1,949 acres of federal land in the Nevada desert for $9,745—$5 an acre.[26] The land contains an estimated 22.5 million ounces of gold worth about $9 billion.[27] At about the same time, a South African company bought another 1,018 acres in Nevada for $5,090, containing an estimated $1.1 billion in gold.[28] Additionally, a Montana company paid $10,000 for land containing an estimated $32 billion worth of platinum and palladium.[29] The $5 per acre is all the American people will ever get for the billions of dollars of their property "sold" to these companies by the federal government. Another company bought 17,000 acres in Colorado for $42,500—only $2.50 per acre—and immediately sold it for $37 million.[30] Now that is a real estate deal. The few thousand dollars that the taxpayers receive for their extremely valuable properties does not even cover the government's cost to transfer title to the land. In reality, tens of billions of dollars worth of public property is simply being given away.

In 1990, there were about 1.2 million mining claims on federal lands.[31] While $65 billion worth of hard rock minerals had been identified as of 1990, this undoubtedly represented a small fraction of the hundreds of billions in gold, silver, and platinum that the federal government plans to give away. Would these mining companies pay a royalty if they had to? Absolutely. Most western states charge a royalty on minerals mined on state lands which often border royalty-free federal lands. Is there any reason to sell the land at all, much less give it away? None whatsoever.

The majority of the 1.2 million federal mining claims will never be mined because they do not contain economically recoverable amounts of minerals. And most will not result in dirt-cheap sales of public property because the mining operations will create such a horrendous environmental mess that the operators will simply pack up and leave once they have taken the minerals. They will not want any part of the contaminated land.

Once a mining claim is registered with the Bureau of Land Management (BLM), the miner has the legal right to use the property for mining purposes indefinitely as long as he pays an annual fee of $100. The miner need not take title to the land to mine it, and the vast majority of miners do not bother because then they can get away without "reclaiming" the land. Reclaiming refers to the expensive process of restoring the land after the necessarily substantial disturbances caused by the mining process. Both the U.S. Forest Service and the BLM, the two agencies that administer the lands where nearly all hard rock mining takes place, have regulations requiring mine reclamation, but neither agency takes these regulations very seriously. Consequently, miners literally get the gold and the public gets the shaft. The Mineral Policy Center has estimated that it would cost between $32.7 billion and $71.5 billion to clean up abandoned hard rock mine sites.[32] That cost will have to be paid by the public because the miners are long gone. Even if the taxpayers had received a 10% royalty on the 2,094 tons of gold that the BLM reports was mined between 1982 and 1992,[33] it would have been a mere $2.3 billion, a pittance compared to the clean-up bill. The Mining Law of 1872: another senseless subsidy for which the public is paying dearly.

For many years, federal politicians have held firmly to the belief that economically disadvantaged Americans only need employment training to enable them to join in the American dream. It is one of those simple ideas that seems intuitively obvious. In support of that belief, they have enacted training programs by the dozen. As one after another failed to achieve its objective, Congress simply added more programs. Despite the evidence that individual programs were not working, they were continued; the idea behind them seemed so sensible that politicians felt that they simply had to work. In October 1994, Labor Secretary Robert Reich told Congress that the Job Corps, one of the largest employment training programs, was "one of the jewels in the crown of our work force investment system."[34] This is the same program that Labor Department studies show places only 12 percent of its sixty thousand annual enrollees in the vocational jobs for which they are trained at a cost to the taxpayers of $23,000 each.[35] The program wastes about a billion dollars each year training fifty-three thousand people for occupations that they will not work in. Yet it qualifies as one of the training program "jewels."

By 1994, the GAO had concluded that every year, "at least 154 programs administered by 14 federal departments and agencies provide about $25 billion in employment training assistance."[36] Note that even the GAO could not determine exactly how many programs exist. By any measure, the extraordinary duplication involved is stunning. Consider these GAO findings:[37]

- Sixty-five of the programs served the economically disadvantaged.
- Forty-eight programs targeted out-of-school youth under twenty-two years of age.
- Ninety programs provided career counseling and assessments.
- Seventy-five programs provided occupational training.

At $25 billion dollars per year, these employment programs constitute one of the federal government's largest areas of expenditures and the GAO has found that the number of training programs continues to grow.[38] A taxpayer looking at the sheer number of programs with the same objectives might intuitively suspect that there simply has to be a great deal of waste involved, and indeed, there is. It is very possible that most of that $25 billion is wasted because the GAO found that,

> . . . these agencies do not know whether their programs, as currently configured, are providing assistance that results in participants getting jobs. Even when the participants get jobs, agencies do not know whether employment resulted from participation in the program or if participants would most likely have found the same types of jobs on their own, without federal assistance.[39]

Additionally, the GAO found that the training programs are difficult for job seekers and employers to access, they overlap and duplicate one another, and they fail to meet client needs.[40] Worse, the agency found little reason to expect significant improvements. The staffs of various similar programs are reluctant to coordinate and share information because they compete for funding.[41] Moreover, agency staffs generally do not welcome change—they find it threatening.[42] It is difficult to imagine a more damning assessment of a group of subsidy programs consuming $25 billion each year, yet rather than terminate these programs, Congress continues to fund them and adds new ones almost yearly.

These unrelated subsidies, from sugar to employment, reveal the characteristics consistently found in virtually all federal subsidies:

- Proposed programs sound wonderful and create public perception that the cost of the program to each individual taxpayer is insignificant.
- Regardless of the efficacy, cost, or consequences, subsidy programs are permanent.
- Program costs are much higher than anticipated because the target group expands significantly in response to the subsidy. The true costs and benefits are obscured, either deliberately by the beneficiaries and administering agencies, or by the complexity created by numerous and overlapping programs.
- The programs very seldom achieve their intended purpose, or do so only at extraordinary and unjustifiable cost.
- Unintended consequences frequently require additional subsidy programs.
- Programs are often counterproductive, exacerbating the problem they were intended to alleviate.
- They sustain uneconomic activities and reduce national income by protecting the least efficient and incompetent producers, while effectively constraining the output of the most efficient.

Let us look at these characteristics a little closer.

Perception

Subsidies arise as a remedy to a "problem" for some group of Americans. At one time, they were usually passed in response to, what was at least thought to be, a situation which had some negative ramifications for the nation as a whole. However, in recent decades, federal subsidies have been routinely handed out to groups solely for their benefit and with the full knowledge that they were not in the best interests of the nation. But there is still an attempt to make the subsidy appear to benefit the public. For instance, Pembroke Rathbone, Director of the American Sugarbeet Growers, claims that, "The sugar program is operated primarily for the benefit of the consumer. It guarantees the consumer a reliable supply at a reasonable cost."[43] In reality, the world is perennially awash in cheap sugar.

Subsidy beneficiaries are usually a relatively small group compared to the number of taxpayers or consumers who are footing the bill for the subsidy. As such, the perception is that a large number of people will pay an insignificant price to provide a substantial benefit to a small group of fellow Americans. This perception is crucial to the passage of the subsidy because the process involves government forcibly taking money from some citizens and giving it to others who are not performing a service in return. This concept is very difficult to defend unless the recipients are receiving basic subsistence aid that they are unable to provide for themselves. However, that is very seldom the case. Federal expenditures in 1993 for the basic cash welfare program, Aid to Families with Dependent Children (AFDC), amounted to $12.3 billion, less than 1 percent of the federal budget.[44] And all the various welfare programs funded by the federal government, excluding Medicaid, came to only 7 percent of the budget.[45] While many of these are failed and wasteful programs, they are not *the* cause of the nation's budget woes, as many Americans believe.

The vast majority of the hundreds of billions of dollars in annual federal subsidies go to those perfectly able to provide for themselves—which is inherently unjustifiable. Thus, the importance of the *perception* that any given subsidy provides substantial benefits to the few at virtually no cost to the many. It makes what largely amounts to government enforced larceny sound harmless. It still might not be an issue if there were only a few subsidies; however, when you are paying a little for each of the hundreds of federal subsidies now in existence, the size of your total bill is a major issue.

Subsidies Are Forever

Regardless of their original objective, once passed, it is almost a certainty that a subsidy program will go on indefinitely. Among the subsidy programs passed under the New Deal in the 1930s was the Rural Electrification Administration (REA). Its objective was to bring electric power to rural areas of America and it accomplished that mission very well. By 1973, the REA had subsidized the development of both electric and telephone service to virtually all of rural America, and President Nixon sought to cut funding for the agency. But the fact that the agency had fulfilled its mission made little difference to Congress, which took the agency off-budget to protect it from a Nixon impoundment[46] Congress again interceded when President Reagan attempted to cut the REA budget in 1981.[47] In 1994, at least twenty-five years after the agency, renamed the Rural Utilities Service, had ceased to have a reason to exist, it made $1 billion in subsidized loans and cost the taxpayers $150 million in direct spending.[48] And not for isolated farm communities. Citizens Utilities Company in Stamford, Connecticut, located thirty miles north of New York City, earned $108 million for the first nine months of 1994, thanks in part to over a billion dollars in subsidized REA financing.[49]

There is no argument about whether the agency has or has not succeeded in achieving its objective, nor is there a question of pressing need. Rather, the basis for the continued funding is that those who have benefited from the subsidies simply want the subsidies continued. They have found it very convenient and beneficial for the rest of America to pay part of their electric bill. Congress accommodates them year after year, just as it has the sugar producers for nearly two centuries. The day after Congress enacts a subsidy program, the reasons for its passage cease to be relevant. The beneficiary group has been given the right to take part of their fellow Americans' income, which they quickly come to consider their own. And Congress agrees with them.

Pass a Subsidy and They Will Come

In theory, subsidies are passed to help alleviate some problem that a group of citizens is having. The affected interest group, whether it be homeowners, farmers, or the unemployed, are usually well defined and identifiable. This should enable the legions of federal bureaucrats and staffers to project a cost for a given subsidy program based on the proposed benefits and the number of expected recipients. However, despite all the available data and resources, the projected costs seldom come within a cannon shot of being accurate—they always miss on the low side. The fact that the sponsors of a proposed subsidy invariably underestimate the actual program cost clearly indicates built-in biases in the procedures used to produce cost estimates.

The most obvious bias is that intentionally underestimating the cost makes passage of the program easier in a competitive budget environment. The Pentagon and defense contractors consider it an article of faith that all projected costs are low-balled. Then too, assumptions about how the program will be administered, and the efficiency of program operations are, as a rule, wildly optimistic. These biases are hardly surprising given that the bureaucrats and politicians who propose the subsidies stand to benefit directly in terms of increased budgets, votes, and political contributions.

Another major reason why actual program costs greatly exceed projections is that far from reducing the problem targeted by the subsidy, the availability of the subsidy attracts more people to the "problem." No doubt the most spectacular case was President Johnson's 1965 estimate of $500 million annually for Medicare,[50] which actually came in at $208 billion in 1997.[51] Congress set out to subsidize a few hundred sugar producers, but now the government forces Americans to transfer billions of dollars to 1,705 sugarcane growers and 13,731 sugar beet farmers[52]—virtually all of them far wealthier than the average American. Indeed, how could they not be?

Subsidies attract people like picnics attract flies. While that seems like a simple enough idea, it is lost on Congress. Through two centuries and a myriad of subsidy programs (nearly all of them still in existence), Congress seems not to have learned the simple fact that subsidies create their own constituencies. The programs seldom reduce the scope of the targeted problem, but they always expand the base of those deemed affected by it. As such, they inherently expand to the limit of available funding. And, as the number of beneficiaries increases, their growing political power puts added pressure on politicians to increase funding. It does not take long for the number of beneficiaries to reach critical mass. At that point, their subsidies are sufficiently large that they can organize to recycle a small percentage—but nonetheless a substantial amount of money—back to the politicians in the form of campaign contributions to assure program immortality. Their objective then becomes to freeze the system in place and avoid cutbacks or reforms, no matter how sensible. As Peter Drucker notes,

> *The single cause group derives its power from being a minority, and usually a very small one. Its strength lies in its single purpose rather than in numbers. Its task is almost never to get something done. It is to stop, to prevent, to immobilize.*[53]

In this manner, the National Electric Cooperative Association has preserved the Rural Utilities Service and their subsidies despite widespread recognition that the agency has long since outlived its purpose.[54]

The Subsidy Tangle

Subsidy programs seldom end, while new ones are added regularly by Congress. Thus, some activities are subsidized by so many different programs that no one inside or out of government knows the total subsidy being received by beneficiaries, or the total cost of all the subsidies being provided. Clearly, that is the case with employment training programs. In trying to evaluate the jumble of 154 programs, the GAO found that, "In some instances, the relationships between the programs was so close that it was difficult to determine which program was providing which services to the client."[55] Moreover, less than 60 percent of the programs could provide accurate data on how many people they were serving,[56] much less who they were serving. So, not only do we not know if these programs are actually helping, we do not know how many people they are trying to help and how much is being spent per person. The GAO was able to ascertain that the aggregate cost of all 154 programs was $25 billion, a great deal of taxpayer money. But we know little about who is getting what for all that money, or why.

As little as we know about training subsidies, it is vastly more than we know about the cost of agricultural subsidies, where programs have been piling up for two centuries. Government budget figures show that in 1996, farm income stabilization cost $17.7 billion,[57] and that is the figure that farm interests and their proponents point to as the cost of agricultural subsidies. However, that is just the tip of the iceberg. Most agricultural subsidies simply are not counted or are not classified as subsidies. For instance, as we have seen, the government restricts the supply of sugar and imposes import tariffs on foreign sugar to force domestic prices higher. Thus, American sugar producers are paid artificially high prices due to government action, but the government does not collect and redistribute the money. Rather, it is paid directly by consumers in the marketplace. Because the government is not involved in the money transfer, sugar subsidies are not counted in the official farm price support figures.

In support of American agribusiness, the U.S. Department of Agriculture (USDA) spends more than $55 billion annually[58] and maintains fifteen thousand offices,[59] including operations in almost every one of the nation's 3,150 counties.[60] The 108,000 USDA employees [61] provide an astounding array of services, unheard of in any other sector of the economy, to the farm sector. In addition, other federal departments provide still more services such as heavily subsidized irrigation water. Yet none of these are categorized or counted as subsidies; the costs are simply classified as domestic discretionary spending. How much do the taxpayers really spend on the dozens of programs that subsidize agriculture? No one knows, but it certainly far exceeds the figure reported in the federal budget.

Shameful Success

Some subsidies are far more successful than their architects ever imagined. That is, the target group receives benefits far exceeding what is necessary to alleviate their original "problem." But these programs can only be considered successes as long as the cost of the program is either understated or ignored. Certainly, the prime example of such a program is Social Security. It is quite remarkable to still hear some politicians refer to Social Security as a model social program or the most successful program in the history of this country. The basis for these assessments is that it has largely eliminated poverty among the elderly. Nevertheless, if a program can be a success regardless of cost, then we can solve all our problems with lavish spending; just mail a generous government check to all Americans seeking government help. Simplistic foolishness aside, someone has to pay to fund all subsidy programs, try as we might to evade the responsibility by deficit spending. And we are well aware of who that someone is: our children and grandchildren.

Social Security has created a window of windfall that began in 1940 and will end shortly after the year 2000. Retirees who make the window will receive benefits wildly out of proportion to their contributions, while those who miss the window will receive less than they contributed and, ultimately, little or nothing if the system collapses. And the system is headed for collapse. While Social Security is said to be running a surplus, it has a staggering unfunded liability that will be our legacy to our children. Consider the following prediction by former Social Security Commissioner Dorcas R. Hardy for Social Security spending,

> *Expenditures will double every ten years until we talk about trillions the way we used to talk about billions . . . benefit payments in 1991 were $275 billion; they will be $500 billion at the turn of the century, and $20 trillion by 2050.*[62]

But where will tens of trillions of dollars come from? Seniors in 2040 and 2050 will demand the benefits they are entitled to, just as today's seniors do, but there are only IOU's in the Social Security trust fund. Those trillions will have to be paid through punishing tax rates on workers in 2040 and 2050. However, those presently too young to vote and those not yet born will reject tax slavery, violently if need be, long before the bill gets to $20 trillion. Nonetheless, it appears that we intend to use Social Security to confiscate their earnings for as long as we can. The proper word for such a policy is shameful, not successful.

Unintended Consequences Beget Additional Subsidies

The Mining Law of 1872, termed the "Last Great Giveaway" by *Newsweek*,[63] is one of America's richest subsidies, but it is also one of the primary sources of growth for a relatively new, government-sponsored industry, hazardous waste management. Nearly all of the $15 billion in revenues chalked up by this industry in 1991 came from tax dollars.[64] The Mining Law is another "successful" program in that it did induce hundreds of thousands of miners to take free minerals from federal lands. For over a century, miners have taken the valuable minerals and frequently left an environmental disaster behind. In 1996, the GAO attempted to determine how many abandoned mines there were, but it concluded, "there is no definitive inventory available."[65] Yet many subsidized mines are continuing to create serious public health and safety risks which will require additional tax dollars to clean up. As is nearly always the case, getting something for nothing precludes responsibility.

It has long been known that acids and toxic metals from mining operations have been poisoning water supplies and wildlife. Fish in the Carson River in Nevada are still contaminated with mercury from Comstock mining operations over a century ago.[66] But it is just in recent years that the full magnitude of the problem has become known. An Environmental Protection Agency (EPA) Report to Congress estimated that non-coal mining generates about as much hazardous waste as all other industries combined.[67] That is a truly staggering prospect, especially when you consider that 18,846 manufacturers, reported (under requirements of the Emergency Planning and Community Right-to-Know Act) releasing seven billion pounds of toxic substances into the environment in 1987.[68] That is just a portion of American industry. According to the EPA then, non-coal mines are producing more than seven billion pounds of toxic waste per year.

These poisons threaten the water supplies of millions of Americans. Wastes from the Iron Mountain Mine near Redding, California, deliver an average daily dose of 4,800 pounds of iron, 1,466 pounds of zinc, 423 pounds of copper, and 10 pounds of extremely toxic cadmium into the Keswick Reservoir on the Sacramento River.[69] The reservoir is the city of Redding's water supply. The Clark Fork, Montana's largest river, was virtually sterilized along its ninety mile length by toxic mine wastes. Nearly all the pollution came from the vast Anaconda copper mines on federal lands, purchased for $2.50 an acre from the federal government.[70]

The EPA estimates that there are 557,650 abandoned hard rock mines in the nation that, along with active mines, are pouring poisons into ten thousand miles of streams.[71] The tens of billions of taxpayer dollars that it will take to clean up this mess are, in effect, another subsidy for the mining industry. As noted earlier, cleaning up the hazardous waste from these mines could cost over $70 billion.[72] The father of the 1872 Mining Law, Nevada Senator William Stewart, may well have intended that his great giveaway of federal property would bring wealth to miners at public expense. However, he surely could not have intended that taxpayers also spend many billions of dollars to reclaim their own land and remove toxic waste from their drinking water.

Unfortunately, this is not an uncommon scenario with federal subsidy programs. A well-intended subsidy produces unintended consequences requiring further subsidies to correct. The new subsidy program results in the creation of an industry specifically to mitigate the problems resulting from the initial subsidy. That new industry soon becomes a significant employer and a powerful interest group, enabling them to insure the immortality of the new program. Be assured that the multi-billion dollar toxic waste industry will do everything in its power to protect its taxpayer funding—even if we get to the point when there is nothing left to clean up.

Counterproductive Programs

During the depression years of the 1930s, mortgage lenders were having a tough time. The government responded with the creation of a number of federal agencies to prop up the mortgage and construction industries through federal insurance and credit subsidies. The National Housing Act of 1934 created the Federal Housing Administration (FHA). Its purpose was to insure private mortgage lenders against losses on mortgages that financed purchases of one to four units,[73] and it was intended to be a temporary program to get lenders through the depression.[74] In 1938, the Federal National Mortgage Association (Fannie Mae) was chartered to provide a secondary market for residential mortgages.[75]

While these agencies did stabilize the mortgage industry, the housing market remained sluggish through World War II, leading to a housing shortage by 1950. Again the government responded—with the help of real estate developers. The role of the FHA was expanded to providing insurance for low down payment, low-interest mortgages to greatly increase the number of Americans who could buy homes. A similar program was set up through the Veterans Administration. As the GAO has noted, "The single most important determinant of a loan's foreclosure, is the borrower's equity in the property . . . ."[76] Private mortgage lenders prudently deemed low down payment loans too risky, so the government agreed to have U.S. taxpayers assume the risk through the FHA and VA. As with most subsidy programs, it seemed to work perfectly for a time. Developers suddenly had so many buyers they could hardly build homes fast enough. Mortgage lenders enjoyed a boom in virtually risk free loans, and great numbers of middle class Americans became homeowners. Buying a house was often cheaper than renting, and the percentage of families who owned homes jumped from 44 percent in 1940[77] to nearly 66 percent in 1980.[78]

An essential part of the federal housing policy was an idea called "filtering."[79] The idea was that as middle-class families moved from the cities to the "suburbs," a ready supply of housing for the urban poor would be created. These homes did indeed filter-down to the poor—which proved to be a major factor in bringing about the decline of America's cities. With the aid of federally subsidized highway construction and subsidy-driven demand for houses, suburbs sprang up all around major cities. And the mostly white, middle class headed for these shiny new communities in droves, changing the demographics of the cities to communities increasingly comprised of a mix of black social classes.[80] Until the 1960s, places like New York's Harlem and Chicago's South Side were black communities with a middle class and ample job opportunities. Then the middle class blacks also began moving to the suburbs.

In 1968, Fannie Mae was converted to a private company, but while it lost its explicit government guarantee for its debt, it essentially retained its interest subsidy because of implicit government backing.[81] In addition, it still enjoyed Congressionally mandated tax exemptions. In 1970, the thrift industry convinced Congress to charter another government-sponsored enterprise, The Federal Home Loan Mortgage Corporation (Freddie Mac), as a source of subsidized credit for Savings and Loans, similar to that supplied by Fannie Mae to banks.[82] Through the FHA, VA, Fannie Mae, and Freddie Mac, the federal government was pumping hundreds of billions of dollars into the mortgage market—and incurring an equal liability for U.S. taxpayers.

In the 1970s, retailers started following the flow of disposable income and shopping malls began to dot suburbia. One of the first things the new Reagan Administration did in 1981 was enact generous tax subsidies for commercial and industrial real estate developers.[83] The Depository Institutions Decontrol Act of 1982 freed Savings and Loans to invest their taxpayer insured deposits in commercial and industrial real estate (and virtually anything else).[84] With much of the risk being borne by taxpayers, construction of suburban shopping centers and industrial parks exploded. By the mid-1980s, downtown shopping areas were withering, and employers had joined the exodus from the cities. What evolved were doughnuts of prosperity surrounding hollow cores. The cities were stripped of their diversity and vitality as well as their tax base. Attempts to increase tax rates to make up the lost tax revenue only resulted in further erosion of the tax base. A classic death spiral.

Writing in *Time*, Jack E. White described Atlanta in 1993: "The city's population has dwindled from 495,000 in 1970 to 394,000, as the middle class of both races fled to the suburbs, leaving behind a large residue of poor people."[85] Most of the nation's major cities suffered a similar decline. Some like Camden, New Jersey—a once thriving industrial city—fared far worse. By 1992, half of the city's 100,000 residents were under twenty-one, yet it had two hundred liquor stores and bars and not a single movie theater.[86] Many cities became the all-too-familiar images on the six o'clock news: poverty, drugs, gangs, unwed mothers, welfare, and decay. Sociologist William Julius Wilson of the University of Chicago contends that the problem is not a culture of poverty as is commonly claimed, but social isolation that is the root cause of the tragic state of those left behind in the cities.[87] They have lost all contact with those who have succeeded at life through hard work and decency, because the black middle class lives in suburbia along with their white counterparts. The young, having no other role models, are absorbed into the culture of crime, violence, and welfare that surrounds them. A rule of thumb on Chicago's south side is that if a boy acts delinquent by the age of eight, the drug gangs will have him by the time he is ten.[88] Our history is full of those who rose from abject poverty to achieve greatness, but they were exposed to successful people who inspired them. The urban underclass is exposed only to itself, where the successful are usually drug dealers who live flashy and often short lives. This social isolation, resulting from the intentional suburbanization of America, is costing hundreds of billions of dollars annually in poverty programs, crime, devalued and abandoned real property, and lost productivity.

The federal suburbanization policy was a giant mistake according to Charles L. Leven, a Washington University economics professor.[89] He notes that the housing shortage was over by the end of the 1950s, but we still had a mechanism that made it profitable to give up a house in the city and move to the suburbs. Urban housing units abandoned since then easily number in the millions—over two hundred thousand in St. Louis alone.[90] In New Orleans, where 10 percent of the population lives in ten run-down housing projects, there are an estimated thirty-seven thousand abandoned houses.[91] Most abandoned buildings become property of the city due to unpaid taxes. In 1987, the City of New York owned, or was in the process of acquiring, over eleven thousand residential buildings, totaling a quarter of a million housing units due to tax liens.[92] By 1989, there were twelve thousand empty buildings in Detroit with an additional two thousand being abandoned every year.[93] These figures don't count the tens of thousands of units that the cities had already demolished. Detroit, which, since the 1950s, had lost 42 percent of its population to the suburbs, was tearing down buildings at the rate of three thousand per year.[94] Camden's population dropped nearly 30 percent, and as of 1992, it had razed 5 percent of its housing stock, with many more buildings yet to go.[95]

While federal subsidies are not the only cause of urban decline, they certainly bear the lion's share of the responsibility. Without the subsidies, there is simply no way that Americans would have relinquished valuable existing housing and infrastructure and undertaken the expensive task of replicating much of it twenty miles away. Miami University of Ohio geographer James M. Rubenstein observed that we are the first society in history to create a surplus of housing, and that's why we throw it away.[96] Housing is too expensive and valuable for sensible people, using their own money, to produce a surplus; only government action can create throwaway housing.

At the same time that we were throwing away millions of housing units, the federal and local governments were using tens of billions of taxpayer dollars to build new housing—much of it in the same places. Between 1976 and 1985, the federal government alone, through its notorious Department of Housing and Urban Development (HUD), spent $96.8 billion on the construction of new subsidized housing.[97] Another case where the unintended consequences of one federal policy implemented through a group of subsidy programs created the conditions for instituting another subsidy-based federal policy.

Local governments are now building apartments on the very lots where they demolished units a few years ago. New York City undertook a $5.1 billion program to provide 252,000 affordable housing units on tax-defaulted property.[98] While the construction industry and politicians might like to think so, housing does not need to be replaced every thirty years or so. One can travel all over the world and see houses that are several centuries old and still in very good condition. Maintaining and periodically updating them has made all the difference. The same would be true in the United States if not for counterproductive government policies that discourage maintenance and encourage new construction. Federal policies and subsidies have created disposable housing and, consequently, disposable cities.

Despite the catastrophic results of these policies, they remain in effect, and not surprisingly, they are continuing to produce the same results. We are now seeing the first ring of suburbs going through the same demographic shift as the cities did. The middle class is leaving for a second ring of suburbs, and suburban squalor is replacing them just as it did when they moved from the central cities. Nor is there any reason to expect any change. A number of groups are benefiting from the subsidies that support the existing policy, and as always, they will fight to protect them. The construction and real estate lobbies are among the most powerful in Washington, but so, too, is the poverty lobby. There is a massive conglomeration of public and private agencies, bureaucrats, and service providers "whose business literally rides on the backs of the poor . . . ," according to Robert Woodson, president of the National Center for Neighborhood.[99] He adds that 75 percent of the aid to the poor goes not to them, but to those who serve the poor. Then there are the government agencies like HUD who depend on a continuation of housing problems to justify their existence. Additionally, government-sponsored enterprises such as Fannie Mae and Freddie Mac would be threatened if all the mortgage business associated with the over-production of housing was eliminated.

Penalizing Competence by Subsidizing the Incompetent

Without a doubt, the biggest direct hit that the taxpayers took from the government sponsored real estate boom of the 1980s was from the collapse of the Savings and Loan (S&L) industry. While the economy, foolish federal tax policy, and fraud all played a part, the primary contributor was plain and simple, subsidized incompetence. After the Depository Institutions Decontrol Act of 1982 turned the industry loose, S&L lending for land acquisition and development and other nonresidential real estate purposes skyrocketed to $74.1 billion in 1983 and $142.1 billion by 1986.[100] This speculative frenzy was a direct result of that Act and the Deregulation and Monetary Control Act of 1980. Between the two, provisions were enacted into law that:

1. Raised deposit insurance from $40,000 to $100,000 per account.
2. Removed the limit on the interest rate payable on deposits.
3. Reduced net worth requirements to 3 percent.
4. Allowed lending 100 percent of appraised value for

almost any purpose.
5. Allowed lenders to charge a loan origination fee of 6 percent.[101]

Thus, a person or group with $3 million could open an S&L, pay a very high rate of interest, and attract $100 million in deposits. Lending all of it out on highly speculative developments would generate $6 million in origination fees, or a 200 percent annual return on investment. Whether any of the loans were repaid was irrelevant because the federal government insured all depositors for $100,000 per account. Anyone with more than $100,000 simply opened several different accounts. It was a real estate developer's dream come true. All he had to do was open his own S&L, and he could finance his wildest projects, and those of his friends, absolutely risk free. It was an opportunity that many developers, and others with no banking experience, could not turn down. Commenting on the impact of the S&L "disaster," the CBO noted,

> *The incentives that federal deposit insurance created for the S&L industry have caused it to channel some of the nation's saving into inefficient and sometimes entirely worthless projects instead of into household and business assets that would have expanded national welfare and GNP*[102]

By the end of 1987, the 40 million square feet of empty office space in the Dallas market exceeded all the office space in Boston's central business district.[103] But that was just a fraction of the 540 million square feet of vacant office space across the country in 1991, which translated to an annual loss of $65 billion in property values.[104] Sensible individuals, using their own money, simply would not engage in such lunacy. Senseless projects were being built by inexperienced developers, financed by incompetent lenders, and underwritten by federal subsidies, which assured that only the taxpayers could lose. It was an orgy of incompetence that only large federal subsidies could sustain.

The GAO has estimated the taxpayer cost of the S&L bailout at $132 billion.[105] Since we borrowed the entire amount, the final cost will be much higher. And while the S&L industry has been seriously tarnished by this debacle, much of the industry has been branded unfairly. In 1980, there were about 4,000 thrifts, and 1,223 of these failed,[106] meaning over 2,500 did not. Moreover, 100 thrifts in six states accounted for over 50 percent of the losses while thrifts in thirteen states had no failures at all.[107] Nonetheless, the survivors are all being penalized for gross lending incompetence made possible by government subsidies so generous that the disastrous outcome almost seems to have been the objective. Since the late 1980s, both banks and S&L's have been required to pay higher insurance premiums to replenish the insurance funds of the Federal Deposit Insurance Corporation (FDIC). In mid-1995, the bank fund reached its required reserves of 1.25 percent of insured deposits, and then premiums dropped from 23 cents per $100 of deposits to 4 cents per $100 of deposits.[108] Because the S&L insurance fund is saddled with some of the debts of failed thrifts, it will be approximately 2004 before the surviving S&L's replenish their fund.[109] Until then, they will have to continue paying an average of 23.7 cents per $100 of deposits, which will put them at a competitive disadvantage compared to banks.[110] Responsible thrift operators are being penalized for government-sponsored incompetence of those long gone from the industry; this creates additional risk for the taxpayers who provide a minimum of 98.75 percent of the backing for the FDIC insurance funds.

Virtually all federal subsidy programs suffer from several or more of the characteristics detailed in this chapter. In the following chapters, we will examine all significant federal subsidy programs, including several mentioned in this chapter, in more detail.

3

A NATIONAL DISGRACE:

SOCIAL SECURITY, MEDICARE, AND MEDICAID

Shortly after World War I, a financial wizard in Boston began producing spectacular returns for his investors. His investment plan, which was based on the purchase and resale of European postal-reply coupons, earned investors a 100 percent return in only ninety days.[1] Money poured in as delighted investors spread the word, and the total quickly reached $15 million. But it turned out that there was no investment miracle; Charles Ponzi had been simply paying the early investors with funds collected from later investors. It was a simple pyramid scheme where the initial investors make out like bandits at the expense of the suckers who come in after them. All pyramid schemes—frequently called Ponzi Schemes—collapse after those at the top of the pyramid fleece those at the bottom, and they are illegal in every state in the union. Nonetheless, less than twenty years after the Boston scam, the federal government passed what has become the world's greatest Ponzi scheme: Social Security. And since it is government operated, it is completely legal.

In 1935, President Franklin D. Roosevelt could not possibly have imagined the monster that the Social Security system would become, but he was less than honest about it from the beginning. It was sold to the American people as insurance, which it most certainly is not. Nonetheless, the payroll deductions that fund the system under the Federal Insurance Contributions Act (FICA)[2] are called insurance contributions, not taxes. And the benefits are termed Old-Age and Survivors Insurance or Disability Insurance. The insurance theme was concocted to gain public acceptance for what was really a social welfare program, at a time when public sentiment was strongly against welfare.[3] Insurance was deemed acceptable because it implied a return in proportion to investment, and it was, therefore, not considered a handout. It was a ruse that worked on both the American people and Congress, and which many people still believe today.

In true insurance, policy holders purchase coverage to avoid the experience of a large sudden loss that would produce severe financial strain, and the insurer charges a premium for assuming the risk. The size of the premium is computed by first multiplying the probability that the particular event will occur in a specified period by the financial value of the loss, then subtracting the expected income the insurer derives from investing the premiums received until payment is required, and finally adding the costs of operations and a target profit amount.[4] Properly done, the premiums should produce a profit on the policy, or in the case of a government insurance program, the policy should break even. Social Security bears no resemblance to true insurance. Indeed, back in 1967 Nobel economist Paul Samuelson sarcastically noted that, "The beauty of social insurance is that it is actuarially unsound."[5] The benefits are essentially unrelated to the premiums, the length of time payments are paid, and the probability of collecting benefits. Nor does the government invest a citizen's FICA contributions to enable it to pay future benefits to the citizen. On the contrary, about 85 percent of a citizen's FICA contributions are used to make immediate payouts to present retirees, and the remainder is used to pay completely unrelated government expenses.[6] A virtually identical scheme to the one used by Charles Ponzi in Boston.

When the federal government is the culprit behind a Ponzi scheme, who protects the unsuspecting victims? No one, when the scam serves the interests of politicians, bureaucrats, and subsidy seekers alike. Rather, it is given an air of legitimacy through terms like the Social Security trust fund. Section 401 of Title 42 of the U.S. Code gives the lengthy details of the Social Security trust fund—as if Social Security was a real insurance program. It provides for a Board of Trustees to oversee the fund's investments and requires them to make an annual report to Congress on the actuarial status of the fund. That report must be certified to be based on reasonable cost estimates and assumptions, and must meet actuarial professional standards. All very official, and all little more than part of the ongoing effort to disguise Social Security as an insurance program. Interestingly, that effort does not extend to the U.S. Code itself because the politicians know that almost no one (including themselves) ever reads it. Section 401 does not bother calling the money deducted from paychecks for Social Security insurance contributions, as it is on the paychecks of Americans. It comes right out with it—they are taxes.

The Social Security trust fund contains no money and never has, despite all the talk by politicians of a "surplus." In 1997, Americans paid $402 billion in Social Security taxes, and $362 billion of that was used to pay current retirees.[7] It did not even make a momentary stop in the trust fund. The $40 billion cash surplus did not make it to the trust fund either; it was spent by the federal government for everything from stealth bombers to Congressional salaries. Every penny of the $402 billion was spent virtually as soon as it was collected. The $40 billion not needed for benefit payments was borrowed to help finance the government's $62 billion budget deficit, thereby reducing the demand on the financial markets by the same amount. In place of the cash, the government deposited $40 billion worth of IOU's in the trust fund. The IOU's are special government bonds, and that is all that ever has been, or ever will be, in the Social Security trust fund. Not one dollar, just $631 billion (including $66 billion in the Disability Insurance trust fund) in special government bonds as of 1997.[8] The entire Social Security trust fund in 1998 consisted of 174 certificates in a filing cabinet on the third floor of the Bureau of Public Debt in Parkersburg, West Virginia.[9]

The fact that there is no cash in the trust fund is not the problem. By law, any Social Security funds in excess of those needed for benefit payments must be invested in government bonds and there is nothing wrong with that. Indeed, prudent financial management requires that cash held by any entity for a long period be invested. While companies and individuals have a broad range of investment alternatives, the federal government is limited to investing in its own debt because of the magnitude of the funds involved and the inherent problems that would arise if it became a significant investor in any company. The problem is that rather than investing the surplus funds in existing government bonds and reducing the national debt, the politicians have borrowed the funds to pay for increased spending, thereby increasing the gross debt. The combination of debt owed to the public and debt owed to the Social Security trust fund continues to grow; both forms of debt represent obligations of the U.S. Treasury that will have to be paid by future taxpayers.

Federal officials and politicians routinely refer to the pile of trust fund IOU's as the Social Security "surplus" and contend that it will provide the funds to pay benefits to future retirees. The trust fund will supposedly fund benefit payments to baby-boomer retirees. That, of course, is complete nonsense, or "fraud," as Senator Kent Conrad more accurately termed it.[10] Following that line of reasoning, you could mortgage your house and then use the mortgage note to pay for a new car. Perhaps some in Washington, D.C. have managed to do just that, but it does not work anywhere else in America where cash, not influence, is legal tender.

Presently, annual Social Security tax collections are projected to exceed that necessary for benefit payments to retirees until about 2012.[11] Thereafter, the shortfall will grow each year and is projected to reach $475 billion by 2025.[12] To make up the deficit, Social Security officials will begin redeeming government bonds from the trust fund by presenting them to the U.S. Treasury for payment. However, the Treasury has no cash because it has trillions of dollars in additional debt and will have been using Social Security trust funds to help pay its bills for eighty years. Therefore, to pay back the trillions it owes Social Security, Congress will have to either raise taxes or borrow an equal amount in the world financial markets. That is the exact same action the Treasury would have to take if there was no trust fund, and Social Security benefits and taxes had simply been handled in the same fashion as other revenues and expenditures. In other words, the trust fund is nothing more than an accounting gimmick. Even Social Security's fiercest defender, the American Association of Retired Persons (AARP) recognizes that fact. Its Legislative Director John Rother admitted, "Whether we finance it out of payroll taxes, income taxes or some other revenue, the burden will be the same with or without the fund."[13]

Because the government immediately spends all money earmarked for the trust fund and plans to raise taxes or borrow the money later, when those funds are needed, what is the purpose of the trust fund? Why not simply admit that Social Security "contributions" are, in fact, no different than income taxes which are collected and spent for various government programs, one of which happens to be Social Security? And that in the future, as always, the government will borrow whatever it needs to cover its deficit? Because such an admission would reveal that Social Security is not an earned benefit but a massive Ponzi scheme, and that tens of billions of dollars in taxes collected in the name of Social Security are being diverted to fund other subsidy programs. As former CBO Director Rudolph G. Penner tactfully observed, "The trust fund is mainly political symbolism."[14] Symbolism indeed, but one that politicians have found immensely useful. There are ten major federal trust funds; among them: highway tax, airport tax, veterans' benefits, and unemployment insurance, in addition to Social Security. The government claimed that in 1997 these funds held a combined 1.21 trillion dollars.[15] The actual cash balance was zero; every penny had been spent and replaced with laser printer generated IOU's. Symbolism.

In 1990, Senator Patrick Moynihan went against the political grain and attempted to end the trust fund myth by proposing that the Social Security tax rate be lowered so that annual collections would equal benefit payments. This simple change would mean that the Treasury would collect Social Security taxes and disburse benefit payments just as it does with other government revenues and expenditures. There would be no "surplus," and, therefore, no need to pretend that funds were being deposited in the trust fund for the benefit of future retirees. With the deception ended, the true nature of Social Security would become apparent. As *Business Week* noted, Moynihan was blowing the lid off of Social Security's "dirty little secret."[16] Coming clean was the last thing on the mind of the Senator's colleagues.

The Senate Finance Committee produced a report warning that Moynihan's proposal would cause the trust fund to run out of funds by the year 2005.[17] And Social Security Commissioner Gwendolyn S. King said, "To reduce the tax rate at this time . . . could seriously jeopardize the Social Security system."[18] Government officials, fully aware that every cent destined for the trust fund was appropriated for other purposes, mounted a furious campaign to protect the myth that there was money in the trust fund. A few politicians, including House Speaker Tom Foley, addressed what most were trying to hide: ". . . where are you making up the revenue? It is a very, very substantial revenue loss."[19] Foley alluded to the real problem with Moynihan's proposal: the government was hooked on Social Security taxes to mask its subsidy-induced deficit spending, and without the trust fund deception, the public might just learn the truth. Moynihan's proposal was buried under a mountain of government disinformation. Unfortunately, it is all too easy for Congress to deceive the public.

Politicians have always preferred indirect taxes, such as excise taxes and tariffs to direct taxes, which are levied directly on people. The rationale is very simple: indirect taxes tend to be buried in prices and are, therefore, less visible. On the other hand, the income tax is very visible since taxpayers must frequently send the government payments and file a tax return that shows exactly how much was paid. (Payroll withholding was initiated to make it less visible.) The U.S. government was funded primarily by indirect taxes until the passage of the Sixteenth Amendment to the Constitution in 1913 authorized the collection of income taxes. Since then, the income tax has become the largest source of revenue with individual and corporate income taxes amounting to 46.7 percent and 11.5 percent respectively of 1997 federal revenue.[20] While they love the huge amounts of revenue that direct taxes produce, politicians hate their visibility; it is much more difficult to camouflage hikes in direct taxes. Therein lies the beauty of the Social Security payroll tax: it is camouflaged as an "insurance contribution," so the taxpayer feels that it is not quite a *real* tax. This ruse has enabled Congress to dramatically increase payroll taxes to the point where now, including Medicare taxes, they comprise 34 percent of federal revenues.[21] During the 1980s, Ronald Reagan slashed federal taxes—or so the story goes. In reality, while income taxes were being reduced, payroll taxes were substantially increased, with the result that the total federal tax burden of most Americans actually went up. The poorest 20 percent of Americans got the worst of it—a 28.5 percent increase according to the CBO.[22]

While disguising a regressive income tax as a social insurance contribution was clever, it pales next to the sleight-of-hand of the employer matching contribution. According to the government, workers pay a Social Security payroll tax (including Disability Insurance) of 6.2 percent and their employers match this with an additional 6.2 percent.[23] There is hardly an economist in the country who believes that the employer pays any payroll tax. In his economics textbook, former Federal Reserve Vice-chairman Alan Blinder states, "The incidence of a payroll tax is the same whether it is levied on employers or employees."[24] Payroll taxes simply increase the cost of labor, and it makes little difference whether the cost increases due to higher salaries or payroll taxes. As such, the real cost of both the employee and employer share of the Social Security tax is borne by the worker. The portion of the tax that the employer pays is money not paid to the employee. The camouflage effect of the employer paying half of the tax on behalf of the employee is very significant since very few workers understand that they bear the full burden of the employer's share in the form of lower wages. The government is thus able to collect a 12.4 percent Social Security tax from workers while they believe that they are only paying 6.2 percent. This, coupled with the "insurance contribution" euphemism, has removed most of the political risk of raising payroll taxes compared with income taxes, which explains why politicians and government officials work so hard at maintaining the Social Security deception. It further explains why, since 1991, more than 70 percent of American families have paid more in Social Security taxes than in income taxes.[25]

The truth about Social Security is ugly. It is a fatally flawed subsidy system that has transferred enormous amounts of wealth from the young to the old. Furthermore, it will collapse without some combination of tax increases and benefit reductions.[26] The recipients of this wealth did not earn their benefits as many claim, they simply were at the top of the pyramid. Social Security, like all Ponzi schemes, will leave those at the bottom, today's young, shortchanged and saddled with the debt being left behind by their elders.

Since Ida Mae Fuller received the first Social Security check in 1940, the system has been "pay-as-you-go," meaning the benefits of current retirees are paid from the taxes of current workers. Ms. Fuller contributed $22.00 to the system and received $20,000 in benefits before she died, a 90,900 percent return on her investment.[27] That is not insurance, nor is it a pension program; it is a massive subsidy. Alan Blinder advises college students:

> *The benefit checks that your grandparents receive each month are not, in any real sense, the dividends on the investments they made while they were working. Instead, they are the payroll taxes that you and your parents pay each month.*[28]

As we have seen, Social Security taxes were never set aside for future benefit payments in the first place; in addition, the amount paid into the system by present retirees was nowhere near sufficient to yield the benefits they receive. In 1991, former Social Security Commissioner Dorcas R. Hardy wrote, "Today in almost every case, every retiree gets back *all* of his own taxes in three or four years."[29] The average retiree now receives benefits for 12 to 14 years that will total five times what he or she paid into the system. For a retiree with a nonworking spouse, the return is much higher. The couple receives back every dollar that the working spouse paid into the system in less than two years, and they will get back almost 7.5 times the worker's contributions.[30] These figures did not reflect the annual cost of living adjustments, which significantly increase the total return. There is no large-scale investment plan that can produce that kind of a return, and most certainly not one run by a government.

Social Security is the nation's largest subsidy program, and one that is so generous and unfair that it is doomed in its present form. The system's inequity is apparent in figures calculated by former Council of Economic Advisers Chairman Michael Boskin. He estimates that a worker who retired in 1980 received a net wealth transfer of $63,000 (in 1985 dollars), while one born in 1960 will suffer a net loss of $48,000.[31] It will have been a bonanza for those fortunate enough to have retired between 1940 and the mid-1990s; a poor investment for those retiring from then until 2010; and a financial disaster for every one after that. Former Commissioner Hardy writes,

> *. . . the current generation of retirees is enjoying a level of prosperity unknown to previous generations and unlikely to ever return again. This prosperity does not derive from hard work and savings in years gone by. Rather, today's retired people are living on a government dole, and that dole is paid for by people now working. . . .*"[32]

The prosperity of present retirees has been made possible by growth: population growth, economic growth, payroll tax rate growth, and, of course, inflation. A rapidly expanding population, especially after World War II, greatly expanded the number of workers paying Social Security taxes, while rising wages and increases in the tax rate considerably increased the amount each worker paid. The maximum tax for the year 1950 was $90 (employee and employer taxes), but by 1998, it had risen to $8,481.[33] In the 44 years between 1950 and 1994, Congress raised the maximum tax by 9,423 percent, a testament to the politician-friendly nature of Social Security "contributions." Over the same period, the population of the United States grew from 151 million to 260 million, a 72 percent increase.[34] The combination of many more workers and much higher Social Security taxes enabled Congress to increase benefit payments from less than $1 billion dollars in 1950 to $362 billion in 1997 and still have a $40 billion surplus to pay for other subsidy programs.

But sooner or later, even the world's greatest pyramid scheme gets so large that there simply are not enough people at the bottom to support all those at the top, and that day is drawing near for Social Security. Birth rates began slowing in 1958. The fertility rate of 3.6 children per woman in 1960 declined to 2.0 in 1997 and is projected to decline to 1.9 by the year 2020.[35] Wage growth slowed in the 1970s and only resumed growing recently.[36] How long that will last is yet to be seen. In 1950, there were 16 workers supporting each retiree; by 1997, it had dropped to 3.3 workers.[37] Projections are that by 2030, there will be only two workers per retiree, and the ratio will drop to 1.5 to 1 by 2050.[38] Of course, without significant changes, the system will not survive nearly that long. George Mason University economics professor Walter Williams calculates that workers by the year 2030 would have to pay a Social Security tax of at least 48 percent under the present system.[39] Our children will not pay anything close to that; they will revolt first, and they would be justified in doing so.

The U. S. government has promised retirement benefits to present retirees, plus all those workers paying into the Social Security system that could amount to $6.7 *trillion* more than the system can pay.[40] Each year, buried deep in the president's budget, there used to be a small section called "Generational Accounting." President Bush's 1993 budget contained a table showing that males who turned thirty in 1990 would pay $201,130 more in taxes (in 1993 dollars) than they got back in Social Security.[41] President Clinton's 1995 Budget contained a calculation showing that a continuation of existing government policies would result in a tax rate of 94 percent for future generations.[42] This is not the type of data that politicians trying to maintain the grand deception like to see made public, so when more horrifying data was prepared for Clinton's 1996 budget, the White House threw out the whole Generational Accounting section. However, try as they might, the truth is getting out. A poll by the group Third Millennium found that only nine percent of Americans ages 18 to 34 believe that Social Security will pay them anything.[43] That is easy to say for those not facing retirement for more than thirty years. When they get older, they will change their tunes, especially when they see how much they have paid to support the retirees ahead of them. And anyone who seriously believes that those presently over 50 will accept significant cutbacks in future benefits is deluded. Even at the present rate of benefit payments, those over 40 in 1998 will not come close to getting their Social Security investment back. Every year the formidable army of those closing in on retirement swells. Cut benefits? Really.

Social Security today bears little resemblance to the program passed in 1935. Like most subsidy programs, over time Congress found numerous ways to expand the number of beneficiaries and to increase the level of benefits well beyond the intent of the original legislation. Retirement benefits were increased in 1939, 1950, 1956, 1961, and 1965.[44] In 1972, Congress decided to make benefit increases an annual event, and it mandated yearly cost-of-living adjustments (COLAs), beginning in 1975, tied to increases in the Consumer Price Index (CPI). This placed benefit increases on automatic pilot and caused payments to skyrocket from $63 billion in 1975 to $186 billion only ten years later.[45] The annual increases considerably exceeded increases in the cost of living—economists generally agree that the CPI overstates inflation. Federal Reserve Chairman Alan Greenspan estimates the overstatement at .5 to 1.5 percent,[46] meaning that a COLA based on a three percent CPI could be overstating inflation by as much as 100 percent.

In 1956, Congress enacted the Disability Insurance (DI) program as an addition to Social Security. It provided benefits to workers between 50 and 65 years old "unable to engage in substantial gainful activity by reason of a physical or mental impairment."[47] The 1958 Social Security Amendments added benefits for the dependents of disabled workers over 50, and finally, the 1960 Amendments provided disability benefits for workers under 50.[48] Disability Insurance added another camouflaged tax and another trust fund. The tax went from .5 percent in 1957 to 1.8 percent in 1998 (employer and employee tax).[49] The 1.8 percent DI tax plus the 10.4 percent Old Age and Survivors tax equals the 12.4 FICA tax paid by workers—commonly called the Social Security tax. The DI tax brought in $60.5 billion 1997, while benefits paid amounted to $47 billion.[50] The surplus supposedly went into the DI trust fund, which had $66.4 billion at the end of 1997, but, of course, that was just IOU's, not cash.[51]

By 1992, the DI program was out of control. While it was supposed to provide benefits only while the recipient remained disabled, the GAO reported in 1993,

> *Today, almost all the terminations are due to the beneficiaries' deaths or their leaving the program at age 65, when the Old Age and Survivors Insurance Fund begins to pay retirement benefits.* [52]

In other words, once someone qualified for DI benefits, they could continue to collect benefits for the rest of their lives, or until Social Security kicked in, even if they completely recovered from the condition that caused the disability. An injury or temporary impairment to a 20 year old, which left him or her unable to work for a year, would likely result in lifelong benefits, unless they were voluntarily terminated. Indeed, the GAO found that between 1987 and 1997, "not more than one in 500 DI beneficiaries . . . left the roles to return to work."[53]

The Social Security Administration is required by law to conduct Continuing Disability Reviews (CDRs) at least once every three years where medical improvement is either possible or expected, to preclude the payment of benefits to those who no longer qualify.[54] However, due to budgetary constraints, 4.3 million CDRs were due or overdue by 1996.[55] The situation was so bad that Congress appropriated an additional $4.1 billion to the Social Security Administration, which administers the DI program, to implement a seven-year program—just to catch up on CDRs.[56] The almost total failure of the CDR process had been previously brought to the attention of Congress by the GAO in 1987 and again in 1991, to no avail.[57] Finally, Congress decided to do what it does best: throw a few more billions of dollars at the problem. By substantially expanding the Social Security Administration bureaucracy, the politicians can expect the number of program beneficiaries to grow even larger. That is one of the primary means by which subsidy program administrators insure their job security. They do not intend to put themselves out of business.

Federal subsidy programs are inherently inefficient at their inception, and with time and the inevitable expansions, they become grossly inefficient and riddled with abuse. Though repeatedly advised of these serious problems, Congress will seldom take serious action, because it is considered "political suicide" to terminate subsidy payments, even those obtained through fraud. Federal subsidies are forever.

Still not satisfied with the now colossal Social Security system, Congress added the Supplemental Security Income (SSI) program as part of the 1972 Social Security Amendments. This program provided almost $29 billion in cash payments to "needy, aged, blind, and disabled persons" in 1996.[58] For whatever reason, Congress elected not to use the trust fund ruse for SSI, but specified that the benefits be paid from general tax revenues. Essentially, SSI is a means-tested welfare program, but its provisions allow some well-off individuals to qualify for benefits. As of 1998, a single person could have no more than $2,000 in assets other than a house, household goods, and a car, and there were maximum limits on the value of the household goods and car.[59] However, the value of a house is not limited. As such, someone with a $250,000 house owned free and clear could qualify for taxpayer-funded welfare benefits through the SSI program. This despite the fact that he or she is clearly wealthier than many of the people footing the welfare bill. The house could later be sold, and the suddenly wealthy (according to the government), former welfare recipient could keep every penny of the proceeds. From a political standpoint, the "success" of a subsidy program is primarily determined by its size; by that standard, SSI was another winner. Between 1974 and 1996, the cost of the program increased nearly 640 percent from $3.8 billion to over $28 billion.[60]

It is interesting to compare SSI with what are considered the primary federal welfare programs: Aid to Families with Dependent Children (AFDC) and its successor Temporary Assistance for Needy Families (TANF), Family Support, and Job Opportunities and Basic Skills. Together, these programs accounted for $17 billion in federal spending in 1997.[61] Many Americans think that these "family support" programs, and AFDC in particular, are largely responsible for much of the nation's budgetary woes (a 1994 poll found that 46 percent think that welfare or foreign aid is the biggest item in the federal budget[62]), but they could not be more wrong. Combined, all the family support programs amounted to just 1.1 percent of 1997 federal expenditures, and that makes it particularly interesting.[63]

Although AFDC was replaced by the Temporary Assistance for Needy Families (TANF) block grant program in 1996, the history of the AFDC is very instructive. AFDC was created by the Social Security Act in 1935, but it was not generally considered part of the Social Security system, nor was it funded by payroll taxes. It was an optional program administered by the states, and all fifty states elected to operate an AFDC program. The federal government paid from 50 to 80 percent of each state's benefit costs, and 50 percent of their administrative costs. Unlike the federal SSI program, the states were "at liberty to pay as little or as much as they choose."[64] But despite having been in existence for sixty years, three times as long as SSI, federal AFDC expenditures amounted to only about $14 billion in 1996,[65] about half of SSI's cost. The federal SSI program grew at about six times the rate of the federal-state AFDC program.

The enormous tax base available to the federal government, and its ability to borrow huge sums of money, produces irresponsible, and frequently irrational, expansion of federal subsidy programs. SSI, for example, was enacted as an assistance program for "adults whose disabilities precluded work."[66] Yet inexplicably, benefits were extended to children who are too young to work, leading some, including the GAO, to "question the underlying rationale for providing benefits to children through this program."[67] Meanwhile, the program, which is riddled with fraud, paid $4.5 billion to 900,000 children in 1994.[68] States have far more modest means, and they cannot easily disguise the taxes that fund state benefit payments. The result is greater responsibility or perhaps just the lack of the opportunity to be as reckless as their federal counterparts.

The GAO has reported that the SSI program is at considerable risk for waste, fraud, and mismanagement,

> *because of an agency culture . . . which places emphasis on making payments to an "entitled" population rather than as a welfare program that requires stronger income and asset verification policies . . . . Thus, annual overpayments have increased steadily, program abuses continue to occur . . . . Since 1989, SSA has written off more than $1.8 billion in SSI overpayments.[69]*

It is this culture which, between 1986 and 1995, managed to expand the number of SSI recipients between the prime working ages of 30 and 49 by 1.6 million people, or 46 percent of all beneficiaries, at the same time that the Americans With Disabilities Act considerably enhanced the likelihood of those individuals finding jobs.[70] Unfortunately, the expansionist culture typified by SSI bureaucrats is the rule at federal subsidy program agencies.

Social Security was never intended to be retirement income. Indeed, the program was designed so that most people would not live long enough to collect benefits. A man who was 25 years old when Social Security was enacted in 1935 had a life expectancy at birth of 48.6 years, and one born in 1930 still only had a life expectancy of 59.7 years.[71] The law was specifically written to provide benefits to the minority of people who lived to be 65 years old, which is why the statute refers to payments as "old age and survivors benefits."[72] The program was intended to enable those who managed to survive to be 65 to live out the last few years of their lives, during which they were likely to be frail and suffering from one disease or another. But rapid advances in medical technology and better nutrition dramatically increased life expectancies, and by 1995, a 65 year old man could expect to live another fifteen years, while a woman could expect to reach her 84th birthday.[73] Had the frequent amendments to the Social Security Act been made consistent with the original intent of the program, the retirement age in 1992 would have been raised to about 80 years old![74] Raising it to 75 years old still would have been a generous expansion of benefits. However, once passed, the original intent of a federal subsidy becomes irrelevant, and Social Security is one of the premiere cases of the irresponsible expansion of a subsidy program by Congress. Not only was the retirement age relative to life expectancy significantly reduced, but benefits were recklessly increased. What was intended to be a short-term old age benefit was transformed into long-term "retirement income" and has led many Americans to believe that they have a "right" to live in leisure at taxpayer expense for the last 20 years of their lives. If that is what Franklin Roosevelt had in mind in 1935, the Social Security Act would have specified a retirement age of about 49 years old. That seems preposterous, and indeed, it would have been, but it is the equivalent of today's situation.

Rather than increasing the retirement age as life expectancies increased, Congress amended the Social Security Act to do the exact opposite; it lowered the minimum age for collecting benefits to 62. Although there is a modest decrease in benefits for "early retirement," the net effect of the lowered age was to increase the already heavy burden on young workers. Every time someone retires, there is one less worker paying into the system, and one more retiree that remaining workers must support. Today, 70 percent of all workers start collecting benefits before they are 65, while in 1948, half of all men over 65 (who could have been collecting Social Security) were still working.[75] The dramatic change reflects the attitude shift engineered by Congress over the last forty years. In 1948, individuals felt they were responsible for themselves, today, many Americans believe that society should support them. In more basic terms, it has been a change from a belief that you are entitled to the fruits of your labor to you are entitled to whatever you can get away with. Earlier generations took very seriously their responsibility not to burden their children and grandchildren with debt; today, generous subsidies that will impoverish future generations are selfishly defended. That is the incredibly destructive power of federal subsidy programs; they are not unlike a progressive disease.

The confiscation of wealth from those least able to afford it, and those least able to protect their interests, underscores the callousness that has displaced the deep sense of personal responsibility of previous generations. All workers, even those below the poverty level, pay Social Security taxes. Unlike the progressive income tax, FICA taxes are taken regardless of the economic condition of the taxpayer, and there are no deductions or exemptions. On the other hand, retirees are paid benefits regardless of how wealthy they are. One could certainly argue that since wealthy retirees paid into the system, they are entitled to receive benefits, but, as we have seen, the benefits received far exceed the taxes paid into the system. The net result is that poor workers are taxed to subsidize wealthy retirees—those least able to afford it are supporting those who do not need it. As Harvard economics professor Robert J. Barro has observed, "The [Social Security] program produces nothing, and most of the transfers are not from the rich to the poor (which is one reason the program is so popular.)"[76] Adding insult to injury, younger poor workers will not be able to collect the same benefits as those they are paying to provide for today's affluent retirees. Their children will be either unwilling or unable to pay the crushing taxes that would be required, and benefits will have to be sharply curtailed.

It is hard to imagine a more difficult dilemma for our children and grandchildren than to force them to choose between a life of involuntary servitude, paying for the irresponsible excesses of their elders, or voting to eliminate many of the benefits that their elders will insist that they are entitled to. On the one hand, they would be agreeing to shoulder a punishing tax burden that could force them to live in poverty. On the other, they would be forced to tell their parents that they had foolishly invested hundreds of thousands of dollars in a Ponzi scheme that was now defunct. Consider the outrage of an elderly couple who had paid over $200,000 into Social Security when they are informed by their grandchildren that the system has collapsed due to a $10 trillion unfunded liability[77] engineered by their parents. They will feel abandoned by their progeny and exploited by their progenitors. Those mostly responsible for the problem will be gone, so their bitterness will be unfairly directed at their descendants who will have played no role in the fraud. Realizing that the perpetrators have made a clean getaway, they will shoot the messenger.

Senator Warren Rudman was one of the few in Congress who stood for responsibility, and after retirement, he continued to champion the cause of future generations. He warned,

> *The bottom line is that the federal government is making promises that it either cannot keep or that jeopardize the well-being of future taxpayers. This intergenerational compact has been made without the consent of those whom ultimately will bear its burdens.*[78]

The tragic result is likely to be an intergenerational war in which both sides must lose. All because of the irresponsible subsidies that previous generations voted for themselves in a gross abuse of governmental power. As Thomas Paine observed in 1776, "Government, like dress, is the badge of lost innocence."[79] This developing tragedy is being forced on those who are now young children and those not yet born. Indeed, an injustice of this magnitude could only be imposed on children without risking violent resistance. It is taxation without representation in its purest form. But when the crises comes, those children will make up much of the government, and they will be aware that in 1960 (Fleming vs. Nester), the Supreme Court ruled that the government has the power to renege on paying Social Security.[80]

While Social Security will be one of the major burdens for our children, one program benefit is specifically aimed at children. The unmarried children of deceased workers are entitled to a monthly payment until they reach 18 years old, or 19 if they are in school. This "child's benefit" was intended to preclude a child, who's working parent had died, from becoming destitute, and, in 1998, 1.9 million children were receiving $3.7 billion in annual benefits.[81] The program has no doubt helped many needy children, but it has been like winning the lottery for many others. The child's benefit is paid regardless of the income of the surviving parent and continues through at least age eighteen even if the parent remarries.[82] Again, the system provides for a situation where poor workers (and all other workers) are taxed to provide a subsidy to the well off. In this case, the parents of poor children are simply providing extra spending money for children who are already well provided for. Sadly, it is precisely this type of subsidy provision that will preclude these workers from getting back what they pay into the system during their working lives.

The problems with Medicare are considerably worse. When he signed the Medicare Act in 1965, President Johnson defended it, claiming that an extra $500 million in spending would not create a problem.[83] In 1997, the federal government spent $208 billion on the program, 416 times Johnson's estimate. Truly frightening is that the 1997 program cost doubled from 1990 and is projected to more than double to $447 billion in 2008.[84] That increase of $239 billion in only eleven years is before the 76 million baby boomers arrive at Medicare's doorstep. Like so many other government subsidy programs, Medicare sounded like a wonderful idea: providing health care for the elderly and disabled. Most Americans over 65 are automatically entitled to "Part A" coverage for hospital and home health care costs, and in 1996, almost 37 million aged and disabled Americans were covered.[85] Part B covers doctor bills and generally pays 80 percent of reasonable or approved charges. It differs from Social Security and Part A coverage in that it is voluntary and not automatic. Virtually all those eligible for Part B coverage elect to participate; one would have to be a damn fool not to. Federal subsidies are like that.

Part A coverage is funded by a payroll tax of 2.9 percent (employee and employer share), bringing total federal payroll taxes (Old Age, Disability and Hospital) to 15.3 percent.[86] Unlike the Social Security and Disability taxes which are only imposed on the first $65,400 of wages (1997), the Hospital Insurance (HI) tax has no upper limit. There is a separate trust fund for HI taxes which had a mythological $116 billion balance at the end of 1997.[87] The CBO projects that the trust fund will go bankrupt about 2009.[88] Officially.

Part B coverage is funded partially by premiums paid by those in the program, and partially by the taxpayers. The premium is adjusted annually, based upon the projected costs of the program for the upcoming year, with the original intention of premiums funding half the costs.[89] However, original intentions and federal subsidies being what they are, and the taxpayers being what they are, the adjustments have not kept up with increasing costs. Not by a long shot. In 1997, Part B enrollees paid just 27 percent of the cost of the program—$19.1 billion compared with the $52 billion that the taxpayers kicked in.[90]

Although many Part B enrollees understand that their $43.80 monthly premium (1998) only covers a fraction of their medical benefits, they, like Social Security recipients, believe they earned their hospital benefits; the hospital portion of Medicare (Part A) was masquerading as insurance. Like Social Security, the insurance concept was a deception. According to Guy King, former actuary of the Health Care Financing Administration, new retirees will receive about $5 in hospital benefits for every dollar they contributed.[91] Medicare is another massive subsidy program, which, in 1997, was 91 percent funded by payroll and income taxes.[92] Moreover, the taxpayer cost of the program is expected to continue its explosive growth. Total costs in 2008 are projected to be $447 billion, while dedicated Medicare tax revenues and Part B premiums will total $262 billion.[93] The anticipated $185 billion shortfall, which could easily turn out to be double that, will have to come from additional taxes.

Although held in check through the mid-1990s, medical inflation began accelerating again in 1998. Nationwide health insurers' 1999 premiums were increasing five to seven percent, double the 1998 increase.[94] In 1997, Congress attempted to limit Medicare's growing cost by legislating a cap of about two percent annually on health service provider premiums.[95] It was an attempt to transfer some of the Medicare subsidy from taxpayers to health providers—as if passing a law could induce them to operate at a loss. In response, during 1998, some 96 health plans either withdrew from Medicare or reduced their service areas, thereby terminating their services to nearly a half million Medicare beneficiaries.[96] Congress is not going to get off the hook that easily.

By 2015—shortly before Social Security becomes a punishing burden on workers—Medicare costs become overwhelming. Under CBO's middle-of-the-road assumptions, Part A costs alone will exceed revenues by $431 billion, while under its pessimistic assumptions (which have historically proven more accurate), the deficit reaches a stunning $742 billion.[97] Now add an additional $300 to $500 billion for Part B; it is likely that our children will be looking at a trillion dollar Medicare shortfall. That is after accounting for the $208 billion in HI taxes that they will have paid that year.[98] Victor R. Fuchs of Stanford University predicts that annual health care spending for each senior citizen will soar from $9,200 in 1995 to almost $25,000 in 2020, an ultimately unsustainable burden.[99] Testifying in September of 1998 before the National Bipartisan Commission on the Future of Medicare, Dr. Timothy Flaherty of the American Medical Association warned that unless action is taken, a Medicare payroll tax of 30 percent might be required to support the system.[100] That is just Medicare alone! Bruce Vladeck, head of Medicare until 1997, echoes Flaherty's concerns: "You can't make the numbers add up without [higher] taxes."[101]

As a financial disaster, Medicare could hardly have been better designed. The basic design incorporated the flaws of the private health insurance system, which was a distorted product of federal regulations. During World War II, employers faced with federal wage and price controls began offering health insurance in lieu of higher wages to attract workers. With wages fixed and labor in short supply, employers competed for workers by offering better health benefits. The Internal Revenue Service made this benefit even more attractive by ruling that employers could deduct the cost of health insurance premiums, and employees did not have to count the value of the premium as taxable income. This made employer provided health care more attractive than increased wages for both the employer and the employee. Thus, it led to a mushrooming of the number of Americans, from seven million in 1942 to 26 million in 1945, enrolled in group hospitalization plans.[102] From an average of 10 percent in 1945, employers continually increased the portion of health care premiums they paid—until the United Steelworkers negotiated a contract in 1959, requiring steel companies to pay the full premium.[103] Other major industries soon followed. In concert with the expansion of health insurance, Congress passed the Hill-Burton Act in 1946, which financed a massive hospital construction program to add 500,000 new hospital beds by 1978.[104] The foundation for a wasteful and expensive health care system was now in place.

There were a number of serious flaws with this system of providing health care. The tax benefits encouraged employees to seek more generous health insurance rather than increased wages. This resulted in employer-paid health insurance that provided little or no deductible and paid for a broad range of services, including routine medical care. Workers were buying more insurance than they needed or than was reasonable. It was also a new approach to insurance, which usually covered major losses while leaving the insured to cover minor or routine expenses. Freed from any financial responsibility, those with employer paid health insurance greatly expanded their use of medical services and sought unwarranted hospitalization and medical treatment. Doctors and hospitals were eager to oblige; under the fee-for-service arrangement, the more treatment provided, the more they could bill. Moreover, patients were completely insulated from the costs of services by the "third-party payer" arrangement where the insurer was billed directly by the health care provider. Because they never saw a bill, patients never bothered to inquire about, much less question, the cost of services. That left the medical establishment free to implement a cost-plus reimbursement system with no checks on costs. University of Texas economist Stan Liebowitz has estimated that excessive third-party insurance adds $33 billion, just in unnecessary administrative costs, to the nation's health care bill.[105] Moreover, a 1994 study by the National Center for Policy Analysis concluded that the adverse consequences of third-party insurance unnecessarily increased national health spending by 16%, or $140 billion.[106]

The private health insurance system effectively eliminated the cost, price, and availability mechanisms critical to maintaining discipline and efficiency in any market. All that was necessary to set off a wild price spiral was a little fuel for the fire. The government provided two supertankers—Medicare and Medicaid. While Medicare provides health care for the aged, Medicaid pays for medical care for low-income persons who are aged, blind, disabled, members of families with dependant children, and certain other pregnant women and children. Medicaid is a federal program administered by the states with a combination of state funds and matching federal funds. The federal government makes the rules and reimburses the states for 50 to 80 percent of their costs. Nonetheless, the program places a heavy burden on the states. The states incurred $72 billion in federally mandated Medicaid costs in 1997.[107]

Senator Jay Rockefeller has termed Medicaid "a vile program, a horrible program," and it most certainly is.[108] It is the paramount example of an irrational, inefficient, and stunningly complex federal subsidy program. And, of course, it is very, very expensive—$96 billion in 1997 according to the CBO.[109] That is in addition to the $72 billion spent by the states. The CBO projects that federal Medicaid costs will more than double to $210 billion by 2008 and that combined state and federal costs will reach $369 billion.[110] However, it could be much worse. An estimated 25 percent of those eligible for Medicaid have not enrolled in the program.[111] If the government undertook an "outreach" program to enroll those currently eligible but not receiving Medicaid benefits, the $369 billion could approach $500 billion. In 1997, Congress authorized $20 billion over five years to fund state expansion of Medicaid and other subsidy programs.[112] Both SSI and DI costs increased significantly because of prior outreach programs.[113]

While childless American couples cannot qualify for Medicaid benefits no matter how poor they are, illegal immigrants qualify for emergency health care, including childbirth costs.[114] Children born under these circumstances are U.S. citizens, which qualifies them, and their mothers, for more benefits. Not surprisingly, there were an estimated 5.1 million illegal aliens with their 550,000 U.S. born children living in the United States in 1994 according to Donald Huddle, an economics professor emeritus at Rice University.[115] The arcane provisions of the program have made it an easy target for fraud. Medicaid pays for nursing home costs for the poor, which has given rise to a booming business for lawyers who advise middle-class elderly how to hide their assets so they can qualify as poor.[116] For about $1,000 per year, a 65 year old person can obtain long-term care insurance,[117] but many would rather bilk the system. That way, the taxpayers pick up the tab for their nursing home costs, and their hidden assets get passed on to their children. Even the states have defrauded the Medicaid program. In December 1994, the Department of Health and Human Services charged eighteen states with illegally shifting $3 billion worth of medical services to the federal government.[118] Previously, Federal Health Care Financing Administration Administrator Gail Wilensky had complained that the scam by the states could destroy the program because, "the requirement for a state share of payment has always acted as a restraint on the otherwise open-ended Medicaid program."[119] A revealing admission of the nature of federal subsidy programs.

Largely due to health care industry influence in the Senate, both Medicare and Medicaid incorporated the basic defects of the private health insurance system that was so profitable for the industry.[120] It also focused the full inflationary power of the federal government on the health care market. Congress needed to insure that there were enough doctors to staff all the new hospitals and care for the millions who were suddenly entitled to taxpayer-funded health care. Therefore, a subsidy was created to fund an increase in the number of doctors, from eight thousand to sixteen thousand, graduating from medical schools each year.[121] It also added an additional subsidy to encourage hospitals to purchase high-tech equipment. When it was enacted in 1965, government actuaries projected the cost of the Medicare program to be $9 billion in 1985; they were short by $54 billion.[122] This reflects not only a suspicious and consistent pattern of grossly underestimating subsidy program costs, but also the persistent foolishness of pretending that a federal subsidy program will not drive up demand, and consequently, prices. The massive infusion of federal dollars pushed hospital expenditures up by nearly 15 percent per year between 1965 and 1970.[123] By then it was clear that the government had let the subsidy genie out of the bottle, and federal politicians have been trying, in vain, to get it back in ever since.

In the absence of market discipline mechanisms, the increased supply of doctors produced more services rather than competition as Congress had anticipated. According to former Department of Health, Education, and Welfare Secretary Joseph Califano, "the increased number of doctors only meant more care and more health care costs . . . and more specialists meant more referrals to specialists and a spiraling medical bill."[124] And he laments that the cost-based fee-for-service reimbursement system became a blank check for American hospitals and doctors.[125] As costs continued to skyrocket, Congress passed one cost-containment measure after another, resulting in a mountain of regulations under constant revision. This paperwork jungle spawned an army of bureaucrats and administrators in the health care industry, which drove up costs even further. (In 1998, it took four thousand government employees and an additional 22,000 contract employees just to process Medicare claims.)[126]

Doctors reacted to restrictions on medical procedures by creating new procedures or renaming old ones, and the added complexity increased the already incredible overhead cost of the system. When Congress cut doctors' fees, physicians reacted by performing more procedures to make up for the lost revenue. The CBO concluded, "Studies of the effects of fee freezes or controls on physicians' prices indicate that they result in a pronounced volume offset."[127] Further cuts, to levels that forced doctors to treat patients at a loss in some cases, caused doctors to shift costs to privately insured patients. Shocked by the rate at which lucrative federal subsidies were causing hospitals to expand and invest in expensive equipment, Congress reversed policy and passed the Health Planning Act in 1974 to constrain hospital expansions.[128] That set up an additional bureaucratic hurdle, which led to the creation of "an industry of consultants, lawyers, and lobbyists" who were necessary to get the approvals needed for expansions or equipment purchases, according to Peter J. Levin, former Chairman of the Florida Hospital Cost Containment Board.[129] Each attempt by Congress to contain the health care monster they had created made it worse, and costs continued their relentless climb. In 1997, federal costs for Medicare and Medicaid combined amounted to $304 billion, and the CBO projects that to rise to $658 billion in 2008, an increase of 216 percent in just 11 years.[130] Figure in the $159 billion for state Medicaid costs, and the total comes frighteningly close to one trillion dollars. Perhaps it was this prospect that led Nobel laureate economist Milton Friedman to call for ending Medicare and Medicaid in 1991, when federal costs were *only* $160 billion.[131]

While the primary unintended consequence of the Social Security, Medicare, and Medicaid programs is the unsustainable cost and unconscionable liabilities that are being passed on to our children and grandchildren, there are many others as well. These programs are the driving force behind the record federal spending that is exacerbating the depletion of national savings. The engines of the nation's economy—its factories, machinery, and technology—are financed either from national savings or foreign borrowing. By inhibiting these investments, the nation's productivity growth is reduced, leading to slow growth in real wages. Partly due to federal spending, and partly due to record consumer spending, the household saving rate in the U.S. turned negative in September 1998 for the first time since the Great Depression.[132] Coincident with the decline in national savings, Labor Department reports indicate that wages stayed flat or declined from the early 1970s through 1994.[133] While real wages did grow in 1997 and 1998, it is yet to be seen whether that can be sustained. To make up for the dearth of national savings, America has been importing huge amounts of foreign capital. Over the long term, however, that also leads to a lower standard of living because eventually the foreign investors must be repaid.

Low wage growth only exacerbates the problem we have created for future generations. We are passing them enormous financial obligations, while at the same time undermining their ability to pay those obligations. In inflation adjusted dollars, the median income of families headed by someone under thirty in 1990 was 13 percent lower than such families earned in 1973, according to an analysis of 1990 Census Bureau statistics by Northeastern University's Center for Labor Market Studies.[134] The high taxes we are expecting them to pay can only come from earnings, and by using most of our national savings for instant gratification, we are limiting investment, future productivity, and the incomes of our children and grandchildren. Yet, we still fully expect them to shoulder the debts and obligations that we have incurred. It is difficult to see how we could have made their burdens much heavier.

Should they be foolish enough not to revolt and throw off the yoke, future Americans will only be able to offset slow wage growth by working longer hours. But the very system that will enslave them encourages today's 62 year-olds to retire early and claim more unearned benefits. They cease paying payroll taxes, and, instead, add to the drain on the system. In addition, their contribution to the economy is lost along with the income taxes on the fruits of their labor. While 54 percent of males age 65 and older were working in 1930, largely due to the Social Security's perverse incentives, only 17 percent were working in 1996.[135] Just as ludicrous, those Social Security recipients who choose to work are severely penalized through a combination of loss of benefits and taxes that effectively translated to a 33 percent marginal tax rate[136] on annual earnings over $14,500 in 1998.[137]

The government claims that this provision saves the system over $5 billion per year, but that is questionable.[138] Boston University economist Laurence Kotlikoff believes that a good number of the elderly arrange their work to earn just under the amount beyond which they will start losing benefits; they would work more if they were not penalized.[139] There is no doubt that Social Security recipients are advised to avoid the penalty by limiting the amount they earn. Money Magazine gave this advice to retirees:

To stay ahead, your best strategy is to increase wealth in the early years by working part time (provided, of course, your added earnings don't cause an offsetting reduction in Social Security benefits). . . .[140]

Even the conservative World Bank has weighed in on the disincentives of pay-as-you-go social security systems like ours. Its report, "Averting the Old Age Crisis," states, "Such social security arrangements have discouraged work, saving, and productive capital formation." The authors of the report found that "the history of publicly managed [retirement] systems has been disastrous."[141]

Social Security's work disincentives have helped create a retirement mind-set in older workers that encourages them to retire as soon as possible and begin consuming, although it is frequently not in their best interest. As *Money* cautioned, "You need to plan for age 90, at least."[142] Many retirees are not prepared for 25 or more years of retirement, but Social Security's perverse incentives encourage them to stop working and to further burden a system that is already collapsing.

Many of the older "baby boomers," the 76 million Americans born between 1946 and 1964,[143] have been led to believe that Social Security will provide a nice retirement income for them, as it has for their parents. It surely will not, and Princeton University economist B. Douglas Bernheim estimates that the typical boomer family is saving at only one third the rate necessary to maintain their standard of living in retirement,[144] the same rate predicted by the Merrill Lynch Baby Boom Retirement Index.[145] To compound matters, burdensome government regulations are causing tens of thousands of companies to eliminate their pension plans.[146] And the Social Security retirement income illusion is being reinforced by a program started in 1995 when the Social Security Administration began sending statements to workers detailing what benefits they can expect from the system. Those statements constitute an official act of fraud by the U.S. government because the promised benefits cannot be delivered. Moreover, Professor Bernheim worries that they will tend to diminish retirement saving even further by increasing confidence in the system.[147] Those lulled into a false sense of social security will be hit doubly hard because not only will they have insufficient savings, but also the benefit levels promised in the annual statements will certainly be reduced in the future. It may be the younger boomers who will be the best prepared because many of them don't believe that they will get any benefits, and it is the non-believers who are doing nearly all the saving according to Professor Bernheim.[148]

While younger workers are wise not to trust their government, they will nonetheless pay twice for their retirement benefits: once through Social Security taxes which are being transferred to current retirees, and a second time through their own savings. Those not yet in the work force will fare even worse; increasing taxes will leave less and less for them to save. Moreover, America's children are already feeling the effects of the massive wealth transfer from the young to the old. The CBO found that 29 percent of federal spending goes to people over 65 while only seven percent goes to those under eighteen.[149] The direct result is that the proportion of children living in poor households has increased by a third, to 20 percent, since 1973, while the poverty rate for the elderly has fallen from 10.5 percent to 6.6 percent.[150] As Robert J. Samuelson writing in the Washington Post has observed, ". . . the moral claims of the old on the young—through government programs—have lost much of their original power."[151] Indeed.

Perhaps the greatest defect with Medicare and Medicaid is that they indemnify those covered against the consequences of their own actions, thereby subsidizing self-destructive behavior. It is inconceivable that someone who repeatedly sets their house on fire could buy fire insurance, except at an exorbitant rate, yet the American taxpayers subsidize comprehensive health care for millions of people who are doing the equivalent to their own bodies. That is true even for employer-provided insurance, where the cost of health insurance is reflected in the price of the company's products and is consequently paid by consumers. However, if a company's health care costs force its prices too high, the company goes out of business. We have no such check on Medicare and Medicaid; the government simply commands more taxes and more borrowing to fund higher subsidies.

Alcohol and drug abuse, poor diets, smoking, obesity, and sedentary lifestyles have all been proven to significantly increase the risk of developing serious disease, yet the perverse Medicare and Medicaid incentives encourage such behavior which, not surprisingly, is increasing. Louis Harris and Associates have found that the number of Americans who were overweight increased from 58 percent in 1983 to 66 percent in 1992, and that only 51 percent made any attempt to avoid fats in their diets.[152] Essentially, the giant government health care programs are, in large measure, "disease subsidies," which transfer money from the health-conscious to those leading unhealthy lifestyles. Together, they may constitute the federal government's largest subsidy. The

Health Care Financing Administration projects that the nation's health care bill will increase from $1.0 trillion in 1996, to $2.1 trillion in 2007.[153] In addition, Aetna Insurance Company, one of the nation's largest group health insurers, has concluded through analysis of government data and its own studies that "illnesses related to lifestyles account for half of our health care costs."[154] That would indicate that about $500 billion in health care costs in 1996 were attributable to self-destructive lifestyle choices made by Americans, most of whom were indemnified against the consequences of those choices by private or government health coverage. Based on its nearly 50 percent share of the nation's health bill,[155] the federal government's disease subsidy for that year was about $250 billion, and it will double by 2007.

The obvious result of subsidizing self-destructive lifestyle choices is that such behavior is encouraged, and concerns about the prospect of huge, lifestyle-related health care bills are virtually eliminated. There is no doubt that having to bear the financial consequences would change many minds. Instead, too many Americans fully expect someone else to pay the bills and that is what typically occurs. Much of that money will come from those who are making the effort to protect their own health—the healthiest 50 percent of Americans who account for just three percent of annual health costs.[156] The net effect of Medicare and Medicaid policies is to encourage the behavior that results in health problems, which the programs are intended to remedy. Additionally, they subsidize the programs through taxes extracted from those who reject the perverse incentives and are not, therefore, part of the problem. The programs are perfectly designed for uncontrolled growth.

The sheer size of our health care system—with over four billion claims per year[157]— makes it very difficult to operate efficiently, thus creating an easy target for fraud. Approximately 10 percent of all health costs are attributable to fraud and abuse,[158] and for 1996, that would translate to $100 billion. Eliminating that, and then subtracting 50 percent for self-inflicted disease, yields the "unavoidable" portion of the nation's 1996 health bill: $450 billion, half of which would be Medicare and Medicaid cost. While the $450 billion is an idealized objective, it is certainly true that Medicare and Medicaid and their perverse incentives are responsible for much of the size, inefficiency, and vulnerability of the system. Consequently, elimination of the disease subsidies would go a long way in moving costs toward the ideal.

4

SUBSIDIES FOR ALL:

THE FEDERAL TAX SYSTEM

"As soon as a government activity has more than one purpose, it degenerates," according to management expert, Peter F. Drucker.[1] If ever there was a textbook case of this theory, it is the federal income tax system. Of course, the original purpose of virtually all taxes is to raise revenue, but the U.S. tax system has become as much a vehicle for dozens of federal subsidies as it is for raising revenue. The GAO estimated that federal subsidies implemented through the tax system amounted to $400 billion in 1997.[2] In addition, the incredible complexity of the system has created an industry of lawyers, accountants, and tax preparers who do nothing but tax work. The tens of billions of dollars paid to these individuals are, in effect, another federal subsidy. Jimmy Carter appropriately termed the U.S. tax code a disgrace to the human race, and it has only worsened since he was president.[3] Shirley Peterson, who was Internal Revenue Service (IRS) Commissioner under President Bush, says she "would repeal the IRS Code and start over."[4]

It is indeed ironic that Americans should find themselves with an oppressive tax system used by their government to subsidize favored interests, because that was precisely what triggered the American Revolution. While it is widely believed that the Boston Tea Party was a reaction to the imposition of taxes on tea by King George III, that is not the case. The colonists reacted to imposition of the tax on tea imported from Britain by switching to smuggled Dutch tea. By the time of the Boston Tea Party, the British tea tax had been in effect for five years, and Dutch tea was widely available throughout the colonies.[5] The British government responded by removing the duties on East Indies tea imported into Britain so that it could be sold in America at a price cheaper than the smuggled Dutch tea.[6] Essentially, the government granted British tea merchants a tax preference in order to undercut their American competition. This threatened American merchants who were selling Dutch tea and raised fears that the British might try the same approach with other products. At the same time, British revenue agents were given nearly unlimited search and sei-zure power, which they fully exercised. It was to protest these policies that a group of Boston merchants threw the British tea into the harbor in 1773.[7] Some 200 years later, Americans are still faced with tax favoritism; this time, it is by the government that they themselves formed after revolting against those prac-tices by the British. However, their own government has progressed far beyond anything King George III ever dreamed of.

Any discussion of tax fairness is difficult because taxes inherently involve forcible confiscation of a citizen's property. Making each citizen pay the same amount is fair in one sense, but many would argue that it is unfair to the poor. On the other hand, Internal Revenue Service (IRS) data shows that in 1990 the top 5 percent of earners paid 44 percent of all income taxes while the bottom 50 percent paid only 5.6 percent.[8] A case could certainly be made that such a skewed distribution is also unfair. It is terribly easy for those with a class-warfare agenda to mislead with fairness arguments. This is especially true when the issue is whether the government should allow citizens to keep more of their own property. For example, a hypothetical tax cut that reduced the average tax bill for the top five percent by $3,500, but only $45 for the lowest 50 percent would bring howls of protest from those who espouse a "tax the rich" philosophy.[9] They would pronounce such a tax cut "unfair" and a "giveaway to the rich." But that would have been the result of a simple 10 per-cent income tax cut for *everyone* in 1990. The top 5 percent would have still paid an average of $31,500 in taxes while the bottom 50 percent would have had their tax bill reduced to an average of $401.[10] The former group's average tax bill would still have been 7,800 percent of the latter's. Is the tax cut for the top five percent unfair or is their tax burden unfair?

While reasonable people can differ in their opinions on how the tax burden should be divided among citizens of different means, there can be no question that the subsidies built into the federal system are unfair. "Tax expen-diture" is the euphemism that the government uses for subsidies implemented through the tax system and which the House Ways and Means Committee *Green Book* notes, ". . . are similar in nature to entitlements."[11] The GAO de-fines tax expenditures as "reductions in tax liability that result from preferen-tial provisions in the tax code, such as exemptions and exclusions from taxa-tion, deductions credits, deferrals, and preferential tax rates."[12] And the GAO notes that ". . . studies by GAO and others have raised concerns about the ef-fectiveness, efficiency, or equity of some tax expenditures."[13] Indeed. As is frequently the case with government subsidies, many tax expenditures origi-nated for some ostensibly good reason, while others were simply subsidies passed under the cover of a noble intent. In any event, the result has largely been the same. The claimed benefit for society seldom materialized, but special groups of citizens nonetheless ended up receiving benefits at the expense of the rest of the nation. Quite simply, if a group of taxpayers is given a tax prefer-ence, resulting in lower payments, the lost revenue must be made up by all other taxpayers. That is nothing more than a federal subsidy for the special interest group. The trillions of dollars in taxes that certain taxpayers have been exempted from paying has been made up with increased taxes on other taxpayers, and by shamefully increasing taxes on future taxpayers.

The $400 billion in tax subsidies compares with $1.04 trillion in non-Social Insurance taxes that the government collected in 1997.[14] Corporate and personal income taxes accounted for $919 billion while excise, estate, gift, customs, and miscellaneous taxes made up the remaining $121 billion.[15] It is interesting to imagine what could be done with the additional $400 billion in revenue. Sixty-two billion dollars would have wiped out the budget deficit (the true, non-Social Security-masked deficit), and the rest could have been used to retire debt, making it feasible for the next generation to avoid servitude. Alternatively, part of it could have been used to lower tax rates. The resulting decline in interest rates would significantly reduce federal interest payments while the increased economic activity unleashed by the lower rates would further increase federal revenues. Lower expenditures and higher revenues would enable another tax rate cut which would . . . . Of course, that is not what the politicians would actually do. The minute they got their hands on the additional revenue, they would turn right around and pass new subsidy programs. Even more likely, the new subsidies would begin before the additional revenue came in.

When the federal income tax was passed in 1913, the mortgage interest deduction was intended to allow family farmers and small business owners to pay down their debts. After World War II, the subsidy was expanded to help American families buy homes. The idea seemed intuitively obvious: if you provide tax incentives to own a home, more people will be able to do so. Indeed, it has become an article of faith for the vast real estate, mortgage, and construction industries. Howard J. Levine, President of ARCS Mortgage Inc., a national mortgage affiliate of the Bank of New York, found President Clinton's 1993 plan to raise income tax rates nothing but good news for the real estate industry. His reasoning: "The President's economic plan, which would raise personal income-tax limits as much as 36 percent, will make the home mortgage deduction even more valuable," and he predicted that, ". . . many more consumers will be looking to enter the housing market to take advantage of the mortgage deduction."[16] The tax savings incentive of the mortgage interest deduction is considered to be so potent that a tax increase (Clinton's tax increase was passed by Congress) only serves to make it more effective.

Consider the five-point plan proposed to Congress by the National Association of Home Builders in 1992 to help the supposedly depressed real estate industry:[17]

1. A $2,000 tax credit for first-time homebuyers.
2. Permanent extension of low-income tax credits and mortgage revenue bonds.
3. Allow the use of IRA funds for the down payment on a first house.
4. Liberalize the deductibility of real estate losses.
5. Lower the capital gains tax rate.

The plan proposed additional tax subsidies for housing, which would cost billions of dollars on top of the tens of billions that homeowners already receive. The argument was that the mortgage interest deduction has considerably expanded home-ownership, and therefore, more tax subsidies will have an even greater effect. (Congress did not enact the plan.)

The problem is that there is little evidence that the hallowed mortgage interest deduction has expanded home-ownership. In 1991, more than eighty years after the introduction of the mortgage interest deduction, 59 percent of Americans owned their own homes.[18] At the same time, 64 percent of Canadians were homeowners, although they could not deduct the interest on their mortgages.[19] Additionally, Canadian homes were, on average, 13 percent larger than American homes.[20] Australians had about the same home-ownership rate as Americans, yet they could not deduct mortgage interest either.[21] Remarkably, despite a number of federal homeowner subsidies, America's rate of home-ownership in 1991 was lower than that of Ireland, Spain, Japan, Luxembourg, Norway, Belgium, Greece, Italy, Denmark, and Great Britain.[22]

Between 1992 and 1998, home-ownership in the U.S. increased to 66 percent, but it was clearly not due to the mortgage interest deduction. Rather, the vibrant economy and low interest rates accomplished what the mortgage interest deduction failed to achieve. Ironically, it is subsidy programs like the mortgage interest deduction that result in higher interest rates and slower economic growth. While the mortgage interest deduction may have failed to achieve its stated goal, it has nonetheless grown to be one of our largest subsidy programs, costing over $50 billion per year.[23] One of the definitions of insanity is doing the same thing repeatedly and expecting a different result. After more than 80 years, the mortgage interest deduction is a clear indication of government insanity. Unless you analyze the real reason for the deduction; then it changes from insane to unconscionable.

Most Americans probably believe that the mortgage interest deduction has actually expanded home-ownership, but the mortgage, construction, and real estate lobbies that staunchly defend it know better. They know the data does not support the theory. The real story is about $50 billion per year that is channeled through homeowners and directly into the pockets of these industries. This is why they expend millions of dollars lobbying Congress, not only to protect the mortgage interest deduction, but also to push for additional subsidies, such as those contained in the Home Builder's 1992 plan. The "expanded home-ownership" theme allows the industry to seek additional subsidies for itself while claiming to improve the quality of Americans' lives.

The Home Builder's plan was proposed to stimulate the economy and, of course, expand home-ownership opportunities, but by October of the following year, the Associated Press was reporting, "The housing industry, particularly the single-family sector, has been one of the strongest sectors of the economy."[24] That was without Congress passing their proposed plan. A major election year had just been an opportune time to push for more subsidies. Subsidies have made America the first nation in history to produce a surplus of housing, yet have left us behind many other industrial nations in the rate of home-ownership. Rather than expanding home-ownership, these subsidies are going to the real estate industry to produce surplus housing. Older housing is then discarded to allow continued over-production. Only government subsidies can produce such lunacy.

The fact that the mortgage interest subsidy has failed to achieve its intended purpose, and that it has come to be little more than a $50 billion annual gift to the well-off, should be enough to embarrass those in government for not putting an end to it. However, the terrible inequity of the subsidy makes it unconscionable. It is a program where non-homeowners (the poor and lower-middle class) subsidize homeowners (the upper-middle class and rich). Indeed, the 11 percent of households with incomes over $75,000 reaped 58.9 percent of the subsidy in 1993.[25] Not surprisingly, Joint Committee on Taxation data shows that only two percent of taxpayers earning less than $20,000 per year receive a mortgage interest subsidy.[26] Since nearly all of these people are renters, they do not qualify. However, the rhetoric of politicians and the real estate industry would lead one to believe that the main purpose of the subsidy is to help those in the $20,000 to $40,000 bracket become homeowners. Yet only 23 percent of these taxpayers claim a mortgage interest deduction, because many of them are either renters or do not itemize their deductions.[27] Even those in the $40,000 to $50,000 bracket derive little benefit from the mortgage subsidy. Only 28 percent claim the deduction, and the average value of their subsidy in 1994 was only $944 compared to $8,348 for those earning more than $200,000.[28]

Rather than expanding home-ownership for average Americans, the mortgage interest subsidy primarily expands the size of the homes of those perfectly able to foot the bill themselves. Interest on up to $1 million of mortgage loans on a primary residence and a second home are fully deductible. (A 1993 proposal to limit the interest deduction to the first $300,000 of a mortgage on a primary residence was vigorously opposed by the real estate industry, despite CBO estimates that the limit would affect only about one million taxpayers.[29]) In case that is not enough, the interest on a home-equity loan up to $100,000 can also be deducted. Those who rent because they cannot afford a $75,000 mortgage and cannot even imagine a million dollar loan, are helping to pay for a subsidy for the wealthy that they themselves cannot qualify for because they do not earn enough. There is no deduction for rent payments, so those at the bottom—renters—end up subsidizing those at the top—homeowners. It is reverse welfare. The inequity of this situation is even more disturbing when you consider that only 20 percent of families below the federal poverty line receive federal housing aid, while 75 percent of those earning more than $100,000 benefit from the mortgage subsidy.[30]

There is still more. Under legislation passed in 1997, a homeowner is allowed up to a $500,000 tax-free capital gain on the sale of a primary residence, and a taxpayer can use the exclusion repeatedly every two years.[31] The capital gain, regardless of the amount, on the sale of a primary residence is completely tax-deferred if another home of equal or greater value is purchased within two years. When a homeowner dies, the gain on the current home, plus any accrued gain on previous homes, escapes taxes permanently. (All capital gains escape taxation at death.) The capital gains subsidy for homeowners came to almost $20 billion in 1997, and the death exclusion for all other capital gains added about another $13 billion.[32]

To homeowners, of course, this seems only "fair." And because much of the increase in value of assets reflects not a true capital gain, but inflation, there is some merit to this claim. However, the issue is of the sensibility of taxing capital gains, and more particularly, inflation, which is a creation of government. Allowing governments to benefit from taxing a byproduct of their own irresponsibility sets up a dangerous reinforcing loop. However, as long as there is a capital gains tax, any tax preference is nothing more than another subsidy. The generous subsidies showered on homeowners are more than just an equity issue. They are working against the long-term best interests of even those who presently benefit from them. As the CBO notes,

> *The tax advantages for owner-occupied housing encourage people to invest in homes instead of taxable business investments. That shift may contribute to a relatively low rate of investment in business assets in the United States compared with other developed countries. . . .Currently, about one-third of net private investment goes into owner-occupied housing. Consequently, even a modest reduction in housing investment could raise investment significantly in other sectors.[33]*

Almost as unfair, and even more expensive, is the tax exemption for employer-paid health insurance. The GAO calculated that this subsidy cost the government $79 billion in reduced income and payroll tax revenues in 1998.[34] As we saw in Chapter 3, the tax-exempt status of employer-provided health insurance had its origins in the wage and price controls of World War II when employers, unable to increase wages, used health insurance to attract workers. The practice grew enormously, and its inherent incentives to overconsume health services became a major, fundamental problem of our health care system. It is also a deceptive and fundamentally unfair provision of the tax code.

The deception arises from the fact that the revenue lost to the exemption is partly made up by increased taxes on the same people who benefit from the exemption. For those without employer-provided benefits, the situation is considerably worse. The exemption essentially shields part of the income of those lucky enough to have an employer-provided health care plan from income taxes. Those who pay for their own health insurance get a reduced tax break, and those without insurance get no subsidy at all. Nevertheless, they pay taxes to subsidize those who do. The CBO summed up the twin problems as follows:

> *. . . the money taxpayers save because of the exemption must be made up through other taxes, higher deficits, or reduced government spending. Thus the direct benefits of the tax exclusion are less than they might appear to be. Although part of the tax*

subsidy for people with comprehensive employment-based health insurance comes at the expense of the uninsured and underinsured, part of it comes in the form of higher taxes (either direct or indirect) on the people who benefit from the exclusion. Moreover, some would view it as unfair to tax uninsured people to subsidize insurance for those with the most generous coverage.[35]

Big business and the big labor unions are fast supporters of the health insurance subsidy because they are the primary beneficiaries. Most union contracts provide for generous employer-paid health coverage, which is nothing more than tax-free income. The tax subsidy typically equals 26 percent of the value of the insurance according to the CBO.[36] While employers decry the spiraling cost of providing health insurance, they like the idea of having a portion of the salaries they pay exempt from payroll taxes. Moreover, producing the same after-tax compensation solely through taxable wages would raise their total labor costs. However, the significant benefits accruing to these selected employers and employees are due to a tax subsidy from U.S. taxpayers.

In 1994, some of the health-care reform plans discussed in Congress proposed ending the employer-provided health insurance tax exemption, which led AFL-CIO President Lane Kirkland to protest, "The real burden will fall squarely on the backs of working families."[37] The implication being, again, that the average American is the primary beneficiary of this subsidy. Not quite. While 60 percent of the population is covered by employment-based health insurance,[38] the subsidy is heavily skewed in favor of higher wage earners. CBO figures show that for families with employer-provided health insurance who earn less than $10,000 per year, the tax subsidy is worth 11 percent of their insurance premiums. For covered families earning over $200,000 annually, the subsidy amounted to 33 percent of their premiums.[39] Sixty percent of the subsidy ends up in the pockets of the highest paid 20 percent of Americans.[40]

The GAO found that 85 percent of the 34 million Americans without health insurance in 1989 were either working or living in a household headed by a worker.[41] These uninsured families, while exposed to potentially catastrophic health care expenses, were nonetheless paying to subsidize the comprehensive health insurance for upper-income Americans. Moreover, the subsidy is not limited to individuals. The CBO also found that the health insurance exemption effectively creates a labor subsidy for large employers at the expensive of small ones.[42] Therefore, not only are poor Americans subsidizing the health care of the rich, small businesses are subsidizing the labor costs of large businesses. Remember, the market distortions caused by the health insurance subsidy are a primary driving force behind the nation's spiraling health care costs. It is the perfect perverse subsidy. In the face of such obvious market inefficiency and inequity, the CBO concluded that the health insurance tax subsidy was "hard to justify given the available information."[43] How about *impossible*?

The second largest federal tax subsidy program is another employer-provided tax exemption—the exclusion for pension contributions and earnings. This provision defers, until retirement, taxes on employer contributions to qualified retirement plans and exempts income earned by the funds in those plans from taxation. The GAO put the cost of this subsidy at $57 billion in 1993.[44] The *Green Book* states, "The tax treatment of pension contributions and earnings has encouraged employers to establish qualified retirement plans and to compensate employees in the form of pension contributions to such plans." Sounds terrific: employers help employees save for their retirement. Indeed, it would seem like a particularly wise policy given the future of Social Security. Nevertheless, as with all federal subsidies, there is more and less than meets the eye.

In 1988, 48 percent of full-time workers in the private sector were covered by an employer-sponsored pension.[45] By 1998 that had dropped to 42 percent, and nearly half of all pension plans, 43,000 in all, had been terminated.[46] As you might guess, there are definite characteristics of those with coverage and those without. Younger workers were much less likely than middle-aged or older workers to be covered. And while only 13 percent of those earning less than $10,000 per year in 1988 were covered, 72 percent of those making more than $30,000 had employer-sponsored pensions.[47]

Sixty percent of the companies in the manufacturing, mining, financial services, transportation, and public services industries provided pension coverage, but the rate drops to less than 30 percent for agriculture, retail trade, and services other than financial and professional.[48] A familiar picture emerges of those in the higher paying union and professional jobs receiving the lion's share of the subsidy. As with the health insurance subsidy, the 58 percent who receive no benefit from the pension tax subsidy must still pay taxes to help subsidize those who do. The young, those without pensions, and those in lower-paying jobs, pay taxes to subsidize the pensions of their older, wealthier, more fortunate fellow citizens. Not only are young workers forced to provide a massive Social Security subsidy for their elders, but they are also required to subsidize their pensions. And that is not the end of it.

The Studebaker Company, a sizable automobile manufacturer, went bankrupt in 1963. The pensions of 6,900 employees under sixty years of age and with less than ten years experience went down the tubes with the company.[49] This focused the attention of Congress on the security of private pensions, and it was one of the factors resulting in the passage of the Employment Retirement Security Act of 1974 (ERISA). One of the provisions of this act established the Pension Benefit Guarantee Corporation (PBGC), a government-owned corporation to insure the defined-benefit pensions of workers against the failure of their employers. It was another well-intentioned idea, specifically designed not to cost the taxpayers a dime. Companies operating pension plans were to pay insurance premiums "to provide for sufficient revenue to the fund for the corporation to carry out its functions under this title," according to the legislation.[50]

In 1993, the PBGC insured $900 billion in pension assets, and the present value of its deficit was estimated to be $35 billion.[51] The CBO noted, "The federal government is almost certainly responsible for those liabilities of PBGC that exceed PBGC's assets, even though ERISA states that the United States is not liable for any obligation or liability incurred by PBGC."[52] The agency also flatly stated that the reason for the PBGC losses is that Congress specifically permits companies to underfund their pension plans,[53] and then to buy subsidized federal insurance backed by U.S. taxpayers. This sorry state of affairs led to the passage of the Retirement Protection Act of 1994, which, along with a booming economy, improved the PBGC's financial situation considerably.

Nevertheless, the PBGC is still a very real liability for the taxpayers. As of December 1997, the multi-employer insurance fund—the one that covers most large, unionized employers—had assets of $596 million and liabilities of $377 million.[54] The PBGC had $219 million of capital to cover its insurance of hundreds of *billions* of dollars of large-company pension benefits. In October 1998, the GAO reported, ". . . underfunding among some large plans continues to pose a risk to the agency;" and, "Despite improvements in PBGC's financial condition, risk to the agency's long-term financial viability remain."[55] While all taxpayers are on the hook, those whose pensions are insured by the PBGC also benefit from the insurance subsidy. Those without pensions just get the liability. Half of the American people, who have only the teetering Social Security system to look to for their retirement, not only subsidize the pensions of those considerably better off then they are, they also subsidize the federal insurance that protects those pensions. Such multiple subsidies are commonplace and are frequently just as irrational.

Having to pay taxes on taxes must be a violation of one of the Laws of Nature that the founders referred to in the Declaration of Independence. Perhaps that was the thinking behind the creation of the federal income tax deduction for state and local income, real estate, and personal property taxes. Before the Tax Reform Act of 1986, state and local sales taxes were also deductible.[56] In 1998, state and local tax deductions resulted in $48 billion worth of lost revenues to the federal government.[57] But while the deduction might seem in the spirit of the nation's founders (more likely they would be horrified that there is an income tax at all), the resulting subsidy certainly conflicts with their strong belief in self-reliance and their view of the relationship between the federal and state governments.

Virtually any tax deduction encourages the use of the deductible activity because the federal government effectively picks up a part of the cost of the activity. The reduced cost makes the activity more attractive and increases its usage. It makes no difference whether the activity is health insurance or state income taxes. As such, the federal deduction for state and local taxes subsidizes state and local taxes, thereby increasing their use. Those governments can raise revenues by increasing tax rates higher than they could without the federal subsidy, or by imposing new taxes that would meet stiff opposition if the federal government were not picking up part of the tab. This in turn allows state and local governments to increase spending at the expense of the federal government. For all practical purposes, they spent $48 billion in 1998 that they did not have to raise in taxes from their own constituents. That would have produced a call-to-arms from the founders: taxation without representation. State and local governments are essentially taxing Americans outside of their jurisdiction who have absolutely no say in how much they are taxed or how the money is spent.

Tax expenditures are like entitlements; there is no upper limit on the amount of the expenditure. This is in contrast to defense spending, for instance, which has an annual budget. Thus, there is no ceiling on the amount of state and local taxes that citizens of any state or locality can claim. The higher a state raises its income taxes, the higher the federal tax subsidy it receives. That subsidy is paid, in part, by the federal taxes of citizens of other states; those living in low-tax states often subsidize those living in high-tax states. While the federal government acts as the tax collector, the net effect is that high-tax states are taxing the citizens of low-tax states. Clearly, allowing politicians to tax people they need not be accountable to, nor face on Election Day, is a prescription guaranteed to produce inefficient and irresponsible government.

The inequities associated with the other tax subsidies we have looked at are also manifested in the state and local tax deduction. The deduction is only available to the 30 percent of taxpayers who itemize their deductions, and of course, those are mostly the highest income taxpayers.[58] Again, the 70 percent who do not itemize subsidize itemizers who live in states and localities with taxes higher than their own. Moreover, wealthier communities make out the best. As the CBO found, communities with higher than average income levels have more residents who itemize and are more likely, because of deductibility, to spend more then lower-income communities.[59]

We have already seen that the Social Security system transfers massive amounts of wealth from the young to the old. But the subsidy does not end there. Most Social Security benefits, as well as Railroad Retirement benefits (a federal program, similar to Social Security, for railroad employees), are tax-free—a tax subsidy that amounted to $25 billion in 1998.[60] Couples with incomes below $32,000 pay no tax on their benefits. For higher incomes, taxes are paid on a portion of their benefits, but, regardless of how much they make, some of their benefits are exempt from taxes. Three-quarters of Social Security recipients pay no taxes on their benefits.[61] The same people paying for their Social Security benefits pay for this $25 billion subsidy. For workers without pensions, this is the fourth subsidy they are funding for other people's retirement.

If Social Security was as it was originally sold—a system whereby workers fund their own retirement—then there might be some grounds for special tax treatment. However, it is anything but that. As we have seen, most present retirees are receiving benefits far exceeding their contributions; their benefits are little more than gifts from today's workers. The tax subsidy amounts to free icing on the free cake. Fully taxing these benefits would have a negligible effect on those whose sole income is Social Security. In 1998, a couple over 65 paid no tax on an adjusted gross income—including half their Social Security benefits—of $32,000.[62] Because the average benefit for a retired couple in 1998 was $14,115, nearly all of those solely dependent on Social Security would still receive their benefits tax-free.[63] Clearly, the exemption is not aimed at protecting the incomes of the poorest retirees.

In 1917, Congress was preparing to raise taxes to help pay for World War I, but some members feared that the higher revenues would come at the expense of churches, colleges, and charities. Because it was anticipated that higher tax rates would be temporary, a temporary charitable deduction was added to the Revenue Act of 1917.[64] Thus was born the nonprofit tax subsidy, which, over the years, became very permanent. In 1998, it cost $21 billion.[65]

The argument from 1917 through 1986 (the last time nonprofit deduction provisions were amended), has been that without the deduction charitable groups could not survive. Not surprisingly, armies of charitable and nonprofit organizations were the proponents of this theory. Although it had no basis, it was, nonetheless, an argument that seemed plausible, and the ramifications, if the deduction were eliminated and the argument proved correct, were more than most politicians wanted to think about. Therefore, through numerous revisions of the tax code, the deduction remained.

The Tax Reform Act of 1986 eliminated charitable deductions except for those who itemize, again, limiting the subsidy to 30 percent of all taxpayers. More importantly, it was a meaningful test of the dire predictions of the consequences of eliminating the deduction. The deduction had previously been eliminated for non-itemizers in 1977, which brought heavy pressure from the nonprofit lobby to restore it in 1978. United Way Vice President Jack Moskowitz testified before Congress that, ". . . all of those financially fragile entities so important to American life, such as local community centers, small colleges, day care centers, halfway houses, co-ops, little theaters, will surely go under."[66] The Economic Recovery Tax Act of 1981 restored the deduction to all taxpayers within certain limits, presumably averting the predicted disaster.

Just a few years later, Congress again elected to court disaster by eliminating charitable deductions for non-itemizers once more, and if the predictions were correct, the landscape should have been littered with the carcasses of dead charities. Not quite. By 1992, the assets of nonprofit organizations had reached one trillion dollars,[67] and in 1997, donations to charitable organizations reached a record $130 billion.[68] In 1992 alone, 29,000 new nonprofits came into existence, and that segment of the economy was growing four times faster than the economy as a whole.[69] A study conducted by Independent Sector, an organization of some 800 charitable groups, found that 73 percent of American households gave an average of $880 to charities in 1993.[70] Another study found that more than half of charitable giving comes from Americans earning less than $50,000 a year.[71] That is despite the fact that most of them could not deduct the contributions since they did not itemize.

What about those who can take advantage of the tax deduction? Peter Dobkin of the Yale Program on Nonprofit Organizations states that, "The vast majority of the very rich show, if anything, less of a philosophical inclination to give than their predecessors."[72] Again, the arguments about the critical importance of government subsidies proved to be nonsense. Clearly, Americans are supportive of nonprofit organizations, with or without tax deductions.

Probably the images that most often come to mind for most Americans when they think of nonprofit organizations are those of groups like the United Way, the Girl Scouts, or the American Cancer Society. But how about the Workplace Health and Safety Council? Despite its pro-worker-safety-sounding name, it is comprised of a group of businesses opposed to efforts to strengthen worker-safety regulations. It is nonprofit, and donations to the Council are tax deductible. How about People for the Ethical Treatment of Animals (PETA), a group opposed to the use of any animal products for food or clothing. Their tactics have included spray painting McDonald's restaurants and harassing people who wear furs.[73] This is another tax-exempt nonprofit. You are supporting these groups along with the other one million organizations that have 501(c)(3) tax exemptions from the Internal Revenue Service.[74]

Every time someone deducts a contribution to a nonprofit, it translates into a subsidy from the U.S. government. In 1994, $70 billion was deducted by taxpayers.[75] But while the taxpayers foot the bill, they get no say in which organizations receive the federal subsidy. That is determined solely by the person making the deductible contribution. If John Doe, who is in a 30 percent tax bracket, makes a $1,000 donation to Citizens for Sensible Control of Acid Rain, the effect of the deduction is that his net contribution after taxes is $700––taxpayers pick up the remaining $300. Whether you like it or not, your tax dollars are supporting an organization which is comprised of companies from the coal and electric industry opposed to the Clean Air Act.[76]

It is illegal to use federal money to engage in political activity, but consider the Civic Events Corporation of San Diego and Chicago '96 of . . . Chicago. The former is a nonprofit that funneled "charitable contributions" to the Republican presidential nominating convention in San Diego in 1996.[77] The latter served the same purpose for the Democratic convention in Chicago.[78] By forming these "non-profits," the political parties set up a conduit for big political donors to make charitable contributions to the nonprofit organizations, which were then funneled into the political conventions. The politicians received about $20 million (in addition to the $12 million from the U.S. Treasury that each party receives, by law, for their nominating conventions).[79] The big donors got tax deductions and the taxpayers further subsidized the conventions. But remember, using federal money for political purposes is illegal.

Even if the organization is one that you wholeheartedly support, you still might not find tax subsidies necessary or appropriate. Consider the nation's largest nonprofit, Catholic Charities. In 1994, it raised $339 million in donations, some portion of which was federal subsidies.[80] The organization also received $1.2 billion directly from federal, state, and local governments in grants and contracts.[81] About half of the nation's one million nonprofits are charities, and they received $40 billion the same way.[82] With over 70 percent of Catholic Charities' $1.9 billion budget coming from governments, the organization is very close to becoming a pseudo-government agency. Many other big charities, including The United Cerebral Palsy Association and CARE, are in the same situation.[83] Given the extraordinary level of direct nonprofit government funding, it becomes even more difficult to justify additional support through tax subsidies.

Compared to the $57 billion in tax subsidies, grants, and contracts, the $1 billion postal subsidy for nonprofits almost seems insignificant; except that it is one billion dollars.[84] While soliciting tax-deductible contributions, 400,000 nonprofits mail twelve billion pieces each year at a Congressionally-mandated discount rate that results in a billion dollar loss for the Postal Service—and another billion dollar subsidy for the nonprofits. The subsidy is paid by other postal users who are forced to pay higher rates. Most of the burden falls on first-class mailers who paid 138 percent of their fair share in 1992, according to a study by the U.S. Postal Rate Commission.[85] Part of the postage you pay to mail a first-class letter is further subsidizing nonprofit groups whose objectives you may vehemently oppose. Alternatively, you could be helping a worthy charity defray its expenses—like the $630,192 salary, $208,947 in benefits, and $21,867 expense account allowance that the Ford Foundation paid its president in 1996.[86]

A charitable deduction can be claimed not only for cash contributions, but also for items of value that are donated. The law allows the market value of the item to be deducted, and this has inspired some very imaginative tax planning. An investigation by the *American Spectator* found that Bill and Hillary Clinton donated their used underpants to charity and deducted one dollar per pair from their taxes.[87] Expensive artwork is a favorite donation of the wealthy. Since the market value of a piece of art is quite difficult to determine, it allows the donor to value it very dearly; and it makes no difference what the donor paid for the piece. Thus, a piece purchased for $50,000 might, in the eyes of the owner and a friendly art dealer, be worth $200,000 several years later. The owner could then donate the piece to charity, escape paying any capital gains tax, and claim a $200,000 tax deduction. Another scheme that has been spreading is donating cars to nonprofits that then auction them off. The law allows the donor to claim a deduction for the "blue book" price of the vehicle––regardless of its condition. This provision allows people to "donate" cars that are little more than junk to charity, and then to claim a deduction for far more than the actual value of the vehicle. An auctioneer who handles cars donated to the Kidney Foundation estimated that 60 percent of donated cars were seriously in need of work. Regardless of the intention of a tax subsidy, it will generate abuse.

There are many more federal tax subsidies. For 1993, the Joint Committee on Taxation listed 124 separate exemptions, exclusions, deductions, credits, deferrals, and preferences.[88] However, the nine just detailed are the heavy-hitters for individuals, comprising over 70 percent of the $350 billion in 1997 individual tax expenditures. In 1998, Corporations received tax subsidies estimated to be worth $50 billion, with some estimates as high as $75 billion.[89] A typical provision is the tax exemption for "controlled foreign corporations," which allows American businesses to incorporate in other countries to escape

U.S. taxes. Royal Caribbean and Carnival Cruise lines are examples of companies that are essentially owned by Americans, are based in America, but have
paid no U.S. taxes on hundreds of millions of dollars in profits because they
are incorporated in foreign countries.[90] Another example is Section 936 of the
Internal Revenue Code, which, since 1976, has allowed companies with facilities in Puerto Rico to escape taxation on $35 billion in profits.[91] The program
was intended to create jobs, but after nearly twenty years and billions in subsidies, Puerto Rico's per capita income is less than that of the poorest state, Mississippi, and manufacturing employment has decreased.[92]

As with income taxes on individuals, the revenue lost by a tax preference granted to one corporation must be made up through additional taxes on
others (or individuals). Economists agree that the corporate income tax is
among the least efficient ways for governments to raise revenue. There is considerable debate about who really pays corporate taxes because corporations
are fictitious persons, and only real persons can be taxed. Corporate taxes are
actually paid by employees in the form of lower wages, stockholders in the
form of lower dividends, or the corporation's customers in the form of higher
prices. To the extent that a tax is shifted to customers, it is really a hidden tax
on individuals. Taxing dividends subjects a corporation's profits to double
taxation—once at the corporate level and again when they are paid as dividends to individuals. The United States is the last industrial country that taxes
corporate profits twice. Nonetheless, many economists support the corporate
income tax. Economist Joseph A. Pechman writes,

> *Data for the United States indicate that, without the corporation
> income tax, the tax system would lose the tax that contributes
> most to progression in the top brackets. (Even if half the corpo-
> ration tax is assumed to be shifted [to consumers], the other
> half—which is borne mainly by middle- and high-income share-
> holders or holders of capital in general—is still significant.) The
> corporation income tax is needed, therefore, to safeguard much
> of the progression the system possesses.*[93]

Mr. Pechman argues that the corporate tax helps restore the progressivity—
where the rich pay a higher percentage of their income in taxes than the poor—
to the tax code that the plethora of individual tax subsidies has diminished. In
essence, one bad idea deserves another.

While the tax code penalizes corporate profits by taxing them twice, it
also provides a mechanism for making those profits disappear: the interest deduction. To arrive at their taxable income, Corporations are allowed to deduct,
from their gross revenues, the reasonable expenses they incur in the course of
business operations. Interest on debt is one of those expenses, and there is no
limit on how much interest can be deducted. Regardless of how profitable its
business operations are, a corporation can minimize profits, or even produce a
net loss, simply by borrowing money and then using its profits to make deductible interest payments. While some borrowing is done for legitimate busi-

ness reasons, corporations have borrowed hundreds of billions of dollars primarily to take advantage of the tax deduction, and their interest deductions now run more than $200 billion each year.[94] Whenever a corporation takes on debt, it receives a government subsidy. The business pays most of the interest cost, while the taxpayers pick up the rest.

Corporations have two mechanisms, other than profits, for raising capital: issuing stock and borrowing. The tax subsidy lowers the cost of debt thereby encouraging the use of the riskier mechanism. Investors buy stock with the anticipation of receiving dividends, but a corporation is not obliged to pay them. On the other hand, lenders must be paid—in good years and bad—or the firm can be forced into bankruptcy. However, because interest is deductible, the taxpayers pick up part of the interest tab, reducing the effective interest rate of debt. Thus, the effect of the corporate interest subsidy is to encourage businesses to raise funds in the riskier debt market rather than the equity market. Not only do the taxpayers lose, but investors are also exposed to additional risk, and the economy is made less efficient.

Between 1960 and 1991, corporate revenues grew from approximately $448 billion to $4,953 billion, an eleven-fold increase.[95] Yet, over the same period, corporate profits only increased from $42.9 billion to $348 billion, less than a seven-fold increase.[96] The data suggest that revenues grew nearly twice as much as profits, but the tax subsidy-induced increase in debt and the resulting higher interest deductions can account for most of the discrepancy. Federal Reserve figures show that between 1979 and 1989 alone, corporate debt nearly tripled from $774 billion to $2.1 trillion.[97] By 1989, corporate interest payments exceeded after-tax profits for the first time since 1934, and debt was beginning to bankrupt otherwise sound businesses.[98] LTV Corp., Southland, Integrated Resources, Campeau, Federated, Circle K, Ames Department Stores, Resorts International, Greyhound, Drexel Burnham Lambert, Jim Walter Corp., and Pan American are just a few of the large companies where excessive debt led to bankruptcy or a major restructuring to avoid bankruptcy. They were typical of companies that had expanded through debt, which the tax code subsidizes, rather than equities, which the tax code penalizes. In 1989 alone, 68,112 companies with assets totaling $67 billion entered bankruptcy.[99] Most of these companies did not have a business problem, they had a debt problem. As New York bankruptcy lawyer Brad E. Scheler noted, "You can still have a good business, but be in trouble and drowning,"[100] Ironically, many companies were drowning despite the tax subsidies that had induced them to get in over their heads in the first place. However, as long as subsidies are available, businesses will continue to pursue them. In 1994, AMR Corp., the parent of American Airlines, converted some of its equities to debt specifically to take advantage of the interest deduction.[101]

Solely on the basis of their adverse consequences, tax subsidies are indefensible. They produce more inequity, economic distortion, nonproductive and wasteful allocation of resources and inefficiency than any other government subsidy mechanism. In addition to their $400 billion annual cost, there is the economic cost, easily hundreds of billions of dollars, to the nation. Entire industries, such as the real estate tax shelter industry of the late 1970s and early 1980s, have been created to take advantage of tax subsidies. When Congress abruptly eliminates a tax preference, as it very occasionally does, the dependent industry collapses. Congress has enacted 140 tax revisions since 1976,[102] nearly all of which contained tax subsidy provisions. The economic inefficiency that results from this constant state of flux, and the regular enactment and repeal of tax incentives, cannot be overstated. However, without a doubt, the worst consequence of tax subsidies is the Internal Revenue Service (IRS) and the burden of complying with IRS regulations.

In his history of how great societies tax themselves to death, *For Good and Evil, the Impact of Taxes on the Course of Civilization*, Charles Adams concludes,

> *The most crucial problem, seldom addressed by any tax reformers, concerns not the question of rates—for we cannot judge a system by rates alone—but the dangers created by the growing powers of spying and tough penal laws used to enforce tax compliance.*[103]

This is an issue of no small consequence for a nation founded on the principle of liberty. Much of what we have successfully defended against external threats has been lost to the Internal Revenue Service. Congress has granted the agency extraordinary powers to lien and seize property, while at the same time limiting the rights of courts to review IRS enforcement actions. In 1990, the agency seized the bank accounts or paychecks of 2,631,000 taxpayers.[104]

Until the Internal Revenue Service Restructuring and Reform Act of 1998, the law allowed the IRS to seize the property of a taxpayer who failed to pay any tax thirty days after it mailed a "Notice and Demand." The new law requires the IRS to obtain the approval of a federal judge before seizing a taxpayer's personal residence, but the agency can still seize personal assets and business property without court approval. In contravention of the basic principles that this nation was founded on, the IRS presumed taxpayers were guilty until they proved themselves innocent. The 1998 Reform Act shifted some of the burden of proof to the tax collectors—but only for individuals and businesses with assets under $7 million. The IRS is still free to presume guilt for businesses worth more than $7 million.

Congress claims that the exceptional powers granted to the IRS are necessary to insure funding for important government services, and on the face of it, that almost seems reasonable. Nevertheless, an incredible percentage of what the agency does is in error, and that changes the situation from reasonable to frightening. The GAO found that 47 percent of the IRS communications that it sampled, including tax assessments, contained errors, 66 percent of which were termed "critical."[105] Now consider that the IRS assessed over 32 million penalties in 1995, according to Dan Pilla, author of *How to Fire the IRS.*[106] The tax collecting agency of the U.S. government, not some foreign nation, poses the greatest threat to the freedom of Americans, and the incomprehensible, subsidy-laden tax code is the primary reason. The 1981 tax act contained 185 pages.[107] The Tax Reform Act of 1986—which was called "tax simplification"—ran 879 pages, and the House resolution just to correct the errors in the 1986 Act contained 960 pages.[108] In 1997, Congress enacted legislation that added more than 800 pages to the tax code, bringing the total to 9,400.[109] The IRS is simply doing the bidding of an irresponsible Congress. As Senator David Boren remarked, "Political expediency has been the prime determinant of tax policy; not what was good for the country."[110]

Despite its extraordinary power, the IRS is losing the tax collection battle. It estimated that taxpayers did not report and pay $127 billion in taxes in 1992—a figure that the GAO contends is too low[111]—while the IRS reported that it was owed $214 billion in unpaid assessments in 1998.[112] While Congress has approved funding for additional compliance staffing each year from 1990 to 1995, compliance has not improved.[113] Partly out of desperation, Congress has appropriated $23 billion for the Tax Systems Modernization program (TSM) since 1990. This computerized information system is supposed to enable the IRS to collect tens of billions of additional dollars. But in 1993, the GAO found ". . . little basis for confidence in estimates of TSM program costs and benefits. In fact, the likelihood is slim that the currently projected TSM costs and benefits are accurate."[114] GAO's opinion had changed little by February of 1995.[115] Congress appropriates more and more money in a hopeless effort to force compliance with a tax system that is widely acknowledged, by those in and out of government, to be blatantly unfair and virtually impossible to comply with. In 1993, forty-one professional tax preparers, including twenty-five CPAs, answered *Money* magazine's challenge to prepare a tax return for a fictional American family. Just two were able to come within $500 of the target tax, and the calculated tax ranged from $31,846 to $74,450.[116] And these were professionals.

While former IRS Commissioner Peterson thinks the tax code is already beyond comprehension, Congress, on the other hand, seems to believe that endlessly manipulating an already impossibly complex tax code to subsidize favored interest groups need not affect tax compliance as long as the IRS is provided with enough authority and funding. Our politicians are simply repeating the mistakes of King George III. As Charles Adams observes,

> *A government that shackles its people with grossly inequitable tax laws and despotic enforcement practices loses all moral persuasion with respect to compliance and can hardly complain if its taxpayers resort to all kinds of schemes to protect themselves, including illegal ones.* [117]

A sure sign that moral persuasion is indeed being lost is the IRS finding that small corporation voluntary compliance dropped from 81 percent in 1980 to 61 percent in 1987.[118] In addition, between 1990 and 1998, the gross inventory of tax debt nearly tripled from $87 billion to $214 billion.[119] Though it has been bringing its might to bear—the number of levies has quadrupled since 1980[120]—the IRS is losing ground, and the GAO has advised Congress that noncompliance threatens our tax system.[121] However, the lessons of history and the advice of its own experts are no match for political expediency—particularly for members of the tax writing committees. The members of the House Ways and Means Committee make up only 10 percent of the House, but they take in 25 percent of all PAC contributions.[122] The explanation is simple, according to Law Professors Richard L. Doernberg and Fred S. McChesney of Emory University: the committee members are selling tax changes to special interest groups.[123] Unfortunately, selling subsidies has become the primary business of Congress.

While noncompliance is increasing, most Americans are still attempting to pay the taxes they owe. The IRS estimates that in 1992 taxpayers voluntarily paid 82 percent of their income tax liabilities.[124] However, the cost of trying to obey U.S. tax laws is steep. Arthur Hall of the Tax Foundation has estimated that the 1996 cost of compliance with the income tax laws came to $157 billion, $52 billion for individuals and $105 billion for businesses. That is very close to the $159 billion estimate of James L. Payne, author of *Costly Returns: The Burden of the U.S. Tax System*.[125] That $159 billion represented the expense that taxpayers incurred in record keeping, learning about tax requirements, preparing tax returns, and tax planning.[126] While $159 billion in costs for $828 billion in income tax revenue collected in 1996 seems excessive, Payne has determined that compliance costs are actually a small portion of the total cost burden of our tax system. Additional costs include enforcement, disincentives to production, the disincentive cost of tax uncertainty, evasion and avoidance, and government costs.[127] All told, Payne suggests that the real cost of our tax system is 65 percent of revenue collected *on top of the tax revenue*.[128] In other words, Americans incurred about $538 billion in costs in addition to the $828 billion they paid to the IRS in 1996. Our subsidy-ridden tax system has become so complex and inefficient, and has so many economic disincentives, that it costs $1.65 to produce each dollar of tax revenue. In its endless and irresponsible pursuit of subsidies, Congress has undermined the tax system to the point-of-no-return. As King George III learned, no amount of force will remedy the problem.

5

STEALTH SUBSIDIES: DEFENSE SPENDING

In the early 1980s, public attention was focused on waste and fraud in the Department of Defense (DOD) budget by revelations that the Pentagon had purchased hammers for $435 and coffee pots for $7,662. The usual explanation for very high prices for many military contract items is specialization and "equal allocation." Equal allocation refers to an accounting practice whereby the contractor adds up all its overhead costs, such as utilities, taxes, administration, and employee benefits, and then spreads this sum equally over all the items on a contract. As a legitimate contract expense, overhead must be paid either as a lump sum or spread over the contract items. Thus, if a contract called for a truck and four spare tires, 20 percent of the overhead cost would be allocated to each of the five items. This could result in the tires "costing" $1,000 each, with $800 of that price consisting of equal allocation of overhead. While this is a plausible explanation and one that has mollified Congressional and media critics, there is no basis in reality for the theory. Ernest Fitzgerald, author of the *The Pentagonists* and an Air Force cost analyst, has spent years investigating the concept, but has been unable to find any factual basis for equal allocation.[1] It is simply a cover story for Pentagon waste and inefficiency. The truth is that defense contractors load virtually everything they sell to the Pentagon with enormous amounts of real and imagined overhead. For example, jet engine maker Pratt and Whitney charged the Pentagon $20.79 for every dollar it spent on labor for TF33 engines.[2] Each dollar actually expended on labor was loaded with $19.79 of overhead, nothing out of the ordinary at the Pentagon.

Of course, defense contractors are not solely responsible for Pentagon waste. The DOD does its share. In their book, *The Defense Revolution*, Kenneth Adelman and Norman Augustine provide the following example of how a simple item can cost the DOD so much money.[3] The Pentagon wanted a missile manufacturer to supply six rolls of tape with the word "vent" printed every few inches for identification purposes on its missiles. Since the manufacturer did not make tape, it referred the government directly to the tape company. For an order of only six rolls, that company would not even read the Pentagon's nearly half-inch thick specification for tape and refused to make the numerous required certifications (mostly mandated by Congress). However, it indicated that the tape was available for $13.45 per roll. No good. The government needed all the paperwork, so it went back to the missile manufacturer and asked it to buy the tape and resell it to the Pentagon with all the certifications. The company indicated that its legal and administrative costs to do so would be about $441—bringing the cost of each roll to $87. In the end, the taxpayers paid $87 for each roll of tape that was worth, and could have been readily purchased for, $13.45. There is no doubt, Pentagon procurement is terribly inefficient and consequently, very expensive. Nor is it a secret. At least twelve studies of the defense acquisition process between 1960 and 1987 reached the same conclusion.[4] The last major study, the Blue Ribbon Commission on Defense Management (Packard Commission) termed the excessive costs and inefficiency "disastrous."[5]

Defense contractors have frequently been more than willing to milk this system for all it is worth. In 1985, House Oversight and Investigations Subcommittee Chairman John Dingell protested to then Defense Secretary Caspar Wineberger that his committee had discovered that Westinghouse had charged 63 hours of engineering time to develop a three-inch piece of common wire for use as an "assembly pin"—at a cost of $14,835.[6] For the five years before the "development" of the simple piece of wire, Westinghouse had used a wooden peg to do the job. There is no plausible explanation for that, except billing whatever you think you can get away with. Unfortunately, Mr. Dingell would have found it difficult to find a major defense contractor who had not done essentially the same thing many times. In 1988, over one thousand defense contractors were banned from receiving government contracts for at least part of the year for violations including bribery, bid rigging, and overcharging.[7] Remarkably, the defense industry had two years earlier created an industry ethics policy, the Defense Industry Initiative, specifically to preclude these types of problems. However, only thirty-nine of the one hundred largest defense contractors actually signed the initiative.[8] As Secretary of Defense Frank Carlucci told the Senate Armed Services Committee in 1988, "In the end, we may find that greed, not the system, causes most of the misdeeds."[9]

Defense contractors are by no means alone in violating the law for their own benefit. Frequently, the Defense Department itself is a partner in crime, and violations by Pentagon program and procurement personnel are routine. In a system loaded with perverse incentives, Pentagon managers are rewarded for getting weapons programs funded through completion, regardless of how far over budget the program is and whether the system works at all. As Harvard Professor Ronald Fox notes, "Indeed, if good management results in exposing problems in a program to public or Congressional criticism, a defense manager is likely to be criticized by his superiors."[10] In 1990, Captain Lawrence Elberfeld, director of the Navy's A-12 bomber program, went so far as to hide from Defense Secretary Dick Cheney that the program was a year behind schedule and a billion dollars over budget.[11] In March of 1990, when Cheney visited the McDonnell Douglas plant to review the progress on the A-12 program, Pentagon and company officials loaded various defective parts and incomplete assemblies into the main aircraft assembly area to hide the fact that there were no aircraft under construction. The following month, Cheney assured Congress that the program was on schedule and within budget and stated that building 620 A-12s for $100 million each was "the only sensible option."[12] Five weeks later, McDonnell Douglas and General Dynamics, the prime contractors, admitted the truth.

Elberfeld had likely viewed the A-12 as his ticket to becoming a rear admiral, and it very nearly was. (Promotions depend on the officer's military superiors, not the civilians nominally in charge of the Defense Department.) Just before the A-12 fraud was disclosed, the Navy announced Elberfeld's promotion, but Cheney's anger at being duped ended both the A-12 program and Elberfeld's navy career. Also forced into retirement was the head of the Naval Air Systems Command, Vice Admiral Richard Gentz.[13] Due in part to the actions of these officers, the taxpayers had wasted over $3 billion on the canceled program and still had to pick up the tab for their navy pensions. The Pentagon system offers substantial rewards for protecting a program by almost any means, with the maximum risk being early retirement with full benefits and likely a cushy job with a defense contractor. It is not difficult to see why the same pattern occurs repeatedly.

As for the co-conspirators, McDonnell Douglas and General Dynamics went on getting more Pentagon contracts even as they sued the government for an additional $2 billion on the A-12 contract. There is virtually nothing that a major defense contractor can do that would threaten its defense contracts. Northrop is certainly proof of that. The company, which Congressman John Dingell called a "continuing criminal enterprise," pleaded guilty in 1990 to 34 felony counts of falsifying test results on cruise missile and Harrier jet components and was fined $17 million.[14] Because the company has virtually no commercial business, the $17 million fine was, in effect, paid by the taxpayers through defense contracts. As part of a plea bargain, the government dropped 141 other criminal charges and discontinued investigations into fraud on the MX missile program and B-2 bomber.[15] Since then, the Pentagon has nonetheless paid billions of dollars to Northrop (now merged with Grumman), which continues to be one of the nation's largest defense contractors.

These patterns of waste and abuse have been documented in scores of reports and studies by various government and non-governmental entities over the past thirty years. Many of them have proposed reforms, and reform programs at the Department of Defense have become routine. Almost every new Secretary of Defense implements a new set of reforms, and we have a new Secretary about every three years. Yet why does nothing change? After leaving office in 1981, Defense Secretary Harold Brown concluded that the Pentagon was beyond reform.[16] George Washington University Professor Ralph Nash gave a frank explanation in testimony before the Senate Armed Services Committee in 1985:

Let me close by saying I have no illusions. None of the things I have suggested can be accomplished. The Pentagon is fully staffed with experts on why significant changes are impossible. . . . I wish you luck in your task, but I feel the best you will get is more studies of the problem.[17]

That is a very disheartening conclusion given that defense analysts have estimated that one-third of the defense procurement budget—nearly $100 billion each year—is wasted.[18] However, even a modest examination of the problem leads to the conclusion that Nash is correct. Reforming the Defense Department is a complete waste of time; reform programs have no effect because the source of the problem is not Pentagon procedures; it is the U.S. Congress.

Article one, Section eight of the Constitution makes it clear that the power and responsibility for raising and supporting armies and providing and maintaining a navy resides in Congress. The president, as Commander-in-Chief, commands our military forces, but Congress is fully responsible for maintaining and provisioning them. As such, that body, through self-serving appropriations and gross negligence, bears full responsibility for the unconscionable defense waste and abuse of recent decades. Politicians have long sought to bring defense spending and facilities home for their positive impact on local economies. Until the last thirty years or so, they squabbled over largely necessary defense programs. Historically, peacetime national defense spending was between one and two percent of Gross National Product (GNP).[19] Since Congress transformed the defense budget into a massive subsidy program, this has ballooned to between four and ten percent of GNP.[20] Enormously expensive weapons systems are evaluated primarily for their impact on local constituents and only secondarily, if at all, for their military value and necessity. The defense budget is the perfect subsidy program because self-serving politicians can engage in criminally wasteful spending while hiding behind the flag. As Samuel Johnson observed two hundred years ago, "Patriotism is the last refuge of scoundrels." More recently, Ronald Fox has updated Dwight Eisenhower's 1961 warning to guard against the military-industrial complex to a warning to guard against the "Congressional-industrial complex."[21] It is a warning that we can ill afford to ignore.

The problem goes well beyond simply buying more weapons, ships, and aircraft than are needed. Congress routinely appropriates tens of billions of dollars for weapons systems that do not work or that have no real military justification. And they do so with the full knowledge that the money will not enhance the defense of the nation. Rather, the expenditures are fully intended to be subsidies for local defense contractors and constituents because nothing produces campaign contributions like defense spending. Federal politicians are practically part-time Pentagon employees working on commission—a percentage of all the defense pork they bring home is recycled back to them by contractors and defense workers who are clearly intending to buy votes for additional defense spending. While providing jobs may seem to some a defensible position for members of Congress, it is well known that defense spending is the least beneficial economic activity because it produces few goods that are of use to the general economy. A dollar will produce far more benefit if it is left in the economy rather than being collected through taxes and expended on a defense program. M.I.T. economists Jerome Wiesner and Kosta Tsipis have concluded that the same amount of money that produces one job in the defense industry will produce two jobs in the non-defense sector.[22] As such, the profligate defense spending of Congress actually reduces the number of jobs in the economy, but the massive subsidies serve the interests of individual politicians exceedingly well.

That is not to say that Congress has undermined the nation's security, although, as we shall see later, it has precluded the possibility of fighting and winning two regional conflicts simultaneously as called for in President Clinton's "Bottom-Up Review." On the contrary, it is the vast superiority of America's armed forces that has enabled Congress to transform a significant portion of the defense budget into one of the nation's largest and least questioned subsidy programs. By any measure, the U.S. stands alone in the world militarily. While Russia retains a potent nuclear capability, its armed forces are a mere shadow of those of the former Soviet Union. With the Russian government's annual revenues less than what the U.S. Treasury collects in one week,[23] the plight of its military is likely to worsen. Indeed, things have gotten so bad that in the fall of 1998, the Pentagon was considering sending millions of Meals Ready to Eat (standard military field rations) to the Russian Army to help its soldiers survive the winter without having to sell their weapons.[24]

At close to $300 billion a year (including the Energy Department's nuclear weapons programs), our defense budget is seven times higher than major European countries[25] and nearly six times greater than Japan's.[26] China spends about $32 billion a year on defense,[27] and its two million-man army is the "world's best military museum," according to Robert A. Manning of the Council on Foreign Relations.[28] While China is making significant efforts to modernize its People's Liberation Army (PLA), Eric McVadon, a former U.S. Navy Admiral and defense attaché in Beijing notes that, "the PLA is coming from a position of truly extraordinary backwardness and obsolescence."[29] Two countries that we are greatly concerned about, Iran and Iraq, spend less than 5 percent of what we spend on defense.[30] According to the International Institute of Strategic Studies, the United States and its allies spend about $563 billion annually on defense, while our potential adversaries spend a total of just $92 billion.[31] Our military technology is at least a decade ahead of other countries and growing.[32] Indeed, we are building defenses against weapons that are not even on the horizon. The GAO reported that our best existing fighter, the F-15, "exceeds the most advanced threat system expected to exist,"[33] yet the Air Force is already committed to retiring these aircraft in favor of new F-22s, at a cost of up to $62 billion.[34] Congress has overwhelmingly supported the program despite the fact that there is no mission for the F-22 and that as a pure air superiority fighter, it is less capable than the multi-role F-15.[35] In fact, it is the $62 billion subsidy that Congress was voting for.

The story of the B-1 bomber is a capsule summary of how the nation's defense planning has been transformed into a quest for subsidies, which is manipulated by vested interests for self-serving purposes. The B-1 design began in the 1960s as a replacement for the venerable B-52, a 1950s heavy bomber. The plane was to be supersonic (faster than the speed of sound) and capable of penetrating Soviet air defenses to deliver a large nuclear payload. Initially, the Defense Department claimed the cost would be $37 million each,[36] but the actual cost, including the program to convert the B-1 from a nuclear to conventional bomber, exceeds $330 million each.[37] It has long been standard operating procedure at the Pentagon to propose weapons systems with wildly exaggerated capabilities at a fraction of the real cost. The GAO has politely pointed out this ongoing fraud to Congress: "Over the years, DOD has employed a systemic bias toward overly optimistic planning assumptions."[38] Annually, after huge sums of money have been invested, the Pentagon raises the cost and lowers the performance. It seeks ever more funding on the basis that it would be foolish to abandon a system on which we have spent so much. It virtually always works. Everyone in Congress is well aware of this practice, and nearly all support it as a very effective mechanism for quietly passing multi-billion dollar subsidy programs. In 1971, Senator Thomas McIntyre, then Chairman of the Senate Subcommittee on Defense Research and Development, noted:

> *We have been unable to either eliminate or substantially affect a single program getting ready to emerge from the far end of the pipeline. I have discovered, much to my own frustration, that the present viewpoint seems to be that we are committed to a system's ultimate production as soon as we have sunk virtually any money into it.*[39]

In 1973, when it became apparent that the cost of the B-1 would well exceed the Pentagon's understated price, that the plane would not be able to perform as advertised, and perhaps most importantly, that advances in Soviet air defenses made it very doubtful that it would be able to successfully complete its mission, it was still most unusual that the Senate Armed Services Committee cut $100 million from the Pentagon's requested B-1 funds. This action shocked Air Force officials, and a subsequent attempt in the House of Representatives to kill the B-1 entirely galvanized them into action. The Air Force and Rockwell International, the prime contractor for the B-1, undertook a coordinated effort to insure full funding for the program. This pioneering effort set the standard for future Pentagon-defense contractor strategies for major weapons systems procurement, and it is routine procedure today.

While the Air Force directed a major (and illegal) lobbying campaign, Rockwell developed a strategy to generate political pressure and campaign contributions all over the country. In this subsidies-across-America strategy, Rockwell and the Air Force sought to spread B-1 subcontracts from coast to coast. This necessarily meant selecting subcontractors based on Congressional District rather than best price and quality, but neither of those were the primary, or even important, objectives. Having different parts built all over the country may have decreased efficiency and increased costs, but it made for a very large and politically powerful group dedicated to the procurement of the B-1. As Frank Spinney, a cost analyst for 20 years with the Air Force and Defense Department, writes in his pamphlet *Defense Power Games*, "By designing overly complex weapons, then spreading subcontracts, jobs, and profits all over the country, the political engineers in the Defense Department deliberately magnify the power of these forces to punish Congress."[40] From Rockwell's standpoint, there was another significant advantage to this strategy: higher profits. They were able to add their "standard overhead" and profit percentage to the higher subcontract prices, thereby generating higher profits. As with nearly all defense contracts, the higher the costs, the higher the profits. As Ronald Fox has observed, "The Defense Department customarily does business with an inverted system of rewards and penalties. Contractors are often rewarded for higher than planned program costs with increased sales, contributions to overhead, and profits."[41]

When all of the subsidies had been passed out, contracts had been given to over five thousand contractors in forty-eight states and in nearly every Congressional district.[42] The addition of such big names as Westinghouse, IBM, Sunstrand, Airborne Instrument Labs, Avco, LTV, Garrett, General Electric, Goodyear, and Boeing to the alliance resulted in the combined weight of most of the military-industrial complex being brought to bear. The Air Force had invited Boeing to the party. Boeing had bid against Rockwell for the B-1 primary contract and lost. To insure that the influential Washington state Congressional delegation (who were big supporters of Boeing) got behind the program, Boeing was awarded a fat contract for guidance and weapons control electronics. Rockwell gave a contract to LTV of Texas for fuselage parts that it could have built in its own facility, but the Texas company could influence two powerful Texas politicians, John Tower and Jim Wright.

Many of the defense contractors now on the B-1 payroll were large corporations with well-funded political action committees (PACs) and even many smaller contractors had PACs. Together with individual employees, the contractor PACs were recycling vast sums of defense money into the reelection campaigns of B-1 supporters and the challengers of B-1 opponents. This was one of the primary objectives of the subsidies-across-America strategy. Having a large number of defense contractors involved in the program broadly expanded local political support, which greatly increased the political contributions that could be generated to buy votes for the B-1. Because nearly all of the companies involved derive substantial income from government contracts, their political contributions are little more than recycled tax dollars. The cost of buying political support for weapons systems is simply built into the price of the system, and of course, the more the Pentagon spends, the more contributions the politicians get. Thus, the Congressional-industrial complex was formed. While there has been much debate in Washington recently about public financing of Congressional elections, the truth is that the taxpayers have been financing most incumbents' campaigns for years.

In a thorough manner not often seen in its procurement program, the Air Force wanted to be certain that they brought all possible vested interests into the act, and labor unions were another significant source of political pressure and funds. They would be especially effective with Congressional liberals who tend to support labor and are often critical of large defense expenditures. Air Force Chief of Staff, General David Jones, personally met with the presidents of the Autoworkers and Machinists unions to solicit their support. Both unions represent large numbers of aerospace workers, and after meeting with the General, the union heads promptly directed their unions to join the lobbying effort.[43]

Having marshaled all their forces, the Air Force and Rockwell began the hard sell on Capitol Hill. Some hearings were held in Congress on the capabilities of the B-1 and the viability of its stated mission, but the B-1 forces knew that they would not likely prevail on those issues. Continuing the subsidies theme, they focused on jobs. They carefully calculated how many jobs would be brought to each Congressional district and produced a report (making a mockery of economic principles) showing that $15 billion spent on the B-1 would increase the nation's total output by over $41 billion and create nearly 200,000 jobs.[44] They did not point out that far better results would be achieved by simply allowing the taxpayers to hold on to their $15 billion and save it or spend it as they see fit. Not only would American citizens be $15 billion richer, but that money would be channeled into plants and equipment, producing products that are useful to the public. In response to the flawed economic report from the B-1 forces, the University of Michigan undertook a study showing that the $15 billion invested in defense spending actually produced *a loss of 150,000 jobs* as compared to the same amount of money spent on other public sector and private sector investments.[45]

A funding problem turned out to be about the only problem that the B-1 did not have. In 1987, a B-1 crashed after it hit a single pelican on a low-level flight. This is extraordinary for a four engine military aircraft. It is not unusual for military aircraft and commercial airliners to hit a whole flock of birds without catastrophic effects. Another B-1 crashed in 1988 after a fuel line ruptured. Again, this is remarkable for a combat aircraft. Incredibly, after more than twenty-five years of development and operation, the B-1 is very susceptible to engine damage in icing conditions. Icing conditions exist when the air is cold and the humidity is high, generally when the air temperature is below freezing and there are clouds. An aircraft flying in clouds in cold air can accumulate ice, which, if ingested into an engine, can cause damage sufficient to shut down the engine. The old B-52 bombers and commercial airliners have had very reliable anti-icing systems for many years. Without them, many scheduled airline flights from October through April would have to be canceled. The B-1, on the other hand, is prohibited from operations when the temperature is below forty-seven degrees and humidity is above 50 percent because its anti-icing system does not work.[46] That makes it essentially a sunny-day bomber. The Air Force states that this restriction would be lifted under wartime conditions, but an Air Force study showed that without the icing restrictions, 16 B-1s would only be able to make seven flights a day between them because of all the repairs resulting from engine damage.[47] Because the study was done by Rockwell, the prime contractor, the findings are probably optimistic.

The B-1's primary defense mechanism is an electronic system intended to confuse enemy radar and thus protect it against radar guided missiles. The original system, which was supposed to be able to detect and jam attacks from fifty types of threats (various types of missiles, fighters, and air defense systems) did not work.[48] A second system developed at a cost of $3.2 billion and designed to jam attacks from only ten types of threats failed as well.[49] And a third system also proved ineffective,[50] meaning that if a B-1 was not incapacitated by ice, it could very likely be downed by a missile, because while the Air Force was decreasing the number of the threats that the B-1 had to defend against, the number and sophistication of the air defense threats it would have to face was constantly increasing.[51]

If a B-1 did manage to survive long enough to reach its target, it still might not make it back. The entire B-1 fleet was grounded between December 19, 1990, and February 5, 1991, while temporary devices were installed to keep the engines from disintegrating.[52] This "fix" did not decrease engine failures; it just kept the engines from exploding.[53] A permanent fix was estimated to cost up to $500 million and take years to develop.[54] The never ending maladies of the B-1 and its unavailability for the Gulf War in 1990 led Senator Patrick Leahy to comment that "the best chance the B-1 has of getting to Saudi Arabia safely is if the Navy transports it there."[55] Certainly, the timing of the Air Force grounding of the B-1 fleet is curious, coinciding almost exactly with the Gulf War. It may have been a prudent action to protect a very vulnerable and unreliable aircraft. The GAO reported, "The B-1 did not participate in the campaign because munitions limitations, engine problems, inadequate crew training, and electronic warfare deficiencies severely hampered its conventional capabilities."[56]

The truth about why the B-1 sat out the Gulf War may have come out on March 5, 1991, when Congressman John Conyers, Chairman of the House Committee on Government Operations, disclosed that the Air Force had admitted to him in writing that the fully mission capable rate for the B-1 fleet was zero.[57] (The mission capability rate is an evaluation of an aircraft's ability to perform during combat.) However, despite the fact that the Air Force admitted that the B-1 had virtually no real combat capability, it continued to heap high praises on the plane. The following day in testimony before Congressman Conyer's committee, General Richard Hawley, Director of Operations for the Air Force, said that the B-1 is "the most accurate long range bomber in the world."[58] That might have been true. The B-1 might be very accurate on sunny days in non-combat situations if the engines hold out.

Additionally, there is the question of what we do with B-1s if they are ever really fixed? The aircraft was designed to drop nuclear bombs on the Soviet Union, a mission that many defense experts, Congressmen, Senators, and President Carter determined back in the 1970s could not be accomplished due to advances in Soviet air defenses. As early as 1971, the Pentagon Office of Systems Analysis, the National Security Council, and the White House Office of Science and Technology unanimously recommended that President Nixon cancel B-1 development based on their conclusion that the Air Force had understated the cost by 100 percent while overstating its performance by 50 percent.[59] Of course, they were wrong; it was much worse than that. Nonetheless, through 1985, the Air Force continued to maintain that the B-1 was fully capable of penetrating Soviet defenses and delivering its load of nuclear weapons. When the first squadron of B-1s went into service in 1986, General Lawrence Skantze called the B-1 "the best, most capable manned penetrating bomber in the world."[60] He was well aware that his statement was untrue. For the next five years the Air Force maintained that the B-1 just needed "one more fix" to make it a real nuclear threat, but the breakup of the Soviet Union pulled the rug out from under that approach.

With no other choice, the Air Force began touting the B-1 as a conventional (non-nuclear) bomber, and in 1992 it issued *The Bomber Roadmap* in which it indicated that the B-1 would become the nation's primary conventional bomber[61]—a mission for which it had virtually no capability. It was only capable of dropping small 500 pound "dumb" conventional bombs, the type that had an accuracy rate of just 25 percent in the Gulf War.[62] While the old workhorse B-52 bomber could carry four types of precision munitions (cruise missiles and smart bombs), the B-1 could deliver none.[63] But for just a couple of billion dollars, the Air Force assured Congress, it could solve that problem.

As always, Congress was happy to appropriate the money. The program to modify B-1s to allow them to carry 2,000 pound precision bombs will cost at least $2.4 billion.[64] At about the same time that Congress was approving the funding, the GAO was reporting that the nation had more than adequate interdiction capability (the ability to disrupt or destroy enemy targets), and that converting the B-1 to a conventional bomber simply added "more redundancy at a high cost."[65] But Congress has never been concerned about the military necessity of the B-1. In voting to appropriate the additional $2.4 billion to convert the bombers for an unneeded interdiction role, the politicians were simply continuing to fund a nearly 30 year-old defense subsidy program.

The GAO also has concluded that the B-1 will be less deployable in a conventional role than it was in its nuclear role[66]—which was effectively zero. Therefore, we got absolutely nothing for an investment approaching $35 billion, because the B-52 is a more capable and far more reliable bomber. During the Gulf War, B-52s flew just three percent of the air combat missions, but accounted for 30 percent of all the bombs dropped.[67] The B-1, which Congressman John Conyers called a "$300 million paper weight,"[68] has been carefully restricted from combat situations by the Air Force. When Iraqi forces again moved towards the Kuwait border in October of 1994, the U.S. mobilized hundreds of combat aircraft in preparation for a massive strike against Iraq. B-52s and every other type of U.S. Air Force combat aircraft were sent to the region—all except the B-1s.[69] They stayed home again. Finally, in 1999, a few, well-protected B-1s made a highly publicized appearance in Kosovo where their safety was virtually assured. After claiming in 1976 that the B-52s were wearing out,[70] a 1991 Air Force structural analysis showed that B-52s could continue to serve the nation well into the next century.[71] It is a damn good thing. One might think that, at this point, the B-1 subsidy program has just about run its course, but such is not the case. In addition to the billions of dollars being spent for B-1 upgrades and repairs, U.S. taxpayers continue to pay nearly $1 billion annually to operate the 95 bombers.[72] While they may not pack much punch, there is still plenty of pork left in them.

Tragically, many in the defense industry, the Air Force, the Pentagon, the White House, and Congress knew a decade before 1981, when the bomber finally went into production, that it could not perform its mission and that all the publicly stated cost figures were outright lies. Senator Dale Bumpers has stated that in the late 1970s, the GAO reported to Congress that the B-52s could have been inexpensively modified to extend their service life to 2020. The Pentagon and Congress rejected that option because "they wanted to spend billions."[73] In 1981, the Air Force Systems Command insisted that 100 B-1s could not be built for less than $27 billion. Air Force superiors, determined to build the B-1, forced the analysts to come down to $20.5 billion, the maximum price that the Reagan Administration and Congress would accept.[74] At the same time, the GAO informed Congress that the real cost of 100 planes would be at least $35 billion.[75] Nonetheless, the Air Force proposed, and the politicians approved, a contract for $20.5 billion. The GAO estimate turned out to be accurate, but most of those involved knew that at the time. The record showed that, almost without exception, costs for defense programs are always greatly understated and that the GAO produces far more accurate cost estimates.

In voting for the B-1, the politicians were not acting to enhance America's security, they were engaging in a subsidy orgy. In their never-ending quest for subsidies, the scoundrels conspired to defraud the American people, while hiding behind the flag. Moreover, by treating the defense budget as a giant cookie jar, our elected leaders are exacerbating one of the most serious problems with our armed services: their narrow pursuit of gold-plated weapons systems that enhance the prestige and budget of the individual services, whether or not they contribute to the overall military capability of the nation. This intense competition between the Army, Navy, and Air Force has resulted in extraordinary duplication in some areas while less glamorous, but critical, functions are dangerously shortchanged, and nearly always leads to the most expensive solution to every real, and frequently imaginary, threat. In a 1997 report, the GAO summarized the defense subsidy situation,

> . . . the underlying cause of these persistent and fundamental problems [is] a prevailing culture dependent on continually generating and supporting the acquisition of new weapons. Inherent in this culture are powerful incentives and interests that influence and motivate the behaviors of participants in the process—including components of DOD, the Congress, and industry.[76]

In the 1960s, when the B-1 was first envisioned, the Air Force was responding to a very real Soviet threat. Of equally great concern was the threat that American cruise missiles posed to the Air Force. Cruise missiles are highly accurate and inexpensive guided missiles that can deliver nuclear or conventional warheads over distances up to 1,000 miles. The Tomahawk missiles used with great success against targets in Baghdad in the Gulf War were U.S. Navy cruise missiles, and both the Navy and the Air Force used cruise missiles in the war against Serbia in 1999. There is no greater threat to the Air Force than these cheap, accurate, unmanned, jet-powered bombs. Quite simply, if you can deliver a bomb with a cheap missile more accurately than with a manned aircraft and without jeopardizing an air crew, why do you need terribly expensive, manned bombers? This question haunts the Air Force. So much so that for years it vehemently opposed all research and development of cruise missiles.

In the late 1960s, the Air Force developed a short-range cruise missile, the subsonic cruise armed decoy (SCAD), to help penetrate Soviet defenses, but it promptly canceled its own weapon once it realized that it might lead to support for a longer-range cruise missile.[77] According to the GAO, land attack cruise missiles "are very difficult to detect, track, and intercept under the best conditions."[78] A low flying cruise missile cannot be detected by ground-based radar until it is about 20 miles away, while an aircraft flying at ten thousand feet can be detected about 150 miles away.[79] Because of these capabilities, the U.S. Air Force lives in fear not of enemy missiles, but of American cruise missiles. Reflecting on the Air Force's attitude toward unmanned weapons systems, Former Director of Air Warfare in the Office of the Secretary of Defense John Transue noted, "The Air Force wants pilots to fly sorties through dangerous territory. It is almost a cultural thing with them."[80] The only reason that the Air Force has cruise missiles today is because Defense Secretary Melvin Laird ordered their development in 1972 and placed a Navy Captain in charge of the program to insure that the Air Force could not sabotage it.[81] Defense Secretary John Lehman described the cruise missile as "a classic civilian weapons system . . . invented by civilians and kept alive by civilians because it never fit into the services' agendas."[82]

An aircraft is a much better cruise missile platform than a ship because it is already moving at high speed and at a high altitude. Sea launched versions have to carry a launch motor and more fuel. As such, air-launched cruise missiles carry a 2,000 pound warhead compared to 1,000 pounds for a Navy version. Nonetheless, the navy has procured thousands of Tomahawks while the Air Force has done everything in its power to keep them out of its arsenal. That explains why, after launching a few dozen cruise missiles during the first week of the air campaign against Serbia in 1999, the Air Force had only 100 missiles left in inventory.[83]

During the Gulf War, both the Air Force and the Navy used cruise missiles against Iraq and gained valuable performance information. Based on the new data, the Navy immediately upgraded its Tomahawks, but the Air Force refused to request funds for an improved CALCM cruise missile.[84] Nor is any cruise missile program under Air Force control likely to succeed. In 1986, the DOD undertook the development of an advanced cruise missile called the Tri-Service Standoff Attack Missile (TSSAM) to be used by the Army, Navy, and Air Force. Unfortunately, the Air Force was designated as the lead service. By 1994, the usual problems were apparent: the missile was behind schedule, having reliability problems and the program cost had risen from $8.9 billion to $13.7 billion.[85] This was par for the course and better performance than many other programs. Nonetheless, the Air Force-directed program was canceled in December 1994, despite the following facts:[86]

- Although only thirteen of twenty-two test flights were successful, the GAO found that the failures were due to correctable manufacturing problems, not design problems.
- Both the Air Force and Navy expressed confidence that the TSSAM would meet their performance requirements.
- A March 1994 DOD report concluded that the TSSAM was still the most cost-effective of several missiles examined for a broad band of applications.
- The Air Force admitted that it had a requirement for a system with the TSSAM's characteristics and that it had no readily available alternative.

Given the dogged determination of the Air Force to build the B-1 and B-2 bombers despite staggering cost overruns, serious performance problems, and unanswered questions regarding their missions, the ease with which the TSSAM program was canceled is nothing short of extraordinary. That is, until you realize that advanced cruise missiles posed the single biggest threat to the B-1 and B-2 programs and the TSSAM was perilously close to being a successful program. Furthermore, if these bomber programs were cut back, the Air Force would have a tough task justifying the senseless and budget-busting F-22 fighter program. As far as the Air Force is concerned, these manned fighters and bombers *are* the Air Force; being reduced to a missile launching service is anathema. This "white scarf syndrome" is needlessly continuing to require aircrews to put their lives on the line and costing the nation hundreds of billions of dollars.

There is little doubt among dispassionate military experts that cruise missiles are a key to future military power. John Hopkin's Eliot Cohen writes:

As the defense budget falls, the tendency will be to concentrate on smaller numbers of high value platforms. These are not only aesthetically more satisfying and imposing, but politically more comprehensible. But the true indices of power in the future may lie in the possession of large numbers of cruise missiles and sensors.[87]

In the mid-1980s, U.S. analysts concluded that a heavy cruise missile offensive launched against the Soviet Union in 1995, with advanced cruise missiles, would hit 70 to 90 percent of their targets despite very heavy Soviet defenses.[88] (A similar attack by unescorted B-1 bombers would likely have wiped out the fleet, mostly before they delivered their bombs.) In a 1995 report, the GAO concluded:

> *Therefore, most future strike aircraft, if employed in conjunction with cruise missiles and a limited number of highly capable aircraft, may not require as long a range or as high a degree of stealth as originally planned. In addition, fewer strike, tanker, command and control, and electronic warfare aircraft may be required if cruise missiles are used to strike a larger portion of enemy targets.[89]*

That is, of course, the last thing that the Air Force wanted to hear. While the Navy has supported cruise missiles (partially because of the threat they posed to Air Force bombers), it has now come to perceive them as a potential threat to its precious aircraft carriers. Thus, the Navy has become tepid in its support for advanced cruise missiles, which helps explain why the TSSAM program was so easy to cancel. The response of the DOD to the GAO conclusion about cruise missiles is most revealing and reflects the serious threat that the Air Force and now the Navy think they pose to their expensive, manned platforms. The GAO report contains the DOD response:

> *DOD agreed that cruise missiles provided many useful capabilities and that new generations should be more flexible and versatile than existing missiles. However, DOD said that cruise missiles had inherent limitations that precluded them from successfully performing some strike missions; therefore, even though cruise missiles represent an important supplement to U.S. air power, they cannot replace manned aircraft. It also said that the Bottom-Up Review process took into account the capabilities of cruise missiles and other advanced munitions when it set forth its goals and modernization priorities.*

One would expect cruise-missile opponents to say that, but the GAO's observation on that response is particularly interesting:

> *Although DOD said it considered cruise missile capabilities as part of the Bottom-Up Review process, GAO found no analysis that specifically made the assessments it recommended. DOD did not provide any documentation to support its statement that cruise missile contributions were considered.[90]*

In fact, time after time, the GAO has reported to Congress that DOD analyses have been carefully constructed to support the "need" for ever more expensive manned weapons systems. Just as in preparing the *Bomber Roadmap* in 1992, the Air Force concluded that the B-1 should be the backbone of the nation's bomber fleet by conveniently ignoring the impressive performance of the more capable B-52s in the Gulf War about a year earlier.[91] Quite simply, a thorough analysis would not have supported the Air Force's plans for the B-1 and B-2 bombers. Despite full knowledge of the skewed and deceptive analyses upon which the DOD bases its weapons proposals, Congress continues to appropriate hundreds of billions of dollars for what amounts to a giant stealth subsidy program. In essence, the Pentagon has bought off the politicians with subsidies for their constituents. However, by sanctioning wholesale deception on the part of the DOD, Congress has encouraged and fostered dangerous misinformation efforts by the Pentagon against the citizens it is supposed to protect.

Saddam Hussein's 1990 invasion of Kuwait posed a serious threat to the United States because of its dangerous dependence on imported oil. However, it was a godsend for the Department of Defense, which was facing dramatic cuts in defense spending, and the Pentagon took maximum advantage of the opportunity. As most Americans sat glued to their TV sets, the U.S. military fed a round-the-clock stream of propaganda to its captive audience. It was a well-orchestrated disinformation campaign for the purpose of building popular support for expensive and unjustifiable new weapons systems. The press was expertly manipulated to deliver the message. Although virtually none of the reports so indicated, all news reports were censored by the military. David Evans, a U.S. Marine for twenty years and an analyst in the office of Secretary of Defense Caspar Weinberger, covered the Gulf War for the *Chicago Tribune*. He was shocked to find that hundreds of military officers were sent by the Pentagon solely to handle public relations—"a professional cadre of commissioned officers whose job it [was] to protect their institution."[92] Tom Wicker of *The New York Times* observed that "the Bush Administration and the military were so successful in controlling information about the war that they were able to tell the public just about what they wanted the public to know."[93] What the Pentagon wanted the American public to know was that its weapons systems all worked wonderfully, and that we clearly needed bigger and better versions that would be even more wonderful. What the Pentagon did not want Americans to know was the truth. Retired Army intelligence officer Phillip Davidson remarked, "The public only knows a fraction of what's going on. In terms of quantity, 75 percent of the information is not making it to the public. In terms of quality, 90 percent."[94]

It is important to understand that the Gulf War was not really a war at all. Rather, it was what retired colonel David Hackworth, writing in *Newsweek,* termed the "mother of all military anomalies."[95] After invading Kuwait, the Iraqis sat back and watched for nearly six months as a massively superior multi-national force was assembled around them. They neither attacked nor hindered the operation in any way. As Vice Admiral Paul D. Butcher noted,

"We had the luxury of time—161 days to land all that stuff with nobody firing a shot."[96] Then, too, in five military conflicts before the Gulf War, Iraq's military forces had a very poor record. An analysis of Iraqi forces versus Israeli forces in the 1973 Arab-Israeli War concluded that 100 Israeli soldiers were the combat equivalent of 330 Iraqis.[97] As for Saddam Hussein's ability as a military leader, General Norman Schwarzkopf had this to say, "He is neither a strategist, nor is he schooled in the operational art, nor is he a tactician, nor is he a general, nor is he a soldier. Other than that he's a great military man."[98]

Though very large, much of Iraq's army was poorly trained. Indeed, such was the state of Iraq's forces that Trevor Dupuy, author of *How to Defeat Saddam Hussein: Scenarios and Strategies for the Gulf War*, is confident that even if Iraq had been armed with our weapons and equipment, and the multinational forces had fought with theirs, the outcome would have been exactly the same—it just would have taken a little longer.[99] Finally, a House Armed Services Committee report estimated that at the beginning of the ground war the Iraqis had less than half the troops claimed by the Pentagon, and the U.S. and its allies had a five to one advantage in troop strength.[100] Perhaps military historian Major Ken Sheldon gave the best analogy. He compared the war to a Super Bowl game where only our team showed up.[101] In reality, the Gulf War was a thoroughly one-sided affair where most U.S. weapons systems were utilized under nearly ideal conditions against incompetent or nonexistent opposition.

The disinformation campaign began with the first combat action of the war. The story of the initial attacks of the air campaign at 3:00 AM Baghdad time on January 16, 1991, by Air Force F-117A stealth bombers, was widely reported in the media and repeated in a number of books written after the war. Countless articles told how the F-117As, invisible to radar because of their stealth technology, attacked the most heavily defended targets without the aid of fighter escorts, electronic jamming planes, or ground radar attack planes. A *Newsweek* article was typical:

> *Stealth bombers hit heavily defended targets near Baghdad. Because the stealths could elude radar and needed no fighter escort, eight with two tankers could do the job of seventy-five warplanes and support craft.*[102]

This was virtually word-for-word Pentagon propaganda, and it was repeated countless times in print and on TV. The Air Force took every opportunity to laud the invulnerability of the F-117. Americans had it drilled into them repeatedly: stealth aircraft are invisible to radar, making all non-stealth planes obsolete. The Air Force even went so far as to provide Congress with a chart showing that F-117s received no support from electronic combat planes during the war.[103] It was an absolute lie, but well within the bounds that Congress has set for the DOD when lobbying for new weapons/subsidy programs. The object of the disinformation was to build support for the B-2 bomber and the F-22 fighter, both of which employ stealth technology. And both of which have no definable missions, but astounding price tags.

Of course, the truth was a far different story. In fact, the Air Force was well aware that F-117s do show up on radar. During the war, U.S. Navy E-2C Hawkeye early-warning aircraft were able to detect them from up to 100 miles away.[104] (In 1999, the Serbians were able to shoot down an F-117 with an old, Soviet, radar-guided SA-3 missile.) Months after the war ended, Air Force officials quietly conceded that the F-117s did indeed receive protection from Air Force EF-111 Ravens that jammed Iraqi radars.[105] In addition, Air Force combat aircraft were used to set up diversions to draw the attention of Iraqi radars away from F-117s.[106] In its full-court-press to win funding for the B-2 bomber shortly after the war, Air Force General Charles A. Horner, who commanded air operations in the war, inadvertently confirmed the totality of the misinformation. He stated that one of the reasons that the B-2 was needed was that he had to send tankers and radar jammers along with the F-117s to attack targets in northern Iraq that were beyond the unrefueled range of the F-117s.[107] His statement confirmed that the DOD had lied about the radar invisibility of the F-117, had deliberately falsified a report to Congress about the plane's capability and operations in the war, and that the frequent representation that eight F-117s were the combat equivalent of seventy-five other aircraft was a complete fabrication. On the contrary, in many cases because of their very limited bomb capacity and range, it took more total aircraft to attack a target with the F-117 than with the Air Force's primary fighter-bomber, the F-15E. Many F-117 missions consisted of illuminating a target with a laser designator from a high (safe) altitude while F-15s, F-16s or F-111s actually delivered the bombs from a lower (exposed to ground fire) altitude.[108] The one thing that Iraqi forces did was put up intense ground fire.

Technically, the Air Force claim that the F-117s did not require fighter escorts on their missions was correct. What it did not say was that none of the attacking aircraft needed fighter protection because Iraq's Air Force sat out the war. In computer simulations before the first air attack, the Air Force concluded that it could lose as many as 150 planes on the first night.[109] However, only a few Iraqi fighters took off, and they quickly fled or were shot down. The Iraqi Air Force spent the rest of the war either hiding or trying to escape to Iran. To avoid having their air defense radars targeted and destroyed by U.S. F-4G "Wild Weasels," the Iraqis had turned most of them off two months earlier, and many remained off on the night of the initial attack. Those that were still active focused on the dozens of ground-launched pilotless drones (normally used as targets) that were sent in just ahead of the attack aircraft. As the Iraqi radars targeted the drones, F-4Gs launched 200 anti-radar missiles that homed in on the radars and destroyed most of them.[110] The few that remained were jammed by EF-111s. The still active early warning radars had been destroyed by U.S. Army helicopters minutes before the attack aircraft crossed into Iraq.[111] From the very beginning of the air war, Iraq's air defense system was either out of service, destroyed, or rendered useless, virtually eliminating the threat of missile attacks. Yes, the F-117s came through the first night's attack unscathed; but of a thousand aircraft involved in the attack,[112] so did all but one aircraft, a U.S. Navy F/A-18.[113] During the rest of the war, the Air Force lost fourteen aircraft—all to ground fire.[114] None were lost to missiles that stealth technology helps protect against. No F-117s were lost because they operated exclusively at night and at high altitude, not because of their stealth as the Air Force propaganda machine insisted. No F-111s, A-10s, or F-16s were lost on night missions[115] and not a single aircraft operating at high altitude was lost either.

Perhaps the most honest Air Force assessment of the F-117 again came inadvertently, as it was desperately trying to win funding for the B-2 bomber in September of 1991. Two months earlier, tests of the B-2's stealth characteristics had shown that the bomber was far more visible on radar than expected. Pentagon spokesman Pete Williams indicated that if the problem continued, then it was a "major problem."[116] Air Force Secretary Donald B. Rice rushed to the defense of the B-2, but in the process, he let truth about the F-117 slip out. He stated that while the B-2's radar-evading capability rated a grade of "D," its survivability still exceeded that of the F-117.[117] This, only nine months after the Air Force had maintained that the F-117 was invisible to radar. Surely the Secretary of the Air Force knew that there is only one grade lower than a "D," and his statement was another unintentional admission that the Gulf War hype about the F-117 was nothing more than a massive disinformation campaign to obtain funding for the B-2. Perhaps the best assessment of the F-117 was provided by a former Pentagon analyst and fighter designer, Pierre Sprey, who observed that the war showed it was "not really stealthy, with poor payload and poorer range."[118]

In June 1997, the GAO issued a comprehensive report on the air campaign in Operation Desert Storm. The following are a few of its findings on the F117: [119]

- The bomb hit rate was between 41 and 60 percent as opposed to the 80 percent stated in the DOD's Title V report to Congress.
- The Air Force claimed that the F-117 was the only aircraft it dared risk over downtown Baghdad, but the greatest concentration of air defenses was clearly not in the center of the city, but rather in its outlying regions where five other types of aircraft made repeated strikes.
- The F-117s never faced the defenses that proved to be most lethal in Desert Storm—daytime antiaircraft guns and shoulder-fired, heat-seeking missiles.
- Contrary to DOD claims, the F-117 was not the most effective bomber used in the war. The Vietnam-era F-111, which also had no losses, was 20 percent more effective, dropping the same laser-guided bombs on the same targets as the F-117.

It is notable that, for all the effort spent promoting the F-117, almost nothing was said about the Air Force's real star performer in the Gulf War: the A-10. This relatively slow (420 mph), ugly attack plane, nicknamed the Warthog, devastated Iraqi armor. While A-10s made up only 140 of the 1,800 attack aircraft involved in the war, they claimed 70 percent of the Iraqi tanks destroyed by planes.[120] In total, A-10s destroyed nearly 1,000 tanks, over 900 artillery pieces and 750 other vehicles.[121] One team of two A-10s destroyed 23 tanks in just one day.[122] Heavily armored, they are tough to bring down, extremely reliable, and possess fearsome firepower. Iraqi prisoners said that it was the plane they feared the most.

The A-10 was as effective as the Air Force pretended the F-117 was, yet the propaganda machine was silent about its achievements because the Air Force despises the A-10. It simply does not fit the Air Force image: sleek, stealthy, and supersonic. The Air Force accepted the plane reluctantly, primarily to keep the Army from getting it. For years, it has been trying to retire the A-10 in favor of an antitank version of the F-16, a mission for which it is wholly unsuited. The F-16 is too light, fast, lightly armored, and underpowered for the job, but it has the all-important Air Force look. Image is that important. Despite the fact that Iraq had 7,500 tanks and armored personnel carriers,[123] the Air Force refused to bring A-10s to the Iraqi theater until General Schwartzkopf, head of all American forces and an Army General, ordered them to. It planned to use less capable and more vulnerable but sexier aircraft to attack the tanks. In the end, Air Force General Charles Horner admitted to his staff that the A-10 saved his air campaign.[124] But for the public, it was the F-117.

In its efforts to manage the war as a propaganda tool, the Air Force was even willing to sacrifice the lives of its pilots. Many of the A-10s sent to the Gulf had a green camouflage paint scheme intended for service in northern Europe. However, this made them stand out in the desert against both the sand and the sky. Since the A-10s were primarily attacking tanks, often during the day, they were far more exposed than other aircraft to Iraq's most effective air defense—ground fire and shoulder-fired, heat-seeking missiles. (A-10s comprised 25 percent of all the aircraft hit during the war.[125]) To reduce their exposure, some A-10 units repainted their aircraft the same light gray color as most other Air Force aircraft. But the Air Force did not even want the A-10 to be there, much less to be the star of the show, and they were enjoying far too much success. Incredibly, the units that had changed their aircraft color to gray were ordered by the Air Force to repaint them green, thereby making it easier for Iraqi gunners to zero in on them.[126]

One of the most dramatic scenes ever to be shown on television has to be the footage of laser-guided bombs being delivered with unbelievable precision on targets in Iraq—usually by F-117s, according to the Air Force. One incredible shot showed a bomb going down the air shaft of a building. Most of the daily press briefings in both Saudi Arabia and the U.S. included video of such precision bombing missions. While the Iraqis complained that allied bombers were hitting schools, hospitals, and residential areas, the Pentagon produced the videos to backup its reports of precision bombing. More propaganda: the Pentagon had clearly and deliberately represented that the precision bombing it showed daily were typical bombing runs, but nothing could have been farther from the truth.

Shortly after the war ended, and after Americans had turned their attention to other matters, Air Force General Merrill A. McPeak held what he called the "Mother of all Briefings" to boast: "For the first time in history, a field army has been defeated by air power."[127] But an analysis of the data he was so proud of revealed that only 7 percent of the 88,500 tons of bombs dropped on Iraq were laser-guided bombs like those that showed up in the daily briefing videos.[128] Yet footage from those 7 percent had made up 100 percent of the video beamed daily to tens of millions of Americans. In its 1997 report on the Gulf War, the GAO reported that rather than the "one target, one bomb" image of laser-guided bombs that the Pentagon had carefully crafted during its TV propaganda blitz, the average number of precision bombs dropped per target was four.[129] However, by that time, Congress had already approved the tens of billions of dollars that the defense industry and the Pentagon had been seeking.

The data from the Mother of all Briefings also revealed that only 25 percent of the 82,000 tons of "dumb" bombs hit their targets. This was in sharp contrast to the image of consistent pinpoint accuracy that the daily war briefings *always* portrayed,[130] meaning that the reports of frequent "collateral" damage to nonmilitary targets were true. The daily press briefings had indeed been a concerted disinformation campaign, not aimed at the Iraqis, but at Americans. In addition to fraudulently attempting to convince Americans that stealth technology played a significant role in the success of the air war, the briefings were intended to portray an image of manned aircraft as the critical element in precision strikes. All to convince Americans to spend over a hundred billion dollars for more manned, stealth aircraft. However, with the war over and other pressing matters to attend to, few members of the media and even fewer Americans took note of later revelations. As David Letterman said, expressing a sense of relief shared by many Americans, "Finally, we can go back to ignoring CNN."[131] The Pentagon propaganda was left firmly in place.

The Air Force was not alone in using the war as a propaganda opportunity. Perhaps the weapon system that received the most accolades was the U.S. Army's Patriot missile. The Patriot was an antiaircraft missile that had been modified to enable it to be used against short-range missiles like Iraq's Scud, a primitive surface-to-surface missile. Tens of millions of Americans watched dramatic TV footage that showed Patriots intercepting Iraqi Scuds launched against Saudi Arabia and Israel. Thousands of newspaper and magazine articles dutifully reported the Army's accounts of the Patriot's success. In January 1991, *USA Today* reported, "The United States' new Patriot missiles are overwhelming Saddam Hussein's fabled Scuds in the skies over Saudi Arabia. The Patriots simply outmatch and outgun the aging Soviet-designed rockets . . ."[132] The following month it published a scorecard showing that Patriots had downed thirty-eight of forty-eight Scuds for a very impressive 79 percent success rate.[133] Again, it was all disinformation. An argument could certainly be made that deceiving the Iraqis into believing that their Scuds were being destroyed—and thus wasted—served a valid military purpose: convincing them not to fire any more. However, the Army kept the disinformation campaign going long after the war ended, thereby confirming that Americans were its real target.

In fact, the $1 million Patriots destroyed few, if any, Scuds. Two months after the war ended, Theodore A. Postal of M.I.T., an authority on tactical missile defenses, testified before Congress that many, if not most, of the Patriots failed to destroy the Scuds they were fired at.[134] And an Israeli analysis of the missile's success against Scuds fired at Israel, found that damage from Scuds *increased* several fold after the Patriots began trying to intercept them,[135] possibly because both the Scud and Patriot warheads were exploding on ground impact. Professor Portal also suggested that rather than decreasing the damage from Scuds, they may have actually increased it.[136] After hearing the testimony and reviewing secret performance information, the House Armed Services Committee concluded that the Patriots' greatest contribution was psychological rather than military.[137] Despite mounting evidence that the effectiveness of the missile had been greatly exaggerated, the propaganda remained firmly implanted. Five months later, in September of 1991, David Brock, writing in *Insight* stated, "The Patriot knocked down almost all of Saddam's Scuds."[138]

In February 1992, the Project Manager of the Patriot program released his report on the effectiveness of the missile, which concluded that it had been successful against 70 percent of Iraq's Scuds.[139] The GAO reviewed his report and found the following:[140]

- The first of two documents, which were cited as the basis for the conclusion, was "an inaccurate summary of information . . . [with] many gaps and inconsistencies between the data presented on the spreadsheet and the supporting records."
- The System Manager who prepared the document told the GAO that he was not surprised at the gaps and inconsistencies, and that it was never intended to be an analysis of the Patriot's performance.
- The second document was a draft report concerning impact points and the magnitude of high explosives. It had little to do with the Patriot's performance, and in fact, had a built-in assumption of successful intercepts.
- While the second report contained information on only one-third of the Saudi engagements, it was cited by the Project Manager's report as a source for all the engagements.
- Typically, two Patriots were fired at each Scud, but the number launched was considered irrelevant.

- Patriots were fired at false targets, but these were omitted from the assessment.

In short, the Project Manager's report was indefensible and could only be considered a deliberate attempt to produce a document that   supported and sustained the disinformation of the previous year. Several days before the GAO debunked the report as a fraud in testimony before the House Subcommittee on Legislation and National Security (and only because of it), the Army decided to revise the report to indicate that it had high confidence, but not certainty, that 25 percent of the Patriots successfully intercepted Scuds.[141] A remarkable "revision." Not surprisingly, the Chairman and ranking member of the Subcommittee requested that the GAO review this new assessment as well. Its report, issued in September of 1992, indicated, "About 9 percent of the Patriot's Operation Desert Storm engagements are supported by the strongest evidence that an engagement resulted in a warhead kill."[142] Eighteen months after the war ended, the truth was finally out; but not before Congress had appropriated an additional $215 million for more Patriots. Chicken feed; the real object of the Patriot campaign was the Strategic Defense Initiative (SDI) (which was subsequently renamed Ballistic Missile Defense (BMD) by the Clinton Administration). As *Insight* reported, ". . . the Patriot is everybody's darling and the Strategic Defense Initiative is riding its coattails."[143]

SDI was the naive vision of Ronald Reagan: to build a space-based umbrella over the U.S. as protection against nuclear missiles. Its detractors gave the program the nickname "Star Wars". Through 1997, the SDI and BMD together had consumed $50 billion without producing a single usable device.[144] Rather, they have proved to be one of the nation's richest defense subsidy programs. Fanciful projects such as the X-ray laser and the Free Electron laser wasted billions of dollars.[145] But they were unprecedented windfalls for research institutions, which politicians could not resist. Typical of the subsidy grab was a 1990 bill by Senators Jeff Bingham and Richard Shelby to direct most SDI funds away from spaced-based weapons and towards research on small land-based missiles and laser weapons—a move that, coincidentally, would shift billions of dollars to research facilities in their home states of New Mexico and Alabama. Senator Malcolm Wallop objected that the bill would turn SDI into "an entitlement program for special R&D interests that pour billions of taxpayer dollars down a bottomless pit, with no promise that we will ever achieve anything."[146] Of course that is what the program already was; the bill was passed into law.

Despite its tremendous subsidy appeal, by 1990, nearly $30 billion had been spent on SDI, and it was becoming increasingly difficult to hide the fact that the program had produced absolutely nothing. At the same time, the nuclear missile threat was dissipating as the Soviet Union unraveled. These factors, along with the ballooning budget deficit, created considerable pressure on the SDI budget, much to the distress of many in Congress and those who had been the recipients of the largess for nearly a decade. In August 1990, the House delivered a body blow when it voted to cut President Bush's 1991 SDI request by nearly 40 percent to $3 billion.[147] SDI was headed for oblivion, and proponents desperately searched for a means to protect the program. Saddam Hussein and the Patriot provided it. Making the most of the DOD Patriot propaganda, in December 1991, Congress passed the Missile Defense Act, which appropriated $4.1 billion for SDI and mandated the rapid development of a 100 missile system at Grand Forks, North Dakota, to protect against small-scale nuclear missile attacks.[148] The Act specifically stated that this deployment was "the initial step of an antiballistic missile system . . . designed to protect the United States against limited ballistic missile threats."[149] It authorized the first phase of a $35 billion nationwide network of 700 antiballistic missiles,[150] a system that would, by definition, spread billions in defense subsidies from coast to coast. This had been the real objective of the Patriot disinformation campaign.

Under the umbrella of BMD, a host of redundant antimissile systems is being developed with funding between 1998 and 2002 approaching $20 billion.[151] In addition to the national missile defense program, the Army is developing the Theater High-Altitude Area Defense (THAAD), the Medium Extended Air Defense System, and the Patriot Advanced Capability 3 (PAC-3).[152] The Navy (naturally) is developing two antimissile systems of its own, and the Air Force is developing the Airborne Laser program.[153] The GAO has reported that all these programs are high-risk and based on unproven or nonexistent technology. The most advanced of the programs, the Army's $18 billion THAAD system[154] finally had two successful tests in 1999 after six successive failures.[155] However, they were conducted under idealized conditions. Whether the system will be militarily useful has yet to be demonstrated. Nonetheless, Congress is pushing deployment of the more complex and only partially developed National Missile Defense System, against the advice of the GAO and a panel of former senior military, government, and industry officials.[156] Even the system's program manager, usually an unabashed cheerleader, stated that the planned flight test program was "anemic."[157] But House and Senate staff members involved in setting defense budgets have been told not to worry about how the money is being spent and to just "throw more money into it."[158] That is what Congress does best. In March 1999, both houses of Congress overwhelmingly passed legislation that authorized spending whatever it takes to develop an antimissile system. Even long-time Democratic critics of the program joined in, and President Clinton, who had attempted to kill the program in 1993, indicated enthusiastic support. The reason? Not a new threat to national security, but the beginning of the presidential campaign for the 2000 elections. Subsidy programs are, after all, the primary source of campaign financing.

The U.S. Navy is certainly the equal of the Air Force at the propaganda game, but the Gulf War provided it little opportunity. The Air Force and the Army played the leading roles in the war, while the Navy's carrier-based attack planes were not very effective. The Navy was unsuccessful in its attempts to destroy bridges in Iraq, which then had to be attacked again by Air Force bombers, resulting in an embarrassing average of twenty-four bombing missions per damaged bridge.[159] The highlight of the Navy's combat perform-ance was the impressive effectiveness of its Tomahawk cruise missiles. During the war, a variety of Navy ships launched a total of 288 Tomahawks.[160] Nev-ertheless, like the Air Force, the Navy has since come to consider the cruise missile a threat to the aircraft carrier—its heart and soul. The war presented the Navy with the worst possible public relations scenario: Its piloted attack air-craft were ineffectively dropping dumb bombs from extremely expensive car-riers. Meanwhile, its relatively cheap, unmanned Tomahawks, fired by inex-pensive carrier escort ships, were scoring precise hits on the most heavily de-fended targets. Not surprisingly, the Navy maintained an unaccustomed low profile during the war. However, after the war, it wasted no time resuming its all-out campaign for more carriers.

There is no question that a modern American aircraft carrier, its flight deck loaded with jets, is a truly impressive sight. Even more so when you con-sider that these behemoths are among the fastest ships in the navy, capable of speeds over thirty knots. Their awesome presence has, for many years, caused serious second thoughts for nations considering making trouble for the United States. However, much like battleships prior to World War II, their size and reputation belies their military value and vulnerability. Pearl Harbor abruptly ended the battleship myth, just two years after U.S. Navy Admiral Clark Woodward assured Americans, "As far as sinking a ship with a bomb is con-cerned, it just cannot be done."[161] Yet, the carrier myth lives on, largely be-cause of its enormous subsidy value. The estimated final cost of the U.S.S. Ronald Reagan (CVN-76), including its complement of aircraft, is $10 bil-lion.[162] With the escort ships that it requires, the cost for a carrier battle group approaches $20 billion. The 12 to 15 ships of a carrier battle group require 10 to 15,000 sailors and marines, and cost about $1 billion per year to operate.[163] It takes two years and costs $2.7 billion just to refuel a nuclear carrier.[164] There is simply no greater source of defense pork than an aircraft carrier.

For many years, the Navy was organized around the task of countering the huge Soviet Navy on the open seas. The big-deck, nuclear-powered carriers and their aircraft equipped with nuclear weapons were at the center of its stra-tegic plan. However, that mission ceased to exist when the cold war ended; since then, the Navy has been desperately searching for a role for its carriers. The combat value of aircraft carriers has been declining since World War II primarily because of their ever-increasing vulnerability. Additionally, despite their fearsome appearance, they pack a very modest punch unless they use nu-clear weapons. And under a U.S. policy announced by Defense Secretary Wil-liam Perry in 1994, nuclear weapons have been removed from all carriers.[165] In conflicts employing conventional weapons, such as the Gulf War, their contri-bution to the military effort was minor, although they were largely safe from attack. Nevertheless, the cost was great and disproportionate.

There is an old Navy saying that the reason you build an aircraft car-rier is so that you can launch planes to defend it. There is a great deal of truth to that saying. Carriers are generally escorted by one or two attack submarines and six surface warships, usually cruisers and frigates, which are there to protect the carrier.[166] Of the 80 aircraft on a carrier, almost half are also used primarily to protect the carrier.[167] Thus, most of the nearly $20 billion cost of a carrier battle group is expended to protect the carrier. The problem is that weapons technology has advanced to the point that protecting a very large and expensive asset like a carrier has become a daunting task. Adelman and Augustine note that the balance of power between large capital items and the systems that threaten them has shifted substantially; the advent of antiship missiles has meant that surface ships can now be threatened by a relatively weak enemy.[168] Adding ever more defensive capability to the carrier and its escorts only makes them more complex and more expensive—and makes them even more attractive targets. At the same time, the proportion of the battle group's resources designed for offensive operations decreases, meaning that the mission of an aircraft carrier has increasingly become to defend itself. Nonetheless, its vulnerability is continuing to increase. On that subject, the *Economist* observed,

> *So it sails with escorts: cruisers and destroyers with the most sophisticated air-defense capabilities in the world; anti-submarine-warfare frigates; and a submarine or two of its own. The escorts are worth more than the carrier itself. And still, a lucky cruise missile, or one with a nuclear tip, could put paid to the whole thing.*[169]

For attack capability, carriers rely on the F/A-18 Hornet. The A-6 Intruder, the Navy's most effective attack plane, was phased out in 1997. The F/A-18s can carry four 1,000-pound bombs and have a combat radius of 170 miles,[170] while the A-6s could carry twice as much about twice as far. (The combat radius of an Air Force F-16 is 500 miles, an F-15E is 650 miles, and an A-10 is 600 miles.)[171] During the Gulf War, A-6s dropped nearly all the laser-guided bombs delivered by the Navy, while the F/A-18s dropped old style gravity bombs.[172] The lack of a laser target illumination capability precluded the F/A-18s from using precision bombs. Nonetheless, the Navy retired all its A-6s and is adding laser capability to some F/A-18s, a decision that led Former Navy Secretary John Lehman to comment,

> . . . *the navy aviators are appalled. They've almost had open revolt in the F-14 and A-6 communities. It's because they understand their mission and they know they can't do it with F/A-18s.*[173]

Today, a carrier's offensive largely amounts to forty F/A-18 Hornets with a very short 170 mile combat radius; it comes down to a huge amount of money for not much punch.[174] For all the efforts of the Navy and Congress to obfuscate the facts, the hard realities are inescapable and beginning to surface. A 1993 Rand Corporation study concluded that even a large carrier force would make relatively little contribution after the early days of a regional conflict.[175] A report issued about the same time by the Henry L. Stimson Center reached the same conclusion.[176]

The combat efficiency of carriers is actually much worse. Because of Navy operating, maintenance, and personnel policies, it takes at least three carriers for each one deployed.[177] That translates into about $50 billion worth of ships and planes, with operating costs of at least $3 billion per year, to keep 40 light attack aircraft on station. Given the modest success record of carrier aircraft in delivering bombs on target, the cost per bomb accurately delivered is astronomical. It is many times the cost of a Tomahawk cruise missile, which can be launched from a lone, submerged submarine, and can fly accurately at night and in bad weather to targets more than twice as far away—without escort fighters, radar jammers, and refueling aircraft. More importantly, Tomahawks do not risk the lives of aircraft or ship's crews. Rather than expand the use of submarines to perform some traditional carrier duties, as the GAO has repeatedly recommended, the Navy is pursing the opposite strategy. It is retiring relatively new nuclear attack submarines[178] in favor of more carriers and manned aircraft—items that support its budget and image. Because that strategy maximizes defense subsidies, Congress is all for it.

Without the Soviets to counter and despite the sharply increased risk, the Navy came up with the only strategy it could devise to save its carriers: it would become a "brown water" navy. It would shift from "blue water" operations on the open seas to "projecting power and influence across the seas in response to regional challenges."[179] This fundamental change meant deploying carrier battle groups in littoral (coastal) waters where both costs and risks are maximized and where F/A-18 Hornets have not proved effective. Indeed, during the Gulf war, although the Navy moved some of its carriers into the Persian Gulf to get as close as possible to Iraq, it still had to restrict F/A-18s to an average of only six minutes over their targets, due to their very limited range.[180]

Bordering Iran and Iraq, the Persian Gulf is the most dangerous body of water in the world. It varies from 35 to 210 miles wide, averages only eighty-four feet in depth, has many shoals and islands, and bristles with hostile high-technology anti-air and anti-ship weapons systems. The thirty-five mile wide Strait of Hormuz, the entrance to the Gulf, has several islands on which the Iranians have installed artillery, anti-ship missiles, and chemical weapons.[181] In just the first half of 1997, they launched sixty sea-based missiles in training exercises and fired their first air-launched cruise missile.[182] Iran has twenty patrol boats armed with missiles with a range greater than 20 miles.[183] Even if the Iranians failed to sink a carrier, they could easily sink oil tankers to block the strait, thereby trapping it in the Gulf. Yet under the Navy's new strategy, this is the type of deployment envisioned for its carriers. The only thing it does not put at great risk is the Navy's budget.

The aircraft that Iran is using for its air-launched cruise missiles are American-made F-4s that were sold to Iran when it was considered an ally back in the 1970s. It is not the first time that our own weapons have come back to haunt us. Nonetheless, in 1997, the DOD approved the sale by Lockheed Martin of eighty F-16s, a front-line U.S. Air Force fighter, to the United Arab

Emirates (UAE), a tiny Middle Eastern country that is presently an ally.[184] Beginning in 2002, the fighters are to be delivered with equipment so advanced that it will not be installed on U.S. fighters until 2007.[185] At the same time, the U.S. Navy is planning to deploy its carriers in and around the Persian Gulf. What happens if the UAE, armed with more-advanced F-16s than the U.S Air Force, goes from ally to enemy as Iran did? Unfortunately, our aircraft carriers may be the first to find out.

The threats to capital ships operating in littoral waters grow almost daily. Some sixteen third world nations have or are developing nuclear weapons, while eighteen have chemical weapons programs, and thirteen have biological weapons capability.[186] Sixteen third world nations, including most of those with nuclear, chemical, or biological weapons programs, also have ballistic missile capability.[187] And they don't need long-range delivery systems to hit a carrier in sight of their coast. It is estimated that, in addition to the industrialized nations, at least several dozen third world nations have advanced anti-ship missiles which are readily available on the world arms market.[188] Indeed, twelve nations acquired them before the U.S. Navy.[189] Several third world nations including Iran and North Korea—whose waters are primary areas of U.S. carrier deployment—have purchased modern diesel-electric submarines from Russia. These subs are capable of carrying nuclear tipped torpedoes as well as mines and are very quiet and difficult to detect. In addition, the Navy acknowledges that shallow coastal waters have poor sound propagation, and that varying temperature, depth, and underwater terrain make submarine detection considerably more difficult than in deep water.[190]

Admiral Joseph Lopez, Deputy Chief of Naval Operations, expresses confidence in the Navy's ability to track diesel subs, but then adds, ". . . allowing some potential enemy to lay mines, or to get his diesel submarines under way undetected, then the problem becomes more complicated."[191] In fact, the Navy is not prepared to handle diesel submarines. In 1993, the GAO reported that the Navy did "not have documented and approved requirements for undersea surveillance systems to counter the regional submarine threat" and "was continuing to build . . . ships designed for the Soviet submarine threat."[192] In 1996 and again in 1998, the GAO reported that critical mine countermeasures capabilities were unmet and that the Navy's twelve brand new minehunter ships lacked the speed and endurance to accompany carrier battle groups.[193] It is no wonder that Adelman and Augustine warn that, "In any operation that places ships near shore, even against nations with a second-rate military, naval forces should be prepared to take losses."[194]

The underlying theory behind having twelve Carrier Battle Groups dates back to World War II, and during the cold war, the Pentagon claimed that the same number were needed to protect vital sea lanes. But back in 1993, Secretary of Defense Les Aspin admitted, ". . . these missions are no more. Without the Soviet Navy, no one challenges us for control of the seas." There is a legitimate need for the U.S. to maintain a forward presence in areas of vital interest such as the Arabian Sea. The Mediterranean Sea is another matter. The nations of the European Union have over two million active-duty military personnel and an economy about the same size as the U.S.[195] The combined defense budgets of Western European nations is about two-thirds of U.S. defense spending,[196] and they do not have the problem of patrolling waters a couple of thousand miles from home. It would seem that they are perfectly capable of patrolling their own backyard. But whatever the actual "need" for U.S. forward presence, there are militarily capable and far less costly alternatives than the Navy's big-deck carriers. In 1993, the GAO reported:

> . . . there are opportunities for using less costly ways to meet overseas presence requirements without unreasonably increasing the risk to U.S. national security. Using groups centered around highly capable surface combatants and amphibious assault ships could provide a very credible and capable presence under most circumstances at a much reduced cost. . . . We believe that expanded use of noncarrier groups is possible because of the increased capabilities of the ships and weapon systems in these groups.[197]

Specifically, the GAO has pointed out:

- In addition to its twelve big-deck carriers, the Navy currently has eleven highly effective amphibious assault ships, which carry AV-8 Harrier attack aircraft and attack helicopters. These moderately sized aircraft carriers are comparable to the carriers of the other navies of the world.[198]
- Many Navy surface combatants (cruisers, destroyers, and frigates) can provide significant strike, anti-air, anti-surface, and anti-submarine capabilities.[199]
- Since the 135 Navy warships carrying Tomahawk cruise missiles have shown that they can conduct forward presence missions and crisis response without the presence of carrier-based air forces, they are a viable option for those missions.[200]
- The average strike by carrier based aircraft takes twenty-four hours or more to plan and launch, whereas a Tomahawk can be fired in about an hour.[201]

It is simply not a matter of capability; the Navy has plenty of it without its big-deck carriers. The smaller carriers with their AV-8 Harriers (more versatile and in some ways more capable than F/A-18s) can handle most of the big carrier missions. The real issue is maintaining the enormous budget of the Navy. Having retired its A-6 Intruders in favor of the less capable F/A-18 Hornet, the Navy now has declared an urgent need for a new attack aircraft. It plans to spend $85 billion for a new, larger version of the Hornet, the F/A-18E/F. This, despite the fact that the Vice Chairman of the Joint Chiefs of Staff acknowledged, "the main consideration in the timing of the need for the F/A-

18E/F is not an emerging threat nor a declining inventory of existing aircraft, but the approaching limit in F/A-18C/D growth potential."[202] In other words, the Navy retired its most capable attack aircraft, only to request $85 billion for a new one for which it has not identified any need. This is strikingly similar to the Air Force ploy of eliminating most of its radar suppression capability by retiring the highly effective F-4G Wild Weasel[203] and then claiming an urgent need for $100 billion for F-22 and B-2 stealth aircraft to evade enemy radar. It is a money chase involving hundreds of billions of dollars where the services, in hot competition with each other, simply come up with ever more expensive weapons systems, primarily to maintain their budgets. In addition, Congress, well aware that there is no real defense requirement, will approve almost anything if it brings defense pork back home. However, it is a system collapsing from its own weight. Adelman and Augustine have come up with a sobering calculation: at the rate the cost of new military aircraft is increasing, *the entire defense budget* will buy just one bomber in the year 2020.[204] And the DOD will insist that it must have that one bomber although it will not be able to identify a mission for it.

The present public justification for the wholesale looting of the U.S. Treasury for unneeded weapons systems, facilities, and manpower is based on two "reviews" of the nation's military requirements, the 1993 Bottom-Up Review (BUR) and the 1997 Quadrennial Review (QDR). Both documents were based not on assessments of threats to the nation's security, but on threats to the budgets of the military services. They are both based on the preposterous supposition that the U.S. needs to be prepared to fight and win two regional wars simultaneously *without the assistance of our allies*. The only examples that the Department of Defense could come up with are simultaneous wars with North Korea and Iraq. In its analysis, the Pentagon assumed that Iraq could again seriously threaten oil supplies, but that this time our oil-dependant allies would simply do nothing. Pentagon analyst Franklin Spinney calls the two war strategy "just a marketing device to justify a high budget."[205] Indeed, one of the original architects of the two-war strategy, former Defense Secretary William Perry, told Congress, "Nowhere in our planning do we believe that we are going to have to fight two wars at once. . . . I think it is an entirely implausible scenario that we would have to fight two wars at once."[206]

The Bottom-Up Review was much more top-down than bottom-up. It was first proposed by Under Secretary of Defense Frank G. Wisner who suggested that the review would provide "more thorough and compelling descriptions of the New Dangers."[207] In other words, it started with the conclusion that all the services' major new and existing weapons platforms had to be preserved and progressed backwards from there. The BUR was not intended to be a review, but another propaganda tool. When facts got in the way, the DOD simply made favorable assumptions, no matter how ludicrous, to allow it to proceed to the predetermined conclusions. For instance, the DOD assumed that as much cargo could be moved in six weeks as was moved in the first six months of the Gulf War despite the fact that it does not have nearly enough ships and transport planes to achieve that.[208] Indeed, General Joseph P. Hoar, head of the U.S.

Central Command, which includes the Middle East, stated, "Strategic lift in this country is broken right now."[209] The GAO confirmed that the review was deeply flawed in a 1995 report and noted that many of the DOD "questionable assumptions" were not even analyzed until nearly two years after the BUR was released.[210] Further, the GAO found that the DOD analysis of those assumptions was based on the very same favorable assumptions.[211]

The Department of Defense press release announcing the completion of the Quadrennial Defense Review called the document,

> . . . *a comprehensive assessment of the nation's defense requirement, based on emerging threats to U.S. security over the next two decades. . . .*[212]

But rather than addressing the future, the review concludes that we should continue to buy hundreds of billions of dollars of weapons systems designed to fight the old Soviet Union. Commenting on the QDR, Rutgers University Professor Ann Markusen, a Senior Fellow on the Council on Foreign Relations, noted,

> *It suggests that peacekeeping, urban terrorism, and information warfare are apt to become increasingly important challenges, but then grandfathers in every existing, inappropriate Cold War weapons system.*[213]

Essentially, the only thing that the QDR did was stretch out the delivery schedules and reduce the numbers of each aircraft the Pentagon intends to purchase. That has become standard procedure: initially overstate the number of aircraft to be purchased, allowing a low projected unit price, then, after substantial funds have been appropriated, significantly reduce the number to allow the contractors to justify hefty price increases. The Pentagon and defense contractors have used the same strategy on every aircraft contract for decades.

After two "comprehensive reviews" of our national security needs, the Department of Defense insists we need the following new aircraft:

Air Force F-22 Fighter

The GAO has repeatedly reported that we already have the best fighter in the world, the F-15, and that no nation will be able to challenge it in the foreseeable future. There is literally no military reason to build the F-22. Nonetheless, the Pentagon plans to replace the $46 million F-15 with the F-22.[214] The BUR called for purchasing 438 F-22s at a cost of $160 million each.[215] True to form, the QDR reduced the number to 339. We can expect that number to be further reduced in the future, and that the final F-22 cost will exceed $200 million each. It still will not have a mission.

Navy F/A-18 E/F Carrier Multi-role Aircraft

The E/F model of the F-18 is a bigger, more powerful version of the C/D model presently used on Navy aircraft carriers. The E/F version was developed to address the serious range, survivability, and payload problems of the C/D model. Nevertheless, the GAO has reported on numerous occasions that the E/F model "will be only marginally improved over that of the less costly C/D version."[216] Even worse, a Navy board assessing the E/F program in 1997 reported that the E/F version may prove to be *less capable* than the C/D model.[217] However, the Navy needs new, expensive aircraft to justify its carriers, just as it needs carriers to justify new expensive aircraft. Missions and effectiveness are irrelevant. The BUR projected the acquisition of 1,000 aircraft at a cost of $67 million each.[218] The QDR reduced that number to between 548 and 785. Of course. We can expect the actual cost of the E/F model to exceed $75 million, compared to $28 million[219] for the quite possibly more capable C/D model.

Army Comanche Helicopter

The Comanche is a ground attack helicopter that the Army intends to use as a replacement for its existing Apache and Kiowa helicopters. The projected cost for 1,292 aircraft is $45 billion, or about $35 million each.[220] The GAO has reported that the Comanche will perform essentially the same functions as the existing Apache, Kiowa, and Marine Corps Super Cobra helicopters and that just upgrading the Kiowa helicopter would remedy many of the deficiencies the Comanche is expected to resolve.[221] Moreover, the combined armed services already have at least ten different ways to hit 65 percent of the thousands of expected ground targets in fighting two major regional wars.[222] All of which is beside the point. The Army needs to grab its share of the procurement budget, and that is what the Comanche is all about.

In addition to those programs, the Pentagon is also planning to buy 3,000 Joint Strike Fighter (JSF) aircraft for the Air Force, Navy, and Marines at cost of $165 billion.[223] Total expenditures planned for just the F-22, F/A-18E/F, Comanche, and JSF come to $310 billion, and very clearly, little of that has anything to do with the our national security. Indeed, in January 1998, retired Admiral William Owens, former vice chairman of the Joint Chiefs, testified before a Senate committee that that the Pentagon already has 40 percent more air power than is needs.[224] A Navy analysis of the nations that both the BUR and QDR claimed as our primary threats, Iran, Iraq, and North Korea, found that their Air Forces will shrink by about 20 percent while we are spending hundreds of billions of dollars for new aircraft.[225] Further, many of their aircraft are old and not very capable to begin with.[226] The GAO confirmed that finding, noting that, ". . . the United States has over 2,000 front line fighters, but potential adversaries have few."[227] The real security issue involved in these enormous expenditures is the career security of senior military officers and Pentagon bureaucrats, the financial security of defense contractors, and the political security of Congressional incumbents.

While new attack and fighter aircraft comprise the largest segment of the Pentagon's procurement budget, there are plenty of other questionable or redundant weapons systems. For example, the Navy's New Attack Submarine was supposed to be a smaller and less costly replacement for the nearly $2 billion Seawolf submarine. Partly because Congress insists that the program subsidize two big defense contractors, Electric Boat and Newport News Shipbuilding, the New Attack Submarine is turning out to be considerably less capable, but just as expensive as the Seawolf.[228] To top it off, submarines that have only recently been put in service will be retired to make room for the new ones. Admiral J.L. Johnson, Chief of Naval Operations, has told Congress that the Navy could operate effectively with fewer Trident ballistic missile submarines and save as much as $7 billion. Congress, however, has mandated that the Navy upgrade all eighteen of its Tridents to keep the pork flowing.[229] There is much more. As Army intelligence analyst Lt. Col. Ralph Peters observed, "We can beat the Chinese or the Russians, but we cannot beat Lockheed Martin or Ingalls Shipbuilding."[230]

For all our very expensive hardware, American forces would be hard pressed to fight just one regional war because of critical shortages in training, transport, and supplies, often due to funding shortages.[231] Nearly half of the Air Force's anti-radar aircrews were unable to complete their training requirements in the first half of 1994, while two of the Air Force's newest F-15E squadrons have had to forego training in their primary mission, precision weapons delivery.[232] One-third of the $3.6 billion provided for Army training in 1993 and 1994 was used for other purposes such as base operations and property maintenance.[233] An infantry division based at Fort Riley, Kansas, had to stop training in 1994 because it couldn't pay for fuel and ammunition, while the 4th Infantry Division at Fort Carson, Colorado, had to forego advanced training at the National Training Center due to lack of funds.[234] Navy and Marine Corps pilots have had their flight time cut by as much as half, and Army M1 tank crews have had their training miles cut by nearly 40 percent.[235] The GAO found that, for 1993, Army National Guard combat platoons, a key element in the two regional war strategy, "mastered an average of just one-seventh of their mission-essential tasks, compared with a goal of 100 percent, and less than one-third of the battalions met gunnery goals."[236]

By 1998, nearly 200 Navy planes were out of commission awaiting repairs and 25 percent of Air Force equipment was not fully mission capable.[237] Admiral Johnson blames the Navy's 82 percent increase in accidents in 1998 on parts shortages, while Air Force Chief of Staff General Michael Ryan reported that stripping Air Force planes for parts has increased 78 percent just between 1994 and 1998.[238] The 69th Fighter Squadron prepared to leave its U.S. base for a 60-day rotation enforcing the Iraq no-fly zone in January, 1998, with 25 percent of its fighters cannibalized for spare parts to keep the other 75 percent flying.[239]

Despite spending nearly $300 billion annually on defense—a sum almost equal to the total of all other nation's defense budgets combined[240]—the nation is barely prepared to fight one regional conflict. Clearly, it is not that

Americans are not spending enough for defense. Rather, because U.S. weapons systems are superior and the politicians do not really expect the U.S. to become involved in a major conflict, real military readiness is considered secondary to defense subsidies. As budgetary constraints have forced reductions in defense spending, the big subsidy programs have been preserved, while operations and maintenance (O&M) have been increasingly underfunded. This has become so serious that the GAO estimated the O&M shortfall for just the years 1994 through 1999 to be as high as $241 billion.[241] While pilots are having their training time reduced in the F-15, a fighter that "exceeds the most advanced threat system expected to exist,"[242] the Air Force is spending nearly $60 billion for the F-22, a fighter that has no foreseeable mission—except to pad the Air Force's budget and insure fat campaign contributions from happy defense contractors.

Although it has huge backlogs of equipment awaiting repairs and troops unable to train for lack of funding, the Pentagon has consistently reported to Congress that U.S. forces were prepared to fight two regional wars. To do otherwise would have risked having funds transferred from procurement to O&M. In April 1998, Secretary of Defense William Cohen wrote, "Our forces are in good shape now, but without the necessary O&M funding, their readiness would erode quickly. . . ."[243] But just a few months later, the Joint Chiefs of Staff changed the story to one of serious problems with present readiness.[244] What change motivated the DOD to start telling the truth? The reported budget surplus. It presented the opportunity to increase total funding rather than O&M funding at the expense of new weapons systems. Congress, which little more than a year earlier in the 1997 Budget Agreement had agreed not to increase defense spending through 2002, promptly increased the 1999 defense budget by $9 billion.[245] But then again, Congress has never abided by a budget agreement. Just a few months later, when President Clinton asked for additional funds for the war against Serbia, Congress appropriated another $9 billion—twice what Clinton requested.

Major weapons systems are subsidy programs that keep on giving. All those B-1s, F-22s, aircraft carriers, and Comanche helicopters have to be based somewhere. Military bases are the equivalent of having a direct pipeline to the federal treasury for local communities—which translates into additional money in the bank for politicians. A valid military requirement has much less to do with bases than their subsidy value, which makes it very difficult to close unneeded facilities. In 1988, Congress passed legislation (P.L. 100-526) to begin closing surplus bases and to insulate themselves from making decisions to end base subsidies. Additional Base Realignment and Closure (BRAC) rounds were held in 1991, 1993, and 1995; while some bases had some functions terminated, relatively few bases were actually closed. A study by Business Executives for National Security found that one-third of the sixty-seven bases supposedly closed during the first three rounds either never closed or reopened with a new name or function due to political pressure.[246] And not one of the many major military installations in the Washington D.C. area had been closed because members of Congress and the military brass like to use their clubs, tennis courts, swimming pools, and golf courses.[247]

The GAO found that "it is generally recognized that much excess capacity will likely remain after the 1995 BRAC round."[248] The Pentagon projects that it will still have 23 percent more base capacity than it needs in 2003.[249] While the number of military personnel has declined by 33 percent since the mid-1980s, the number of civilian defense jobs, primarily at military bases, has only dropped by 14 percent.[250] Congress simply refuses to close the hundreds of unneeded military installations. In 1997, the U.S. had 1.44 million active-duty military personnel, but only 20 percent of them were combat forces.[251] Our troops do not have sufficient funds for parts, fuel, and ammunition for training, but billions of defense subsidy dollars are being used to keep tens of thousands of civilians and military personnel in make-work defense jobs at useless military bases.

The list goes on. From the B-2 bombers that cost $2 billion each, yet lose their stealth capability in the rain (meaning, like the B-1, they are useful in fair-weather wars), to the $2 billion Seawolf submarine that the DOD did not want, but that Congress funded solely as a defense subsidy program. In all, despite having no significant threat to its national security and not being well prepared for war, U.S. defense spending still stands at 92 percent of cold war levels.[252]

The Quadrennial Defense Review pointed out that terrorism will be an increasing threat to the U.S. in the future and indeed, it is already the single biggest threat to Americans. Congress has responded by appropriating more than $1 billion for counterterrorism programs in forty federal agencies,[253] but how serious are the politicians about a very real threat to national security? The State Department's Office of the Coordinator for Counterterrorism is the lead agency for coordinating U.S. efforts to fight terrorism overseas. Christopher Ross, appointed head of this office in March of 1998, had still not been confirmed by the Senate eight months later, and decided to leave the post.[254] Before his appointment, the position had been vacant for over ten months.[255] Evidently, there just was not enough pork involved to interest the politicians. One can only admire the insight of Samuel Johnson; patriotism is indeed the last refuge of scoundrels.

6

FARM INTERESTS: HOW DO I SUBSIDIZE THEE?
LET ME TRY TO COUNT THE WAYS

The U.S. has been subsidizing farmers almost since its inception. We pay farmers not to grow crops in areas with abundant rainfall, while building multi-billion dollar dams so that other farmers can grow water-loving crops in deserts. Then we pay them not to grow crops, too. The taxpayers freely loan farmers money at subsidized rates. If they do not repay the loans, we loan them more money. We pay them to overproduce food and then pay foreigners to take it off our hands. In the name of helping family farmers, huge agribusinesses—corporate food processors and exporters—receive billions of dollars in subsidies. Worst of all, we use school children and the poor to dispose of mountains of surplus fat that result from subsidies to overproduce. Even in times of "serious" budget cutting, these subsidies remain sacred. They are "traditional way of life" subsidies. The recipients and their Congressional supporters claim that to cut these programs would threaten a traditional way of life. The theory being something like: if the taxpayers have supported a group of people in some lifestyle for more than one generation, they become entitled to subsidies ad infinitum, regardless of the merit or adverse consequences. Somehow, this preposterous welfare-for-the-well-off argument is widely accepted.

Orders administered by the government, set market prices, terms and conditions of sale, minimum prices to be paid by plants, and distribution of financial returns among farmers.

A line from the central agriculture ministry in the old Soviet Union or perhaps communist China? Not at all. It came (with the words "U.S. Department of Agriculture (USDA)" substituted for "government") from a GAO report describing the operation of federal dairy policies.[1] Created in 1937, these "marketing orders" allow dairy farmers to set up cartels to control prices. Over the years, the USDA has set up similar cartels for the producers of walnuts, raisins, hops, lemons, oranges, and other fruits and vegetables. All have had the same objective: to minimize competition and force up the prices that consumers pay. Any industry other than agriculture that organized this type of market manipulation in the United States would be breaking the law, and the trustbusters at the Justice Department would be all over them. However, in the case of agriculture, not only are cartels legal, the federal government acts as the enforcer. This is the same government that lectures other nations about free markets.

That is just one example of an astounding number of laws that have been enacted over the last seventy years to enrich farmers at the expense of the American public. The Organization for Economic Cooperation and Development estimates that government direct and indirect farm subsidies since 1986 have cost the American people over $370 billion, almost enough to buy all the farm land in the country.[2] Given the extraordinary amount of taxpayer money that farmers receive directly from the government, one would expect that Americans would enjoy a lower food bill, but such is not the case. Even in communist countries, government agriculture subsidies bring the consumer price of food down, but the USDA found that Americans paid 12 percent more than if there were no farm programs at all.[3] Thus, we have the absurd situation of taxpayers supporting a segment of the economy through government subsidies and being penalized in the marketplace for their efforts.

Farm subsidy supporters and politicians are quick to explain that these policies are meant to protect "family farmers" and assure Americans an adequate food supply. Commenting on proposals to cut farm subsidies in the 1996 budget, President Clinton said, "I don't believe that we ought to destroy the farm support program if we want to keep the family farm."[4] The statement is almost laughable. Despite the hundreds of billions of dollars in subsidies extorted from the public, the number of farms in the United States has declined sharply since the support programs were initiated. The farm population has declined over 80 percent since the 1930s.[5] The reported number of farms in the U.S. has nearly always been a politically generated figure. President Roosevelt claimed that there were six million in the 1930s, and the Commerce Department claimed that there were 1.9 million in 1992.[6] These figures are based on the USDA definition of a farm: any establishment with yearly agricultural sales, including government subsidy payments, of at least $1,000.[7] This definition grossly overstates the number of real farms. Indeed, in the Commerce Department's 1982 Census of Agriculture, one million of the supposed 2.2 million farmers denied they were farmers, claiming some other occupation.[8]

About 1.4 million farm households derived 101 percent of their income from off-farm sources.[9] In other words, these "farmers" spend some of their income from their "real" jobs to offset an average annual $400 loss from their hobby, small-scale farming. In 1996, 74 percent of all farm households relied on off-farm sources for virtually all their income.[10] On average, they lost money farming, but received $45,418 in off-farm income.[11] Clearly, the great majority of those that the government classifies as farmers are something other than farmers. An office worker who is an avid, weekend golfer is not a "professional" golfer. In fact, there are about 500,000 full-time farmers in the U.S., but the politicians and the USDA inflate the number to propagate the myth that huge farm subsidies are preserving the "family" farm.

According to former Deputy Secretary of Agriculture Jack Parnell, 300,000 commercial farms produce 80 percent of the nation's food, and 12 percent of the farms receive 90 percent of all subsidy payments.[12] The data are irrefutable and the subsidies indefensible. James Schaub of the Office of the Chief Economist at the USDA admitted that, "A lot of the reasons for farm programs that existed in the '30s are gone." But most in the department, along with many politicians, are still using the family farm myth to continue subsidizing some of the nation's wealthiest people in the lifestyle to which they have become accustomed. Meanwhile, according to *Farm Aid News*, America is losing almost 600 farmers per week.[13] Nearly all of these are small-scale farmers, the very people that the politicians claim farm subsidy programs are intended to keep in farming. Their claims and their real intentions are two very different things: Farmers with annual sales of over $100,000 receive 65 percent of all subsidies, while those with annual sales of less than $10,000 receive 5 percent.[14]

The image of farmers as among the poorest of Americans is a myth and it always has been. Even the purported desperate condition of farmers in the late 1920s, the basis for most of today's farm subsidies, was a government creation. In the 1930s, a number of economists, including Joseph S. Davis of Stanford University, concluded that farmers in the 1920s fared as well as most Americans.[15] It was statistics concocted by the USDA that made their plight seem so bad, and the situation has hardly changed. Although you would never know it to hear those in the USDA and Congress, full-time farmers—those who receive most of the subsidies—are among the wealthiest Americans. According to the Census Bureau, the median net worth of American families in 1991 was $36,623, while that of full-time farmers was just over a million dollars, nearly 30 times that of the average American.[16] Much of a farmer's net worth is due to the value of the farm, which has been driven up by federal subsidies. The USDA estimates that farm subsidies have added 15 to 20 percent to the value of American farmland.[17] Just between 1992 and 1997, the value of farm real estate rose by one-third.[18] This indirect subsidy further enriches farmers while raising the capital cost of food production and, consequently, consumer prices. Some farmers have done so well that they have left the farming to others and moved to large cities. A study of USDA records by the Environmental Working Group found that between 1985 and 1995 the agency sent $1.3 billion in subsidy payments to "farmers" whose permanent address was in a major city.[19]

While the government has created dozens of complex and expensive subsidy programs for wealthy farmers, it has been conspicuously passive when it comes to even basic protections for their employees. The GAO found, "Hired farm workers are not adequately protected by federal laws, regulations, and programs; therefore, their health and well-being are at risk."[20] According to Philip Martin, a University of California agricultural economist, farm worker's earnings have been declining since the late 1980s and the average California farm worker earned about $8,000 per year in 1997.[21] Far from the mythical image of the poor struggling farmer, the reality is that the average American is nowhere near as well off as the average full-time farmer. It is those farmers' 1.25 million employees[22] that come closest to fitting that image. Yet these employees, as well as average Americans, continue to subsidize wealthy farmers.

As little sense as that makes, the actual subsidy programs are even worse. While nearly all farm products are subsidized by one USDA program or another, the vast majority of subsidies go to just a third of them: wheat, corn, rice, cotton, sugar, peanuts, soybeans, and milk products. Producers of those products and their politicians claim that the extensive price protection and government subsidies are necessary to stabilize prices and supplies. The USDA states that the subsidy programs "help keep enough farmers in business to produce an adequate food supply and to keep consumer prices reasonable."[23] These statements raise a number of questions. Why then, has the number of farmers declined sharply since the subsidy programs started? Why would "too many" farmers go out of business since the business would get increasingly profitable as the number of farmers decreased? How does forcing prices higher keep consumer prices reasonable? Why do we not have a supply problem with products, such as chicken and apples, that receive no direct subsidies? In essence, why would the most efficient price-supply management system ever conceived, the free market, not work for a relatively small number of commodity farm products?

The USDA's answer is that the subsidies for the selected crops "help stabilize farm income, help create a balance between supply and demand, and help farmers at harvest time by providing interim financing."[24] Again, one has to ask how income is stabilized, and supply and demand balance maintained for those crops—and all the other products made in America—that do not have specific subsidy programs? (There does not seem to be an income stabilization or "balance" problem with turkeys, despite the fact that nearly a quarter of the 300 million birds raised annually in the U.S. are consumed between Thanksgiving and Christmas.[25]) Why should taxpayers provide subsidized financing for full-time farmers who are, on average, millionaires? And why should the taxpayers provide financial support for hobby farms or any other hobby?

When all else fails, subsidy proponents roll out the big gun: food supply. This argument is intended to elicit the same emotional reaction that defense subsidy proponents count on when they talk about national security. It might be effective if the government were not paying farmers *not* to grow crops on thirty-one million acres of farmland,[26] and if the U.S. did not produce such an incredible surplus of food. Corn production in 1997 topped 9.3 billion bushels[27] while domestic usage was estimated at 6.8 billion bushels.[28] Similarly, the numbers for wheat were 2.53 billion produced and 1.2 billion used; and soybeans, 2.73 billion produced and 1.4 billion used.[29] One-third of total U.S. farm production is exported, but a considerably higher percentage of the most heavily subsidized crops are shipped overseas.[30] In 1996, 57 percent of the wheat, 47 percent of the rice, and 43 percent of the cotton produced by American farmers was exported.[31]

The U.S. is simply awash in food—with the government paying farmers not to produce. After near record exports in 1997, farmers still had nearly half of their 1997 harvest in storage as they began harvesting their 1998 crops.[32] Even in 1993, when historic rain and flooding damaged or destroyed crops on twenty-five million acres in Kansas, Missouri, Nebraska, Iowa, Illinois, Minnesota, South Dakota, and Wisconsin, and while severe drought was parching the southeastern states, our food supply was hardly threatened.[33] On the contrary, the harvest was down only slightly from 1992's record crop, but in line with the five-year average.[34] Very clearly, we do not need farm subsidies to insure an adequate food supply.

The hands-down winner for crop subsidies is corn. Since 1978, the taxpayers have paid over $68 billion to subsidize corn production.[35] Certainly not to insure an adequate food supply for Americans, given that corn production far exceeded domestic food requirements every year. Just the carryover (excess production) of corn stocks after the 1992-93 crop year, a "disaster" year for farmers, equaled 87 percent of an entire year's usage.[36] Indeed, while the government was paying billions of dollars to subsidize corn production, it was paying billions more, to many of the same farmers, not to produce corn. It was not at all uncommon for a farmer to be paid to produce corn on part of his farm while being paid not to produce corn on another part.

Over the years, the politicians have shown that neither logic nor concern for American taxpayers and consumers could get in the way of programs to enrich corn farmers and producers of corn derived products. The reason for corn subsidies is simply to transfer wealth to a powerful special interest group that can be counted on for political and generous financial support. Between 1985 and 1994, the top 26,000 corn farmers received $7.5 billion in direct corn subsidy payments.[37]

Not surprisingly, generous corn subsidies have resulted in enormous surpluses year after year. Since farmers have been shielded from the normal market consequences of overproduction by government subsidy programs, they have simply produced as much as they could. This in turn flooded the market with corn, which drove prices down. Since the primary objective of farm programs is to keep food prices and farmers' incomes high, the politicians reacted to the depressed market by increasing subsidies, which further increased production and further depressed prices. This obviously self-defeating policy reached the pinnacle of absurdity in 1987 when the government spent $12 billion subsidizing a corn crop worth only $12.1 billion.[38]

No fools, those in Washington realized that too much corn was being planted. Rather than eliminate the senseless subsidy, they turned to working at cross-purposes through programs that offset overproduction with no production. Until 1996, the primary vehicles were the Acreage Reduction Program (ARP), the Conservation Reserve Program (CRP), and Set-asides. All three programs were geared to limiting production by requiring farmers not to plant on a portion of their farms or by paying them not to. Set-asides and the ARP required farmers not to grow crops on part of their land to qualify for subsidies on the rest of it. Nothing could be more irrational: requiring zero production in one place to qualify for an incentive to overproduce in another; except perhaps the 1996 "Freedom to Farm Act" which ended the ARP and set-asides, and in their place, enacted provisions that pay farmers for doing absolutely nothing: no farming, no agreement not to farm, nothing. All they needed to do was sign up to receive their share of $35.7 billion.[39] More on that later. The 1996 farm legislation continued the CRP program, which pays farmers not to grow crops on part of their land for ten years. Farmers thought it could not get any better than that . . . until the Freedom to Farm Act. Nonetheless, being paid not to grow crops is pretty close to getting paid for doing nothing at all.

As with most subsidy programs, the CRP is promoted as something else; in this case, a conservation program. According to USDA Extension Service economists Richard T. Clark of the University of Nebraska, James B. Johnson of Montana State, and Stephen H. Amosson of Texas A&M, the primary objective of the CRP program was to reduce cropland erosion.[40] Secondary objectives were to protect soil productivity, reduce sedimentation, improve water quality, and create fish and wildlife habitat. In sixth and seventh place, were reducing surplus commodities and providing farm income support. The reality is quite different; numbers six and seven are really numbers one and two. Most CRP land is not subject to excess erosion. A 1994 study found that more than 60 percent of the thirty-six million acres then enrolled in the CRP program could be farmed with little or no negative impact.[41] The GAO found that only six million of the thirty-six million acres needed to be removed from production to meet the stated environmental objectives.[42] A five-year study by Philip Gersmehl of the University of Minnesota of the CRP program provided more evidence that the program is simply another farm subsidy and not a conservation program. Among his findings:[43]

- For every eroding acre that a farmer idles, another farmer—–or sometimes the same one—simply plows up nearly as much additional erosion-prone land.
- In the Great Plains, farmers put 17 million acres into the CRP program, but the total cultivated land dropped by only two percent.
- The CRP program typically pays farmers twice what they would have earned farming the land.
- The CRP rewards farmers who manage their land poorly.

Without crop subsidies, it is unlikely that much of the erodible, low-productivity land could be farmed profitably. It would be idled due to the conservation program called market efficiency. However, because crop subsidies drive excess production and make it possible to profit from uneconomic farming, the government found it necessary, and politically advantageous, to institute a new subsidy program to offset the unintended consequences of another. Much to the delight of farmers who are being paid 20 billion tax dollars by the CRP program not to farm.[44]

Despite numerous regulatory and legislative attempts to counteract subsidy-driven corn overproduction, large crop surpluses have persisted. Rather than recognize that farmers respond very effectively to government subsidy programs by milking them for all they are worth, the politicians have elected to enact additional subsidy programs to "absorb" the surplus production. The massive subsidy program for American sugar farmers discussed in Chapter 2 has proven to be a bonanza for corn producers. By creating an artificial shortage of sugar in the U.S. and forcing the price of domestic sugar to more than double, the government not only has funneled billions of dollars to wealthy sugar producers, but also created a market for high fructose corn syrup (HFCS)—a sugar substitute.

There is no way that HFCS can compete with sugar at world market prices, but with the USDA restricting the sugar supply in the U.S., sweetener users, such as candy and soft drink producers, are forced to use the expensive, corn-based sweetener. The GAO estimates the extra cost paid to HFCS producers by American consumers at $548 million per year.[45] Eighty-seven percent of this half-billion dollar annual subsidy goes to only four agribusinesses.[46] But the corn farmers and HFCS producers are certainly not ungrateful. They pay the politicians handsome commissions on the subsidies they receive. While the politicians pass subsidy after subsidy, which only exacerbates the "problems" they claim to be attempting to solve, agricultural interests keep recycling some of each new subsidy back to the politicians, thereby reinforcing their penchant for more new subsidy programs. It is a near-perfect relationship . . . unless you happen to be footing the bill.

There is no better example of this cozy relationship than ethanol. Long used as a fuel (and for other purposes), ethanol is simply grain alcohol. In the U.S., nearly all ethanol is distilled from corn. While it may be competitive for alcoholic beverages, it is far too expensive for use as a motor fuel—unless it is heavily subsidized. In the 1970s, when OPEC drastically raised oil prices, corn interests and politicians found it another good reason for a new subsidy program: a domestically-produced gasoline substitute. Blending one part ethanol with nine parts gasoline gives you gasohol. Because the ethanol is produced from American corn, each gallon of gasohol reduces the usage of fossil fuels by 10 percent. So the story goes. In any event, it was a story that could easily carry a new subsidy program.

President Carter got gasohol exempted from the federal fuel excise tax, which now amounts to a 54 cent a gallon subsidy for ethanol, about equal to the wholesale price of gasoline.[47] In the late 70s and early 80s, hundreds of millions of tax dollars were loaned to build ethanol distilleries. Most of them went bankrupt. Even with a subsidy equal to 100 percent of the cost of gasoline, ethanol cannot compete because the USDA estimates that it costs about $1.60 a gallon to manufacture.[48] Nevertheless, many states, mostly large corn producers, also subsidize ethanol, bringing the total subsidy to nearly a dollar a gallon. With the dollar a gallon subsidy, it is a damn competitive product. The federal ethanol subsidy alone costs the taxpayers $700 million annually,[49] but the program has also created artificial demand for an extra 450 million bushels of subsidized corn.[50] Agriculture Secretary Dan Glickman proudly boasted that the extra demand raised corn farmers' net income by $720 million per year.[51] Some of this extra cash comes from corn subsidies and some results from government policies. For instance, the USDA has a mandatory internal requirement to use gasohol in all Department vehicles.[52] (Not surprisingly, it is the only federal agency with such a policy.[53]) Most of the extra cash comes out of the pockets of consumers who are forced to pay higher meat prices due to the government-engineered increase in demand for corn. Most corn is used for animal feed.

No one argues the fact that ethanol is highly subsidized; the arguments of the corn lobby center on the claim that ethanol is an environmentally friendly fuel and that it reduces reliance on fossil fuels. The question becomes, are the subsidies worth the gains in environmental quality and energy independence? An analysis by agribusiness giant Archer Midland Daniels Company (ADM) of one of its distilleries showed that it was consuming energy in the form of natural gas and electricity equal to 85 percent of the energy content in the ethanol.[54] The process of converting corn to ethanol, therefore, was yielding a small 15 percent fuel gain. However, the analysis did not include the substantial amount of oil and gas consumed in the form of fuel and fertilizer used on the farms in the production of the corn. Accounting for this additional energy consumed, the total process of raising corn for ethanol production results in a net loss of energy and a net increase in fossil fuel usage. Clearly, it would be considerably cheaper for Americans, and would likely require less imported oil, if the ethanol program was terminated. However, neither of those results are significant concerns in Washington, D.C.

During the 1992 presidential campaign, Bill Clinton criticized President Bush for proposing changes in clean-air rules to promote the use of ethanol to "buy the votes of corn growers."[55] The Clean Air Act Amendments of 1990 required that reformulated gasoline (RFG), special oxygenated gasoline, be used by 1996 in the nation's nine most polluted cities. Neither regularly formulated gasoline nor ethanol could be used. However, those nine cities also happen to constitute a large percentage of the national motor fuel market, and the ban on ethanol would significantly reduce total demand for that fuel. President Bush had proposed relaxing the regulations to permit the continued use of ethanol.

After becoming President, Clinton jumped on the corn bandwagon with both feet and an open hand. In 1994, he announced rules that would grant ethanol a minimum 30 percent share of the RFG market. The sole reason for Clinton's blatant action was to stuff an additional $350 million into the pockets of the corn industry. Coincidentally, he received a $100,000 contribution from Archer Midland Daniels at about the same time.[56] ADM just happens to produce 60 percent of the nation's ethanol, and consequently receives over $400 million each year in federal ethanol subsidies.[57] Nearly $200 million of the additional $350 million in subsidies from Clinton's 30 percent mandate would also go to ADM. Just one year later, the same Bill Clinton who chastised George Bush for trying to buy the votes of corn farmers, expressed strong opposition to Congressional Republican efforts to reduce the ethanol tax subsidy. His Agriculture Secretary Dan Glickman stated,

> *We believe that Congressional efforts to reduce or repeal the alcohol fuels tax exemption would reduce or eliminate investment in ethanol production facilities, effectively halting a period of unprecedented growth in the industry. As a result, ethanol production would decline by as much as 50 percent from current projections.*[58]

In June 1994, when President Clinton announced his 30 percent mandate policy, he explained that "this policy is good for our environment, our public health, and our nation's farmers, and that's good for America."[59] He brought up one of the primary justifications for the ethanol program: it is a clean fuel, good for the environment and our health. This claim is based on the fact that burning gasohol produces about 25 percent less carbon monoxide than gasoline. However, it also produces as much as 50 percent more hydrocarbons and 15 percent more nitrogen oxide.[60] Consequently, gasohol did not qualify as a cleaner burning fuel under the Environmental Protection Agency's (EPA) requirements for the nation's nine smoggiest cities. The EPA's Martha Casey noted, "The Clean Air Act said that there can be no increase in nitrogen oxides. Unfortunately for the ethanol industry, ethanol would increase those emissions."[61] It was President Bush's proposed waiver from this requirement that brought Bill Clinton's charge that the president was trying to buy the votes of corn farmers. Of course, he was right. Clinton's attempt to buy corn farmer's votes through the 30 percent mandate came undone because it conflicted with the same law. In an April 1995 ruling, that the Clinton mandate exceeded its statutory authority, the Washington D.C. Circuit Court of Appeals noted, "EPA admits that the [ethanol rule] will not give additional emissions reductions for VOCs or toxics . . . and has even conceded that the use of ethanol might possibly make air quality worse."[62] The court ruled that Clinton could not use the Clean Air Act to buy the votes of the corn lobby.

The ethanol program clearly demonstrates that politicians of both parties consider subsidy programs important tools for generating campaign funds and votes. During 1997 and 1998, the chairman and employees of Archer Daniels Midland Company made nearly $530,000 in political contributions[63] as part of a multi-million dollar effort by ethanol interests to buy an extension of the ethanol tax break—and they got it. An extension through the year 2007 was added to the 1998 highway funding legislation. Republicans and Democrats know it is wrong, because they chastise each other for pandering. Nor is it a minor transgression. A USDA study found that the ethanol program cost American consumers and taxpayers four dollars for every additional dollar of farm income.[64] The politicians know how dearly Americans are paying to support their subsidy programs, just as they know that the programs do not serve the national interest and that the arguments they put forth to justify them are either false or, at best, half-truths. In the absence of any remotely defensible basis for their subsidies, they prattle about preserving "traditional ways of life." Quite simply, neither party is capable of putting the best interests of the nation above their own political interest. The rich commissions that subsidies generate are as addictive as any drug.

Dairy support programs demonstrate the irrational extremes that politicians have been willing to go to please a small, but powerful and generous farm interest. For decades, American dairy farmers have produced a preposterous oversupply of milk and milk products in direct response to very generous federal subsidy programs. In just the decade between 1980 and 1990, these subsidies cost Americans $65 billion.[65] The Agricultural Adjustment Act of 1933[66] obligated the federal government to purchase all the diary products that farmers could produce in excess of the supply necessary to meet private sector demand. Not surprisingly, dairy farmers wildly overproduced. During the 1980s, the USDA bought an average of 11 billion pounds of surplus milk, cheese, and butter annually.[67] Eleven *billion*.

Nearly all (98 percent between 1985 and 1989)[68] of this surplus was then given away to domestic and foreign "nutrition" programs. Indeed, most of these programs, such as the School Lunch Program, Food for Progress, and the Special Supplemental Food Program for Women, Infants, and Children (WIC), were devised largely as noble-sounding mechanisms to dispose of the government's mountains of surplus dairy products. The WIC regulations specifically require that the food distributed through the program contain protein, iron, calcium, vitamin A, and vitamin C.[69] Because that specification was obviously tailored to dairy products, it is not surprising that the primary program foods are infant formula, milk, cheese and eggs. Applying the term "nutrition" to a program intended to clog the veins of recipients with fat, adds insult to injury. WIC, which is categorized as a federal assistance program rather than a dairy subsidy program, cost the taxpayers over $2.7 billion in 1996.[70]

The fact that WIC is administered by the Agriculture Department, rather than the Department of Health and Human Services, reveals its primary purpose: to increase demand for surplus dairy products. From that standpoint, the program has been fabulously successful: In 1997, the program had 7.4 million beneficiaries, including 1.9 million infants, 46 percent of all the infants born in the U.S. in 1996.[71] However, studies have found no strong evidence of health benefits for children who participate in the WIC program, except for a five percent decline in anemia.[72] Why then, is the federal government feeding half of the nation's infants? And since the program provides higher benefits to mothers who do not breast-feed, it discourages what has been determined to be the most nutritional and hygienic method of infant feeding. Indeed, half of all the baby formula sold in the U.S. is purchased with WIC vouchers, and just four percent of women participating in the WIC program in 1994 were breast-feeding.[73]

Faced with the truly monumental problem of disposing of nearly a billion pounds of unneeded dairy products every month, the politicians did not even consider simply eliminating the source of the problem: the absurd dairy subsidy system. In typical fashion, they responded to the unintended consequences of one subsidy program by inventing a host of new ones. While the poor were being stuffed with fat through "nutrition" programs, other programs were devised in an attempt to reduce the surplus. Because it was now clear that paying farmers to produce mountains of unneeded milk was literally beginning to bury the country in butterfat, the obvious solution was to begin paying some farmers to stop producing milk—while continuing to pay others to overproduce. This is the same senseless system that assures endless surpluses of corn and billions in subsidies for corn farmers. Under the 1984 Milk Diversion Program, farmers could reduce their production by up to 30 percent for fifteen months. They would be paid 81 percent of the going price for the milk they *did not* produce, while receiving full price for the milk they did produce.[74] The theory was that farmers would slaughter the cows that were not producing milk, thus reducing the size of the dairy herd. While a number of farmers did slaughter some cows, others increased their herds. The net reduction in the herd from the billion-dollar program turned out to be only 10,000 cows, and taxpayers ended up paying nearly $100,000 per cow to achieve that reduction.[75] Dairy subsidy supporters claimed that this program saved the taxpayers money, because it would have cost more to purchase the four billion pounds of milk that the farmers did not produce, than it cost to pay them not to produce it. In Washington, D.C., that passes as a rational argument.

Promptly after the Milk Diversion Program ended, milk production rebounded, presenting the opportunity for another subsidy program: the 1986 Dairy Termination Program. Instead of paying farmers to stop producing milk, this program had the government pay farmers to go out of business for at least five years. The taxpayers paid fourteen thousand farmers $1.55 billion, or an average of $110,000 each, to agree to retire for five years.[76] In addition, the taxpayers paid them another $400 million to buy the extra 400 million pounds of meat that resulted from the slaughter of the "terminated" dairy herds.[77] An already wealthy group of 144 farmers received over a million dollars each and one received ten million.[78] The taxpayers did not even get the farms or the dairy herds; rather, the farmers collected the proceeds from the slaughter of their cows along with the termination payment, and they were able to keep their farms. The net effect on production of these subsidies-to-counteract-subsidies was minimal. Through 1995, the USDA was still purchasing eight to 10 billion pounds of surplus dairy products annually.[79] It is certain, however, that the programs had their intended effects on dairy farmers and politicians.

Given the serious oversupply situation in the U.S., the government also found it necessary to sharply limit dairy imports. The GAO described the dairy import quota system as " . . . established in the 1950s to limit foreign producers from competing in the domestic market and interfering with the government-established minimum price."[80] This method of creating subsidies by government regulation is a favorite method of politicians because of their stealthy nature. The effect of the import quota is to shield farmers from competition, thereby allowing them to charge higher prices. As with sugar, the subsidy is paid directly by consumers to the dairy farmer, rather than through taxes. Since there are no payments from the government, the extent of the subsidy and its cost are far more difficult to track. Politicians and farmers both like that, but the USDA estimates that the import quota subsidy costs Americans between five and seven billion dollars per year.[81] And as farm subsidy critic James Bovard points out, while the U.S. is providing billions of dollars in foreign aid to east European countries, they are prohibited from selling any dairy products in the U.S.[82] We will give them money, but we will not let them earn that money. Americans end up paying twice.

The granddaddy of consumer-to-farmer dairy subsidies is the Federal Milk Marketing Orders (FMMO) pricing system whereby the federal government sets the price of milk in the U.S. based on the distance from Eau Claire, Wisconsin. The FMMO system was enacted in 1937 to boost dairy farmers' incomes when Wisconsin was the center of milk production and there was no refrigeration to speak of. The theory was that the greater the distance from Eau Claire, the greater the expense to deliver milk products. Today, California is the nation's largest producer of dairy products and refrigeration is cheap and plentiful, yet the federal government still enforces price controls based on the 1937 FMMO system. Consequently, in 1998, Americans in Texas and Florida paid 30 to 35 cents more per gallon for locally produced milk than those in Wisconsin and Minnesota.[83] Nationally, according to USDA calculations, the FMMO system forces milk-product consumers to subsidize dairy farmers to the tune of $2.7 billion annually. The taxpayers spend an additional $40 million each year to pay the federal bureaucrats who administer and enforce the price controls.[84]

Still not done, the government also determined that dairy exports needed to be subsidized. The logic here is easily understood: in 1992 the world price for bulk cheddar cheese was eighty-one cents per pound while the USDA was buying all the cheese American farmers could produce for $1.11 per pound.[85] Federal dairy subsidy programs protected America's inefficient dairy producers while limiting the production of those who could compete in world markets. With U.S. prices inflated above world prices by the government, there was little opportunity to export the enormous surpluses . . . unless they were subsidized.

The solution, enacted in 1985, was the Dairy Export Incentive Program (DEIP). The U.S. Department of State candidly described the DEIP as a program that "enables U.S. exporters to miss prevailing world prices for targeted dairy products and destinations."[86] One provision of this program gave away dairy products, purchased by the government, to companies that would export them. The taxpayers purchase the unneeded milk products, which are then given, at no cost, to exporting companies that sell them overseas. Another provision required the Agriculture Department to export minimum levels of dairy products, regardless of the price. Through this program, U.S. taxpayers effectively pay about $135 million annually[87] to foreigners to take some of the surplus dairy products that result from the generous subsidies paid to American farmers to overproduce. The foreigners get the dairy products paid for by American taxpayers at a price cheaper than the U.S. government will sell it to its own citizens—who have already paid for it through taxes.

A good example of the absurd consequences of federal dairy subsidy policies occurred in the summer of 1998. Wholesale prices of butter skyrocketed to $1.95 a pound—about twice the usual price—due to a shortage of butter.[88] It turns out that the USDA, in its never-ending effort to boost milk prices, had subsidized about 35 million pounds of butter and milkfat exports during the preceding twelve months, double what it had done during the previous corresponding period.[89] Because of import restrictions, only 12.7 million pounds could be imported with low tariffs, and that level had already been reached. Consequently, a nation with chronic surplus butter production was now faced with a nearly 100 percent price increase due to a shortage, and import restrictions precluded increasing the supply. Dairy processors—makers of foods like ice cream and cream cheese—petitioned the USDA to allow increased imports, to no avail. Agriculture Secretary Dan Glickman explained that he was reluctant to take any action that might reduce prices paid to struggling dairy farmers.[90] Of course, the only reason there are struggling dairy farmers is that federal subsidy programs keep inefficient producers in the business at the expense of efficient farmers, American consumers, and U.S. taxpayers. That, however, is what USDA bureaucrats firmly believe they are supposed to do.

Unfortunately, they are quite right; they are simply carrying out Congressional mandates. All of this bipartisan foolishness, subsidy after subsidy, is intended to counteract the logical consequences of a basic policy that rewards inefficiency and pays farmers to overproduce. The politicians have simply been unable to abandon that policy. The 1996 Freedom to Farm Act preserved dairy import restrictions and export subsidies, and left the Federal Milk Market Order system largely intact. While the law provides for the elimination of dairy price supports in the year 2000, it is unlikely that they will actually be allowed to expire. Just as Congress could not resist adding $6 billion in additional farm subsidies to the 1999 budget[91]—subsidies that the Freedom to Farm Act was supposed to preclude—Congress will decide that eliminating price supports would be too much for "struggling dairy farmers."

A similar scenario applies to wheat, but the government spends three times more subsidizing foreigners. Since 1917, the government has paid farmers to grow wheat and they produce plenty of it: more than twice the nation's annual consumption. During the 1950s, the overproduction was so great that the USDA began having wheat farmers who exceeded their quotas arrested. The government has not had to go quite that far lately, but between 1985 and 1994 the taxpayers spent $18.2 billion on direct wheat subsidies.[92] The 1996 Freedom to Farm Act authorized another $9.4 billion for wheat farmers for the years 1996 through 2002.[93] To qualify for the new subsidy, a farmer must have been either paid by the government to grow wheat or paid by the government not to grow wheat for at least one year between 1991 and 1995.[94] All who qualify receive seven years of wheat subsidy payments—whether or not they grow wheat. Not only is this senseless, but remarkably inefficient as well. The GAO found that wheat subsidies costing taxpayers an average of $2.2 billion annually were only producing an average of $1.4 billion in yearly economic benefits for wheat producers.[95] Nearly a billion dollars a year extracted from the taxpayers for the benefit of mostly wealthy wheat producers was simply disappearing. This dismal 63 percent efficiency rate was achieved through the brilliant idea of requiring wheat farmers to idle some of their land to qualify for subsidies on the remainder. Such reverse alchemy could only emanate from a subsidy program. The 1996 Freedom to Farm Act took the absurdity one step further: a wheat farmer could pack up, move to the city, and still receive seven years of subsidy payments.

With subsidies driving annual wheat production at about 2.5 billion bushels, twice domestic usage, we had another situation where, without additional government action, mountains of grain could begin to pose a safety hazard to American citizens. Fortunately, the politicians came up with the Export Enhancement Program (EEP), a subsidy that cost over $8 billion from 1985 to 1998.[96] Among the consequences of the EEP, noted in an analysis by Texas A&M University[97] were that it:

- *Invites complaints from trading partners and allies such as Australia and Canada.*
- *Reduces government stocks of commodities and increases price variability.*
- *Violates the spirit of GATT* [General Agreement on Tariffs and Trade].
- *Invites public image problem and undermines U.S. efforts in GATT.*
- *Offsets commercial sales of U.S. products.*
- *Places upward price pressure on domestic consumers.*

Since 1985, more than one-half of all American wheat has been exported, and more than half of those exports have received EEP subsidies.[98] From 1985 through 1994, these subsidies totaled $4.8 billion.[99] After buying wheat from American farmers at an inflated price, the U.S. government sells it to agribusinesses for about one-third the world market price.[100] They then reap a handsome profit while selling it to foreign countries for about a third less than U.S. citizens pay for it. The exporters and the foreign buyers are both subsidized by American taxpayers. Adding insult to injury, 39 percent of the EEP contracts go to foreign-owned exporters.[101] The EEP subsidy is the second time that the same wheat has been subsidized because the taxpayers also paid the wheat farmers. Essentially, the government buys wheat to force the price up, and then subsidizes wheat exports to force the price down. It is an irrational phenomenon, which turns up repeatedly with government subsidies.

Federal export efforts have reached the pinnacle of perversity with cotton programs. In their analyses, the GAO generally seems to accept that the political objectives of subsidy programs have some sort of merit, even if they make absolutely no sense from any other standpoint. The fact that the agency is an arm of Congress, and subject to Congressional appropriations, no doubt accounts for a certain amount of diplomacy in its reports. On the subject of cotton exports, however, the GAO is unusually blunt:

> *Although exports are usually considered to be beneficial, this is not true for cotton. While the cotton industry benefits from the exports, during the period covered by our review, production costs and government payments, taken together, were consistently higher than the adjusted world price. As a result, the United States sold cotton on the world market for less than it cost.*[102]

As with other subsidized commodities, domestic cotton production vastly exceeds usage. For 1997, estimated production was 19 million bales while usage was 11 million.[103] Cotton farmers benefit from virtually every variety of farm subsidy, and they very likely profit more than any other farm group. One subsidy, the 50/92 program, allowed cotton farmers to plant 50 percent of their acreage yet receive a subsidy as if they had planted 92 percent.[104] From 1986 through 1993, cotton subsidies totaled $12 billion, with only nineteen thousand farmers receiving 79 percent of that.[105] The GAO also determined that counterproductive cotton subsidies are even less efficient than wheat programs. Subsidies that cost taxpayers $12 billion, produced just over $6 billion in net benefits for cotton farmers, a miserable 51 percent efficiency.[106] Six billion tax dollars produced no benefit for anyone. Even more incredible, the GAO found that the $12 billion expenditure only reduced cotton prices by $131 million from what they would have been with no subsidies at all.[107] One can only stand in awe of a system that can achieve the seemingly impossible task of devising a $12 billion subsidy program where $6 billion disappears into thin air and results in only a one percent change in the commodity price. But Congress still was not finished. Import restrictions on foreign cotton pushed domestic prices to a level well above world market prices. Because neither domestic nor foreign mills could afford the government-inflated price of U.S. cotton, the 1990 farm act added a "Step 2" subsidy for domestic mills and exporters to bring the price down to world market levels.[108] Between 1992 and 1996, Step 2 subsidy payments cost the taxpayers $701 million.[109]

The cotton provisions of the 1996 Freedom to Farm Act do not appear quite as ridiculous as those it replaced; then again, it was a very tough act to follow. Nonetheless, cotton farmers who received subsidies in any year between 1991 and 1995 will receive over $4 billion in additional subsidies under the legislation, even if they stop growing cotton.[110] It is a true entitlement: They get the future subsidies solely because they received past subsidies. Import restrictions, export subsidies, and the Step 2 subsidies remain. The GAO predicted that continuing federal subsidies would keep American cotton prices above world prices.[111]

Then there is rice. American taxpayers have been subsidizing rice farmers since 1941. In both the 1985 and 1990 farm bills, "reforms" were introduced to reduce the government's costs and increase the U.S. share of the world rice market.[112] Indeed, reforms with similar objectives for various crops are usually a part of each five-year farm bill. However, the proof is in the pudding, and "reform" is as often as not a euphemism for increasing rather than decreasing subsidies. Taxpayers paid far more for rice pudding after the reforms were enacted. Annual subsidies averaged $594 million before the 1990 reforms and $863 million after, a 45 percent increase.[113] The 1996 Freedom to Farm Act guaranteed rice farmers a minimum of $3 billion in additional subsidies.[114] In yet another example of a senseless attempt to increase the export of commodities with subsidy-inflated prices, despite $157 million in additional export subsidies, the U.S. share of the world rice market declined from 24 percent in 1980 to 15 percent in 1992.[115]

Of course, the program is very beneficial for rice farmers—between 1985 and 1994, a no doubt very happy group of 895 rice farmers received an average of $434,840 each from the taxpayers.[116] But what do the taxpayers get in return for their $1 billion annual rice subsidy? According to the GAO, they get to pay $12 million *more* for rice at the market than if there was no rice subsidy program at all.[117] In 1997, the GAO reported that Americans could expect to continue to pay more than world prices for rice, thanks to the determination of their government to subsidize wealthy rice farmers.[118]

Nothing exposes the prevarication in the USDA's claim that farm subsidy programs are intended to insure adequate supplies of food at reasonable prices like the sugar program. As discussed in Chapter 2, by establishing a minimum support price and strict import quotas, the USDA works deliberately and effectively to accomplish exactly the opposite. The agency, politicians, and sugar producers are quick to point out that the government's sugar program operates at no cost to the taxpayers, and they are largely correct. Rather than direct government payments, this subsidy operates by increasing the prices that consumers pay for sugar. The world is awash in sugar, and corn sweeteners have significantly decreased sugar demand. As such, world prices are low. But Americans are forced by their own government to pay over twice the world price of sugar directly to a handful of wealthy sugar producers. The average price set by the USDA between 1991 and 1995 for Americans was twenty-two cents a pound while the world price was just over eleven cents,[119] and this government-enforced extortion costs consumers an average of $1.8 billion annually.[120] Incredibly, 158 sugar farmers receive over $235 million per year in sugar subsidies,[121] and one family receives $60 million every year.[122] As we have already seen, the government-created, artificial sugar shortage has allowed the producers of corn-based high fructose corn syrup (HFCS) to collect an extra $548 million per year, of which $476 million goes to only four producers.[123] Annually.

Despite the extraordinary amount of money indefensibly being channeled to a tiny number of sugar and HFCS producers, USDA Under Secretary Gene Moos told Congress in May 1995 that the U.S. sugar policy is "an important part of U.S. agricultural policy and should be continued in order to provide American sugar producers the safety net their industry deserves."[124]

This statement is a testament to how federal subsidy programs seriously distort reality for both the subsidized and the government agencies responsible for administering the programs. Mr. Moos believes that average Americans should provide a "safety net" for sugar producers, the vast majority of whom are millionaires. Such irrational thought has become the norm in Washington, D.C.; indeed, the Congress and President Clinton demonstrated their agreement with the Secretary by extending the sugar program in 1996 with minor modifications. They also contend that by severely restricting the availability of readily-available sugar and forcing the price up by more than 100 percent, they are protecting U.S. consumers from a "relatively volatile world market," according to Moos.[125] While I am unaware of any research in this area, there is strong, circumstantial evidence that involvement with federal subsidies, in any capacity, somehow disrupts the normal functioning of the human brain.

The peanut subsidy program provides evidence that the affliction is irreversible. In 1949, the government introduced a peanut quota system based on allotments to those farmers who were growing peanuts at that time. Fifty years later, the basic system is still in place, despite the concentration of benefits into the hands of an astonishingly few farmers. In order to sell peanuts in the United States, a farmer must have "quota" derived from the original 1949 allotment. A corn farmer who decided to switch to peanuts would be charged with a federal crime by the USDA if he tried to sell his crop inside the U.S. The number of allotments when the program started was about 173,000, however, by 1991, only 6,182 producers controlled over 80 percent of the quota.[126] What a fortunate group they are. In 1995, the government guaranteed them $678 per ton for their peanuts, which netted them an 84 percent profit margin.[127] At the same time, those farmers without quota, who by law can only sell their peanuts outside the U.S., were only guaranteed $132 per ton, well below production cost.[128]

The world price for peanuts in 1995 was $415 per ton while the average cost of production for U.S. farmers was $369 per ton.[129] American peanut farmers are world competitors; U.S. non-quota farmers export nearly five hundred million pounds of peanuts annually, which clearly demonstrates that there is absolutely no need for either the quota system or the USDA price support. Nevertheless, this absurd system, benefiting fewer than seven thousand farmers, is further buttressed by a virtual prohibition on imports. Annual peanut imports amount to less than one-tenth of one percent of the total output from quota allotments.[130] Once again, American consumers are forced to pick up the tab for the government's extraordinary generosity. The GAO estimates the program increases the price Americans pay for peanuts, peanut butter, and other foods containing peanuts, by as much as $513 million per year.[131] The 1996 Freedom to Farm Act made only a small change in the peanut program, dropping the support price from $678 to $610 per ton[132]—and decreasing, to only 65 percent, the government-guaranteed profit margin for the very fortunate six thousand odd farmers with peanut quotas.

After the government has forced farm commodity prices up for Americans through price supports, and then lowered them for foreigners through export subsidies, farmers still face a potential problem: What if the foreign buyer doesn't have the money to pay even the bargain-basement subsidized price? Of course, the government has a subsidy program for that situation, too: the GSM-102 and GSM-103 Export Credit Guarantee Programs. The GAO states that these programs "aid U.S. commercial agriculture exports to countries experiencing hard currency constraints."[133] Translated, that means countries that do not have cash and have lousy credit as well. In Congress' view, there is nothing the taxpayers should not do to enhance farm income, including guaranteeing very risky loans to countries that no commercial (and therefore somewhat sensible) lender would touch. Under the GSM programs, commercial lenders make the export loans, but U.S. taxpayers guarantee a minimum of 98 percent of the principal.[134] There is not much more principal than that. For many exports, a GSM loan is the third subsidy, after price supports and EEP, for the same commodity.

An interesting insight into the irrational thinking at the USDA is revealed by the claim by the agency's Foreign Agricultural Service (FAS), which administers the GSM programs, that they are "fully commercial," because the loans are made by commercial lenders at market interest rates.[135] There is not a lender on the planet that would touch those loans if they were not guaranteed by U.S. taxpayers. The GAO has noted, "Because of the riskiness of the borrowers, these programs have a very high cost."[136] They know that at USDA. From the 1980s, when the GSM programs began, through 1992, these "fully commercial" loans cost the taxpayers $5.7 billion because of loan defaults by the foreign buyers, and the GAO has warned of "significant future increases in defaults if high-risk foreign buyers continue to participate."[137] The agency was quite right. In August 1998, Russia defaulted on its $2 billion GSM-102 debt.[138]

Three hundred and sixty million tax dollars were paid to the Gulf International Bank in Bahrain in 1992 after Iraq defaulted on a GSM guaranteed loan.[139] The bank that received all its money back from U.S. taxpayers is partly owned by . . . Iraq.[140] After spending billions of dollars in the Gulf War against Iraq, we promptly turned around and reimbursed the Iraqis for a loss due to their own default! They got their GSM cake and got to eat it, too. A GAO analysis of USDA credit guarantees for Iraq revealed that various high-level government officials in the USDA and other agencies were well aware that Iraq was not creditworthy, but the guarantees were approved to further the USDA's "market development objectives."[141] By 1989, due to defaults, few government agencies other than USDA continued to extend credit to Iraq.[142] Perhaps those other agencies did not consider loans guaranteed by U.S. taxpayers to be fully commercial.

Even more risky than its GSM program is the massive, domestic, credit-subsidy operation run by the USDA's Consolidated Farm Service Agency (CFSA), formerly known as the Farmers Home Administration (FmHA). The GAO calls loans through this program "among the riskiest in the federal government."[143] Indeed, CFSA's credit program is very likely the most preposterous large-scale lending program in the history of the United States. As best the GAO could determine, the CFSA is supposed to provide "temporary financial assistance to farmers who are unable to obtain commercial loans at reasonable rates and terms."[144] The agency's uncertainty arose because it concluded that legislation had not established clear priorities for the agency's fundamental role and mission.[145] But Congress has made it clear that CFSA's job is to lend taxpayer money to almost any farmer, regardless of competence or creditworthiness, and that borrowers are not required to pay back one cent of principal or interest. Moreover, even if farmers fail to make any payments, CFSA is to lend them more money if they request it.

The Agricultural Credit Act of 1987 mandated that FmHA forgive such debt as deemed necessary to allow a delinquent farmer to continue farming.[146] And if a farmer defaulted and quit farming, the agency was simply to write-off the remaining debt. Better yet, farmers who received debt relief under the Act were not barred from obtaining additional loans, and Congress required the FmHA to make "continuation loans" to cover operating expenses of farmers who were delinquent on their existing debt.[147] As is always the case, a subsidized group's response is to maximize the benefits received, and farmers do not look a gift-horse in the mouth. Regarding the clear message being sent to CFSA borrowers, the GAO's Patrick J. Sweeney noted, "It tells them 'I don't have to pay.'"[148] Indeed. With the blessing and encouragement of Congress, farmers have borrowed and failed to pay back billions of dollars. Between 1987 and 1990, taxpayers lost $7.7 billion.[149] Between 1991 and 1994, another $6.3 billion was lost.[150] As of March 1995, 32.6 percent of the CFSA's $17.8 billion in outstanding loans were in default, another $5.8 billion.[151]

The politicians claim, and reasonable people might assume, that there just was no other source of farm financing, but that is far from the case. The American Bankers Association and USDA Economic Research Service both reported that agricultural credit was generally available for creditworthy borrowers in 1991.[152] The Farm Credit System, comprised of 258 non-government agricultural banks, had net income of about $1 billion or more in each of the years 1993,[153] 1994, and 1995.[154] The system is financially sound and a ready source of credit for farmers. However, these loans have to be repaid. As of September 1995, the Farm Credit System had $56.2 billion in outstanding loans and only two percent were delinquent.[155] Now consider this insanity reported by the GAO:[156]

- *From 1989 through March 1995, CFSA made a half a billion dollars in new loans to farmers after it had incurred losses on their previous loans. As of March of 1995, 42 percent of the borrowers were delinquent.*
- *CFSA made an additional $130 million in continuation loans between 1989 and March 1995 to farmers who were already delinquent on their existing loans. As of March 1995, 53 percent of these new loans were also in default.*

Congress *mandated* that tax dollars be handed over to farmers who had not paid back previous loans and, in essence, told them they did not have to pay back the additional money either. That should remove any lingering doubts about the intent of Congress to transfer large amounts of the taxpayer's money to farmers.

Two additional transfer mechanisms used to subsidize farmers are the Crop Insurance and Disaster Assistance programs. The Federal Crop Insurance Act was passed in 1938 before subsidies were the primary business of Congress. During its first six years, the program lost money, and a sensible government canceled it, but in 1947, it was reinstated with new provisions intended to insure that the program would not need subsidies.[157] By 1980, only about seven percent of planted acreage was covered by crop insurance,[158] partly because of program restrictions, but mostly because disaster assistance was a much better deal for farmers. Congress regularly provided direct cash payments to farmers under disaster assistance programs, which cost farmers nothing and made crop insurance largely unnecessary because all the risk had been transferred to the taxpayers.

In 1980, Congress redesigned the Crop Insurance program to expand coverage to more farmers and to make insurance, rather than disaster assistance, the primary subsidy mechanism. Politicians prefer disguised subsidies such as crop insurance to highly visible, overt ones like disaster assistance. One of the stated objectives of the Federal Crop Insurance Act of 1980 was to decrease insurance costs for farmers by providing a 30 percent federal subsidy.[159] Previous Crop Insurance programs had been specifically aimed at eliminating subsidies. The 1980 Act was a manifestation of the transition Congress had made from primarily governing in the 1940s to primarily subsidizing beginning in the 1960s. For all their efforts, insurance enrollment still lagged because, despite the 30 percent subsidy, farmers knew that the politicians would still provide disaster assistance with a 100 percent subsidy. Of course, they did just that and more. Average annual disaster assistance increased 1000 percent for the 1987-1990 period compared to the period from 1982-1986.[160] Just as it made little sense to pay back USDA loans, there was little reason to buy insurance when the taxpayers would effectively provide it for free through disaster assistance. Between 1981 and 1993, these two subsidy programs cost taxpayers more than $19 billion, $11 billion in disaster assistance and $8 billion in crop insurance.[161]

In 1994, Congress declared itself addicted to disaster assistance subsidies and passed the Federal Crop Insurance Reform Act to force itself to go cold turkey. The Act eliminated the legal authority for future off-budget disaster assistance programs.[162] The $11 billion paid to farmers through 1993 had been "off-budget," meaning that it did not count in the official budget deficit calculation. The cost to the taxpayers was still $11 billion. Under the 1994 Act, Congress could still pass disaster assistance, but they could no longer claim that it did not count. In another attempt to force all the subsidies into the insurance program, the new law provided a 100 percent insurance subsidy. The only cost to the farmer for multiple-peril crop insurance is a $50 administrative fee that can be waived.[163] Essentially, disaster assistance was transformed into a permanent insurance subsidy that is essentially free of charge to farmers. It took numerous attempts, and fifty-six years, but finally Congress perfected the Crop Insurance program.

On November 5, 1997, Roger Swartz of American Farm Bureau Insurance Services Inc. testified before the House Subcommittee on Risk Management and Specialty Crops that the new crop insurance program had "saved taxpayers $2 billion annually since agricultural disaster aid was repealed." The idea being that previously farmers were somehow entitled to disaster aid, and so a couple of billion dollars annually was to be expected ad infinitum. However, Congress does not really repeal subsidy programs. In October 1998, Congress passed a $6 billion farm disaster aid package, thereby largely eliminating all the "taxpayer savings" that Mr. Swartz had boasted about.[164] On the other hand, the commercial insurance companies, like Mr. Swartz's, that issue Multiple-peril policies for the government, made out like bandits, reaping $750 million in profits from federal crop insurance between 1994 and 1997.[165] The companies are paid fees by the government to handle the paper work and have no liability under the policies. All the risk is shouldered by U.S. taxpayers, who lost $8.9 billion on federal crop insurance programs between 1990 and 1997.[166] Of course.

Foreign market development has been a major objective of Congress and the USDA. Having enacted subsidies for growing, exporting, and financing farm products, about the only thing left to subsidize was their promotion in foreign markets. Congress would not let farm interests down. In 1985, it enacted the Targeted Export Assistance Program, followed by the Market Promotion Program (MPP) in 1990.[167] Together the two programs cost taxpayers nearly $1.5 billion between 1986 and 1995.[168] Incredibly, American taxpayers are paying wealthy farmers and large companies to advertise their products in foreign markets. That is what the MPP does—it pays for foreign advertising. The politicians' rationale is that because European countries do it, so must we. However, the GAO found that MPP subsidies are two to four times greater than those provided by European governments.[169] In truth, it's just one more program to fatten the bank accounts of farm interests. Even more incredible is the list of subsidy recipients, including already heavily subsidized Sunkist, E.J. Gallo, Tyson's Foods, Pillsbury, Dole Co., Welch's, M&M/Mars, Joseph E. Seagram Co., Wrangler Co., Fruit of the Loom, Sara Lee, Jim Beam, Ocean Spray, Campbells Soup, Nestle, Hershey, Ralston Purina, and McDonalds.[170] That is just a partial listing of the companies that were given tax dollars by the federal government to advertise their products overseas. In 1996, the MPP was replaced by the Market Access Program, which prohibited direct assistance to large companies, but continued subsidies for agricultural cooperatives. As such, big brands, such as Sunkist, Blue Diamond, Sunsweet, Welch Foods, and Ocean Spray, continue to have American taxpayers funding their foreign advertising.[171]

It is not difficult to understand why farm-state congressmen continually vote for nonsensical farm subsidy programs, but it takes a majority in each house to pass bills, and it is less clear why urban representatives agree to give tens of billions of taxpayer dollars to generally wealthy farmers. The answer lies in "nutrition" programs, which cost U.S. taxpayers $36 billion in 1996.[172] There is a long-standing quid pro quo where urban lawmakers vote for farm subsidy programs in exchange for farm votes for federal free-food programs, usually mischaracterized as nutrition programs. The cities get food for their poor (and not so poor) at the expense of federal taxpayers, while farmers get the federal government to buy more food, and perhaps more importantly, they get an outlet for the mountains of surplus food the government pays them to produce. It is a classic federal subsidy tangle where one subsidy breeds another, which breeds another, and on and on. Each new subsidy creates another beneficiary group with an interest in preserving its claim to live off the labors of others. And, of course, the more they become accustomed to enjoying unearned benefits, the less inclined they are to earn their own. In a very short time, they become firmly convinced that they have a right to live at the expense of others because it is their way of life. Politicians consider subsidized "ways of life" sacred, and they tread very lightly.

The largest of the free-food programs is the Federal Food Stamp program, which, in 1996, provided benefits to 26.9 million Americans, about 10 percent of the population, at a cost of $27.3 billion.[173] According to the House Ways and Means Committee *Green Book*, "Food stamps are designed to increase the food purchasing power of eligible low income households to a point where they can buy a nutritionally adequate low-cost diet."[174] The assumption is that these households are undernourished and cannot afford a nutritionally adequate diet. While that is no doubt true for some Americans, it is certainly not true for 10 percent of the population. In an effort to maximize the number of Americans who qualify for food stamps, as well as other welfare programs, the federal government uses an intentionally dishonest definition of poverty. It does not count non-cash benefits from subsidy programs such as Medicaid, public housing, and free-food benefits as income. In 1992, the government refused to count $183 billion of the $305 billion spent on welfare programs as income,[175] despite the fact that it was clearly income to the recipients. As such, families in the lowest fifth income bracket of the population, who the Census Bureau claimed averaged only $7,263 in income in 1991, spent $17,804, on average, when all their subsidies were counted.[176] That was the average; while some families at the low end were poor by any measure, many at the higher end clearly were not. In 1991, 40 percent of those classified as poor by the government owned their own homes and 64 percent owned a car.[177] Honest accounting would greatly diminish the number of Americans who qualify for anti-poverty subsidies.

While free-food program proponents like to portray a picture of millions of poor in the U.S. going to bed hungry, the reality is largely the opposite. The poor have a higher rate of obesity than those with above-poverty incomes. They are overfed. In addition, poor children eat more meat than higher-income children and have average protein intakes 100 percent above recommended levels.[178] Rather than a "nutritionally adequate low-cost diet," government subsidies are fostering a high-cost diet rich in protein and fat—exactly the opposite. This in turn helps fuel the rampant growth in the Medicaid and Medicare subsidy programs due to the inevitable health problems resulting from such an unhealthy diet. But the Food Stamp program, like all free-food programs, is administered by the Agriculture Department and encouraging a diet rich in fat and protein fits well with its programs that pay farmers to overproduce such foods. Farm interests staunchly protect the Food Stamp program to prop up farmers' income, which was the primary intent of the program. In *Feeding the Poor: Assessing Federal Food Aid*, Peter H. Rossi notes,

> *The political support from agriculture, food processors, and food*
> *merchants suggest that the Food Stamp program may also have*
> *been intended to bolster the market for agricultural products.*[179]

Several states have attempted experiments with "cashing-out" food stamps—providing cash instead of food stamps—and these programs have been bitterly opposed in Congress because of the threat of reduced food demand. Cash can be spent on anything, but food stamps can only be used for food. The USDA refused to approve welfare reform demonstration programs by the states of Oregon and Mississippi in 1994 because the programs involved cash-outs.[180] The Department of Health and Human Services gave its approval, but for the USDA, the best interest of the poor was not the issue, the best interest of farmers and food processors was. Studies have shown that a dollar in food stamps led to an additional thirty cents in food consumption, whereas a dollar in cash only led to eight cents in additional food consumption.[181] Cashing-out food stamps could eliminate much of the 14 percent in state administrative costs associated with the program,[182] but maximizing the benefits reaching the poor is not the issue; maximizing the benefits to farm interests is.

A sense of the depth of support for the Food Stamp subsidy as a mechanism for supporting farmers can be obtained by analyzing the cost of continuing the program as opposed to simply cashing-out the entire thing. Food stamps are not really stamps, but coupons in denominations from 1 to 10 dollars. They are used just like cash at food retailers and processed by the Federal Reserve System. The coupons are, in almost every respect, currency of the United States, except that they can only be spent for food items. Nevertheless, as has proven to be the case in every subsidy program, a few government regulations are a small hindrance to those who wish to take advantage of the system. The practice of selling food stamps for cash at discounts as high as 40 percent is widespread. The GAO reported estimates of the extent of the trafficking at $2 billion per year, or about 10 percent of all benefits issued.[183] The agency also found that food stamp overpayments came to about $1.7 billion, or eight percent of benefits, in 1992.[184] In total, the program has losses from errors, trafficking, and administrative costs that come to about 26 percent of benefits.[185]

The Food Stamp program is a disaster, and Congress is well aware of that. The politicians are also aware that most of the losses could be easily eliminated. At the state and local levels, the same welfare offices and personnel that handle cash assistance programs administer the Food Stamp program.[186] If food stamps were cashed-out and combined with existing benefit programs, virtually all the administrative cost could be eliminated. So, too, would the losses due to trafficking because there would no longer be coupons. And because many of the overpayment errors are due to complex Food Stamp program regulations, a substantial reduction in the overpayment problem would also be achieved by cashing-out the program. The 26 percent loss rate could be brought down to the 5 percent range that was achieved by the Aid to Families With Dependent Children program (AFDC)[187] for a savings of more than $5 billion per year *without reducing benefits one cent*. However, that would also end about $25 billion annually in federally mandated food purchases. Farmers and food processors will hear of no such thing.

In 1995, when the Republican-controlled Congress considered turning the Food Stamp program over to the states where cash-outs were likely, the food industry stopped the effort in its tracks.[188] A Washington Post editorial noted,

> *The food stamps program is popular among farmers who produce the food and among the grocers who sell it, making it popular with the agriculture committees. This sort of coalition is not usually in favor of programs to give direct assistance to the poor.[189]*

With the subsidy program serving that industry so well, and given that it accounts for about a third of its annual budget,[190] the USDA has become as dependent on its own subsidy as food interests have. The pusher has become addicted to its own drugs. Having spawned such large and powerful vested interests, the Food Stamp program, as counterproductive and inefficient as it is, has achieved subsidy immortality.

If Americans were not so numbed by three decades of ever-increasing federal intervention in their daily lives, they would be incensed by the audacity of the National School Lunch Program (NSLP). The underlying assumption behind this program is that parents are incapable of feeding their own children, and that only the intervention of federal bureaucrats can protect children from their parents' ignorance and neglect. As with all food aid programs, a major reason for the program was to support farmers, but, as always, there was a reasonable-sounding basis for the program when it was enacted in 1946. President Truman saw it as a measure of national security because too many World War II draftees flunked their physicals due to poor nutrition.[191] The nutritional problems that the military saw in the late thirties and early forties were largely a result of the just-ended Great Depression. By the time the legislation was enacted, the problem was history. Nonetheless in 1972, President Nixon greatly expanded the program and came up with the theory that feeding America's children was a federal responsibility.[192] It is difficult to imagine a more damaging governmental action: relieving parents of their most important duty to their children.

Today, the NSLP has evolved into a major subsidy program that serves twenty-five million meals each school day.[193] Poor children get the lunches for free or at a reduced rate, but the subsidy is not limited to the poor. According to USDA figures, the average full price for a program lunch is $1.14, while the average cost is $1.64, meaning that the taxpayer subsidy comes to fifty cents per full-price lunch.[194] The 55 percent of students, or about fourteen million, who do not qualify for a reduced price because their family income is too high are nonetheless subsidized.[195] Parents who are perfectly capable of feeding their children get the subsidy anyway, which costs the taxpayers $1.26 billion per year.

For some unknown reason, NSLP regulations require that all meals be served hot, perhaps to help use the shortening and oil that Congress requires be supplied to schools. In any event, this requirement resulted in tens of thousands of extra school employees to prepare hot meals and created another subsidized, and largely unionized, interest group. In 1994, they demonstrated how subsidy-born interest groups create a feedback loop to achieve endless growth and, eventually, subsidy immortality. Their union, the American School Food Service Association, proposed that NSLP lunches be free of charge to all students instead of just poor children.[196] This would greatly expand the number of lunches served to non-needy children and create tens of thousands of additional food service jobs—at an estimated additional cost to the taxpayers of $7 billion annually.[197] They succeeded in getting a pilot program bill introduced in the House, but it has not been enacted. Yet.

The intent of the School Lunch Program as a government fat disposal mechanism can be seen in various provisions of the law:

- *Lunches served by schools participating in the school lunch program under this chapter shall offer students fluid whole milk and fluid unflavored lowfat milk.[198]*
- *Among those commodities delivered under this section, the Secretary shall give special emphasis to high protein foods, meat, and meat alternates (which may include domestic seafood commodities and their products).[199]*
- *Among the products to be included in the food donations to the school lunch program shall be cereal and shortening and oil products.[200]*
- *Any school participating in food service programs under this chapter may refuse to accept delivery of not more than 20 percent of the total value of agricultural commodities and other foods tendered to it [by the USDA] in any school year; and if a school so refuses, that school may receive, in lieu of the refused commodities, other commodities to the extent that other commodities are available to the State during that year.[201]*

The program absorbs over a billion pounds of government surplus food annually,[202] and, like the Food Stamp Program, it has become a major source of malnutrition. The USDA's own studies have found that School Lunch Program meals are short on carbohydrates and long on fat and salt.[203] In testimony before the House Agriculture Subcommittee in September 1994, USDA Assistant Secretary Ellen Haas reported that less than one percent of the nation's schools meet guidelines of no more than 30 percent of calories from fat and 10 percent from saturated fat.[204] The average school lunch was 50 percent over on fat and 25 percent over on saturated fat.[205] Milk, which is mandatory, is loaded with saturated fat. The law allows "lowfat" milk to be served along with whole milk, but there is nothing low fat about lowfat milk. Many erroneously believe that the 2 percent lowfat milk served in schools is a dramatic improvement over whole milk, however, whole milk derives 48 percent of its calories from fat while two percent lowfat milk derives 38 percent of its calories from fat.[206] Vegetables have represented only 10 to 19 percent of all the USDA commodities donated to schools, and the lion's share of those have been potatoes.[207] While a raw potato has 1.1 percent fat, the processed potatoes served in the School Lunch Program average from 34.8 to 47.3 percent fat.[208] Given the statutory fat-disposal requirements of the program, none of this is particularly surprising.

In May 1996, President Clinton was running hard to win a second term in office, and cattle ranchers were complaining of low market prices. The federal government has subsidized the overproduction of beef for decades, and surpluses lead to low prices. Not wanting to disappoint a subsidy beneficiary group before an election, Mr. Clinton simply ordered $50 million worth of beef purchased for the NSLP.[209] Agriculture Secretary Glickman said the administration was "doing our best to keep the market from falling further."[210] He said nothing about the government using our children to dispose of surplus beef for the benefit of livestock producers. In December 1998, it was the pork producers who needed help, and again America's children were called on to dispose of the bacon. Secretary Glickman ordered that the purchase of $50 million worth of pork for the NSLP be accelerated into December 1998, and that an additional 36 million pounds be purchased in February 1999.[211]

There are, of course, provisions in the law that stipulate that school lunches must meet nutritional requirements:

- *Lunches served by schools participating in the school lunch program under this chapter shall meet minimum nutritional requirements prescribed by the Secretary on the basis of tested nutritional research.*[212]
- *The Secretary of Agriculture and the Secretary of Health and Human Services shall jointly develop and approve a publication to be entitled "Nutrition Guidance for Child Nutrition Programs". . . . In carrying out any covered program, school food authorities and other organizations and institutions participating in such program shall apply the*

nutrition guidance described in the publication when pre-
paring meals and meal supplements served under such
programs.[213]

Both provisions reaffirm the basic assumption that federal bureaucrats are uniquely qualified to determine how best to meet the nutritional needs of the nation's children. Not only are parents unqualified, but so, too, are local school authorities and "other organizations and institutions." Somehow, the Secretary of Agriculture whose primary function is to insure a rich stream of subsidies to wealthy farm interests is enlightened beyond those who are primarily concerned with the children's best interest. Certainly, Congress took no account of the overwhelming body of evidence to the contrary in formulating these audacious policies. The USDA publishes a handbook called *Handbook 8*, which analyzes seventy items of composition for fifty-three hundred food items.[214] According to the GAO, the handbook is the "primary repository of food composition data in the United States,"[215] and it is widely relied upon in the public and private sectors and throughout the world. However, much of the data in *Handbook 8* comes directly from food interests with no supporting data. For instance, data on bacon-cheeseburgers included in the handbook came primarily from brochures provided by fast-food chains.[216] The GAO has concluded, "Consequently, [USDA] cannot be assured that all the data in *Handbook 8*—used in so many nutritional decisions—are reliable."[217] Another government group, the Interagency Committee on Nutrition Monitoring, has also questioned the accuracy, adequacy of analytical methods, and documentation of the data contained in *Handbook 8*.[218] Despite that, and the numerous studies that have found School Lunch program meals to be seriously deficient in nutrition, Congress' faith in the superior wisdom of the USDA remains unshaken.

In reality, and contrary to much public opinion, very few politicians in Congress are stupid or naive. The nutrition provisions in the School Lunch legislation are primarily window dressing for what is really a farm subsidy program. Some provisions are very clever and revealing. Consider the following section,

Students . . . shall not be required to accept offered foods they do
not intend to consume, and any such failure to accept offered
foods shall not affect the full charge to the student for a lunch
meeting the requirements of this subsection or the amount of
payments made under this chapter to any such school for such
lunch.[219]

This "Offer versus Serve" (OVS) provision essentially allows schools to serve high fat meals and still meet USDA nutrition regulations. One regulation requires that students be offered two or more servings of vegetables and/or fruits as part of each meal. However, OVS allows the students to refuse these items and select just the high fat and high protein items. The meal still meets USDA guidelines because the items were offered, and the school receives federal reimbursement. OVS allows the USDA to profess to be requiring meals in the NSLP to be nutritionally sound, while continuing to use the program to dispose of surplus meat and dairy products. In response to publicity about the poor nutritional quality of school lunches, the USDA was forced in June of 1995 to issue a new regulation requiring school lunches to comply with the Dietary Guidelines for Americans which call for a low-fat, low-salt diet that is rich in vegetables, fruits, and grains.[220] However, the rule requires that compliance be on a weekly basis, meaning that half the meals can continue to exceed the guidelines. OVS allows the other half to comply with the rule while exceeding the guidelines.

The consequences of continuing to allow the government to use school children as fat-disposal units are very serious and costly in terms of lives and money. In the last twenty years (corresponding closely to President Nixon's expansion of the NSLP), obesity among six to 11 year-old children has increased 54 percent.[221] Obesity in both children and adults is at record highs.[222] Columbia University Professor Myron Winick calls obesity the "biggest nutritional problem in children today" and warns that it puts them at risk for high blood pressure and heart disease later in life.[223] Writing in the *Journal of the American Medical Association (JAMA)*, Elizabeth M. Whelan and Fredrick J. Stare echo Professor Winick's concerns and add that obesity "intensifies virtually any health problem."[224] Bernard Gutin and his associates also reported in *JAMA,* "Evidence is accumulating that cardiovascular disease begins in childhood, and it is possible that risk factors such as high blood pressure could be influenced by eating and exercise patterns in early life."[225] Kerry J. Stewart and his associates reported in the *Journal of Cardiopulmonary Rehabilitation,* "Fat in young children already shows a relationship with heart disease risk factors."[226]

In addition to excessive amounts of total fat, school lunches contain excessive amounts of saturated fat. Saturated fat (found in meat, cheese, butter, and milk) raises blood cholesterol more than anything else in the diet—even more than eating cholesterol.[227] N.D. Wong, S.L. Bassin, and R. Deitrick reported in *Ethnicity and Disease,* "High total cholesterol is an important risk factor for coronary heart disease, and high levels in adulthood can be linked to high levels in childhood."[228] According to the National Heart, Lung and Blood Institute, "the evidence relating diet to blood cholesterol levels and coronary heart disease is compelling," and ". . .the magnitude of the problem posed by elevated blood cholesterol levels is very clear."[229] In 1990, the Institute recommended that all Americans over the age of two reduce the saturated fat and cholesterol content of their diet, and thirty-eight federal agencies, not including the USDA, endorsed the recommendation.[230] Congress remained undeterred.

Heart disease is the leading cause of death in the United States, claiming more than 500,000 lives every year.[231] More than 550,000 Americans have a stroke each year and of those, 150,000 die, making strokes the third leading cause of death.[232] Among the primary stroke risk factors are high cholesterol and heart disease.[233] A study of more than 100,000 nurses at Harvard Medical School and Boston's Brigham and Women's Hospital concluded that weight-related illnesses now kill 300,000 Americans a year.[234] According to the GAO, fifty-two million Americans are candidates for dietary therapy due to high cholesterol.[235]

Cancer is the number two killer of Americans, and Dr. Barbara Levine of Cornell University Medical College states that one-third of cancers may be linked to dietary habits.[236] A group of physicians testifying before the government Dietary Guidelines Advisory Committee in 1995 stated,

> *The current recommendation of 2-3 servings of meat every day (or any recommendation for meat consumption) contrasts with the preponderance of scientific evidence showing that meat consumption contributes to several serious illnesses and that those who avoid meats are generally healthier than those who consume them.* "[237]

The evidence is overwhelming that poor nutrition—typified by NSLP meals—is a leading, and possibly the leading, cause of serious disease in the U.S. Moreover, many adult-onset problems actually begin in childhood. In addition to the huge numbers of deaths that result from these diseases, the health care costs run into the hundreds of billions of dollars. The cost of the NSLP was $5.4 billion in 1996,[238] but that is not even the tip of the iceberg. The program is a driving force in the nation's one trillion dollar annual health care bill, half of which is paid by federal subsidy programs.

In all, the USDA operates fifteen separate, and often competing, free-food programs that were enacted over forty-six years.[239] The bureaucratic inefficiency is astounding. Three of the programs: the Emergency Food Assistance Program, the Soup Kitchen/ Food Bank Program, and the Commodity Supplemental Food Program have a combined commodity budget of $132.6 million, and a combined administration budget of $56.9 million.[240] Administrative costs equal an incredible 43 percent of benefits. There is little sense nor direction to the haphazard, fourteen-program morass, which cost the taxpayers $40 billion in 1995,[241] except that they all subsidize farm interests. Even those who administer the programs have no idea what the overall objective is, as the GAO discovered,

> *Most of the regional FNS [USDA's Food and Nutrition Service] and state agency officials, as well as most of the interest group representatives, whom we contacted were unable to identify an overarching, cohesive federal food assistance policy or describe how individual food assistance programs interrelate with the overall food assistance effort.* [242]

Had the report's writers interviewed farm interests, they could have easily provided an overarching policy objective. In response to the GAO's findings, the FNS developed the following mission statement:

The mission of the Food and Nutrition Service is to alleviate hunger and to safeguard the health and well-being of the Nation through the administration of nutrition education and domestic food assistance programs.[243]

However, as we have seen, even poor Americans are overwhelmingly eating too much, not too little. They are not underfed, they are under-nourished. And rather than "safeguarding the Nation's health," USDA programs are a leading cause of malnutrition and disease.

The federal government also runs several free—or nearly free—food programs for developing nations, and there is evidence that these programs that cost the taxpayers billions of dollars may be causing long-term harm to those nations. It is a classic case of how even well intentioned subsidies can, and usually do, backfire. The origins of these programs are, of course, rooted in the government's effort to dispose of subsidy-induced farm surpluses. Nonetheless, one would expect that giving food to needy nations would be beneficial, and in some cases, in the short run it is. But not in the long term. In the 1980s, there was so much free-food given to Somalia that it severely depressed prices and drove many local farmers out of business.[244] The result was a further increase of that nation's dependence on foreign aid.

Seven hundred million dollars of food aid to Russia has similarly ended up hurting those it was supposed to help.[245] This Food for Progress aid was supposed to help Russia get through its transition to a market economy. But instead, it ended up making big profits for the old communists in competition with, and at the expense of, newly established commodities exchanges, the very institutions the program was to help foster. One of the largest profiteers, Moscow's Vnesheconombank, had previously defaulted on $410 million in USDA GSM loans.[246] This outcome should not have come as a surprise to either the USDA or Congress. A GAO analysis of our oldest food-aid program intended to influence the policies of foreign governments found that it has been ineffective. Its report on the Agricultural Trade Development and Assistance Act of 1954 (Public Law 480) stated: "the program provides USDA little leverage to influence development activities or initiate policy reforms in the recipient country."[247] However, it does get rid of lots of subsidy-induced surplus farm products.

In 1998, Russia was suspended from receiving additional subsidized agricultural loans because it defaulted on existing loans. But that was not going to deter the federal government from using Russia as another means of disposing of subsidy-induced surplus farm commodities. If the Russians could not afford to pay for the products, or even to borrow to buy the products, we would simply give them the food. During 1998, the Russians were given 3.1 million tons of surplus farm commodities courtesy of American taxpayers, including 50,000 tons of pork and 1.5 million tons of wheat.[248] The story was that it was humanitarian aid—much like the pork pushed on the School Lunch Program. However, Russia sold an identical 1.5 million tons of its own wheat at the same time that it was receiving free American wheat.[249] In essence, American taxpayers bought surplus U.S. wheat and gave it to the Russians who then turned around and sold it on the world market. The Russians simply acted as an agent of the U.S. government in subsidizing American farmers.

One of Russia's primary sources of the hard currency that it desperately needs to pay for imported food is steel exports. By the end of 1998, it was estimated that Russia accounted for about one-third of all the hot-rolled steel imported into the U.S.[250] Now one might think that allowing the Russians to sell steel to generate funds to buy American agricultural products would be quite sensible. Not so. The federal government also has to subsidize the American steel industry by limiting imported steel. In February 1999, the Clinton Administration strong-armed the Russians into cutting back their steel exports to the U.S. by 70 percent.[251] We will not let the Russians earn the money they need to buy American food, but we will give them millions of tons for free.

A byproduct of all these USDA subsidy programs is the secondary subsidy effect of the department's huge bureaucracy. With a $55 billion budget in 1998,[252] the USDA is much like the Defense Department in that it is so large that its very existence constitutes a major subsidy program. It has 108,000 employees[253] working in nearly fifteen thousand offices, largely due to a one hundred year old regulation that stipulated that the travel time between offices should be no more than the distance a horse could cover in a single day.[254] Four USDA agencies that just do research and provide educational and technical assistance cost almost $2 billion annually.[255] Politicians do not even ask why an industry with a trillion dollars in assets[256] needs taxpayer-funded technical assistance or why it cannot do its own research. Whether needed or not, they do not want to end the USDA-office subsidy to their local economies. Huge farm subsidies have produced a massive bureaucracy, which has resulted in billions in secondary subsidies to local economies, which protects and fosters the farm subsidies. The feedback loop is complete.

7

NATURAL RESOURCES AND INFRASTRUCTURE

For nearly two decades, politicians from both parties have made innumerable speeches decrying the nation's huge trade deficit. Most of those speeches laid the problem squarely on the shoulders of the Japanese, who accounted for $55.7 billion[1] of our $113 billion 1997 deficit,[2] and many concluded with foolish calls for "retaliation." Indeed, candidates for federal office regularly battle each other for who can propose the toughest (and most counterproductive) trade sanctions against Japan and other countries. Seldom mentioned is that an equally large share of our trade shortfall is due to imported oil, which poses a far greater threat to the nation than the imbalance with Japan. This is all the more remarkable since the federal government could far more easily and sensibly affect a significant reduction in oil imports than a reduction in the trade deficit. And interestingly, one result of doing so might just be a reduction in demand for the product that accounts for a large percentage of the trade imbalance: Japanese cars. Again, the reluctance of the politicians to address this issue and take actions that would clearly be in the national interest is rooted in massive federal subsidies.

Most energy and infrastructure subsidies share a similarity with Social Security and Medicare in that the primary beneficiary groups constitute a large segment of the population, the largest being motorists. And like the two big social subsidy programs, much of the cost of today's benefits are being passed on to future generations, who will be faced with bearing their own costs as well as those bequeathed by their parents and grandparents. Yet another similarity is that the subsidies, though based on fundamentally flawed reasoning, are generally well-intentioned. Congress has been acting, for the most part, in what is perceived to be America's best interest. That perception is the problem; subsidies are generally counterproductive.

While consumers are the primary beneficiaries of energy and infrastructure subsidies, those industries have benefited handsomely as well. In 1861, Congress imposed a tariff on imported oil, thereby subsidizing domestic producers. By 1865, this tax had been raised to forty cents per gallon. The

Revenue Act of 1918 established foreign tax credits, which provided substantial benefits for oil companies. In 1926, Congress passed the percentage depletion allowance. That, along with the provisions for intangible drilling costs, has allowed oil companies to take tens of billions of dollars in tax deductions. The Revenue Act of 1932 enacted a tariff on imported gasoline, and the following year, the National Recovery Act established oil import quotas. In 1959, the Mandatory Oil Import Program established a second imported oil quota system, which lasted until the "oil shock" of 1973.

Through the 1980s and early 1990s, Congress enacted energy legislation almost every year, some of which bestowed additional subsidies such as Department of Energy funded research programs and an exemption for independent producers from the alternative minimum tax. One study concluded that preferential tax treatment alone yielded between $1.8 and $4 billion for the oil industry in 1989.[3] Although these subsidies directly benefited oil companies, their customers were the primary beneficiaries. As with all corporate subsidies, there is a question as to how the benefits are divided between corporate profits and the corporation's customers. While shareholders certainly derived some of the benefits, Thomas Lee, Ben Ball, and Richard Tabors of MIT contend that the lion's share went to consumers of oil products in the form of lower prices.[4] They cite as evidence the "mediocre return of major international oil companies compared to those of the mining and manufacturing sectors."[5]

Almost from the beginning, federal subsidies for the oil industry have been contrary to the national interest. In the 1860s, import tariffs were aimed at protecting domestic oil producers at the expense of consumers. That turned out to be the equivalent of protecting the foxes from the chickens. In 1870, John D. Rockefeller and his partners formed the Standard Oil Company. Nine years later, these "robber barons" were producing 90 percent of the nation's refined oil and controlled all of its pipelines.[6] In 1882, they formed the Standard Oil Trust, which solidified their national oil monopoly. The Trust strictly limited output to keep prices at levels that yielded monopoly profits.[7] This was the trust primarily responsible for the passage of the Sherman Antitrust Act in 1890, but it took the government until 1911 to effectively break up Rockefeller's monopoly.[8]

While the government moved to increase competition by breaking up the Standard Oil monopoly, it did not want too much competition. Beginning in 1933 with the National Recovery Act and later the Mandatory Oil Import Program of 1958, the politicians provided protection for domestic producers by imposing quotas on imported oil and oil products. This lasted until the Organization of Petroleum Exporting Countries (OPEC) oil shock of 1973. This was no small subsidy. It allowed domestically produced oil to be sold at $3 per barrel, about twice the world price.[9] After providing relief for oil consumers from the monopolistic pricing of the robber barons, the government turned around and forced them to pay a subsidy to the same companies. The effect of both the tariffs and quotas on imports was to accelerate the discovery and consumption of domestic oil, a policy termed "pump America dry first." While the subsidies themselves were counterproductive, a policy of using them intentionally to deplete a critical and limited resource is incomprehensible. Though based on grossly inaccurate forecasts, that was the expected result. In 1939, the Department of the Interior announced that U.S. oil supplies would run out by 1952.[10] Ten years later it announced that the end of U.S. oil supplies was in sight.[11] Washington believed that America was running out of oil, yet it subsidized domestic production, a substantial amount of which was exported through the late 1950s.[12]

Those who had been oblivious to the threat that an oil shortage posed to national security got a rude awaking in 1973. In retaliation for supporting Israel during the 1973 Arab-Israeli war, Saudi Arabia and several other Arab members of OPEC imposed an oil embargo against the United States. America was on an energy binge with consumption up almost 52 percent between 1960 and 1970.[13] By 1973, the U.S. was importing over six million barrels per day of petroleum, half of it from OPEC countries.[14] But between the middle of 1972 and the end of 1974, OPEC's take from a barrel of oil jumped from less than $1 to over $10, and America's bill for imported oil rose from $3.9 billion to $24 billion.[15] The oil shock boosted the rate of inflation in the U.S. to 12 percent, and a punishing 24 percent in Japan.[16]

Nowhere was the shock felt more than in Washington, D.C. Although very ill-prepared, the politicians were determined to take quick action, if for no other reason than that the federal government always responds to any significant event, whether it is appropriate or not. As always, they called in "the experts" to provide guidance. Of course, there were no experts with relevant experience because the situation was unprecedented. As Lee, Ball, and Tabors note, "The energy experts were analytically ill equipped to develop forecasts and scenarios."[17] Nonetheless, they did so based on the totally incorrect but widely accepted assumptions that energy prices would continue to increase long-term, shortages would persist, and, perhaps most importantly, that the world was running out of oil. This led to dire warnings, such as this from Walter Levy who *Time* called "the world's leading oil consultant," "The world economy cannot survive in a healthy or remotely healthy condition if cartel pricing and actual or threatened supply constraints of oil continue."[18] Suddenly, the obvious became obvious: if we are running out of oil, we had better do something about it. Along with a host of complex regulations, the politicians enacted huge new subsidy programs.

In November 1973, President Nixon launched Project Independence to achieve energy self-sufficiency by 1980. He pledged more subsidies for energy research, reduced gasoline production to allow increased heating oil production, and ordered all gas stations closed on Sundays.[19] Petroleum products had been under general price controls since 1971, but with world prices considerably lower than domestic prices, they were of little consequence. After general price controls ended, Congress extended price controls on oil products in 1973 and again in 1974. As world oil prices skyrocketed, the effect of the price controls became dramatic. Now, domestic prices were much lower than world prices. Without market prices to allocate available supplies, the government had to do so. By January of 1974 the Federal Energy Office (FEO) had established a complex system to ration gasoline, aviation fuel, propane, butane, residual fuel oil, crude oil and refinery yield, lubricants, petrochemical feedstocks, and middle distillates.[20] The system failed miserably and even FEO chief James Schlesinger admitted that they were "putting the gasoline where cars are not."[21]

Essentially, government policy was to protect Americans from the real price of oil exactly the same way that the Soviet Union's command and control system attempted to insulate its citizens from economic reality. The result was the same as well: long lines. Americans wasted millions of hours waiting in gasoline lines just like the Soviets waited for food. Market pricing, the most efficient mechanism for rationing scarce products, was abandoned in favor of the least efficient mechanism, bureaucratic allocations and waiting in line. Federal price controls forced the domestic oil industry to subsidize imported oil and motorists, while Americans lost billions of dollars through lower productivity and lost wages. As the University of Rochester's Paul MacAvoy observed,

> *The embargo itself was not effective, due to reduced demands from the downturn of the economy and warm weather, and to reduction of inventories. Regulations created the effects of the embargo, however, and the FEO gets the credit for the energy crisis perceived by consumers in 1974.[22]*

The unintended consequences of many federal subsidy programs is not apparent until the programs have been in effect for some time, but such was not the case with oil price controls. Clearly, the effect of low gasoline prices was to encourage its use at a time when the stated policy of our political leaders was to achieve energy independence. The President's 1977 National Energy Plan stated, "The world's presently estimated recoverable oil resources, at a conjectural growth rate of 5 percent, would be exhausted by 2010."[23] Policy makers believed that not only was the U.S. running out of oil, so, too, was the world. We were already importing a third of our oil usage,[24] yet federal policy was to keep prices artificially low, thereby removing the economic incentive to reduce consumption.

The politicians claimed that they were concerned about fairness and the impact of world prices on the U.S. economy, but since oil imports in 1973 only amounted to six tenths of one percent of our GDP,[25] the economy could have well withstood the higher prices. And the nation would have been far better off. Moreover, because of federal policy, available supplies were not being used in the most efficient manner. Real prices would have encouraged the use of gasoline for purposes with the highest value, personal or commercial. Federal policy encouraged use by those most willing to pay the wait-in-line price. In those areas over-allocated by the energy bureaucracy, it was simply business as usual. Despite the government-induced shortages and lines, total oil consumption in the U.S. only fell from 17 million barrels per day in 1973 to 16.2 million in 1974.[26] And rather than reducing our dependence on foreign oil, subsidizing oil products caused oil imports as a percentage of total usage to rise from 35.4 percent in 1974 to 46.5 percent in 1977.[27] Oil usage followed the subsidies, not the rhetoric.

The more they acted to exacerbate the problem, the more federal policy makers felt compelled to take additional action. In late 1975, Congress passed the Energy Policy and Conservation Act. It continued oil price controls through 1979 and authorized the Strategic Petroleum Reserve to store one billion barrels of oil in salt caves in Louisiana. The two provisions were a classic example of one federal subsidy being enacted to offset the unintended consequences of another. The Reserve was intended to provide a cushion against a severe supply disruption, but continuing the price controls was a furtherance of the existing incentive to consume more oil. The Strategic Petroleum Reserve was partly necessitated by the price controls, which were fostering an ever-increasing dependence on foreign oil. By 1995, the Reserve contained 591 million barrels of oil and was costing nearly $400 million per year to maintain.[28] Much of the oil stored in the Reserve was purchased at an average price of $27.14 per barrel,[29] meaning that its value is much less than the $21 billion that the taxpayers have invested.[30] Indeed, purchases for the Reserve boosted demand for oil, thereby supporting higher prices. While a convincing argument can be made for the Reserve, funding it from general revenues constituted a subsidy from U.S. taxpayers for American consumers of oil products. The very large size of that interest group is all the more reason why the costs should have been borne by them and not the taxpayers.

Another provision of the Energy Policy and Conservation Act mandated Corporate Average Fuel Efficiency (CAFE) standards, which required auto manufacturers to substantially increase their minimum fleet fuel efficiency. It required that the fleet average increase to 27.5 miles per gallon (mpg) from the existing average of less than 14 mpg for American auto manufacturers.[31] CAFE standards were a backdoor attempt by a government firmly committed to subsidized gasoline to reduce its consumption by increasing the fuel efficiency of automobiles. At first glance, it seems to be a sensible approach; if cars go further on a gallon of gasoline, they will use less. In as far as it goes, that is true. However, the real issue was not reducing the amount of gasoline used per mile but reducing the total consumption of gasoline, thereby reducing the need for imported oil. At that, not only did the CAFE standards fail, they backfired.

The real effect of the CAFE standards was to increase the cost of automobiles by $500 to $1,200 per car.[32] Nonetheless, the percentage increase in the cost of a vehicle was relatively small and not enough to impede auto sales significantly. But once the vehicle was purchased, the better fuel economy actually lowered the variable cost per mile of driving. The result was that the CAFE standards provided a perverse incentive to drive more, and Americans have proven to be very astute at taking advantage of incentives. During the 1980s, the number of miles driven climbed at almost four times the rate of population growth,[33] largely offsetting the gain from the CAFE standards. The bottom line remained: as long as gasoline remained subsidized, Americans were going to use more of it.

With federal policy working to support continued high usage of oil, the only way for the nation to reduce its dependence on foreign oil was to produce more energy domestically. Shortly after he took office in 1977, President Carter said, "I believe that we have now got such a horrible conglomeration of confusion in the energy field that nobody knows what is going to happen."[34] While his conclusions were correct, he failed to realize that there was no reliable basis for anyone to predict what would happen, and that most of the confusion was due to federal involvement in the energy market. Like his predecessors, Carter believed that federal involvement was the solution rather than the problem, and he promptly unveiled his National Energy Plan, It was a package of about 100 proposals aimed at reducing energy consumption, implementing conservation, and developing alternative energy technologies.[35] It was a plan for the federal government to consolidate its control of virtually the entire energy sector through regulations and massive new subsidy programs. To manage this ponderous undertaking, Carter proposed a new cabinet level agency, the Department of Energy, with a budget of $10.4 billion and a staff of 20,000 employees.[36]

In August 1977, Carter signed the legislation creating the Energy Department. The following year, many of his proposals were enacted as parts of the Energy Tax Act and the National Energy Conservation Policy Act. These laws provided billions of dollars in subsidies for energy conversion, and research and development at the same time that federal policy was discouraging the efficient use of energy by subsidizing the price of oil products. The government was pressing on the gas pedal and the brake at the same time. While President Carter had thought the nation was engaged in the "moral equivalent of war," he and the nation were totally unprepared for the second oil shock that hit in 1979 when the Iran-Iraq war caused a drastic reduction in the output of Iranian oil. Confusing economic issues with moral issues has been the root cause of many misguided federal policies for decades, and the policies enacted in response to the 1973 oil shock were prominent among them. As the Brookings Institution's Pietro Nivola observed, "The petroleum price and allocation rules not only induced shortages of gasoline; by stimulating and subsidizing imports of oil, they left the U.S. economy more vulnerable to the doubling of world oil prices in 1979."[37] Between 1979 and 1981, the price of oil increased from $13 to $34 per barrel,[38] and six top oil experts, brought together by Stanford University in 1980, forecast an average price of $98 per barrel by 1997.[39] (The actual price was $20.[40]) By that time, the perverse effects of the energy policies had caused U.S. demand for oil to be at least a million barrels per day more than it would have been without controls, estimates Paul MacAvoy.[41] And prices went higher yet; at one point in 1981 the price reached $50.75.[42]

This called for even more subsidized federal energy projects, including the U.S. Synthetic Fuels Corporation (Synfuels Corp.) in 1980, which was authorized to distribute $20 billion in subsidies to private industry.[43] This government corporation was formed specifically to centralize the government's growing number of subsidy programs aimed at producing oil and gas from oil shale, tar sands, and coal. Such processes were not new. By 1920, almost all Scottish oil was produced from shale,[44] and Germany had met a large portion of its fuel needs during World War II with synthetic fuels.[45] However, synthetic fuels were far more expensive than petroleum and could only be produced with large government subsidies. Indeed, in 1926, the federal government built an experimental oil shale plant in Rulison, Colorado, which was promptly closed in 1929 after it was determined that the process was feasible, but not economically viable.[46] Throughout the late 1970s, the government subsidized various synfuels programs while simultaneously subsidizing the increased use of imported oil, which, of course, was the problem that originally necessitated government funding for synfuels. However, the politicians had moved the energy issue out of the realm of economics and into morality, so reason took a back seat to emotion. As Lee, Ball, and Tabors observed, "The question was not, Do synfuels make sense?, but, Do you believe in synfuels? The implication was that not to do so was somehow unpatriotic."[47]

No, they did not make sense. The theory was that if the government paid to build full-scale, demonstration synfuels plants, private industry, seeing the feasibility, would build more and soon the nation would be awash in synfuels. However, feasibility was not the issue, as the Germans had demonstrated forty years earlier. Cost was the issue and industry was not going to build expensive plants to produce noncompetitive fuels. Few of the plants started by the Synfuels Corporation were actually completed and no project could operate without federal subsidies. One of the few projects completed, a coal gasification plant in North Dakota, was constructed beginning in 1980 with a $2.02 billion government guaranteed loan. The plant began operation in April 1984; when the government failed to provide $720 million in price support subsidies in August 1985, the owners promptly defaulted on their federal loan.[48] After wasting billions of dollars, Congress finally pulled the plug on the Synfuels Corporation in 1986. Linda Cohen and Roger Noll of the Brookings Institution assessed the Synfuels program this way, "The entire synfuels program had a quality of madness to it. . . . Goals were unattainable from the start."[49]

Amidst all the madness, Congress had taken some positive steps to address the problem of imported oil. The Energy Conservation Act had mandated that automobile manufacturers increase the fuel efficiency of their fleets, and in 1978, a "gas guzzler" tax was passed on cars with low fuel-economy. Finally, in 1981, oil price controls, and the associated four hundred pages of allocation regulations,[50] were abandoned. Nevertheless, the effects of years of subsidies were apparent. During the first oil shock between 1973 and 1975, U.S. consumers, protected from real oil prices, decreased oil consumption by six percent.[51] During the same period, demand from the rest of the free world, which faced the full brunt of OPEC price increases, declined almost twice that amount.[52] Had U.S. demand dropped by an equal percentage, oil imports would have been nearly seven hundred thousand barrels per day lower. After government policy shifted from subsidizing to discouraging oil consumption, the situation changed dramatically. During the second oil shock from 1979 to

1983, U.S. oil usage dropped 18 percent, and oil imports plummeted 46 percent.[53] Decreased U.S. and world demand, in response to the 1979 oil shock, along with increased non-OPEC production, caused OPEC's production and pricing system to collapse. Prices began declining in 1982 and nose-dived in 1985. Even the *Washington Post*, usually a supporter of regulatory approaches, editorialized,

> *In an energy shortage, the most useful legislation is not the kind that tries to cap prices or allocate supplies, but rather the more modest kind that only keeps the market open and working efficiently.*[54]

　　With the exception of a brief period after Iraq invaded Kuwait in 1990, world oil prices have remained at or below their 1985 level, meaning that the real price of oil has fallen significantly. On an inflation-adjusted basis, the retail price of gasoline dropped to its lowest level ever in 1998.[55] Unfortunately, the result has been sharply increased oil imports. From 1985 to 1989, imports increased 63 percent from 4.9 million barrels per day to eight million barrels.[56] During the period that contained the three oil shocks, 1973 through 1991, U.S. oil imports rose from 36 percent to 50 percent of total consumption while Japan's imports declined 25 percent.[57] Interestingly, despite having no domestic oil resources, Japan's economy grew much faster than ours did during that period. By 1994, imports reached 10.1 million barrels per day, equal to 58 percent of U.S. consumption.[58] Twenty years after the OPEC oil shock, we were more dependent on oil imports than ever thanks to federal subsidies. The world has enjoyed over a decade of very low energy prices, but future oil shocks are a virtual certainty. The World Energy Council foresees global oil demand climbing from about 65 million barrels per day in 1995 to 100 million in 2020.[59] Unfortunately, as we shall see shortly, the U.S. government still maintains policies that subsidize oil consumption. That amounts to nothing less than gross negligence.

　　Congress took much the same approach to natural gas that it did with petroleum. A system of price controls imposed in 1954 had caused periodic shortages of natural gas even before the 1973 oil shock.[60] As always, there was a steep price for the subsidies. The price ceiling at the well constrained new supplies during a period when domestic energy use was rising sharply.

Writing in *Environment*, David Feldman summarized the counterproductive federal policy on natural gas before 1973,

> *By holding the selling price [of natural gas] below market value and replacement costs, incentives for producers to open additional new fields were reduced. Interstate price controls increased consumption and distorted allocation; at the same time, growing demand for gas caused rising prices in unregulated intrastate markets. These markets absorbed new supplies, forcing*

consumers in regulated markets to switch to oil. Demand for this
resource increased rapidly prior to the 1973-74 embargo.[61]

After the 1973 oil shock, the politicians still refused to end the subsidies, further exacerbating the problem. Natural gas shortages on several occasions in the mid-seventies caused thousands of industrial plants in the East and Midwest to close down. Despite the obvious cause of the problem and the equally obvious solution, Congress refused to remove the price subsidies. Instead, it passed the Natural Gas policy Act in 1978, which classified gas under twenty different categories with a complex system of controlled pricing.[62] "Old" gas was to remain under perpetual price controls while newly discovered gas was gradually freed from price controls over seven years.[63] At the same time, the Energy Use Act of 1978, passed on the mistaken belief that we were running out of natural gas, prohibited using gas in any new industrial boilers. Natural gas was considered too valuable for industrial use. The resulting structure left the market in chaos, with field prices varying from $1 to $11 per thousand cubic feet.[64] Just as beneficiaries act to maximize their subsidy benefits, those footing the bill will always act to minimize the amount of a subsidy they have to pay. Gas producers rationally chose to drill in areas qualifying for high prices, while shutting down wells in low-cost, price-controlled areas. The effect was continued supply restrictions and increased cost for natural gas. Because gas supplies are very much tied to existing pipeline networks, some consumers had access to very cheap gas, while the price for others rose sharply. Some companies in the gas industry were forced to subsidize others as well as consumers, while some consumers were forced to subsidize others. Those being subsidized had little or no incentive to do the one thing that made the most sense: conserve gas by using it efficiently. At the same time, the nation failed to take full advantage of an abundant domestic resource to reduce demand for imported oil.

New high-priced natural gas was coming on-line just as demand for energy finally began to fall in 1983, partly in response to the second oil shock and partly due to recession. Since gas could not be used in industrial plants, there was no outlet for the new supplies. The resulting glut, referred to as the "gas bubble," drove many companies out of business. The Wellhead Decontrol Act of 1989 decontrolled gas prices and the nation's 1.2 million miles of natural gas pipelines were deregulated in November of 1993.[65] Nevertheless, between 1984 and 1994, U.S. gas producers experienced a cumulative loss of $151 billion.[66] Much of the carnage was a direct result of the subsidy policies of the federal government. Now convinced that natural gas is abundant (according to Alexander Melamid of New York University, world reserves of natural gas equal those of crude oil on an energy basis [67]), the federal government has done an about face and begun subsidizing the expansion of its use. The Energy Policy Act of 1992 provided up to a $2,000 tax deduction for cars and up to a $50,000 deduction for trucks that convert to using natural gas as a fuel. Companies installing natural gas refueling equipment qualify for deductions of up to $100,000. These subsidies make no more sense than the ones enacted in 1954, but fortunately, their effect is minuscule. Since the federal government essentially ceased its attempts to manipulate the market, natural gas has been both cheap and abundant.

One of the objectives of the Fuel Use Act was to force industrial plants to use coal instead of oil or natural gas. The theory was that while we were short on oil and gas, we had an abundant supply of coal. For once, the politicians' information was correct; the U.S. has about 20 percent of the world's coal deposits.[68] In an all too common exercise at cross-purposes, they sought to force a switch from oil and gas to coal by industrial users, while at the same time subsidizing increased use of oil and gas by consumers. Coal had been the primary fuel for the generation of electricity, and the Fuel Use Act helped keep it that way. In 1989, coal produced about 55 percent of the nation's electrical power.[69] While that seemed like a sensible approach, it became less so when all the subsidy costs were accounted for.

Direct federal energy subsidies are substantial. For example, subsidies for the coal industry amount to about $500 million annually,[70] while the tab for the oil industry, including tax breaks, government funded research, and the Strategic Petroleum Reserve, amount to about $4 billion per year. However, direct subsidies pale next to the indirect subsidies known as "externalities." These are costs resulting from an activity not paid for directly, but, rather, incurred indirectly by society as a whole. Only when the costs of all subsidies, direct and external, are considered can the true impact and economy of a given program or activity be determined. Fully costed, most federal energy policies go from bad to much worse.

The process of converting fuels into energy produces copious quantities of pollutants. The U.S. Centers for Disease Control and Prevention found that in 1991 two-thirds of all Americans lived in areas where air pollutants (ozone, carbon monoxide, particulate matter, sulfur dioxide, lead, and nitrogen dioxide) exceeded national standards, exposing them to a significantly higher risk of illness.[71] A 1996 study by the Natural Resources Defense Council concluded that over sixty-four thousand Americans die prematurely each year of heart and lung ailments caused by particulate air pollution.[72] In addition, USDA scientists estimate that the U.S. loses about $3 billion worth of crops each year to air pollution.[73] When society bears the cost of externalities from some activity, it is effectively subsidizing that activity.

Burning any fuel creates pollution, but some forms are much worse than others: oil and coal in particular. The pollutants of most concern from burning coal are sulfur dioxide (SO_2) and particulates. High-sulfur oil also produces large amounts of SO_2. Sulfur dioxide and rain mix to produce diluted sulfuric acid, which then returns to earth as acid rain. The documented adverse effects of acid rain include eating away at masonry buildings and monuments, killing trees, turning lakes too acidic too support life, and eating the paint off automobiles. All these constitute externalities of burning coal, and the federal government has passed a number of laws aimed at reducing these external costs. Title IV of the 1990 Clean Air Act Amendments incorporated an innovative provision that has put a price on SO_2 emissions. The Act established sharply reduced permissible levels for emissions, which plants can exceed only if they can buy enough federal emission permits from another utility that has reduced its emissions below its allocation or from the EPA, which auctions off 2.8 percent of the total allowance annually.[74] In March 1993, the government auctioned off 150,010 permits, each allowing emission of one ton of SO_2, for $21.4 million.[75]

Beginning in 1995, about 110 electric generating plants came under the law, but in the year 2000, eight hundred additional large SO_2 emitters will be added.[76] Since total allowable emissions are fixed, the total number of emission permits is also fixed. The objective of reducing total emissions is achieved, and those who pollute must buy what amounts to externality permits from the government or from another plant that has reduced its emissions. If the permits become more expensive, it becomes increasingly attractive to reduce emissions rather than pay for permits. Anticipating significant future price increases, Virginia Power paid $5.3 million for permits in the EPA's 1996 auction to emit 83,000 tons of SO_2 in the years 2002 and 2003.[77] The SO_2 market is working efficiently and is achieving the objective of reducing emissions. The GAO reported that trading in permits has been active and that between 1994 and 1996, prices fell, reflecting emission reduction efforts that resulted in total emissions that were 35 percent below the emissions cap in 1996.[78]

This program has used a combination of regulation and market pricing to control the externality, and the players are not limited to polluters. A Cleveland environmental group, the National Healthy Air License Exchange, has spent $120,000 purchasing permits to remove them from the market, thereby reducing the total allowable amount of emissions.[79] Because of this program, the externality is being sharply reduced at the expense of those creating the cost. In 1970, electric power plants, which burn nearly all the coal used in the U.S., emitted twenty-eight million tons of SO_2 into the air, but, that will have been reduced to nine million tons by the year 2000.[80] Sharply reducing the SO_2 subsidy has produced a rational and highly desirable response from those producing the pollutant. The EPA estimates that by 2010, when its acid rain reduction program is fully in place, annual health benefits will range from $12 billion to $40 billion annually, or five to seventeen times the cost of limiting SO_2 emissions.[81]

Unfortunately, the federal government attempts to charge those responsible for externalities only very rarely although it is a fair and efficient approach to several of the nation's biggest problems. In 1991, the National Academy of Sciences made the following recommendation,

> Study in detail the "full social cost pricing" of energy, with a goal of gradually introducing such a system. . . . On the basis of the principal that the polluter should pay, pricing of energy production and use should reflect the full costs of the associated environmental problems. . . . Including all social, environmental, and other costs in energy prices would provide consumers and

producers with the appropriate information to decide about fuel mix, new investments, and research and development.[82]

If there is one area in the world that is the central focus of the Department of Defense, it is the Persian Gulf where the Pentagon fully expects to fight another war. Given that the Department of Energy expects 65 percent of our oil imports to come from the Persian Gulf after the year 2000, the military's concern is justifiable.[83] Large amounts of war materials are already pre-positioned in Kuwait, Bahrain, Qatar, and Saudi Arabia, and powerful U.S. air and naval units are constantly on patrol.[84] The Navy's Fifth fleet, consisting of about 20 warships and 100 aircraft, is now headquartered in Bahrain.[85] The Army and Marines keep an additional 13 ships loaded with enough tanks, artillery, and supplies for 10,000 ground troops stationed nearby, while the Air Force has an estimated 170 warplanes based in the area.[86] In January 1996, Defense Secretary William Perry approved top-secret plan number 1002, detailing a massive commitment of U.S. forces to the Gulf region in the event of another war.[87] The plan was so large in scope that Secretary Perry expressed concerns that it would preclude a U.S. response to another simultaneous regional problem. The percentage of the defense budget attributable to protecting our oil pipeline from the Gulf is far higher than those in Washington are willing to admit. Unfortunately, it is also far higher than most of them even realize, with estimates ranging from $15 billion[88] to $71 billion[89] per year. The actual cost is almost certainly much closer to the higher figure than the lower and, as part of the defense budget, is paid out of general tax revenues. This cost is an externality of petroleum usage. It is a very real cost, and one that is unquestionably attributable to imported oil. In testimony before a Senate Agricultural Committee hearing in October 1996, Former Central Intelligence Agency director James Woolsey stated that accurate calculations of U.S. energy costs should include the military costs of protecting access to Persian Gulf oil.[90] Through the defense budget, U.S. users of petroleum products receive an external subsidy of as much as $19 per imported barrel, which exceeds the cost of the oil.

Motor vehicles account for a very large percentage of the oil used in the U.S., and they emit about seven million tons of hydrocarbons and nitrogen oxides into the air annually.[91] Motorboats are responsible for an additional seven hundred thousand tons.[92] The environmental externalities associated with this consumption have been estimated at between $54 billion and $232 billion annually.[93] Nearly 80 percent of these costs are attributable to human mortality and morbidity.[94] A study by the Harvard School of Public Health of thirteen U.S. cities found that air pollution was linked to up to 50,000 emergency room visits and 10,000 to 15,000 hospital admissions.[95] Since the federal government picks up the tab for about half of the nation's health care, a significant portion of the motor vehicle environmental externality, amounting to tens of billions of dollars per year, ends up being paid by U.S. taxpayers. The rest is picked up by society.

The infrastructure to manufacture and deliver motor fuels throughout the U.S. is extensive. According to the EPA, American refineries emit 216 tons of toxins into the air every day.[96] The U.S. fuel distribution system contains 220,000 miles of pipelines and more than 700,000 storage tanks.[97] According to Jack Doyle, author of *Crude Awakening: The Oil Mess in America*, billions of gallons of oil, gasoline, jet fuel, and diesel are leaking from these facilities every year, and the EPA estimates that it will cost $800 million annually to clean up the resulting groundwater contamination.[98] Because the Superfund Law mandating cleanup of toxic waste does not cover petroleum, again, the taxpayers will likely foot the bill. Added to the military and health externalities, the total cost of American petroleum usage not paid by the users themselves easily exceeds $100 billion annually. This amounts to a massive externality subsidy that, in addition to increasing our dependence on foreign oil, further increases the externality cost.

Transportation consumes nearly three-quarters of all the petroleum used in the U.S. Two-thirds of this is used directly for fuel, and the rest is consumed building and maintaining roads and vehicles and producing the fuel itself.[99] Federal policies have long subsidized the construction of transportation infrastructure, whether it was needed or not. There is no more highly prized pork than infrastructure projects. New construction is hugely expensive, highly visible, and can be named after the pork-procuring politician to remind voters of what a fine job he or she has done. The political cover for the roads, roads, and more roads subsidy programs is that infrastructure is the engine that drives economic growth. While this sounds plausible and certain data appear to support the contention, rigorous analysis shows conclusively that economic growth causes more infrastructure spending, but more infrastructure spending does not cause more economic growth.[100] Maintenance and repairs, on the other hand, seldom bring big headlines. As such, the federal budget is long on new construction and short on maintenance. The result is the same pattern that recurs repeatedly with federal programs: subsidized present consumption at the expense of future generations.

In theory, highway users pay federal excise taxes on motor fuel and tires to pay for the Interstate and National Highways systems, but it is clear that the approximately $23.5 billion per year collected by the Highway Trust Fund (HTF) does not come close. In a speech in late 1995 to a group of state highway officials, Transportation Secretary Federico Pena stated that about $40 billion per year is being spent on the nation's (federal, state, and local) highways, bridges, and transit systems altogether, but $57 billion is needed just to maintain the system in its present condition.[101] He estimated that it would take $80 billion per year to improve the system and predicted that, at current spending levels, 50 percent of the nation's highways and 40 percent of its bridges will be in poor condition within 20 years.[102] He may have greatly understated the situation. A 1993 report of the Secretary of Transportation to Congress concluded that 35 percent of the nation's bridges are already classified as deficient.[103] According to Eric Cooper of the Federal Highway Administration (FHWA), the backlog of bridge repairs in 1992 was $78 billion, which would approach $131 billion if improvements were delayed.[104] It is apparent that the nation's surface transportation infrastructure is already in trouble and is rapidly deteriorating further. Meanwhile, federal, state, and local governments are busy building new roads and expanding old ones while deferring maintenance and passing immensely expensive repair bills on to future generations. Along with all the other unpaid bills.

The $23.5 billion-per-year cookie jar known as the Highway Trust Fund[105] and the subsidy mentality of Congress is the crux of the problem. The federal government is only responsible for 4.8 percent of U.S. highways, but it provides funding and exercises some measure of control over nearly all roads except local streets.[106] Between 1957 and 1990, the HTF provided $213 billion to finance 43,600 miles of the Interstate Highway System and nearly 840,000 miles of other highways. Washington provides 90 percent of the funds for interstates, 43 percent for other main highways, and 31 percent for roads that feed interstates and highways.[107] In typically federal fashion, the funds are doled out under 30 frequently-overlapping programs.[108] Naturally, state and local governments look to leverage their own highway funds by undertaking projects that qualify for federal funds. Federal politicians are only too happy to accommodate—as long as it is a sizable construction project. As Senator Patrick Moynihan remarked, "Nobody ever had a ribbon-cutting ceremony for fixing cracks."[109]

The ribbons that those in Congress enjoy cutting most are those for federal "Demonstration" projects. These are expensive and specifically legislated highway projects of questionable value that primarily demonstrate a politician's ability to deliver pork to his constituents. The Intermodal Surface Transportation Efficiency Act of 1991 (ISTEA) alone authorized 539 Demonstration projects for which $6.2 billion was authorized.[110] The ISTEA Act of 1998 appropriated a record $217 billion, including twice as much pork as all the previous highway bills of recent times combined.[111] However, that is just the tip of the iceberg. As with weapon's systems, the cost of Demonstration projects is usually deliberately and fraudulently understated. The same rationale applies: once the project is well underway, Congress can be counted on to provide enough funding to complete the pork project. The GAO found that for sixty-six Demonstration projects it reviewed, initial federal and state funding combined only accounted for 37 percent of the anticipated project costs.[112] Spending authorizations for Demonstration projects remain valid indefinitely and many of these projects take years to complete. The FHWA, which disperses the funds, has no mechanism to track authorizations and construction progress to completion, so the 1,000 active Demonstration projects, as of March 1994, were largely hidden in a pork black hole.[113] Of course, understating costs is standard procedure for virtually all highway projects, not just Demonstration projects. The Central Artery/Tunnel, a 7.5-mile underground freeway in Boston, was projected to cost $2.56 billion, but the actual cost will approach $12 billion.[114] That is about $1.5 billion of mostly federal taxpayers' money per mile.

Given the hundreds of billions of dollars worth of needed highway repairs and improvements throughout the nation, one would think that Demonstration projects would be the result of Congressmen using their influence to get an urgent local need taken care of. That is seldom the case. The projects are more likely to be for the benefit of a particularly generous contributor or a favored facility or institution, the most indefensible form of subsidy. Consider one of the findings of the GAO review of sixty-six Demonstration projects:

> *Because most of the demonstration projects we reviewed did not respond to states' and regions' most critical federal-aid highway needs, these projects were generally either not included in any state or regional transportation plans or were included without any identified funding. Moreover, the Congress authorized demonstration project funds for 10 projects that would not have been eligible for federal highway program funds, since the projects were for local roads not entitled to receive federal program assistance.*[115]

Since the Highway Trust Fund was designed to finance new, construction not maintenance, and politicians much prefer the former, the national web of highways is constantly expanding while existing roads and bridges fall apart. Transportation officials claim that our highways are crumbling because of unexpectedly heavy loads; but the truth is that, in the scramble to get as much as possible as often as possible from the HTF, American roads are often built cheaply and poorly. Then they are not maintained. Senator Moynihan explained the build-it-cheap mentality as, " . . . the faster it crumbles, the faster we'll get brand new."[116] Many European autobahns carry more traffic and heavier truck loads, but they remain smooth and sturdy. They are simply well built and maintained.

Highway interests claim that they pay far more in taxes and user's fees than are spent for construction, maintenance, and operation. They claim that they are subsidizers not subsidizees. It is true that a small percentage of HTF revenues are used to support mass transit systems, and there is a 2.5 cent per gallon tax on gasoline and diesel fuel that goes to the U.S. Treasury's general fund.[117] However, in total, these "diverted funds" add up to but a few percent of the expenditures for roads and bridges. Various government estimates place the value of the required maintenance that is being deferred on federally funded highways at between $26 billion[118] and $40 billion[119] annually. The cost of the deferred maintenance on the Interstate Highway system alone was $15.8 billion for 1991.[120] That is the cost of the unrepaired damage and wear to the nation's highways annually by highway users. Since users are not paying to make the repairs, the deferred cost amounts to an additional subsidy. One more that is being financed in the manner preferred by our generation: passing the bill on to future generations. Because we are unwilling to properly maintain our infrastructure, they will be forced to rebuild highways that will be beyond repair at a far greater cost. The Department of Transportation has estimated that deferring $1 in highway resurfacing for just two years can require $4 in highway reconstruction costs to repair the damage.[121] In addition, the detrimental impact on quality of life and economic productivity of deteriorated highways is very serious. The FHWA has calculated that highways in poor condition cost users as much as 30 percent more than highways in good condition, and that every one percent increase in highway user costs adds $15 billion to the nation's total transportation bill.[122] An additional 30 percent in cost therefore translates into a staggering $450 billion cost to the nation.

Of course, federal law requires the states to maintain federally funded highways. Title 23 Chapter 1 Section 119(b) of the U.S. Code states,

> *If a State fails to certify as required or if the Secretary determines a State is not adequately maintaining the Interstate system in accordance with such program then the next apportionment of funds to such State for the Interstate system shall be reduced by amounts equal to 10 per centum of the amount which would otherwise be apportioned to such state under section 104 of this title.*

That is the law, but it is rarely enforced. In 1989, 42 percent of the Interstate system was rated as in fair or poor condition, meaning that the "pavement may provide a barely tolerable ride at high speeds," according to the GAO.[123] Yet, the FHWA routinely certifies that states with "significant maintenance backlogs that could affect the integrity of the Interstate roadways and structures and the safety of users" have complied with the law.[124] Nobody wants to disrupt the new construction gravy train. Again, the ever-present perverse-incentive aspect of federal subsidies rears its ugly head. The GAO concluded that the federal highway funding program,

> *provides a further disincentive for states to fund maintenance because unaddressed maintenance items will eventually deteriorate to a point requiring capital-intensive, federally eligible preservation treatments such as resurfacing and reconstruction.*[125]

Whether it is an individual, a business, or a state, the reaction to federal subsidies is to maximize the benefit. States maximize HTF benefits by using federal funds to build highways and then letting them decay until they are sufficiently deteriorated to qualify for federal reconstruction funding. As with all federal subsidies, the intent of Congress is irrelevant, the path of maximized benefits is what is followed. Meanwhile, Senator Robert Byrd has stated that 30 percent of the 42,000 deaths on the nation's highways each year are caused by poor road conditions or poor road design.[126]

Many urban areas have so many highways already that additional capacity is actually counterproductive. According to Sheldon Strickland, former chief of the FHWA's Traffic Management Division, "Building new roads can actually compound congestion, in some cases, by inducing greater demands for vehicle travel—demands that quickly eat away the additional capacity."[127] Traffic jams now cost Americans $51 billion annually in lost wages and wasted fuel,[128] but whether it makes sense or not, the demand for federal highway funds is as strong as ever. Having paid out nearly $300 billion from its inception, the HTF has created a large and very dependent interest group comprised of highway construction interests and state highway departments. Unions also benefit handsomely from federal highway funds. The Davis-Bacon Act subsidizes union workers by essentially requiring that union wages be paid on any project involving federal funding. That provision, plus, to a lesser extent, Buy America and minority set-aside requirements, raise federally-funded highway construction costs by up to 28 percent above state-funded projects.[129]

The primary intent and only legitimate purpose of the trust fund was to build the Interstate Highway system. As Richard D. Morgan, Executive Director of the FHWA, noted, national defense and interstate commerce are the Constitutional basis for federal involvement in highways.[130] Of the Interstate system's 42,795 miles, 98.8 percent, or 42,291 miles, were complete as of 1989.[131] This posed a serious problem for the highway interest group and their Congressional benefactors: what now? From the standpoint of a rational and proper federal role, all highway construction responsibilities should have reverted to the states with perhaps some federal funding strictly for Interstate maintenance. But nearly all federal spending programs either start out as a subsidy program or become one once a legitimate federal undertaking has been accomplished. As such, simply concluding federal funding for highways with the completion of the Interstate system was out of the question. To assure a continued flow of federal highway subsidies, the politicians established the National Highway System (NHS) in 1991. It is comprised of the existing Interstate system, 4,500 miles of highways specifically selected as high-priority corridors by Congress, 17,600 miles of non-Interstate highways and connectors required for national defense, and 91,000 miles of discretionary roads, nearly 159,000 miles in all.[132] Title 23 Chapter 1 Section 103 of the U.S. Code identifies the purpose of the NHS,

> *The purpose of the National Highway System is to provide an interconnected system of principal arterial routes which will serve major population centers, international border crossings, ports, airports, public transportation facilities, and other intermodal transportation facilities and other major travel destinations; meet national defense requirements; and serve interstate and other interregional travel.*

It is notable that the Constitutionally legitimate bases for federal involvement are listed dead last, and were likely added just to provide some cover for what is simply a massive subsidy program. Of course, because the NHS includes the Interstate system, the references in the statute could be based on that inclusion, but that would not justify an expanded federal role. An analysis of data on highway mileage and the number of commercial trucks and buses by John A. Tatom of the Saint Louis Federal Reserve Bank gave no indication that interstate commerce was being constrained by an insufficient highway capacity.[133] The other primary purpose of the Interstate Highway system was to meet national defense requirements. In recent years, our military forces have undergone substantial downsizing, and hundreds of military installations are being closed. In addition to having a considerably smaller military, more of our forces are becoming air-mobile. How, at the same time, can over 17,000 miles of additional roads be declared as necessary for national defense? While it is quite possible that a good case can be made for adding the 4,500 miles of "high-priority corridors" to the Interstate system, the 91,000 miles of "discretionary" roads are just a basis to justify Highway Trust Fund subsidies indefinitely.

Clearly, the primary purpose of the NHS as defined in the statute is to provide federal funds for the construction of state and local highway projects. The GAO found that most states fully expect that the more roads they include in the NHS, the more federal funds they will get.[134] Acting to maximize their subsidy benefit, they sought to include as many miles as possible.[135] Another stated objective of the program is to connect the NHS to all 321 Amtrak stations.[136] In assessing this objective consider the following 1995 GAO conclusion,

> *Amtrak's financial condition has always been precarious, but it has declined steadily since 1990, to the point that its ability to offer service over a national route system of the current size is seriously threatened. Since our earlier testimony, the situation has grown worse. Amtrak's federal support has grown to almost $1 billion annually . . . this assistance has not covered the widening gap between expenses and revenues.*[137]

The objective then, is to spend billions of dollars under the NHS subsidy program to provide local connections to Amtrak stations that are only being kept open through another subsidy program, even though it is increasingly unlikely that enough Amtrak subsidies can be provided to keep those stations open. Federal funds are also supposed to connect airports to the NHS. Apparently, the thinking is that though a city like Denver can afford $4 billion for an airport it did not need, it cannot afford a small fraction of that amount to build a connector to nearby I-70. Cities can also afford hundreds of millions of dollars to replace or rebuild perfectly good stadiums to attract professional sports teams, but they cannot afford to build highways to their ports?

Having eliminated any semblance of a real "national" basis for highway projects, the NHS has transformed the Highway Trust Fund into a slush fund for state and local pork projects. Thus, California, a state with a highway and bridge maintenance backlog in the tens of billions of dollars, has proposed Route 710, a brand new 6.2 mile Los Angeles freeway that would cost $1.1 billion, $177 million per mile.[138] West Virginia's $1.1 billion Corridor H would parallel I-68, and the two largest towns that it would connect have populations under 10,000.[139] Indiana has proposed extending I-69 from Indianapolis, a city already in the center of a web of Interstates, to Evansville at a cost of $800 million.[140] It would be a strictly intrastate extension of an Interstate highway that seven studies since 1966 have concluded would not be economically efficient and should not be built. The only reason for any of these projects is that they qualify for 80 percent federal funding, at least. The objective is to keep the subsidy gravy train rolling; it does not much matter where it is going.

The interaction between various federal subsidy programs is complex, but as a rule, they tend to amplify the unintended consequences of each program. The tens of billions of dollars in federal subsidies that helped pave America have exacerbated the negative effects of other federal subsidies on our urban areas. New highways bisected or destroyed neighborhoods, reduced cities' housing stock, eliminated their parks, and damaged their appearance.[141] About one-third of the land in cities is now taken up by cars, trucks, roads, and parking lots, and nationwide, more land is devoted to the automobile than to housing.[142] In March 1996, the National Capital Planning Commission unveiled a new master plan for Washington D.C. that calls for eliminating the maze of freeways, bridges, and overpasses, and replacing them with a "monumental core" lined with trees.[143] Ironically, the very politicians who channeled tens of billions of taxpayer dollars into the mass conversion of the nation's urban neighborhoods and parks to freeways and overpasses, have now decided that they do not like the result in their own city. President Clinton, commenting on the proposal, stated that the nation "has the resources and the imagination" to make it all happen, and House Speaker Newt Gingrich echoed the President's enthusiasm.[144] Yes, the nation does have the resources, and federal politicians fully intend to confiscate those resources.

The convenience of automobiles combined with the availability of ever-more new, subsidized highways doomed most urban mass transit systems. Suburbs were designed for automobiles, and workplaces are now so spread out that serving them with mass transit is virtually impossible. But jamming more and more cars into cities resulted in ever-increasing traffic congestion, which brought renewed calls for new mass transit systems—federally subsidized mass transit systems. Simply ending motor vehicle subsidies to relieve the congestion problem was out of the question. The solution to the overuse of motor vehicles caused by massive highway and gasoline subsidies was to maintain the existing subsidies while adding transit subsidies in an attempt to persuade drivers not to use their vehicles. It was the standard, countervailing federal-subsidy solution where a second multi-billion dollar subsidy program is passed to nullify the unintended consequences of another.

The Urban Mass Transportation Act of 1964 (UMTA) was the countervailing subsidy program. From its inception through 1991, it provided $62 billion in federal funds to help build, rehabilitate and operate urban mass transit systems.[145] If there was some validity to federal involvement with highways based on the interstate system, no stretch of the imagination could find similar justification for urban mass transit systems. They are, by definition, local and seldom have even statewide significance. That is not to say that they are not beneficial; there is just no basis for federal involvement. But, not surprisingly, federal subsidies have produced extended systems that are frequently not only poorly utilized, but less efficient than automobiles. Mass transit systems require more energy per mile as they move away from the urban core.[146] Fewer people ride the route because it is less likely to go where people want to go, resulting in low-load factors that are very inefficient. For example, an average bus must have a load factor greater than 25 percent to exceed the energy efficiency of an automobile.[147] Left to themselves, cities could not even consider low-load factor service, but with the federal government picking up much of the tab, efficiency is not an issue.

The Los Angeles metropolitan area covers over four thousand square miles, which makes it a most unlikely candidate for a subway system. Nevertheless, the availability of billions of dollars of federal mass transit subsidies meant that rational thinking was not a requirement for the Los Angeles Metropolitan Transportation Authority (MTA). As such, the MTA started building a $5.9 billion subway system[148] that one of its own studies projected would cost from $16 to $98 per passenger trip compared with $1.79 per trip on buses.[149] After two decades and $3.1 billion, only 5.2 miles of the system were in operation, and the rest of the system was in such deep financial trouble that the MTA suspended work in 1998.[150] That the construction has been plagued by huge cost overruns and years of delays is par for the course for a massive subsidy program that is 51 percent financed by federal taxpayers. It is the fact that the program—termed "a crackpot idea through and through" by Peter Gordon, a University of Southern California professor of urban planning[151]—was undertaken at all that is dismaying.

The combination of subsidy-driven, inefficiently-designed systems and automobile subsidies that undermine the use of public transit has resulted in the nation's mass transit systems being so uneconomic that passenger fares cover none of the capital costs and only 37 percent of the operating expenses.[152] The federal government funds up to 80 percent of the capital cost of transit projects through annual appropriations and the two cent per gallon Highway Trust fund fuel tax that is dedicated to the Mass Transit Account. The subsidies average about $5 billion annually,[153] although legislation enacted in 1998 upped that to nearly $7 billion annually for the years 1998 through 2003.[154]

As with highways, politicians much prefer to fund new projects rather than to maintain old ones. The Clinton Administration explains its policy of earmarking 82.5 percent of federal mass transit funds for capital rather than operations as "a more strategic investment."[155] It is certainly a questionable strategy to build more expensive, low-load factor transit systems which cities cannot afford to operate or maintain, especially when the heavily used systems are falling apart. Over 80 percent of public transit agencies surveyed by the GAO indicated that further cutbacks in federal operating subsidies would cause them to curtail existing services.[156] Since one would expect that service would be curtailed first on the least used routes, the net effect could be that service on recent federally funded projects would be cut back while new projects which will have even less usage are being built. That notwithstanding, politicians like the ribbon cutting ceremonies that "more strategic investments" produce. In plain English, big construction subsidies produce big political returns. What happens to the project after that is irrelevant. Despite all the federal spending, public transportation ridership dropped 10 percent between 1980 and 1994 while the average subsidy per rider increased 97 percent.[157] But then federal mass transit funding is mostly about moving contributors, not commuters.

The flagship of subsidized train systems is without a doubt, Amtrak. Between 1971 and 1998, U.S. taxpayers poured nearly $22 billion into that sinking ship.[158] It is still sinking. Amtrak was created by the Rail Passenger Service Act of 1970 to operate and revitalize intercity passenger rail service. It presently operates passenger rail service in 44 states, but despite the massive infusions of federal subsidies, it still loses an average of $47 per passenger.[159] On its Sunset Limited route between Los Angeles, California and Orlando, Florida, it loses a stunning $284 per passenger.[160] The nation does not need Amtrak; it serves just 0.4 percent of Americans who make intercity trips.[161] However $22 billion is a lot of pork, and pork pays.

Amtrak has lost money every year of its existence, and the GAO has warned innumerable times that it faces financial problems indefinitely. Nonetheless, Congress has appropriated billions of dollars to keep it afloat. Such an obvious waste of money has drawn considerable criticism, especially during 1997 when politicians were under great pressure to balance the budget. Unwilling to take the heat, but also unwilling to truly cut the absurd Amtrak subsidies, Congress enacted legislation providing funding for Amtrak that stands out as one of its truly deplorable acts of deception. It provided for $2.3 billion in tax refunds to Amtrak—a quasi-governmental corporation that has never paid a penny in federal corporate income tax.[162] How could the government refund taxes that were never paid? Of course, it could not, and those who voted for the legislation knew that. The politicians handed a $2.3 billion subsidy to Amtrak under the table in what was quite simply an act of fraud. It is both ironic and a testament to the sad state of federal affairs that the legislation containing that provision was the 1997 Balanced Budget Act.

The tens of billions of dollars in mass transit and Amtrak subsidies still pale next to the hundreds of billions that have been spent on highways. Moreover, even as new transit systems that hardly anyone will use are being funded, far more is being spent on highway projects that will further discourage their use. Subsidized highways radiating from cities have provided a route for the middle class that once lived and worked in the cities to use subsidized gasoline to easily access subsidized suburban housing, complete with subsidized utilities. This allowed them to take advantage of the cities' resources without having to pay to support them. That was left to those left behind, increasingly, the poor. Since 1950, eighty-six percent of the population growth in metropolitan areas has been in suburban locations.[163] Since the 1960s, ten of America's twenty-five largest cities have lost population.[164] Atlanta's population declined by 19 percent while its suburbs grew by 396 percent.[165] Between 1993 and 1998, there was a 40 % increase in the jobs in the suburbs north of Atlanta, Georgia, while the central core—the site of the 1996 Olympic games—

–grew only 4 percent.[166] The primary reason? Roads, according to Metro Atlanta Chamber of Commerce president Sam A. Williams.[167]

Businesses followed their employees to the suburbs. Between 1960 and 1980, the number of jobs in the suburbs more than doubled to nearly half of all metropolitan area jobs.[168] This represented a further blow to the cities' revenues, while the loss of jobs added to their social welfare burdens. A city could do little to counteract the generous federal subsidies that powered the exodus to the suburbs. To make matters worse, the federal government takes revenues from many of the larger cities to subsidize rural areas. For instance, economists at Harvard determined that in 1994 New York City generated $9 billion more in federal taxes than it received in total federal benefits.[169] The federal government continues to massively subsidize suburban and rural development at the expense of hundreds of billions of dollars worth of urban infrastructure, housing, and industrial facilities, which are being abandoned or left to decay. Federal tax, highway, gasoline, utility, and real estate subsidies as well as misguided social subsidies have acted in concert to destroy our central cities, leaving the hollow donuts we have today. As long as those policies remain in effect, we will see successive rings of subsidized development creating ever-larger urban donuts with ever-larger cores characterized by crime, poverty, and decay. Our cities cannot survive federal subsidy programs.

Federal utility subsidies date back to the 1930s, a time when electric utilities presented federal politicians with a serious problem; however, the first subsidies enacted made no attempt to solve it. The problem was the rise during the 1920s of giant utility holding companies, 16 of which controlled 85 percent of the nation's electric power by the middle of the decade.[170] With the ready assistance of large Wall Street firms that were major stockholders, the holding companies engaged in wholesale securities fraud and manipulation. Ultimately, that led to numerous bankruptcies and the loss of hundreds of millions of dollars by investors when the bottom fell out during the Great Depression. At the same time, state and local governments were struggling with how to regulate "natural monopolies," especially local power companies that were part of huge, multi-state conglomerates that could easily shift costs to justify rate increases. It is safe to say that abuses, including graft and bribery, were widespread. The concern for the immense power of the holding companies is revealed in this excerpt from a statement signed by 37 leaders of Congress from both parties during the 1932 election campaign,

> *The combined utility and banking interests, headed by the Power Trust, have the most powerful and widely organized political machine ever known in our history. This machine cooperates with other reactionary economic, industrial, and financial groups. It is strenuously working to control the nomination of candidates for the Presidency and the Congress of both dominant political parties.*[171]

The Power Trust nearly kept Franklin Roosevelt from getting the nomination of the Democratic Party in 1932, but they came up just short, and he was elected President. Roosevelt had campaigned against the excess power and abuses of the electric conglomerates, but rather than address that problem, his first priority was to get the federal government into the business of subsidized electricity. During World War I, the federal government had undertaken the construction of a hydroelectric dam and two coal-fired power plants on a site on the Tennessee River at Muscle Shoals, Alabama, to provide power for two munitions plants. The power plants were not completed by the end of the war and construction was halted. For the next fifteen years, politicians debated what to do with the site. Immediately after his election, Franklin Roosevelt proposed the creation of the Tennessee Valley Authority (TVA), a federal agency to finish the plants and to fully develop the Tennessee River for power, flood control, and agriculture—at federal expense. While the original plan had been undertaken as part of a war effort, clearly a federal responsibility, Roosevelt's plan to put the federal government into the local power business was just as clearly well outside the authority of the federal government. Indeed, the Supreme Court ruled that Roosevelt's programs aimed at aiding local economies were unconstitutional.[172] He responded by packing the Supreme Court. Congress refused to allow him to increase the number of justices to 15, but eventually he named eight of the nine justices and initiated the era of unlimited federal authority.[173]

The federal government was now free to spend huge sums of money going into the subsidized electricity and irrigation businesses. At the same time that federal irrigation projects were bringing tens of thousands of new acres into crop production, Congress was enacting farm subsidies to help farmers who had already driven prices into the mud through overproduction. The federal government was doing all it could to make an already bad situation worse. Moreover, there was no demand for the additional electrical power; in 1932, there were only fourteen thousand electric customers in the whole state of Tennessee served by sixteen municipal electric systems.[174] Of course, federal subsidies could change that. The fact that there did not appear to be any justification for the project, and that it did nothing to address the Power Trust problem, did not deter Congress from passing the TVA Act in 1933. In 1955, with the TVA expanding well beyond even Roosevelt's vision, a task force headed by former President Herbert Hoover recommended that it be dissolved.[175] The subsidy interests would not hear of it.

Today, the TVA operates 113 hydroelectric plants, 59 coal-fired plants and three nuclear plants supplying electricity to seven million people in an eighty thousand square mile area covering Tennessee, and parts of Alabama, Kentucky, Georgia, Mississippi, North Carolina, and Virginia.[176] This impressive expansion was made possible by the same mechanism that has allowed the federal government itself to grow from $235 billion in 1950 to nearly $1,700 billion in 1998: debt.[177] In 1959, Congress amended the TVA Act, authorizing the agency to issue $750 million in bonds.[178] The TVA spent every dime it could get its hands on and Congress raised its debt limit four times, finally reaching $30 billion in 1979.[179] It is now nearly $27 billion in debt and in big trouble. The agency only remains solvent because of its huge credit line and the fact that it is hiding billions of dollars in losses through creative accounting.[180] The Energy Policy Act of 1992 deregulated the electricity market, but Congress made sure to protect the TVA from competition because it could not survive competition. The GAO concluded,

> *TVA pays no federal taxes and has access to low-cost financing because of its status as a government corporation. Despite these advantages, given TVA's current financial condition, TVA would likely be unable to compete with its neighboring utilities in the long term.*[181]

To become competitive, the GAO determined that,

> *. . . it would have to reduce its debt by an estimated 50 percent— $13 billion. It is unlikely that TVA can do this on its own. Some form of federal intervention may be required.*[182]

The bottom line is that one way or another, American taxpayers are going to get stuck with a significant portion of TVA's debt. Federal subsidies always come back to haunt the taxpayers, and soon we will get the bill for Roosevelt's grand power subsidy scheme.

Roosevelt and Congress finally did get around to addressing the Power Trust problem with the Public Utility Holding Company Act (PUHC), which they passed in 1935. But in the same year, Roosevelt established the Rural Electrification Administration (REA) by executive order and Congress passed the Emergency Relief Act, which authorized $5 billion in public works projects, including $100 million for rural electrification, to help provide employment for the millions who were jobless due to the depression.[183] The job of the REA was to bring electricity to rural America, and provide customers for TVA to subsidize.

It certainly can be argued that a massive public works program was justified by the desperate state of the economy and rural electrification was not without merit. However, the frequent problem with federal subsidy programs is not that they are not well intentioned, but that they are immortal. Like the "temporary" farm subsidies aimed at helping farmers through the depression, the REA (reincarnated as the Rural Utilities Service in 1994) is still handing out taxpayer dollars decades after its goals were achieved. To keep the program alive, its charter was expanded to telephone service and finally satellite and cable television. With each expansion, the very idea of federal involvement became increasingly preposterous. Exactly what is the basis for the federal government subsidizing cable TV service to rural communities? Especially since there are two active commercial lenders, with $13.1 billion in loans as of June 30, 1997, that specialize in lending to rural electricity and telecommunications providers.[184] Nonetheless, on the same date, RUS had $36 billion in subsidized loans and loan guarantees outstanding to rural utilities.[185] Just during 1996 and 1997, the agency wrote off $1.5 billion in bad loans, but the GAO found that an additional $10.5 billion was either in default or likely to default in the near future.[186] And that was just from its electricity loan portfolio. The RUS, however, is still making loans with 5 percent interest rates—less than it costs the U.S. Treasury to borrow the money—to wealthy resort communities such as Aspen, Colorado, and Hilton Head, South Carolina.[187] There has long since ceased to be any sense to the program. It continues to exist simply because it created a subsidized interest group large enough to insure immortality.

It was a brainchild of another President Roosevelt—Teddy—that ultimately became one of the nation's greatest subsidy machines. Convinced that the American west had vast potential, but only through the widespread use of irrigation, Teddy pushed through the Reclamation Act in 1902, which created what ultimately became the Bureau of Reclamation (BOR). The new law put the federal government in the business of building dams and canals for irrigation, and allowed farmers who used the irrigation water to repay the government for the costs of the projects over twenty years with no interest. Even with the very low interest rates of the day, the interest exemption meant that farmers were only required to repay the government about 75 cents on the dollar, a nice subsidy. Nonetheless, by 1922, sixty percent of BOR's irrigators were in default on their payments.[188]

It apparently did not occur to Congress that the reason that farmers could not afford to pay for cheap, subsidized water was that crop surpluses were driving down prices. The evidence was there: the value of crops raised on Reclamation land fell from $152 million in 1919 to $83.6 million in 1922.[189] Reclamation subsidies were putting more farmers in business to the detriment of all farmers. But the politicians chose a solution that could only exacerbate the problem: they extended the repayment period to fifty years and enacted a provision to charge farmers based on their ability to pay. In the face of huge crop surpluses, Congress dramatically increased irrigation subsidies. As interest rates rose in later decades, farmers were paying pennies on the dollar on their fifty-year, interest-free federal loans—if they bothered to pay at all. In analyzing the government cost versus what irrigators would repay on an Arizona project in 1992, the Interior Department determined that a $25.5 million debt to be repaid without interest over thirty-four years had a present value of $5.8 million.[190] In other words, nearly 80 percent of the government cost of the project would not be repaid. And that was if the irrigators made all their scheduled payments, which is almost unheard of. The GAO summarized the deal on BOR irrigation water as follows:

> *The irrigators do not pay interest on the construction costs associated with irrigation and are required to pay only those construction costs deemed within their ability to pay. When the costs are above the irrigator's ability to pay, they generally are*

paid by the power users at the end of the 40 to 50 year repayment period.[191]

With Bureau of Reclamation water that cost taxpayers sometimes hundreds of dollars per acre-foot (the amount of water necessary to cover one acre of land, one foot deep) being delivered to farmers almost free, the demand for irrigation projects ballooned. Politicians quickly came to realize the political and economic value of federal water projects. They dwarfed all other construction projects and could keep local contractors and businesses awash in federal dollars for years. The nation, or more precisely Congress, went on a dam building binge. Big dams. The first of the giants, the Hoover on the Colorado River near Las Vegas, was started in 1931 and completed in 1936. Despite the irrigation water giveaway, the dam made economic sense based on its enormous hydroelectric generating capacity. The Reclamation Act required that water projects be economically sound, and it did not take long for BOR and Congress to realize that hydroelectric revenues could be used to hide huge amounts of irrigation subsidies. The irrigation requirements and facilities of dam projects often accounted for most of the project cost and they contributed virtually no revenue. However, when the lower cost and high revenues of the hydroelectric portion of the project were included, the overall project appeared to be economically sound. That is, if you did not recognize that about the same revenues could have been achieved with a much lower cost project if it had been built just for hydroelectric generation. But the public did not know that and soon boondoggle dams were being planned all over the west.

In sixty years, the BOR built over 260 irrigation projects,[192] the vast majority of which were economically preposterous. Congress knew it. In the 1950s, while the politicians were authorizing irrigation dams left and right, Illinois Senator Paul Douglas, a former economics professor, performed calculations on the economics of the various projects and reported his findings on the Senate floor. He found that the proposed projects would spend an average of $2,000 per acre (in 1950s dollars) to irrigate land that would be worth only $100-$150 per acre after the projects were completed.[193] In addition, when put into production, much of the land would be used to grow low-value crops that were already in surplus. Congress was already paying farmers on more productive, non-irrigated land not to produce those crops. Even the hydroelectric power was senseless for the later projects. Douglas reported that power from Flaming Gorge dam would cost over $700 per kilowatt and Central Utah project power would cost $765 per kilowatt compared to $112 for power from the Hoover dam.[194] His colleagues listened and then promptly voted for virtually every project that was proposed. They were well aware of the wasteful absurdity of the projects, but there simply was not a more perfect subsidy machine in existence, and it was the excellent returns and efficiency of that machinery that interested them. Forty years later, Congress authorized the Central Utah Project, which would deliver water to farmers that cost the taxpayers $400 per acre-foot. However, it would only be worth $30 per acre-foot to farmers, and they would only have to pay $8 per acre-foot according to a study by the Political Economy Research Center.[195]

The U.S. Army Corps of Engineers has long been in the water project business. It had been building canals and levees for transportation and flood control in the eastern United States since the 1830s. But by the 1920s, it became apparent that the real money was in big dams in the western states. Dams for irrigation were the job of the BOR; the Corps had to justify its dams based on flood control or navigation, which were within its charter. Since all rivers flood on occasion, a flood-control dam argument could be made for virtually any river—except that the Corps had spent decades contending that dams were not effective for flood control. That was when it was primarily in the levee building business. However, once it realized the enormous amount of money to be had building dams, the Corps reversed itself and aggressively began pursuing dam projects for flood control. Shortly after the Hoover dam was started by the BOR, the Corps began construction of the Bonneville dam on the Columbia River in Washington. The two agencies instantly became fierce competitors. The Corps already had an advantage over BOR because it could claim that almost any river needed flood control, but it soon determined that it had another advantage: while the BOR offered nearly free irrigation, the Corps could offer totally free irrigation. By law, farmers had to pay for irrigation projects over fifty years (without interest and only if they could afford it), but flood control projects were paid for entirely by the taxpayers. Irrigation was simply a side-benefit of a flood control project, and farmers who benefited from the water had no obligation whatsoever. In the all-out competition for dam projects, the Corps did its best to co-opt the BOR's farmer constituency by offering free irrigation. However, flood control, navigation, and electric power were the primary arguments used to justify hundreds of dams that Congress was only too happy to fund.

Appropriations for the Bureau of Reclamation and the Army Corps of Engineers came through different Congressional committees, and the intense rivalry for water projects between the two agencies was also carried on by their respective appropriations committees over the multi-billion dollar subsidies. As is usually the case, insuring that both were generously funded was generally the solution to which agency would get what. One particularly thorny issue was over who would get the largest single project: controlling the Missouri River. The Corps proposed the Pick plan (named after Colonel Lewis Pick, its primary architect), which included five huge dams and eight hundred miles of "river-training," mostly through the construction of levees. Its primary objectives: flood control and navigation. The Bureau, claiming that Pick's plan was gross overkill, proposed its own somewhat more modest plan named after BOR engineer Glen Sloan, with the primary objectives of irrigation and electric power. The battle raged in Congress until it finally ended up authorizing the Pick-Sloan plan in 1944, which included most of the elements of the separate plans. The projected cost of $1.9 billion, lowballed in keeping with standard procedure, included $250 million of elements which would, according to the agencies' own previous testimony, cancel each other out.[196] Economist

David Campbell described the plan as "a victory of politics and bureaucracy over economics and nature."[197]

Nearly $4.5 billion was spent, but predictably, many of the exaggerated benefits never materialized.[198] Of the $1.5 billion in cost attributed to irrigation, over $850 million has been written-off as unrecoverable because the millions of acres of land that the proponents claimed would be irrigated by the project turned out to be, not surprisingly, a wild exaggeration.[199] Much of the land that was to benefit from irrigation was too poor for farming. North Dakota was to gain 1.2 million acres of irrigated land, but after fifty years only 9,000 acres, less than 1 percent, have come into production,.[200] In all, only about 25 percent of the acreage planned for irrigation was developed.[201] At the same time, nearly two million acres of the region's best soils were drowned under huge reservoirs.[202] Barge traffic is but a small fraction of that projected by the Corps, amounting to 2.9 million tons by 1984, less than one percent of that carried on the Mississippi.[203] Navigation is only worth $14 million per year and is declining, mirroring the rest of the Corp's inland waterway system. In 1995, taxpayers paid 90 percent of the $786 million cost of operating that system.[204]

Even the flood control elements of the Pick-Sloan plan have proved to be a problem. While the reservoirs and levees have prevented damage during modest floods, they have resulted in much greater damage from large floods, such as those in 1973 and 1993. The levees sealed off the river from its flood plains where the effects of large floods are mitigated naturally. Instead, all the water is forced down stream in the boxed-in river channel, rising ever higher as it goes. In April 1994, after several days of heavy rain, the Missouri River at Jefferson City, Missouri rose seven feet in just twenty-four hours.[205] In a heavy flood, nearly all the water is sent to the lower river basin where nothing the Corps of Engineers can build is going to prevent a devastating flood. Larry Larson, chief of dam safety and flood plain management for the state of Wisconsin, notes that, "The potential for a levee to increase flood elevations upstream and downstream seldom, if ever, was calculated. If they were, it did not deter construction."[206] As with most pork-barrel projects, the benefits were exaggerated while the drawbacks were ignored. It is estimated that the floods of 1908 and 1993 sent about the same amount of water down the river, but the 1993 flood crested eight feet higher because of levees.[207] While the record flood of 1993 was unusual, it does not take that kind of an event to cause problems on the tightly constrained Missouri River. It flooded again in 1994 and 1995.[208]

The great flood of 1993 sent huge volumes of water down the levee-bound Missouri and Mississippi River systems. Virtually all the major tributaries of the Missouri-Mississippi system had been constrained by an extensive system of levees, many built by the Corps. Where a levee was breached, a huge wall of water would emerge causing widespread damage. While the great majority of levees that failed were nonfederal, much of the water flow that caused the failures was due to levees and other river modifications undertaken by the Corps. Property and crop damage exceeded $12 billion.[209] Much of the damage was to farms and structures built on wetlands that were drained after federal levees were built. Harvard economist Robert Stavins has calculated that 30 percent of the conversion of wetlands to farmland in the lower Mississippi Valley was directly caused by federal flood control projects.[210]

Having subsidized the development of the flood plain and then deluged it by the very same device, the politicians felt compelled to pass additional subsidies. Promptly after the 1993 flood, they passed a $5.7 billion flood disaster relief bill.[211] Of course, taxpayers paid for crop losses. Subsidies were provided to purchase over twelve-thousand flood-prone dwellings,[212] many built in harm's way because they were theoretically protected by subsidized federal levees. The purchase of low-lying farms was also authorized, but, incredibly, funds were also appropriated for the Corps of Engineers to rebuild virtually all of the levees that contributed to the problem in the first place. As soon as the farmers found out that the levees would be rebuilt—at taxpayer expense—very few would sell their land. Thus, the subsidy cycle will be repeated over again. The federal government built subsidized levees that made no sense. They resulted in subsidized agricultural production of surplus crops on flood-prone land that made no sense, which, predictably, suffered heavy flood losses, which were largely reimbursed through federal subsidies, after which the government subsidized the reconstruction of the levees. No doubt contemplating this absurdity, University of Illinois Geographer Bruce Hanson posed the question, "What sense does it make for the taxpayer to create private farmland in the bottomlands of the Mississippi when the same taxpayer is paying billions of dollars a year to farmers not to grow crops in nearby unflooded uplands?"[213] To politicians and flood plain farmers relieved of flood risks by U.S. taxpayers, it all makes perfect sense.

The kind of sense that apparently irrational expenditures of vast amounts of tax dollars makes is political sense, and, in America today, that equates to subsidies. Despite the overwhelming evidence that most of the later water projects of the Bureau of Reclamation and the Corps of Engineers were not only a colossal waste of money, but actually did more harm than good, Congress is still at it. While both parties talk of austerity and balanced budgets, they are moving ahead with the BOR's positively indefensible $710 million[214] Animas-La Plata dam and irrigation project near Durango, Colorado. It would largely drain a small river in southern Colorado and consume huge amounts of power to pump the water up a five hundred foot mountain. It would then be used to irrigate very marginal land at seven thousand feet of elevation where little can be grown. Even the BOR, which for decades produced contrived economic analyses showing that its projects were economically beneficial to the nation, could not defend this one. Its analysis showed that every dollar spent would produce 36 cents in benefits.[215] In 1987, the Interior Department testified before the House and Senate committees with jurisdiction over the project that, "the Animas-La Plata Project is not economically feasible."[216]

The project is so widely recognized as being purely a subsidy program that Phil Doe, a staffer in the BOR's Denver office, did not shy away from telling the *Los Angeles Times* that he termed the project "Jurassic Pork," and that "It's clearly a developer's project and taxpayers are going to pay for it."[217]

University of Colorado Economics Professor Charles Howe calls it a "horrible project—ridiculously expensive and blatantly inefficient."[218] Clearly, no one in Washington, D.C. could possibly claim that they thought this project made even the slightest bit of sense. Yet, in 1995, President Clinton and the newly elected and "budget balancing" Republican Congress approved an appropriation to build the Animas-La Plata Project. Perhaps the best explanation of the kind of "sense" that persuaded Congress and the president to fund the project was contained in an advertisement run by proponents in a Durango newspaper:

> *Why support the project? Because someone else is paying most of the tab. We get the water. We get the reservoir. They pay the bill.*[219]

Though politicians would never be so forthright, that is the reason they passed the appropriation. The return on investment from subsidizing the proponents would far exceed any possible losses, because almost none of those paying the tab were aware that they were doing so. At least the local proponents made no pretenses. There were no phony claims about economic benefits; they came right out with it: the project is good for us because it is a massive federal subsidy. Period.

As a result of the great dam-building binge, the federal government controls nearly all the nation's hydroelectric power. In addition to the Tennessee Valley Authority, the government chartered five Power Marketing Administrations (PMAs) to sell the power generated by Bureau of Reclamation and Corps of Engineers hydroelectric plants. The PMAs, which are agencies of the Energy Department, have constructed nearly thirty-three thousand miles of transmission lines to enable them to market their power, which in 1993 amounted to 3 percent of the U.S. total.[220] Of course, they operate in direct competition with the private utilities that supply most of the nation's power. (One can only imagine what the Founders would have to say about that—and their dismay that the Supreme Court actually sanctioned such a clear overextension of federal authority.) Naturally, the PMAs are subsidized and can sell power cheap. The GAO explained how:

> *Their ability to operate as low-cost sellers stems from several factors, including the inherent low cost of hydropower relative to other generating sources, federal financing at relatively low interest rates, flexibility in the repayment of principal on the Treasury portion of the PMA's debt, the PMA's tax exempt status, and operating budgets that seek to break even rather than earn a profit or return on investment. . . . The PMAs other than Bonneville, generally receive [Congressional] appropriations annually to cover operations and maintenance expenses and capital investments in their transmission assets. . . . These financing mechanisms differ from those used by investor-owned utilities. Such utilities generally pay for their operating expenses from op-*

erating revenue and finance capital investments by (1) issuing debt, (2) selling common or preferred stock, or (3) using cash generated from operations.[221]

The federal financing is not just a good deal, it is a fantastic deal: the interest rate on PMA debt to the Treasury averaged between 2.7 and 4.6 percent in 1994.[222] However, the Treasury was borrowing the money it was lending to the PMAs at an average rate of 6.9 percent.[223] Private utilities, with no such taxpayer connection, were paying an average of 8.1 percent to borrow money.[224] Considering that the debt of private utilities equals about 37 percent of total assets, paying interest rates 100 to 300 percent higher than the PMAs puts them at a tremendous competitive disadvantage.[225] Even worse, the PMAs' power is primarily purchased during times of peak demand at rates that are, on average, half the rates charged by private utilities.[226] It is tantamount to the federal government holding a half-price toy sale during the weeks before Christmas.

It should come as no surprise that the GAO concluded that the highly subsidized financing provided to the PMAs has led them to a "high amount of debt in comparison to total investment."[227] The largest of them, the Bonneville Power Administration (BPA), which sells power in Washington, Oregon, and Idaho, had run up its debt to 96 percent of total assets by 1991.[228] The GAO has concluded that in both the short and long run, the BPA's financial condition and very high debt level may lead to default on its debt to the Treasury—despite the low interest rates.[229] Like all subsidy recipients, BPA acted to maximize the subsidies that Congress was willing to provide, in this case, by loading up on bargain-basement debt. And as is usually the case, the more a recipient maximizes its subsidies, the more the taxpayers are exposed to unanticipated additional costs in addition to the cost of the subsidy program.

The BPA is not in trouble simply because it took on too much debt. Just as much, if not more of a problem, is the fact that Congress insists that it subsidize its power users. PMAs are required by law to give preference in the sale of power to public power customers, customer-owned cooperatives, public utility and irrigation districts, and municipally owned utilities.[230] Congress has required the PMAs to sell electricity cheap to these entities, leaving little room to finance capital improvements out of revenues. Indeed, from 1992 through 1996, the taxpayers had to make up a $1.5 billion operating loss from the PMAs.[231] At the same time, because Congress has made it very attractive for them to borrow, they do. In 1990, the BPA proposed raising rates sufficiently to allow it to pay for 35 percent of its capital requirements from revenues, but its heavily subsidized customers howled and the proposal was withdrawn.[232] Again in 1995, Congress mandated that BPA continue to supply subsidized power.[233]

The remarkable thing is that the rates paid by BPA's customers are the lowest in the nation. In May 1995, customers of Boston Edison paid $120.80 per thousand kilowatt-hours, while customers of Jacksonville (Florida) Electric Authority, with one of the lowest rates in the country, paid $69.09.[234] The rate for BPA customer Seattle City Light—$34.55.[235] Yet it is those in the areas with high, unsubsidized rates who put up nearly all the money to build BPA's hydroelectric dams and still pay to heavily subsidize BPA's debt. If any of the government's electric power subsidiaries default on the debt they owe the U.S. Treasury, the same folks will pick up most of the tab for that, too. Nonetheless, BPA's customers protest mightily against increased rates. They stand firm on their tenured subsidy right; having been subsidized for fifty years, they are now entitled to be subsidized indefinitely. The rest of the country should pay two or three times as much for their own electricity and pay extra taxes to insure very low rates for the fortunate few who get subsidized power from the federal government. If that seems ridiculous, there are plenty of people in Washington, D.C. and Seattle . . . and Durango that will gladly explain it.

It is a truism that subsidies increase the demand for the subsidized commodity and electricity is no exception. With dirt-cheap, subsidized federal power, the northwestern U.S. developed the highest rate of electricity consumption in the world.[236] Those who were paying less than the true cost of supplying the power had little incentive not to waste it. About 25 percent of BPA's power is consumed by the extremely energy-intensive aluminum industry. Almost the entire industry is concentrated along the Columbia River because Congress has given it a deal too good to refuse. The price aluminum producers pay for BPA power is indexed to the market price of aluminum.[237] If aluminum prices fall, the already cheap rates get even cheaper. Not only do the taxpayers supply subsidized power, they have assumed part of the market risk for the price of the aluminum. Life is very good for those Uncle Sam favors.

By the 1970s, rapid development and waste had just about consumed all of the prodigious amounts of subsidized hydropower coming from dozens of northwestern dams. There were simply no more sites for new dams, but not a thought was given to ending the subsidies. With Congress and the Supreme Court having decided that there are virtually no limits to what the federal government can do, BPA was authorized to go into the nuclear power business. By the early 1990s, that capacity was about used up as well, but still, no thought was given to ending the subsidies. On the contrary, new subsidies were implemented to offset the overconsumption and waste that resulted from the original subsidies.

Congress created the Northwest Power Planning Council in 1980 to coordinate energy development and policy among the northwestern states served by the BPA. Several federal agencies, including the BPA, Corps of Engineers, and BOR, carry out the Council's policies. In 1993, the Council's Executive Director, Ed Sheets, announced that $7 billion would have to be spent by the year 2000 on electricity conservation measures.[238] Of course, much of that would be tax dollars. After decades of subsidizing profligate energy use, there was to be a new policy: energy waste would continue to be encouraged through power subsidies, but energy conservation would also be encouraged through additional multi-billion dollar subsidies. The theory is that the energy conservation subsidies will negate the waste caused by the electric power subsidies, thereby achieving the same result as having no subsidies at all, but at a cost to the taxpayers of billions of dollars to support both subsidies. The Department of Energy now estimates that the U.S. could save $40 billion annually from investments in energy efficiency in buildings alone.[239] If the federal government had not spent the last fifty years subsidizing energy, many of those buildings would have been built more energy-efficient in the first place.

Federal electric subsidies, mostly in the form of cheap power and tax preferences that benefit about 25 percent of all Americans, cost the U.S. Treasury about $8.4 billion per year, according to the Edison Electric Institute.[240] (That does not include the cost of tax subsidies for energy conservation.) A study by University of Kansas Professor Douglas Houston for the Reason Foundation concluded that a sale of all the federal government's power subsidiaries would bring as much as $30 billion.[241] Not only would the Treasury be that much better off, but "power wheeling," selling power over great distances, would allow all Americans to benefit from the expensive hydroelectric projects that they paid to build. However, to do so, Congress would have to be willing to part with some of its favorite subsidy machines, and currently subsidized electric customers would have to pay a fair price for electricity. With the present federal structure that provides numerous avenues to create subsidies, but virtually none to end them, neither is within the realm of possibility. Indeed, when the Reagan Administration proposed selling the PMAs in the 1980s, Congress responded by prohibiting federal agencies from even studying the idea.[242]

The spectacular success of the atomic bomb that ended World War II set the stage for numerous, very expensive problems as the U.S. tried to adapt the technology to generate electricity. The development of the bomb was a truly remarkable scientific achievement, which had been accomplished in a very short time. During the 1950s, there were great hopes and predictions that nuclear power would soon provide a nearly free and inexhaustible supply of energy. And it was assumed that technical problems would be solved just as easily and on the fly, as they were during the development of the atomic bomb under the Manhattan Project. The project's leaders, Enrico Fermi and Robert Oppenheimer, advocated basic research and cautious development of nuclear power, but their warnings were largely ignored.[243]

Beginning with President Eisenhower's Atoms for Peace program in 1953, the federal government undertook a heavily subsidized and dangerously premature push to develop nuclear power plants. In 1954, the Shippingport reactor in Pennsylvania became the nation's first commercial nuclear plant. The project was a joint venture of the Atomic Energy Commission and Duquesne Light Company, but the federal government paid for nearly 75 percent of the plant's cost.[244] In 1957, Congress passed the Price-Anderson Act, which put U.S. taxpayers on the hook for damages resulting from a nuclear accident at a commercial plant. The Act provided $560 million federal liability-insurance policies for commercial nuclear plants,[245] likely the best insurance deal of all time. During the next two decades, with the Atomic Energy Commission acting as cheerleader, salesman, insurer, financier, and reluctant regulator, construction would be started on over two hundred plants, many before safety and operational issues were adequately researched. The difficult issue of what to do with all the nuclear waste was simply not addressed.

During the 1970s, with many plants nearing completion, a host of environmental, operational, and safety concerns caused the government to issue extensive new regulations that required modifications costing billions of dollars to both new and existing plants. Many plants became so expensive that they were canceled despite multi-billion dollar investments. Between 1974 and 1986, 103 reactors were canceled after an estimated $100 billion had been spent on them.[246] The Long Island Lighting Company is still carrying the $5.3 billion cost of its Shoreham plant, which was completed but never allowed to operate.[247] Consequently, its customers pay some of the highest electric rates in the country. The Tennessee Valley Authority started a stunning seventeen nuclear plants, but between 1982 and 1984 it canceled eight of the plants after investing $5 billion in them.[248] Of the remaining nine units, three are operational, two were still under construction nearly twenty-five years after construction began, and construction on the remaining four had been suspended.[249] In all, as of 1995, TVA had spent $25 billion on nuclear plants, only $5 billion of which was spent on plants that are operating.[250] The Bonneville Power Administration has three nuclear plants, only one of which is operating.[251] One hundred and nine plants actually made it into operation and today supply 22 percent of the nation's electric power.[252]

The federal government led the nation on a heavily subsidized, irresponsible, and nearly disastrous endeavor that proved to be a financial catastrophe. A 1977 Rand Corporation report summarized the misadventure,

> *By the mid-1970s, four flaws in the process of commercialization of light water reactors were retrospectively being attributed to the earlier actions or inactions of the Atomic Energy Commission. The first was that licensing and regulatory delays had slowed the completion of individual nuclear plants. . . . A second was the questionable adequacy of the safety standards . . . Third, changes in AEC requirements, sometimes retroactive, were alleged to have substantially increased the expense and uncertainty of reactor construction. And fourth, the inattention of the Atomic Energy Commission to public demands for more comprehensive safety and environmental provisions was credited with causing a decline in public confidence in the AEC and the nuclear reactor industry.* [253]

In their book, *Power Struggle: The Hundred-Year War Over Electricity,* Richard Rudolph and Scott Ridley conclude,

> *For the commitment of a government subsidy that would total as much as $200 billion by 1980, of the unsolved problems of radioactive waste, and the proliferation of atomic weapons technology*

there had been no public discussion. It was a fateful decision rushed by a few men, willing to risk public security out of a mixed sense of self-interest, dedication to fulfill the corporate vision of the future, and a naive belief in the ability of technology to resolve fundamental social problems. [254]

The tragedy of the federal government's nuclear program goes beyond the waste of hundreds of billions of dollars of both public and private funds, and the risk that the public was exposed to. By undermining public confidence in nuclear power and the government's ability to insure its safe use, federal nuclear policy increased the nation's dependence on foreign oil and coal as sources of electricity. At the heart of the matter was the eagerness of federal politicians to provide massive subsidies to bring a technology into production that had not undergone research and development to insure that it was safe and economically sound, a mistake they later repeated with the synfuels program. The two programs rank among the nation's greatest financial blunders and were precipitated by abuse of the power to subsidize; a power that has defied wise use since the founding of the nation.

After Word War II, when nuclear technology was a government-developed top secret, the government should have undertaken research and development, rather than subsidizing production. Today, the U.S. Department of Energy (DOE) subsidizes research and development of nuclear power, ironically, at a time when that should be left to industry. While basic nuclear research is justifiable on several bases, the DOE is spending billions of dollars on technology for commercial power plants. Ten billion dollars has already been spent on nuclear fusion research,[255] and DOE is currently spending an additional $373 million annually.[256] Consider the findings of the Congressional Office of Technology Assessment,

. . . even the most optimistic supporters of fusion energy concede that many scientific, engineering, and economic challenges remain. Whether these challenges can be overcome is by no means guaranteed. Just developing a prototype commercial power plant may require tens of billions of dollars in research and new facilities over the next several decades. [257]

Between 1978 and 1993, the federal government spent $45.5 billion on energy research and development.[258] Beyond the question of why are more tax dollars being wasted on projects that do not appear remotely feasible is a more fundamental question: why is the federal government subsidizing the research of an industry with $210 billion in annual revenues?[259] The answer is: that is what the federal government does. It no longer governs, it subsidizes.

8

GOOD INTENTIONS

AND OTHER PEOPLE'S MONEY

Americans are compassionate people. A variety of institutions, dating back to the nation's beginning, have been founded to assist those less fortunate. Prior to the 1930s, these were almost entirely private endeavors, but in the last fifty years, the federal government has authorized hundreds of programs aimed at improving nearly every aspect of the lives of American citizens. While a number of programs began during the Franklin Roosevelt Administration, the real impetus began with President Johnson's War on Poverty in the 1960s. Since then, the federal government has spent over $5 trillion in an attempt to eradicate poverty;[1] but clearly, we are nowhere near winning that war. In 1998 alone, federal taxpayers spent about $600 billion on more than 80 social welfare programs,[2] including $220 billion for means-tested antipoverty programs.[3] Unfortunately, the philosophy underlying these programs essentially guaranteed failure. The same perverse incentives that are characteristic of virtually all federal subsidy programs were built into these social programs with predictable results: rather than contract, the target groups expanded. And powerful vested interest groups comprised of beneficiaries, bureaucrats, and program contractors assured continual expansion of benefits even as it became apparent that the programs were a dismal failure.

Starting with the Franklin Roosevelt era, when concerns about the Constitutional limits on federal authority largely evaporated, Congress proceeded to involve itself ever deeper into state and local issues. One of the earliest pieces of legislation was the National Housing Act of 1934, which established the Federal Housing Administration (FHA) to insure private lenders against losses on home mortgages. Today the FHA insures $400 billion in mortgages,[4] and, fortunately, the taxpayers have not yet had to bail out the agency. However, the GAO is doubtful that our luck will hold out. The United States Housing Act of 1937 established local Public Housing Authorities (PHA's) to administer federal housing programs. The National Housing Act of

1949, which included the noble objective of providing "a decent home and suitable living environment for every American family," completed the transformation of housing from a local issue to one largely controlled by the federal government.

The nation's early public housing efforts were not aimed at the poor. MIT's Nabeel Hamdi notes, "Few, if any, public responses to poor housing conditions have been benevolent; their purpose was to prevent disturbance, create jobs, and fuel industry, and, therefore, economic growth."[5] The primary intent of federal programs from the 1930s through the 1950s was to clear slums and to provide temporary housing for the families of workers. President Roosevelt himself presided over the dedication of the nation's first public housing project, the 1,081-unit Techwood Homes in Atlanta, Georgia, built in 1935. Noting the transition from a slum to a brand new complex of brick buildings surrounding a courtyard, the President commented, "Today, these hopeless old houses are gone, and in their place we see the bright, cheerful buildings of the Techwood Housing Project."[6] Sixty years later, another top federal official, Secretary of Housing and Urban Development Henry Cisneros, presided over the demolition of the sprawling slum known as the Techwood Housing Project. During the same year, 31 other federal housing projects were scheduled for demolition.[7] Cisnernos noted that public housing "which began as transitional housing for working people who had come upon hard times, had become a trap for the poorest of the poor rather than a launching pad for families trying to improve their lives."[8] Another well-intentioned, "temporary" federal subsidy program that turned into a disaster.

While Roosevelt pioneered the federal government's move into state and local affairs, President Johnson's Great Society programs formed the foundation of most of the massive, counterproductive programs that we are faced with today. Between 1963 and 1969, his administration saw nearly four hundred categorical programs enacted that were aimed at Americans individually, including programs for housing, welfare, education, job training, and health care.[9] Johnson was also responsible for the creation of the Department of Housing and Urban Development (HUD), one of the most notorious and wasteful of all federal agencies. The University of Colorado's Marshall Kaplan notes, "From the outset, it was a cabinet agency in search of a coherent role and mission."[10] In 1999, while still searching, HUD spent nearly $26 billion.[11]

By 1980, the HUD budget was $35 billion per year,[12] and the federal government was building 125,000 housing units annually.[13] During the 1980s, the Reagan Administration cut HUD funding substantially, but also turned the department into a cookie jar for politically connected real estate developers—especially the Moderate Rehabilitation Program (Mod Rehab). HUD Secretary Samuel Pierce's executive assistant Deborah Dean Gore effectively ran the program, and she publicly admitted that the Mod Rehab program was run as a political program.[14] Apartment developers paid "consultants"—mostly former Administration officials—$1,000 per apartment unit to secure multi-million dollar HUD Mod Rehab loans and guaranteed rent subsidies. That was the going rate, according to Former Interior Secretary James Watt who received

$400,000 in fees for a few chats with HUD Secretary Samuel Pierce.[15] His clients, and former Attorney General John Mitchell's, received their subsidies. A Senate report estimated that HUD handed out $413 million in excess Mod Rehab subsidies during the 1980s.[16]

Throughout the period, the HUD Inspector General was sending routine reports to Congress detailing the Mod Rehab scam as well as other fraudulent activity, including a single HUD lender that was making extremely risky loans that ended up costing the taxpayers an estimated $1 billion.[17] Congress had the information but chose to ignore it because those receiving the subsidies were influential and generous supporters. Indeed, rather than stopping the abuses, members of Congress were actively interceding at HUD to get loans and subsidies approved. The Heritage Foundation discovered that between 1980 and 1988, lawmakers placed an average of more than 2,400 telephone calls per month to HUD personnel requesting meetings or appropriations for projects within their districts.[18] Again, those in Congress clearly demonstrated that they are incapable of exercising oversight, because they are beholden to those who are the beneficiaries of the abuses. When it comes down to protecting the interests of either taxpayers or subsidy recipients, the taxpayers are sure to be the loser.

The lid finally blew off the HUD scandal in 1989, as much for political reasons as any other. The Democratically controlled Congress found the prospect of revealing the huge fees paid to former government officials—who were nearly all Republicans—for peddling their influence at HUD too much to pass up. Eight years earlier, the HUD Inspector General had informed Congress about more than 10,000 cases where the agency paid for work that was never done, but that failed to arouse much interest.[19] After all, the lawmakers regularly passed bills that paid farmers not to work, and those being paid for the phantom HUD work were constituents too. For Democrats, however, the opportunity to expose a Republican scandal was another matter. There were dozens of committee hearings, a special prosecutor, indictments, and even a couple of minor convictions. The Senate committee issued a 300-page report blaming the Reagan Administration for problems that it estimated would cost the taxpayers as much as $2 billion.[20] Not to be outdone, a House subcommittee issued a 270-page report that found, "widespread abuses, influence peddling, blatant favoritism, monumental waste, and gross management," which it also estimated would cost the taxpayers $2 billion.[21] The report concluded that Secretary Pierce, "At best . . . misled the subcommittee. At worst, he knowingly lied." Neither the House nor the Senate reports mentioned that the same Congressional committees had received dozens of reports from the HUD Inspector General and the GAO, over a period of eight years, detailing the very same abuses that they now claimed were so horrific. The indignation was all for political effect. Charles L. Dempsey, one of the HUD Inspectors General who had reported the abuses to Congress years earlier, was left to comment that what was needed was something to "force the damn Congressmen and their lazy staffers to read the IG's reports."[22] Actually, many of them had. But when it was just a matter of waste and fraud, they were not very interested.

Months of Congressional hearings, during 1989 and 1990, kept the HUD scandal in the news, and given the damning reports issued by both houses, one might expect that the department would now be one of the government's best run and most efficient. Not a chance. Four years later, in January 1994, the GAO designated HUD as a "high-risk area," meaning it is an agency that is "especially vulnerable to waste, fraud, abuse, and mismanagement,"[23] the very problems "revealed" in the 1990 Congressional reports. In September of the same year, the Agency's Inspector General issued a report echoing the GAO report.[24] In March 1995, the GAO issued another report stating, "HUD has a long way to go" in resolving its problems."[25] Another GAO report in March 1996 stated "We believe that, for the foreseeable future, the agency will be high-risk in terms of its programs being vulnerable to waste, fraud and abuse."[26] In 1997 and 1999, GAO again reported the same thing,[27] and in March 1998 the HUD Inspector General reported that "management problems continue."[28] During 1996, HUD estimated that it provided almost $1 billion in overpayments on housing assistance.[29] Perhaps most telling, in 1997, HUD discovered that it had unknowingly accumulated $9.9 billion in unexpended budget authority that exceeded known program needs.[30] Almost twenty years after Congress began receiving reports of serious problems at HUD, and nine years after it undertook a major investigation of the agency, little had changed. HUD is a monument to the power and invulnerability of federal subsidy programs.

Much of the power behind HUD comes from real estate interests. The agency has the largest real estate portfolio and operation in the nation, selling about 55,000 properties each year.[31] It effectively provides over $20 billion annually in subsidies for that industry, and some of its most profitable projects are those involving HUD financing and rent guarantees. The nation's 3,400 Public Housing Authorities are vigorous HUD proponents because they are totally dependent on the agency for their existence. Of course, social welfare groups are also staunch supporters. Given this large and varied interest group, it is not surprising that at the same time that HUD is being lambasted by Republicans and Democrats alike, the same politicians are working to insure that its operations—and funding—remain largely unchanged. Politicians from states like New York, which receives $2 billion per year from HUD,[32] forget their ideological differences when it comes to subsidy programs of that magnitude. All the rhetoric to the contrary notwithstanding, Congress—not even one controlled by Republicans—does not really want to derail the gravy train. As conservative Republican and former HUD Secretary Jack Kemp points out, "When you get in power, you come to favor programs where you distribute the largesse."[33]

In support of its efforts to preserve HUD subsidies, the National Association of Homebuilders points out that only 4.1 million of the approximately 13.4 million eligible low-income renters in the U.S. receive housing assistance.[34] But the powerful lobbying organization does not point out that a substantial portion of federal subsidies for housing are primarily intended to enrich those who do not need help. The underlying philosophy is very much like that for highways: lots of funds for new construction and major renovation and little for maintenance. Indeed, the less spent on maintenance, the faster a new project deteriorates into one needing major renovation. The big money is in construction, not maintenance. Thus, we have the situation described by Peter D. Salins from the City University of New York,

A visit to any American city will reveal conditions of housing squalor probably unmatched in other wealthy countries, although even America's worst dwellings are actually quite spacious and amenity-laden by international standards.[35]

Professor Peter Drier of Occidental College and former director of housing for the City of Boston calls our method of providing low-income housing, "the most ineffective and unfair way you can imagine."[36] Take the Casa Gloria Apartments in Los Angeles, for example. The forty-six unit low-income housing project where a three-bedroom, two-bath apartment rents for $353 per month was completed at a cost of $233,000 per unit under the low-income housing tax credit program.[37] Only a federal subsidy program could produce such a preposterous result. For less than that, each family could have been provided a single family home. The approximate value of the rental subsidy can be estimated by calculating the monthly payment on a 30-year mortgage for $233,000. At an interest rate of 8 percent, it would come to $1,725, meaning that the monthly rent subsidy is something more than $1,372 per apartment when operating costs are considered. Even just renovating low-income housing under federal subsidy programs is ridiculously expensive— and incredibly lucrative. The Whiteclaw Hotel in Washington D.C. was turned into 35 apartments at a cost of $100,000 each.[38] The Chicago Housing Authority claims that 15,000 of its 40,000 public housing units need renovation at an average cost of $66,000 per unit.[39] It is interesting to note that, according to the GAO, the estimated replacement cost of the nation's federally supported public housing stock is $90 billion or about $64,000 per unit.[40] Presumably, that is the estimated cost to build new public housing. Yet we are subsidizing new construction at nearly four times that amount and renovations at almost twice that amount.

Only federal taxpayers would accommodate such nonsense. Compare that against some local and private low-income housing programs. The New York City Housing Partnership acquires vacant lots in Brooklyn and the Bronx from the City at no cost and arranges for private builders to erect two- and three-family homes on them.[41] Brand new two-family homes—in New York City—sold for $140,000 in 1993.[42] Even more remarkable, a consortium of New York churches financed the construction of 2,300 small single family row houses that sold for $59,000[43] at the same time that each Casa Gloria rental apartment was costing $233,000 in Los Angeles. For that matter, 84 Lumber Co., a building materials retailer with several hundred outlets around the nation, was selling a complete kit for a 1,200 square foot single family home for $40,000 in 1992.[44] That included everything but the land. While there is no way a federal program could be expected to achieve the efficiencies of a private one, the gross difference is to a great extent because of the different objectives of the two efforts: one is to supply low-cost housing, while the other is to subsidize a large and powerful special interest group.

HUD's low-income housing subsidies are just a part of the maze of federal programs that subsidize real estate. Other subsidizes, such as the mortgage interest deduction, have fueled a wasteful cycle whereby perfectly good housing is routinely abandoned in favor of new housing, creating a large supply of vacant housing throughout the country. According to the 1990 Census, there were over ten million vacant housing units in the U.S.[45] HUD incurs $200 million in subsidy costs annually for 100,000 vacant public housing units.[46] Many of these units are in poor condition because of a host of federal subsidy programs that maximize waste. Once the properties become run down, housing officials claim that it was a poor building design that caused the decay. That self-serving explanation masks the fact that the subsidy programs themselves are producing waste and decay. The programs are designed to support the housing industry, which is best served by construction projects. Atlanta's Techwood homes did not go from Roosevelt's "bright cheerful buildings" that provided quality, safe housing for years, to a notorious slum, that HUD Secretary Henry Cisneros watched demolished, because of the building design. It did so because of Congress's design. A design that included subsidizing the construction of 900 new apartments to replace the demolished Techwood.[47] The truth is that maximizing housing industry subsidy benefits necessitates maximizing waste.

About 30 percent of the households that receive federal rental assistance do so in the form of Section 8 certificates or vouchers, which they can use to rent an apartment of their choosing from the stock of private rental units.[48] The other 70 percent live in public housing units or private projects subsidized by HUD.[49] This latter type of assistance is known as project-based, while the former is called household-based. Project-based assistance programs are a root cause of many of the problems of our inner cities. Ronald Utt of the Heritage Foundation notes,

> By warehousing such large concentrations of the poor, often in deteriorated inner-city neighborhoods where much of the nation's urban public housing is located, Congress has created volatile social environments characterized by high crime, drug abuse, child neglect, and other social pathologies that tend not to occur as frequently with the less costly voucher program that allows assisted households to self-integrate into the community at large.[50]

And Marshall Kaplan states,

> Study after study shows that mobility increases income and job opportunities, . . . that concentrations of low-income people ex-

*acerbate local fiscal conditions, and that healthy central cities
are essential to the economic and social health of their suburbs.*[51]

This is not recently discovered information. For at least two decades, it
has been apparent that project-based assistance was concentrating the poor—to
their detriment—and exacerbating inner-city problems. At the same time, the
scandals surrounding federal housing programs nearly always center on HUD
financing and rent subsidies associated with project-based programs. Just on
the basis of the negative consequences for both the poor and taxpayers, it is
difficult to understand why project-based assistance was not terminated long
ago. However, the case for termination becomes even stronger when compar-
ing the costs of the two types of assistance. As the GAO reported to Congress,

*HUD directly subsidizes and /or insures over 20,000 multifamily
properties with about 2 million units . . . for a large proportion of
this housing, the government is paying more to house low-income
families than it would if these families received tenant-based assistance in the forms of certificates and vouchers to locate alternative privately-owned housing.*[52]

Despite some modest legislative changes recently, Congress continues
to fund project-based subsidies. In 1998, Congress passed legislation "over-
hauling" public housing. Housing Secretary Andrew Cuomo stated that the
objective was to transform projects from "segregated ghettos of poverty and
despair into economically integrated communities of opportunity."[53] The legislation has basically the same stated goals as Franklin Roosevelt's housing
program of the early 1930s. And it aims to achieve them by providing funds to
rehabilitate existing public housing and to tear down some of the projects that
Roosevelt built to achieve the very same thing. Just getting the federal government out of the housing business, which would benefit the poor and taxpayers, would simply be unacceptable to the construction industry and other powerful public housing interests.

In 1995, Secretary Cisneros testified that, on average, it cost $440 per
month to house a family with vouchers (household-based assistance) versus
$481 in public housing (project-based).[54] However, in that analysis, the $90
billion investment in public housing was considered a "sunk cost," and, therefore, was not included in the cost of project-based assistance.[55] On the other
hand, the voucher cost did include the capital cost of private housing, which
was also a sunk cost. To produce an accurate comparison of the relative costs,
Ronald Utt calculated the cost of public housing, including capital cost. He
concluded that the real cost of public housing was $935 per month, more than
double the cost of a voucher.[56]

Now, recall that the Census Bureau determined that there were ten
million vacant, private housing units in 1990. The bottom line then is: project-
based assistance is detrimental to the poor and cities, is riddled with waste,
fraud, and abuse, and costs taxpayers more than twice as much as household-

based assistance. Nevertheless, it has long been popular with Congress because it channels billions of dollars in subsidies to a powerful interest group. The nation's 3,400 Public Housing Authorities support project-based programs because they rightfully fear that conversion to vouchers would put them out of business. Instead of PHA's receiving, from the federal government, funds to mismanage public housing, vouchers would be given directly to those receiving housing assistance, which they could use at any project they desired—public or private. The PHA's would have to compete head-to-head in the market place. Many, if not most, would be driven out of business, much to the relief of the poor and taxpayers alike. Of course, companies involved with the federally-subsidized construction and renovation of low-income housing are staunch supporters of project-based assistance because it channels absurd amounts of tax dollars directly to them. Not in their wildest dreams could they imagine unsubsidized, low-income projects like two that HUD announced for Washington, D.C. and Baltimore with per unit costs of $186,500 and $340,000 respectively.[57] That type of largesse produces the very grateful constituents who are so valued by politicians— Democrats and Republicans alike.

During the 1970s and early 1980s, Congress offered developers some very sweet deals that have cost the taxpayers billions of dollars and now threaten to escalate into tens of billions. To induce developers to build low-income housing, HUD offered guaranteed rents that exceeded market rents. The program was a great success, resulting in 900,000 new project-based, assisted units.[58] As market rents rose, HUD increased its subsidies, when market rents fell, HUD maintained its subsidy level. Some properties received rents that were 75 percent above market rents.[59] Since an income property's value is a function of its income, developers were able to obtain financing well in excess of what market rents would justify. In 1996, about two-thirds of the 8,500 properties in the program were receiving rents that significantly exceeded the market rents for similar non-program apartments in the same housing market.[60] During the same year, total subsidies for these properties, many of which were in poor condition, cost $5 billion.[61] HUD Secretary Cisneros admitted, "We are now paying exorbitant subsidies on those properties, across the street from private apartments that are of the same quality and renting for less."[62] Nevertheless, the federal contracts were expiring and to keep the properties in the program, HUD paid even higher rents. The agency projected an increase in subsidy payments to $7 billion by 2007.[63]

Although HUD realized that the subsidies were scandalous, the government found itself stuck with them. The problem was that the exorbitant rent subsidies allowed developers to put very large loans on their properties, which consume the subsidies in debt service. Those loans are insured by the Federal Housing Administration (FHA), an agency of HUD. Cutting the subsidies could result in defaults on as much as $18 billion worth of insured mortgages.[64] In a classic subsidy-begets-subsidy scenario, in 1995, HUD proposed its Mark-to-Market plan which it claimed would "solve" the problem by reducing the rent subsidies and having the federal government take over part of the mortgage payments directly. According to the plan, not only would the government pay part of the developers' mortgages for them, but a special tax provision would exempt them from having to treat the free mortgage payments as income. It just does not get much better than that! Unless you are a taxpayer.

HUD estimated that the Mark-to-Market plan would cost $2.7 billion *more* over the first five years than continuing the existing scam.[65] But the plan's forecasted twenty-five year cost of an astounding $186 billion was expected to be $36 billion less than continuing the existing program.[66] No doubt delighted by such good news, Congress authorized the Mark-to-Market program in 1997 and established a new temporary bureaucracy, the Office of Multifamily Housing Assistance Restructuring, within HUD to administer it.[67] If history is any guide, we now have another temporary agency that will be around indefinitely.

The Federal Housing Administration was established during the Franklin Roosevelt Administration to insure private lenders against losses on mortgages that finance one to four unit dwellings. From the beginning, the primary mission of the agency was to support the construction industry by making U.S. taxpayers stand behind mortgage loans. The FHA receives premiums from borrowers with insured mortgages, which it uses to cover losses. This program has been self-sustaining since its inception and has not required any taxpayer subsidies.[68] While the federal government has no business being in the mortgage insurance business, the program has not yet been a burden on taxpayers. Nevertheless, with over $360 billion in outstanding single-family-home insurance, the risk to taxpayers is substantial.[69] According to the GAO, "The single most important determinant of a loan's foreclosure is the borrower's equity in the property . . . ," and FHA regulations allow the agency to insure loans where the borrower's equity is a minuscule 2.25 percent.[70] Yet, consider the GAO's opinion of the agency that has to protect the taxpayers from losses on its risky insurance,

> *HUD has had a history of fundamental management and organizational problems that put billions of these dollars at risk: an organizational structure that blurs accountability; inadequate information and financial management systems which make it much more difficult to establish adequate internal controls; and staff without the skills needed to effectively manage programs.[71]*

Virtually all federal programs expand in scope and FHA mortgage insurance is no exception. The agency's multifamily portfolio now includes $43 billion of insured mortgages on nursing homes, hospitals, student housing, co-operatives, condominiums, and apartment properties.[72] Apartments alone make up $32 billion of that amount.[73] While the single-family fund is a risk for taxpayers, the multifamily fund is a disaster. The FHA expects to lose $10 billion because of defaults on multifamily loans between 1995 and 2001.[74] That is over 23 percent of the value of its multifamily portfolio—but not high enough to alarm Congress. That is a large part of the problem. Preserving subsidy programs, even dysfunctional ones, is so important to politicians that it takes stupefying losses to get them to consider termination. FHA insurance for retirement service centers was available through the multifamily program until Congress terminated the coverage in 1991 because of wholesale loan defaults. Through September 1994, 46 percent of retirement service center loans were in default and another 18 percent were expected to default.[75] A subsidy program with a default rate approaching 64 percent is about what it takes to merit termination.

Another HUD agency, the Government National Mortgage Corporation (GNMA), guarantees the timely payment of principal and interest to holders of securities backed by government insured or guaranteed mortgages. Essentially, government-backed mortgages are gathered into pools, which then become collateral for GNMA-guaranteed securities sold to private and institutional investors. In 1997, GNMA had $531 billion in guaranteed securities outstanding, for which American taxpayers are fully responsible.[76] Through the FHA and GNMA, the federal government has transferred the risks of financing housing from bankers and investors to U.S. taxpayers, thereby insuring a virtually unlimited supply of money for the construction industry. Indeed, HUD makes it very plain:

> *The [GNMA] program's purpose is to attract nontraditional investors to the residential mortgage market by offering them a high-yield, risk-free (from loss of principal), government-guaranteed security without the servicing obligation associated with a mortgage loan portfolio.*[77]

Some of the mortgages that back GNMA securities are those issued by the Rural Housing and Community Development Service (RHCDS), which is an agency of the U.S. Department of Agriculture formed by joining two former agencies, the Farmer's Home Administration and the Rural Development Administration. Why the USDA should be in the business of subsidizing the housing industry is not clear, but the RHCDS has made $49 billion in subsidized loans since 1950.[78] A provision of the Housing Act of 1949, which created the RHCDS subsidy program, provides another look at the difference between the intent of subsidy legislation and the reality of how the programs are administered. The law was intended to help rural families buy their first homes, and provided interest subsidies to help with the cost. But the law requires that up to 78 percent of the total subsidy amount be repaid to the government when the house is sold or vacated.[79] As is the case with virtually all federal subsidies, money given is not paid back, regardless of the legal requirement. As of September 1994, RHCDS had recovered less than 10 percent of the $5.8 billion in subsidies on sold or vacated homes, resulting in a loss to the taxpayers of $5.1 billion.[80] With an additional $7.1 billion in outstanding loan subsidies,[81] the taxpayers can expect to lose another $6.3 billion in the future. Even when just a portion of a generous federal subsidy is supposed to be repaid, it does not happen. When Congress is informed that the required repayments are not being made, the response is a collective shrug. The important thing is to keep money flowing to the housing industry. Mission accomplished.

It is interesting to note that according to the *Green Book* published by the House Ways and Means Committee,

> *The primary purpose of housing assistance has always been to improve housing quality and to reduce housing costs for lower income households. Other goals have included promoting residential construction . . . .*[82]

In theory then, the primary objective is to help the poor, while subsidizing the housing industry has been a secondary goal. But the CBO reported that in 1989, "Recipients of federal housing assistance had average income that was 22 percent higher than the average of very low income households that did not receive aid."[83] In fact, the income of housing assistance recipients is likely considerably higher than that. A GAO study of that same year found that 21 percent of recipients examined had understated their annual income by an average of $3,755.[84] As such, federal housing subsidies are not reaching those most in need. At the same time, only 22 percent of those deemed eligible actually receive housing assistance.[85] Based on those facts, federal housing programs are clearly failing to achieve their primary objective. However, based on the extraordinary cost of HUD projects and the enormous surplus of housing in the U.S., the programs have been an unqualified success at achieving their secondary objective.

Another way to evaluate the impact of a federal subsidy program is to estimate the effect that reducing or eliminating the subsidy would have on the beneficiaries of the program. The GAO undertook just such an analysis of FHA mortgage insurance in 1997. It found that reducing the government's share of mortgage insurance to between 25 percent and 50 percent of the loan value—the same level as Veteran's Administration mortgage insurance—and consequently increasing private lenders' risk associated with FHA loans from about 2.5 percent to as much as 50 percent, would result in a increase in mortgage interest rates of just one-quarter to one-half of a percent.[86] Moreover, the agency reported that the increased revenue from a one-quarter percent increase in interest rates would produce more than enough revenue to lenders to cover any losses that they would incur if FHA's insurance coverage were reduced.[87] In other words, neither borrowers nor lenders would be significantly impacted by a major pullback by the FHA from the mortgage market. Indeed, if the FHA were to limit its mortgage insurance to less than 50 percent of loan value, commercial insurers would very likely displace it completely in the market. Nonetheless, the FHA has $1 trillion in outstanding mortgage insurance and federally guaranteed mortgage-backed securities that represent a $1 trillion liability for U.S. taxpayers.[88]

Welfare is certainly another area where it is difficult to find a constitutional basis for the federal government's extensive involvement. As University of Texas Professor Marvin Lansky has observed, the Constitution's charge is to *provide* for the common defense, but to *promote* the general welfare.[89] As in so many other areas, federal politicians optimistically blundered in with both feet. In 1963, President Johnson wrote to Guy Justis, then president of the American Public Welfare Association, about recent expansions of federal welfare programs, including the passage of the 1962 Public Welfare Amendments to the Social Security Act. Johnson noted, "The new Public Welfare Amendments have given us vital new tools with which to reduce dependency where it exists, to help many of our needy to self-reliance, and to prevent poverty where it threatens."[90] During the next few years, he saw several more major federal welfare programs passed as part of his War on Poverty, and spending on social subsidies skyrocketed. Not surprisingly, between 1965 and 1975, welfare caseloads quadrupled. The results have been anything but what President Johnson expected. Rather than promoting self-reliance and reducing dependency, the massive subsidies created pervasive dependence and social disintegration, which has transformed the politics of poverty. As NYU Professor Lawrence Mead writes,

> *Progressive politics [before the mid-1960s] was about how to advance working people while [present] dependency politics is largely about how to cope with nonworking people. Nonwork— by which I mean a failure to work or look for work by the employable—is the immediate reason for destitution and dependency among most of today's working-aged poor . . . poverty is very uncommon among adults who work usual hours at any legal wage.*[91]

Most Americans, including many well-intentioned liberals, are distraught over the dismal results from the expenditure of trillions of tax dollars to fight poverty over the past 30 years. Federal spending on means-tested subsidy programs ballooned from $4 billion in 1960[92] to $222 billion in 1999.[93] Even after one of the longest economic booms on record, which saw unemployment drop to historic lows, the official poverty rate in 1998 stood at about the same level as it was in 1987.[94] While there are 80 federal programs that come under the "welfare" heading, the largest five—Medicaid, Food Stamps, Temporary Assistance for Needy Families (which replaced Aid to Families with Dependent Children in 1996), Supplemental Security Income, and Section 8 Housing Assistance—account for about 65 percent of the spending.[95] All those programs but Temporary Assistance to Needy Families (TANF) have been covered in previous chapters.

For many years, Aid to Families with Dependent Children (AFDC) was the program the public generally associated with welfare. Surveys found that many Americans believed that it was one of the federal government's largest expenditures. However, at about its peak in 1993, AFDC accounted for just $13.8 billion, or just one percent of federal spending.[96] It also amounted to only six percent of total means-tested, low-income federal subsidy spending. Because the states paid from 20 to 50 percent of program costs, total AFDC spending in 1993 came to $25.2 billion.[97] By itself, AFDC was never a significant part of federal spending, nor did it provide a large enough subsidy to induce a significant number of people to choose welfare over work. The average monthly benefit per family in 1993 was only $373, including both state and federal contributions.[98] Almost alone among subsidy programs, AFDC spending declined significantly, an inflation adjusted 45 percent between 1970 and 1993.[99]

It is likely that the disproportionate public attention focused on AFDC was because benefits were paid in cash, and that, although they were able-bodied, the great majority of beneficiaries did not work. The political response was a steady stream of rhetoric and reform proposals, most aimed not at the real source of the problems of dependency, illegitimacy, and social breakdown, but at the tip of the iceberg that caught the public's attention: AFDC. In fact, it was just a very small part of the nation's most serious problem, due in part, to a tangle of 80 federal social welfare programs now costing the U.S. Treasury over $220 billion annually. Together, these programs created serious disincentives against work and marriage that helped to tear apart the social fabric of the nation.

Congresswoman Eleanor Holmes Norton has written, "No reform will work if welfare offers a better break than personal responsibility, as it often does today."[100] Therein lies the real crux of the matter. The wide array of federal social subsidies allowed a large number of Americans to avoid personal responsibility for providing food, shelter, clothing, and medical care for themselves and their children, but the problem goes much deeper. Federal programs also encouraged them to escape the responsibility for properly raising their children, which has devastating consequences for society. It does not take a village to raise a child. It takes two dedicated parents. The role of the village is to lend support to the family, not the child. As sociologist Graham Kinloch writes,

> *The family is vital to primary socialization [of children] for many reasons. One is that it teaches socially acceptable ways of behaving. Another is that its role structure, which is based on parental power and on age and sex roles, represents a microcosm of the larger society—a miniature version that prepares children for later participation in society as a whole.*[101]

Clearly, the most destructive aspect of welfare has been that it subsidizes, and therefore encourages single parenthood. It is not the cause of single parenthood, but it is a significant factor. In 1995, four million babies were born to teenage mothers, three quarters of whom were unmarried.[102] The cost to the federal government for welfare programs for families of teenagers totaled an estimated $39 billion in 1995.[103] Beginning in the late 1960s, Americans began experimenting with alternative family structures. Divorce, out-of-wedlock birth, and single parenthood became acceptable at all levels of society as the focus changed from the well being of children to the well being of adults.

While the lot of many adults did improve, the result for children has been disastrous. As sociologist Barbara Dafoe Whitehead observed,

> *All too often the adult quest for freedom, independence, and choice in family relationships conflicts with a child's developmental needs for stability, constancy, harmony, and permanence in family life. In short, family disruption creates a deep division between parents' interests and the interests of children.* [104]

We now know that children raised in single-parent families are considerably worse off than those raised in two-parent families. They are six times more likely to be poor; two to three times as likely to have emotional and behavioral problems; and they are more likely to drop out of high school, get pregnant as teenagers, abuse drugs, and to break the law.[105] That goes for both rich and poor children, black and white. While wealthy single parents can delude themselves into thinking that they can succeed because they are economically secure, the great majority of single-parents are financially at-risk. Whitehead notes, "For the vast majority of single mothers, the economic spectrum turns out to be narrow, running between precarious and desperate."[106] But federal social subsidies can change that equation. As UCLA's James Q. Wilson observed,

> *. . . most [young girls] would like a separate household as well, out from under the thumb of their parents. Many would like babies because they find babies appealing, and they want to care for them . . . they discover government programs that promise, via AFDC, food stamps, housing subsidies, and Medicaid, that they can have an independent household. They often jump at the chance and take some delight at the fact that they can do this without the services of a male to assist them. The ones who lose are the children.* [107]

Research by June O'Neill, formerly Director of the Congressional Budget Office, showed that after controlling for other factors such as income, parental education, and neighborhood, a 50 percent increase in the monthly value of AFDC and food stamp benefits led to a 43 percent increase in the number of out-of-wedlock births.[108] Other studies show conclusively that after controlling for income, and for every racial or ethnic group, children raised in single-parent families headed by never-married young women are materially worse off in terms of school achievements, delinquency, and emotional problems.[109] Moreover, contrary to popular belief, illegitimacy, not race, is the key correlating factor in violent crime.[110] Whitehead cautions against failing to address the desperate plight of children in single-parent families,

> *If we fail to come to terms with the relationship between family structure and declining child well-being then it will be increas-*

ingly difficult to improve children's life prospects, no matter how
many new programs the federal government funds.[111]

The federal government did not intend to subsidize what amounts to wholesale child neglect. When the Social Security Act was passed in 1935, it included the ADC program—Aid to Dependent Children. It was a fund for widows and orphans, and less than 3 percent of the children receiving benefits qualified because their mother was not married to their father.[112] ADC was later renamed Aid to Families with Dependent Children (AFDC), and Congress greatly expanded the program to provide,

> *. . . cash welfare payments to needy children who have been de-*
> *prived of parental support or care because their father or mother*
> *is absent from the home continuously, is incapacitated, is de-*
> *ceased, or is unemployed.*[113]

It is not difficult to see how such a program could be taken advantage of and how it quickly got out of control. As Missouri Senator John Ashcroft stated, "Current policy encourages parents to abdicate financial and moral responsibility for their children to the government."[114] The provision requiring continuous absence of one parent provided yet another powerful incentive for the formation and continuance of single-parent families. A single mother lost her welfare benefits if she married an employed man—even if he was the father of her children. Therefore, their combined income was significantly higher if they did not marry. By 1992, only 1.6 percent of children on AFDC qualified because a parent was deceased. The program that Franklin Roosevelt designed for orphans was turned upside down as parents responded to the incentives provided by federal subsidies, not as intended by Congress, but as the law allowed. (Similar subsidies in Sweden have produced the same result.) Rather than improving the lot of children, these programs helped sustain large numbers of them in very high-risk family structures for which many of them, and society, are paying a very stiff price. The intentions were good, but as Kay C. James, Dean of Regent University and former Secretary of Health and Human Resources for Virginia, has concluded,

> *Despite the best intentions of those who created these policies,*
> *the government cannot be our parents, cannot teach our children*
> *about responsibility and character, cannot regulate individual*
> *behavior, and cannot create entrepreneurial opportunities.*[115]

The beneficiaries of virtually every federal subsidy program have consistently been able to ascertain how to maximize those benefits. That includes everyone from high school dropouts to university professors. In addition to correctly assessing the incentives of welfare subsidies for family structure, many poor Americans have recognized the incentives provided by federal subsidies for not working, which they often pass on to their children. As Nobel laureate Gary S. Becker has observed, "Children that spend long periods on welfare begin to accept that it is more normal to be supported by the government than to be financially and psychologically independent."[116] Again, welfare was not the sole factor in creating a large class of nonworking poor, but it was a significant factor. Consider the findings of a Cato Institute study, *The Work vs. Welfare Trade-Off*. The study calculated the value of a full package of welfare benefits for every state and factored in the additional value derived from those benefits being tax-free. In 40 states welfare paid more than an $8.00 per hour job; in seventeen states it paid more than $10.00 per hour; and in eight states, welfare paid at least the equivalent of a $25,000 per year job.[117] (While not all welfare recipients receive the full package of benefits, many do, and they tend to be long-term welfare recipients.) The sharp rise in the number of nonworking poor paralleled the dramatic increase in welfare benefits that began with President Johnson's War on Poverty. Lawrence Mead notes that before the 1960s,

> . . . Americans, rich and poor alike, scrambled to support their families on their wages with little expectation of direct help from the government . . . . For the first time [in the 1960s] liberal politicians, intellectuals, and poverty lawyers were prepared to characterize nonworking adults as helpless victims who could not be expected to function.[118]

Many of the poor were not quite as dysfunctional as their supporters contended. They were very capable of determining the value of the subsidy package available to them if they did not work compared to the income available from working. As the Cato study found, not only was the welfare package frequently more generous, but not working meant nearly unlimited leisure time as well. Studies have shown that in the long term, work is more beneficial than welfare, but short-term thinking is clearly widespread throughout the population and is not just a characteristic of the poor. By the mid-1990s, the nonworking poor considerably outnumbered the working poor.[119] In addition, nearly 70 percent of the nonworking poor did not even look for work.[120] As Harriet Dawson, a job counselor for welfare recipients at Chicago's notorious Cabrini-Green housing project observed, "There would be jobs, and even careers, for the chronically poor if they were prepared to work."[121] The poor have proved just as adept as wealthy subsidy recipients at responding to the subsidy incentives rather than the stated intentions of the subsidy programs.

There are those who maintained that the nonworking poor want to work, but that work is either unavailable or other impediments prevent them from doing so. The data suggest otherwise. Lawrence Mead found that none of the so-called "barriers to employment"—young children, child care, employability, and disability—were real barriers to the great majority of welfare recipients.[122] Nor has a lack of jobs been a real problem. Perhaps the best testament to the availability of jobs is the large number of immigrants who enter this country and have no trouble finding work. All around us, we see immigrants comprising an ever-increasing percentage of the work force in lower-end jobs, and studies have shown that blacks are not losing jobs to immigrants.[123] The immigrants are simply taking jobs that poor Americans do not want. It is interesting to note that a study by Barry R. Chiswick of the University of Illinois found that the average pay of *illegal* immigrants was well above the minimum wage.[124] It is, therefore, not surprising that native-born Americans are twice as likely to be on welfare as immigrants, according to the Urban Institute.[125] Indeed, according to the Joint Economic Committee, only 7 percent of nonworking poor adults in 1990 indicated that they were not working because they could not find work.[126] Many claimed they would work if they found the "right" job, but, because of the subsidy option, they did not have to take a job they did not want. The fact is that most who live in poverty and draw on social subsidies could work and lift themselves out of poverty—recall Mead's finding that poverty is very uncommon among adults who work usual hours at any legal wage—but they choose not to.

The concept of poverty is one that is controversial and the federal definition shows clear signs of the powerful influence of those in the poverty industry—the activists, politicians, agencies, administrators, and contractors who depend on massive federal poverty programs for their political support or livelihood. The formula for calculating the official poverty rate was established by Social Security economist Mollie Orshansky in 1963 using data from a 1955 Household Food Consumption Survey.[127] The formula was based on the concept that the average American family spent one-third of its cash income on food. Applying the formula backwards, Eugene Smolensky and Robert Plotnick of the University of Wisconsin found that 70 to 80 percent of all Americans would have been characterized as living in poverty in 1900.[128] Despite the simplistic nature of the calculation, and the fact that today's average family spends only 20 percent of their income on food, the definition of the poverty line remains virtually unchanged.[129]

One of the major flaws with the present formula is that the calculation of family income only includes cash income, while ignoring the considerable value of such subsidies as Medicaid, housing assistance, income from the Earned Income Tax Credit, food stamps, and other in-kind benefits. Thus, over $200 billion in annual welfare program benefits are ignored when determining the number of Americans in poverty. This presents the following conundrum as *National Review* reported,

> *[The Census Bureau] defines as "poor" any family which has an "income" below the official poverty threshold ($14,335 for a family of four in 1992). In 1992 federal, state and local governments spent a record $306 billion on welfare programs for low-income Americans, more than three times the amount needed to lift all "poor" Americans above the poverty threshold. And yet official statistics show that the percentage of Americans who are poor is now at the same level as when the War on Poverty started in the mid-1960s.[130]*

Another significant problem with the official poverty level is that it attempts to measure income rather than consumption, which is a much more accurate measure of standard of living. A study by Christopher Jenks of Northwestern University and Susan Mayer of the University of Chicago found that in 1988-89, the poorest 10 percent of all households with children reported a mean income of $5,588, but acknowledged spending an average of $13,558.[131] Obviously, if the poorest families in America are spending 242 percent more than is reported in income, then they are considerably better off than the income data suggests. Indeed, the per capita expenditures of the lowest-income one-fifth of the U.S. population today exceeds the inflation-adjusted, per capita income of the average American household in 1960.[132] As Nicholas Eberstadt points out,

> *. . . material deprivation and material poverty are conditions defined by consumption levels. They relate directly to a household's purchasing power, to its ability to obtain goods and services. The so-called poverty rate, however, does not even look at consumption levels: it focuses instead on reported income levels.*[133]

Then too, there is the question of what constitutes material poverty. Among Americans below the official poverty line, nearly 40 percent own their own homes, typically, a three bedroom house with a garage and porch.[134] Seventy-two percent own at least one car, 92 percent have color televisions, 60 percent have microwave ovens, and 20 percent have a dishwasher.[135] A European study found that the poorest Americans still enjoy higher living standards than the poor in social-welfare states like Germany and Sweden.[136] Poor Americans eat more meat than the general population in Western Europe,[137] and as we have already seen, their principal nutritional problem is obesity, not hunger. The poor actually have a higher obesity rate than those with above-poverty incomes.[138] The Heritage Foundation's Robert Rector has suggested that if those in poverty were determined by asking who is hungry, who lives in overcrowded or unheated housing, who is inadequately clothed, or who needs a car and does not have one, the result would be a tiny percentage.

All these problems with the definition of poverty are well known in official circles. In fact, the National Research Council undertook a study of poverty measurement, and the two people who directed the study, Constance Citro and Robert Michael, in 1995 concluded,

> *The good news is that these flaws in the poverty measure can be fixed, and at very little cost. Data with which to estimate after-tax income, the value of in-kind transfers, and such nondiscretionary expenses as child support payments and child care expenses are available now—and, indeed, in many instances, have been available for over a decade. What is needed is political leadership to face the facts and fix the official poverty measurement.*[139]

Census Bureau poverty figures for 1995, showed that 38.1 million people, or 14.5 percent of the population, were living below the poverty line. That percentage is unchanged from the number in 1960—before the expenditure of $5 trillion in federal social welfare subsidies. By contrast, economist David T. Slesnick of the University of Texas devised a more comprehensive method of measuring poverty that showed the rate at 31 percent in 1949, 13 percent in 1965, and only 2 percent by 1989.[140] Citro and Michael characterized the Census Bureau's method of calculation as, "so flawed that they cannot possibly reflect the reality of poverty."[141] The obvious question is, why does the government continue to grossly overstate the poverty situation in this country? The answer is that it serves the powerful poverty industry that trillions of dollars in federal social subsidies have spawned.

The poverty industry is comprised of hundreds of government agencies and private charitable organizations (which receive billions of dollars in federal funds), and tens of thousands of social workers, civil servants, and other professionals "whose business literally rides on the backs of the poor," according to Robert Woodson, President of the National Center for Neighborhood.[142] These politically powerful interests need bloated poverty numbers to induce the taxpayers to continue funding for programs that they abhor. Woodson adds that 75 percent of aid to the poor goes not to them but to those who serve the poor, and that, "we are now faced with the problem of how to help the poor survive their champions."[143] Therein lies the answer to the *National Review's* conundrum. Between state, local, and federal governments, over $300 billion is spent each year on the poor; that has created a large and powerful interest group that lobbies heavily for the continuation and expansion of welfare programs, whether they are effective or not. Since many state-administered programs receive federal matching funds, each state's poverty industry also has a vested interest in expanding federal subsidies. As Senator Nancy Kassebaum has observed,

> *The current welfare system is a constant push-and-pull between state and federal bureaucracies. This may suit the needs of government bureaucracy. It clearly is not meeting the needs of children in poverty.*[144]

Clearly, a large number of politicians are also dependent on welfare—for their political lives. Jacqueline J. Cissell, a former welfare recipient and Director of Social Policy for the Indiana Family Institute, suggests that the dedication of liberals to welfare programs that have precipitated widespread dependency has more to do with political support than concern for the poor:

> *The left has developed for itself a large constituency by this so-called care of the poor, and when these people become self-reliant, the left will lose their pets, and then what will they do?*[145]

The core of the poverty industry is a complex web of often-competing bureaucracies within the federal government that frequently have overlapping missions. To protect their funding, they tend to work independently or even at cross-purposes to one another. Consider the following GAO findings:

- *The federal government assists distressed urban communi-ties and their residents through a complex system involving at least twelve federal departments and agencies. Together, these agencies administer hundreds of programs in the ar-eas of housing, economic development, and social serv-ices.*[146]

- *Historically, there has been little coordination among the many federal departments and agencies that have respon-sibility for administering the programs that can be used to assist distressed communities. Agencies have tended not to coordinate efforts with one another because they have been protective of their own resources and separate organiza-tional missions. In addition, efforts that have been under-taken have generally been unsuccessful.*[147]

Federal agencies also act to protect welfare programs that benefit their core constituencies. For example, the Department of Agriculture was reluctant to approve waivers for state welfare demonstration programs that might act to reduce farm subsidies. USDA would not grant approval of plans by Oregon and Mississippi that would have allowed them to "cash-out" food stamps—give recipients cash instead of food stamps—because it would have reduced de-mand for surplus farm commodities.[148] Whether the plans would have im-proved the efficiency of the states' welfare programs or the condition of the welfare recipients was not important.

Other not-so-obvious interests have a big stake in welfare spending. Academia, for example. Between 1973 and 1977 alone, 3,400 evaluation stud-ies were performed for federal agencies, mainly those dealing with social pol-icy.[149] Research spending by federal poverty-related programs rose from $30 million in 1965 to around $300 million in 1980.[150] Public employee labor un-ions have been strong supporters of the status quo and vehement opponents of welfare reform efforts. The 1.3 million-member American Federation of State County and Municipal Employees (AFSCME) strongly opposed the Family Support Act of 1988 because it contained mandatory work provisions.[151] The Service Employee International Union with 1 million public employee mem-bers joined AFSCME in opposing welfare reform efforts in 1994 for the same reason.[152] The unions' concern is that if welfare recipients are forced to work, the new entrants in the labor force could offer competition for their members. Charities that once relied on private donations to help the poor have become increasingly dependent on grants from the federal government for funding.

Some have virtually become federal agencies. In his book *Privatizing Federal Spending*, Stuart M. Butler writes,

> *Research and advocacy, often funded by the federal government itself, have been key factors in lobbying efforts for federal programs. . . . Given that those who choose a career in the federal government generally favor federal solutions to problems, and given that researchers or contractors seeking government work have little incentive to disillusion career officials, it is common for a close working relationship to develop.*[153]

Thus, a diverse group of interests including academics, lawyers, politicians, social workers, government bureaucrats, labor unions, and charities have a strong vested interest in the continuation of massive welfare subsidies. Unfortunately, they have a much larger voice in Washington than either of the interests suffering under the bloated welfare system: the poor and the taxpayers.

Based on reform experiments in several states, Congress and President Clinton proclaimed "the end of welfare as we know it" with the passage of a welfare reform law in August 1996. Democrats were horrified that Clinton signed the bill, with Democratic Party Chairman Senator Christopher Dodd calling his action "unconscionable."[154] Some members of the Clinton Administration resigned after the president signed the bill. The Personal Responsibility and Work Opportunity Act, popularly known as the Welfare Reform Act, replaced the AFDC program with the TANF program that focuses on *requiring the states* to force welfare recipients to find a job after two years or face loss of benefits. However, it is unclear whether even the Republicans really wanted the bill to become law. Many were hoping to gain a campaign issue from a Clinton veto. To their surprise, Clinton signed the bill, which led the *Washington Post* to opine,

> *For only the terminally gullible could think after this much unashamed waffling and gyrating on Bill Clinton's part that his decision to sign the bill has anything to do with principle or substance . . . .*[155]

The law was definitely a step in the right direction, eliminating AFDC's entitlement to cash welfare benefits and reducing the subsidy bias against working. Under AFDC, Americans who met certain criteria were entitled to federal and state welfare benefits. Under TANF, however, the federal government gives a fixed block grant—$16.38 billion annually from 1997 to 2002—to the states. They have considerable flexibility in using the funds to meet broad welfare objectives. The states are required to continue to spend their own funds in what is termed Maintenance-of-Effort requirements. Generally, they must continue to spend at least 75 percent of the amount they spent in 1994 as their share of the joint federal-state AFDC program. The reform law also restricted food stamp benefits for legal immigrants and able-bodied adults without dependents.

When the law was passed, it was claimed that it would cut welfare spending by a projected $56 billion over six years,[156] largely by terminating benefits for about 650,000 legal immigrants.[157] (The politicians did nothing about the problem of the 300,000 illegal aliens that enter the U.S. every year[158]—clearly a federal responsibility—and who Rice University's Donald Huddle estimates cost U.S. taxpayers over $19 billion in 1993.[159]) Indeed, the primary intent of the law was to cut federal welfare spending. But the suddenly-terminated legal immigrants did not just disappear. So an immigration law passed shortly after the Welfare Reform Act created a huge loophole by granting an exemption to any legal immigrant who *claimed* spousal or child abuse.[160] Then, the Fiscal Year 1997 Supplemental Appropriations Act granted the states the authority to purchase food stamps from the federal government— at full cost—to provide state-funded assistance to legal immigrants.[161] Next, the 1997 Balanced Budget Act allowed the states to exempt additional able-bodied adults without dependents from the work requirement contained in the Welfare Reform Act, raising the total number exempted to about 50 percent of the 2.5 million receiving benefits prior to the reform legislation.[162]

The effect of the several amendments was simply to transfer most of the costs claimed as savings from the welfare reform law from the federal government to the states. Finally, the Clinton Administration turned what was now essentially a cost transfer program to one where the states costs increased more than federal costs decreased. It issued a ruling that all federal workplace regulations applied to "workfare"—requiring welfare beneficiaries to perform community service in exchange for their benefits. That meant that payroll taxes, workers' compensation, family leave, job protection, and the Davis Bacon requirement to pay prevailing union wages all applied to workfare participants who were doing such jobs as cleaning up parks. The net effect was to largely kill the states' workfare programs. The Welfare Reform Act's intended objectives of cutting welfare costs and requiring welfare recipients to work were mostly undone only a year after the legislation's passage.

President Clinton and other politicians have claimed that the 1996 Welfare Reform Act dramatically reduced welfare roles, and there is no doubt that it has pushed many people into the workforce. Between 1994 and 1999 the number of welfare recipients dropped 43 percent to about eight million.[163] However, much of that drop was due to the booming economy, and a significant portion of the decline occurred before the reform legislation took effect. For instance, Wisconsin's caseload fell 49 percent between 1987 and 1996.[164] The real impact of the legislation started to be felt in mid-1999 when those families who had received benefits for two continuous years or who had recieved a total of five years of benefits began being cut off. By 2002, half of all single parents on welfare must be working 30 hours per week or they, too, are supposed to be cut off. If that really happens, those terminations will result in some hardship, particularly for the children of the former welfare recipients. Thirty years of perverse welfare incentives have resulted in hundreds of thousands of damaged and abused children that the new law tries to ignore. Regarding these children, Senator Daniel Patrick Moynihan, an acknowledged expert on welfare, said, " . . . the premise of this legislation is that the behavior of certain adults can be changed by making the lives of their children as wretched as possible."[165] Already, an estimated 1.8 million children qualify for welfare although their parents do not.[166] This has set up another perverse incentive situation where frequently middle-class Americans who are raising welfare children of relatives are receiving welfare benefits on the children's behalf. During the period when many welfare recipients are having their benefits terminated, we can also expect the economy to slow and unemployment to increase. As the economy cools off, it is a near certainty that a significant number of recently employed former welfare recipients will find themselves out of a job again.

We have quite a bit of previous experience with many of the training and work provisions that were incorporated into the Welfare Reform Act, and the results were not good. While some of the programs were simply ineffective, a good share of the blame goes to decades of destructive policies that left many welfare recipients so ill-equipped to work that even the best training programs could not help. The Work Incentive Program, passed in 1967, required employable AFDC recipients to look for work. It raised earnings on average by less than $1,000 per year, and there is no evidence that it reduced dependency.[167] In the 1970s, the Comprehensive Employment and Training Act ended up being an additional welfare program—largely for men. The Family Support Act of 1988 also contained a job training program (JOBS) and a work requirement, but $13 billion over seven years resulted in fewer than one percent of welfare recipients going to work.[168]

A frequently cited problem with previous efforts to get welfare recipients to work has been underfunding. Politicians are generally unwilling to acknowledge, for obvious reasons, the size of the dependency problem that decades of debilitating welfare subsidies have brought. Moreover, welfare is a very sore subject with taxpayers—mostly because they tend to overestimate the percentage of their tax dollars that the programs consume. As such, politicians are prone to look for silver bullets that will produce miraculous results for very little money. Thus, we have had one new program after another, none of which is funded at a level that is likely to draw too much attention. But all the research and demonstration programs have found that a substantial increase in spending is necessary to address the existing problem of dependency. Even then, results are modest. Judith M. Gueron is president of Manpower Demonstration Research Corp., a nonprofit research organization that has evaluated the results of a number of state workfare demonstration programs. She concludes,

> *Broader change will require a substantial up-front investment of funds and serious, sustained efforts to change local welfare offices. This may seem mundane, but changing a law is only the first step toward changing reality.*[169]

Perhaps the most significant aspect of the Welfare Reform Act was that it changed the traditional federal-state funding mechanism in favor of federal block grants—annual lump sums paid to the states, which the states must use within federal guidelines. The primary intent was to limit federal liability for future growth in welfare benefits and caseloads by transferring all the responsibility but only a fixed amount of funding to the states, and the block grant mechanism achieves that end nicely. However, for sheer lack of common sense, it is difficult to beat block grants. Because virtually all federal taxpayers reside in states, block grants result in the following inefficient and nonsensical cycle: The federal government collects taxes from residents of a state, expends a portion of the funds on its own bureaucracy, and then sends the balance of the funds back to the state they came from with a bunch of strings attached. Perhaps even worse, the state gets to spend money that it does not have to raise in taxes because block grant funds come from federal not state taxes. There is hardly any greater incentive for government overspending than to give it spending authority over funds for which the elected officials are not accountable to their own taxpayers.

Nor is the history of federal block grants encouraging. Commenting on past federal block grants, John DiIulio, a public policy professor at Princeton University, says "You might as well have taken the money up in an airplane and thrown it out the window."[170] First of all, the federal government does not even know the outcome of much of the spending over which it has direct control. The GAO found that the Department of Health and Human Services (HHS) did not know whether the $8 billion spent on the JOBS program ($5.4 billion of which was federal funds)[171] between 1991 and 1995 was reducing welfare dependency or not.[172] Block grants are much tougher to monitor. The federal government already has fifteen block grant programs with annual funding of $32 billion.[173] In 1995, after reviewing those programs and considering the ramifications for block granting the much larger welfare programs, the GAO concluded,

> *. . . problems persist in the kinds of information available for the Congress and program managers to effectively oversee block grants . . . state flexibility was reduced as funding constraints were added to block grants over time . . . today's challenges are likely to be greater. The programs being considered for inclusion in block grants not only are much larger but also, in some cases, such as AFDC, which provides cash assistance to the poor, are fundamentally different from those programs included in the 1981 block grants.*[174]

A secondary objective of the welfare block grant is to increase the states' flexibility in running their welfare programs. However, the clear implication of past programs is that there is virtually no chance that the federal government will allow the states to run their own programs for very long. Indeed, the Welfare Reform Act had just barely gone into effect when the U.S. Labor

Department ordered the states to adhere to federal employment regulations, a huge setback for many state programs. Thus, after a short period of increased flexibility, states will find ever more strings and constraints attached to their welfare block grant. James L. Sundquist, a former official in the Johnson Administration who helped craft the War on Poverty program, noted back in 1968 that the federal government is loathe to allow local welfare programs to work:

> *The central administrative question is whether the federal government will allow any local system to work. On the one hand it has set up a series of locally based decision-making mechanisms . . . . On the other hand, it has insisted on launching programs that bypass these very structures and upon making the essential decisions itself.* [175]

One outcome is certain: The states, shortchanged from the beginning, will have to come up with more and more of their own funds to handle the many problems created by federal welfare subsidies that were suddenly dumped on them. In the final analysis, the Personal Responsibility and Work Opportunity Act was a little much-needed reform and a lot of welfare dumping. Having created a monster, the federal government devised tough new rules for the states and simply walked away from the intractable mess that it spent decades creating through perverse subsidies. It transferred part of the funds, but all of the problems to the states and declared it to be the end of welfare as we have known it. Then, promptly after enacting the law, the politicians began undoing it—at the expense of the states. As we have seen repeatedly, subsidy beneficiaries and interests skillfully maximize their benefits. After a small step in the right direction, federal politicians quickly backslid under pressure from the welfare industry, and eventually they will find their problem thrown right back in their laps.

Probably the area where the disastrous effects of federal housing and welfare subsidies are most concentrated, is in urban public schools. Nobel laureate Milton Freidman has written that,

> *There is no respect in which inhabitants of a low-income neighborhood are so disadvantaged as in the kind of schooling they can get for their children.* [176]

By concentrating the poor in inner cities and relieving poor parents of much of their parental responsibility, federal social subsidies helped create a situation where teaching and learning has become all but impossible in many urban schools. Physical decay, drugs, violence, disruptive behavior, and lack of parental involvement and support have created environments where education simply cannot take place. Secretary of Education Richard Riley termed many of the nation's classrooms "war zones."[177] Nearly half the students attending public high schools in Los Angeles and more than half in Chicago drop out before graduation.[178] Nationally, two thousand students drop out of school each day.[179] While many in the education establishment blame the disastrous state of our public schools on lack of funding, that is clearly not the case. The performance of public schools has steadily declined even as funding has been skyrocketing. Between 1979 and 1992, while public school enrollment was declining, total expenditures for public elementary and secondary education increased by 40 percent.[180] In total, Americans spent $635 billion on education in 1998.[181] Despite outspending virtually every other nation in the world, America's children simply do not know as much as foreign children. In an international math test taken by thirteen year olds in 1991, the U.S. ranked fourteenth.[182] The results in 1998 were even worse: Out of twenty-one industrialized nations, American high school seniors placed sixteenth in general science, nineteenth in general math and dead last in physics.[183] Fortunately, Asian nations were not included in this test or we would placed even lower. Money is obviously not the answer. The effect of funding levels on success in schools has been studied extensively for several decades, and the results are clear. No systemic relationship between school spending and student achievement has ever been found.[184] Additional funding primarily benefits the education establishment.

What has been shown to be a key factor is family structure and stability. Indeed, a study by Derek A. Neal of the University of Chicago and William R. Johnson of the University of Virginia found that even most of the much-publicized skills gap between black and white students can be accounted for by home and school environments.[185] Harvard's Howard Gardner states, ". . . any successful American education must involve the family and the institutions of the community, not just its school system."[186] And former Education Secretary Lamar Alexander has cautioned, "You cannot talk about achieving 90 percent graduation rates without talking about parents who check on homework and turn off the television and know where their kids are."[187] However, stable two-parent families and vital urban communities are precisely the institutions that have been severely undermined by many federal subsidies.

Federal involvement in education parallels many other questionable federal forays. Nowhere in the Constitution is the word education mentioned, and the Founders clearly considered education to be the prerogative of the states. When Representative Justin Morrill got Congress to pass a bill in 1857 to give federal land to the states for creating land-grant colleges, President James Buchanan vetoed it as an unconstitutional extension of federal power.[188] (The Morrill Act, which established the colleges was later passed as an amendment to war appropriations measure in 1862.) Nonetheless, federal involvement in primary and secondary education remained minimal until President Johnson's War on Poverty. In 1964, the Economic Opportunity Act created the Head Start program and a year later the Elementary and Secondary Education Act (ESEA) was passed. These two laws are still the basis for most federal funding of primary and secondary education, which amounted to $14.6 billion in 1997.[189] The CBO reported that there were over fifty federal education programs up for reauthorization in 1993, about which it had the following comments:

The federal government has never developed an overall plan or a consistent philosophy for the more than fifty programs that the Congress will consider for reauthorization in 1993 . . . . In many cases, data on the programs are limited; for example, current information on participation and effectiveness is not available for all of them.[190]

However, the GAO says that those fifty programs are just the tip of the iceberg. The agency reported,

Hundreds of federal education programs—the specific number differs depending on how education is defined and who is counting the programs—are administered by more than 30 federal agencies.[191]

How can there be that many programs? Simple: duplication beyond belief. For example, the federal government funds 86 different teacher training programs through nine agencies and over ninety early childhood programs through 11 agencies and 20 offices.[192] All told, the federal government appropriates about $73 billion annually for its tangle of education programs.[193] Again, the federal government has created a hodge podge of often competing and duplicative subsidy programs that receive perpetual funding without any indication that they work. Actually, it is even worse than that. Congress continues to fund programs even when there is compelling evidence that the programs do not work.

Head Start has been near and dear to the hearts of politicians of both parties for three decades, and it is not difficult to see why. Poor children do not seem to be as well prepared when they enter school as those from better-off families. Head Start aims to enable poor three- to four-year olds to catch up by enrolling them in preschool for a year before entering kindergarten. Intuitively, it makes as much sense today as it did to Lyndon Johnson, and it has immense political appeal. From its inception in 1965 through 1998, the program served 15 million children at a cost of $35 billion,[194] and in the process, established a sizable Head Start industry. Congress appropriated $4.4 billion in 1998, nearly triple the 1991 funding level,[195] despite the fact that research has shown that the program is ineffective. Such is the power of politically popular subsidy programs.

President Clinton is fond of saying that for every dollar we spend on Head Start today, we will save three dollars later.[196] It is a convenient myth that has been around for a long time and is based on studies of a few programs that had very little in common with Head Start. The one most often cited is the Perry Preschool program in 1980.[197] The GAO noted that a comparison to Head Start is inappropriate because the Perry program spent nearly twice as much per child, had a low child-to-staff ratio, and almost all the teachers had advanced degrees in early childhood education. But politicians and those in the Head Start industry continue to make false claims based on Perry Preschool type programs. It is not because they do not know the real results of the Head Start program. As far back as 1985, a Department of Health and Human Services analysis of studies of actual Head Start programs found,

> *In the long run, cognitive and socio-emotional test scores of former Head Start students do not remain superior to those of disadvantaged children who do not attend Head Start.*[198]

Additional studies have confirmed the finding that after about two years, gains made during Head Start are gone.[199] Another HHS report in 1993 concluded that Head Start programs were having difficulty meeting performance standards.[200] In a 1998 report, the GAO noted that HHS only holds local Head Start programs accountable for complying with regulations, not for demonstrating progress in achieving program purposes.[201] Indeed, the accounting agency found that HHS did not even have a list of Head Start classrooms and their locations![202] The truth is that Head Start is not meeting its statutory requirements and comes nowhere near achieving the exaggerated claims made by its proponents. Congress has been unwilling to appropriate funds to duplicate high-quality programs like the one at the Perry Preschool, which they like so much, and it has also been unwilling to terminate a multi-billion dollar subsidy program that is clearly ineffective. The result is another well-intentioned program that has been transformed into a federally subsidized combination baby-sitting and jobs program.

According to the CBO, "Federal [education] support is concentrated in programs that promote equal educational opportunity."[203] The largest program so intended is Chapter 1 of Title 1 of the ESEA, commonly referred to as the Chapter 1 program. The program is intended to help finance supplemental educational services for educationally deprived children who live in areas with high concentrations of children from low-income families. However, the Education Department, in its publication *Reinventing Chapter 1,* noted that a large-scale study by the consulting firm Abt Associates found that there was no difference between the academic achievement between students who receive Chapter 1 services and comparable students who do not participate in the program.[204] Again the question arises: Why is the federal government continuing to spend over $7 billion[205] annually on a program that is ineffective?

Perhaps termination would be a possibility if all that money was really being spent to "promote equal educational opportunity," but, of course, that is not the case. An analysis of the program by *U.S. News & World Report* found that only two percent of the funds go to school districts in which more than 75 percent of the students are poor, and less than half the funds go to schools in what are considered to be high-poverty areas.[206] In fact, fully 93 percent of all the school districts in the nation, including some of the wealthiest, receive Chapter 1 subsidies while some of the nation's poorest schools receive none.[207] The absurdity of this situation is widely recognized, but the non-poor beneficiaries are not about to part with their subsidies so that the program can benefit the poor. Especially when the program does not work anyway. The reality of

Chapter 1 is that it is simply a general subsidy program for local school districts, and those in Congress have made sure that nearly every Congressional district in the country gets a piece of the pork. In a January 1999 report on federal primary and secondary education programs, the GAO concluded,

> *In fact, many of these programs have been converted into little more than funding streams, distributed through formula-driven funding mechanisms . . . .*[208]

The ugly truth is that poor families are paying federal taxes to support a federal antipoverty program that largely subsidizes the non-poor.

The federal contribution to elementary and secondary education is quite small, accounting for only six percent of total expenditures.[209] But federal politicians and bureaucrats have used that modest contribution to impose a wide range of regulations on local school districts by requiring compliance by states that accept any federal education funds. Not surprisingly, many of those mandates benefited the education establishment at the expense of the education process. Indeed, as the *Washington Post* opined in 1979,

> *The creation of this department [Department of Education] is a response, by both the president and Congress, to one specific organization, the National Education Association."*[210]

The National Education Association (NEA) is the teachers union that represents most of the nation's teachers. There are only fourteen departments in the federal government, and Education is the only one formed specifically for the benefit of a small interest group. But the NEA and the other major teachers union, the American Federation of Teachers (AFT), obviously wield power well beyond their numbers. Between January 1991 and June 1992, the heavy fundraising period before the 1992 presidential election, the two teachers unions ranked third in "soft money" contributions to the Democratic party with $333,530.[211] In 1993 and 1994, the NEA alone gave $2.2 million to Democratic Congressional candidates.[212] The Executive Director of the Democratic National Committee, Debra S. DeLee, was hired from the NEA,[213] and at the 1996 Democratic convention, which nominated Bill Clinton for a second term, the teachers unions controlled 12 percent of the delegates.[214] That is the kind of power necessary to get your own department in the federal government. From there, federal power can be used to mandate programs that effectively force states and local school districts to subsidize the education establishment. Describing this extraordinary power, Milton Friedman wrote that public schools ". . . are really not public at all but simply private fiefs primarily of the administrators and the union officials."[215]

Nothing has benefited the education establishment as much as the Education for All Handicapped Children Act of 1975, which was reenacted as the Individuals with Disabilities Act of 1990. While the law stipulated that the federal government would provide 40 percent of the funding for this program, it has refused to do so, but the mandates remain.[216] Currently, the federal share amounts to about 7 percent, while the states are forced to pick up somewhere between $30 and $50 billion annually.[217] While the program was intended to benefit disabled children, by 1993, 80 percent of the five million Special Education students in the U.S. had no mental or physical disabilities.[218] Most of them were termed "learning disabled," often meaning that they simply have behavior problems or short attention spans.[219] Largely due to the federally mandated Special Education and Chapter 1 programs, 26 percent of American public school students are now in special classes as opposed to one to three percent in other countries.[220] Moreover, the students from those countries consistently outperform ours on international tests. This is hardly surprising given that there is little evidence that the tens of billions of dollars that Washington is forcing the states to spend on these expensive special programs are doing any good. The Education Department admits,

> *Achievement for students with disabilities remains less than satisfactory . . . . Results for students with learning disabilities and emotional disabilities are particularly poor.*[221]

On the other hand, the results for the education establishment have been excellent. Federal regulations have created hundreds of thousands of new jobs providing all the mandated services that have mostly proved ineffective. The cost of supporting the six million people that now work in America's public schools[222] has strained school budgets to the breaking point, while doing little to further the education of American children. While we spend more on education than the rest of the world, only about 52 cents of every school dollar actually gets into the classroom in a typical large school district.[223] And the number of nonclassroom personnel is growing at seven times the rate of classroom teachers.[224] According to the Census Bureau, in 1994 (the latest data), there were 3,763,312 teachers employed by elementary and secondary schools, serving 44,111,482 students, which would suggest a student-teacher ratio of 11.7 to one. But according to the Department of Education, the average public school class size in 1994 was twenty-four while the average private school class size was twenty-one.[225] Accounting for the fact that there two and one-half times as many public schools as private schools yields a weighted average of about 23 students per teacher nationally, meaning that about 1,918,000 teachers are in classrooms. Where are the other 1.8 million teachers? Most are engaged in administration and special services mandated by regulations attached to federal education subsidies, much to the delight of the education establishment.

Despite an investment exceeding $300 billion annually in primary and secondary education, former Education Secretary William Bennett has concluded that 90 percent of students entering U.S. colleges would not be admitted to postsecondary education anywhere else in the world.[226] Moreover, as many as 42 million Americans are functionally illiterate.[227] That compares to the early 1800s—before there was any public education—when Europeans such as

Alexis de Tocqueville and Michael Chevalier found Americans to be among the most literate nations in history.[228] How can we now achieve so little while spending so much? A significant part of the answer is that federal subsidy programs have provided the education establishment with the power and leverage to divert much of the nation's primary and secondary education investment for its own benefit.

President Buchanan would surely roll over in his grave if he could see the extent to which the federal government is now involved in higher education. It started simply. The Morrill Act of 1862 granted federal lands to states in order to establish an agricultural and engineering college in each state. But federal involvement grows like a cancer and no program lasts for long without strings being attached. The second Morrill Act of 1890 introduced federal matching funds, but stipulated that if certain federal standards were not met, colleges would become ineligible for aid.[229] In the early 1900s, the Hatch Act and Smith-Lever Act provided federal subsidies for agricultural research and services, and the Smith-Hughes Act provided subsidies for vocational education and home economics at land-grant colleges. Still, in 1930, President Hoover was sufficiently concerned about the constitutionality of federal involvement in education that he put the question to his Advisory Commission on Education. Of course, that was like asking the Bureau of Reclamation if it was constitutional to build dams. Incredibly, the Commission assured Hoover that there are 31 provisions in the Constitution under which the federal government can find authority to support higher education.[230] The floodgates were open. Through the thirties and forties, numerous federal programs were created that provided direct or indirect subsidies for colleges and universities. By the 1950s, at least 46 different executive branch agencies were administering programs involving higher education.[231]

The launching of Sputnick, the first satellite, by the Soviet Union in 1958 shocked Congress into passing the National Defense Student Loan program, intended to "give assistance to education for programs which are important to our national defense,"[232] specifically math, science, and foreign languages. It was just one of the hundreds of federal subsidy programs that were enacted as a temporary measure, but that became very permanent. If history has proven one thing, it is that there is no such thing as a temporary federal subsidy. In addition, there was no way the National Defense Student Loan subsidy was going to remain so narrowly targeted. President Johnson believed "Every child has the right to as much education as he has the ability to receive."[233] Where they got this *right* is a mystery; certainly not from the Constitution. Nonetheless, Johnson convinced Congress to greatly expand the student loan program with the passage of the Higher Education Act of 1965, which is now the basis for most student financial aid programs. For the 1998-99 academic year, that aid amounted to $47 billion, mostly from Pell grants, the William D. Ford Direct Loan Program (FDLP), and the Federal Family Education Loan program (FFEL).[234] Pell grants primarily target low-income students and are essentially an entitlement, while the FFEL and FDLP programs provide subsidized loans.

Of course, Pell grants, being outright grants, are a direct subsidy. Interestingly, 390,000 legal immigrants received Pell grants in 1993, amounting to about 10 percent of total grants.[235] Thus, after the 1996 welfare reform legislation, the federal government will pay poor legal immigrants to go to college, but it will not pay for food stamps for them.

Subsidized Stafford Loans make up about 60 percent of the FFEL program loans,[236] while most of the rest are accounted for by loans under the Unsubsidized Loan Program—which are, of course, subsidized. Federal taxpayers pay the interest on Stafford loans while students are in school and for up to six months after they graduate, which costs $2.5 billion each year.[237] When they finally begin repayment, the former students pay a below-market interest rate, courtesy of the taxpayers. The interest rate subsidy amounts to almost $2 billion more.[238] Students are responsible for all the interest on loans under the Unsubsidized Loan program, but they too carry below market interest rates, which amounts to a subsidy. Then, the taxpayers have to pick up the tab for a second student loan subsidy: the cost of the huge number of defaults every year. The federal government guarantees all these loans. The Congressional Research Service calculated that if banks did not receive a federal guarantee and instead had to charge enough interest to cover likely defaults, the rate on a student loan would increase by 78 percent.[239] That placed the 1995 subsidy value of the federal guarantee at nearly $6 billion.[240]

By 1990, 22 percent of all student loans were in default. According to the Education Department, as of September 30, 1993, the federal government had guaranteed $69 billion of student loans of which $11 billion were in default, and liabilities for defaulted loans were stated as $14 billion.[241] In 1993, the taxpayers paid out $2.4 billion in default claims,[242] and by 1997, that had climbed to $3.3 billion.[243] The GAO reported that there were $20 billion in delinquent FFEL loans in 1996,[244] but nobody knows what the real liability is. Consider the results of a 1994 joint audit of the FFELP program by the GAO and the Department of Education's Inspector General (IG),

> *The inaccuracies in the data were so pervasive that we could not perform sufficient procedures to conclude whether the FFELP's liabilities for loan guarantees of $14 billion and other related line items were fairly stated as of September 30, 1993, . . . we were unable to determine if Education received or disbursed the proper amounts.*[245]

By 1998, the amount of outstanding student loans had mushroomed to $150 billion.[246]

Billions of federal subsidy dollars always create an interest group to take advantage of the largesse, and education is no exception. Nor is it any more sanctimonious than the others. As the GAO noted,

Since the late 1980s, the [Education] *Department's Office of Inspector General, the Congress and GAO have all concluded after completing several investigations that extensive fraud and abuse exist in student aid programs.*[247]

Of course, that did not deter the politicians from constantly expanding the programs and the role of the Education Department, an agency that former Secretaries of Education Lamar Alexander and William Bennett observe,

. . . has come to contain bad ideas, harmful practices, needless expenditures, obsolete programs, dysfunctional regulations, and the depredations of special interests that care more about the well-being of education's "producers" than for its "consumers."[248]

Congress did take token action to reduce fraud and abuse. When the student loan default rate for postsecondary vocational schools rose to an alarming 41 percent in 1990, Congress passed the Higher Education Act Amendments of 1992 that terminated schools from FFELP eligibility if their default rate exceeded 25 percent for three consecutive years or 40 percent in any single year.[249] The fact that Congress considered acceptable a deplorable 25 percent default rate for two years out of every three, reveals the true nature of the program: Federal student loans are a major subsidy program for the bloated postsecondary education establishment, that requires tens of billions of federal dollars not to further higher education, but just to sustain itself. Education is a distant second and Congress knows it. In 1992, the GAO reported to Congress,

. . . schools use the [FFELP] program as a source of easy income with little regard for students' educational prospects or the likelihood of their repaying loans . . . .[250]

Knowing that, Congress still chose to allow schools with annual 24 percent default rates to continue to ride the gravy train. Quite simply, the politicians recognized that only if they continued to subsidize a steady stream of unqualified students would there be enough warm bodies to keep all the postsecondary institutions in business. Higher education is a $300 billion per year business substantially created by federal subsidies, and it cannot maintain its vast excesses without them.

To justify this wasteful diversion of tax revenues, the education establishment and Congress have preached that the nation's future depends on sending ever-increasing numbers of students to college. But at the same time, the quality and value of a college education is plummeting. In order to accommodate unqualified students and to keep their subsidized tuition rolling in, colleges have trivialized the curriculum. A report by the National Association of Scholars titled "The Dissolution of General Education 1914-1993," indicated that the number of mandatory courses for a college degree had dropped from 9.9 in 1914 to 2.5 in 1993.[251] Now, students can take such courses as "Troubadours and Rock Stars" (Yale),[252] "Race, Gender and the Politics of Rock 'n' Roll" (Columbia), "Unnatural Acts and Split Britches" (Brown), "The Drama of Homosexuality" (Harvard), and "Spirit Possession, Shamanism, Curing, and Witchcraft" (Cornell).[253] Yet when twenty-three Harvard students at their graduation ceremony were asked, "Why is it hotter in summer than in winter?," only two answered correctly.[254] *Harvard* graduates.

In addition to trivializing the curriculum, colleges have insured their flow of federal subsidy dollars by making it all but impossible to fail-out of school. Many, like Stanford, eliminated the grades of D and F.[255] After twenty-four years without handing out an F, Stanford instituted a NP (No Pass) grade in 1994. Over 90 percent of the grades awarded were A's and B's, and the median grade for undergraduate courses was an A-.[256] At Harvard in 1992, 91 percent of undergraduate grades were A's or B's, and 83.6 percent of the seniors graduated with honors—even though many did not know why it is hot in the summer.[257] According to Richard Sabot, a professor at Williams College, professors inflate grades to attract students to their departments and courses.[258] He notes that students pay plenty for a college education and they want the best looking transcript they can get. Colleges are doing whatever it takes to fill their overabundant classrooms, and mostly that involves offering easy courses and easy A's. The higher education establishment now produces lower education in order to maintain its subsidy-driven bloat.

Even if college degrees do not mean what they once did, higher education interests and their politicians still maintain that graduating more students from college is in the nation's best interest. Not only does the data not support that claim, but it reveals that students are being misled just as the taxpayers are. Twenty percent of those who graduated from college between 1984 and 1990 hold a job that does not require a college education.[259] Real wages of college-educated workers rose less than 2 percent from 1979 to 1989[260] and only began rising in the mid-1990s due to the labor shortage created by the booming economy. Michigan State University's Patrick Scheetz offers this simple explanation: "Starting salaries aren't going up because we have a surplus of college grads coming into the market every year."[261]

A study by U.S. Department of Labor concluded that 30 percent of the college graduates entering the work force between 1990 and 2005 will be unemployed or work in jobs that do not require a college degree.[262] On the other hand, degrees in fields where the nation has critical needs are declining. Between 1990 and 1996, the number of degrees awarded in engineering, engineering technology, computer science, and mathematics dropped 3 percent, 16 percent, 1 percent, and 9 percent respectively.[263] Obviously, federal higher education subsidies are not serving the nation's economic interest. Even worse, studies show that 70 percent of students who graduate from vocational schools—the institutions with the highest default rate on student loans—will never work in their field of training.[264] The facts show conclusively that the billions of dollars spent by the federal government to subsidize college graduates primarily serves the interests of the higher education establishment, not students or the nation.

Even the tens of billions of dollars being funneled into postsecondary schools by student aid programs is still nowhere near enough to support the higher education blob. However, there is another rich federal subsidy program: research grants. In 1998, the federal government spent over \$66 billion on research and most of that was channeled into colleges and universities.[265] About half of the total was for military research, while the rest covered a broad range of areas from energy to blueberries. Some universities have nearly become branches of the federal government. During 1993 alone, MIT received \$622.5 million in federal research grants and contracts, Johns Hopkins did even better with \$756 million, the University of Chicago got \$687.5 million, while Stanford only managed \$439.4 million.[266] Incredibly, some of the nation's top universities, despite receiving nearly a billion dollars each in total federal subsidies each year, are losing money. Robert Baker, provost of Cornell University, which received \$211 million federal research dollars in 1995,[267] lamented,

Each term I meet with the provosts of Stanford, Princeton, Columbia, Harvard, Yale, MIT and Chicago . . . we all find ourselves in similar financial situations—expenses outpace revenues . . . [268]

The reason is simple, the more subsidies they get, the more bloated and inefficient they become. One thousand graduate students were entirely dependent on federal research subsidies at Cornell in 1995.[269] Research subsidies serve the same function at graduate schools that student loan subsidies do at undergraduate schools: keeping an overabundant supply of students streaming in. They bring the same unhappy result for both graduate students and taxpayers. Thanks to federal subsidies, graduate schools are pumping out more Ph.D.'s than the nation can employ. Furthermore, a Ph.D. does not mean what it once did. Many receiving the degree are not first rate researchers and are very unlikely to reward the nation's investment in them. As Caltech President Thomas E. Everhart noted, "One outstanding scientist can do 100 or 1,000 times more than someone who is almost as good."[270] A 1995 study by Stanford University and the Rand Corporation concluded that doctoral production in the sciences and engineering averages about 25 percent above employment opportunities.[271] Again, we see the mature phase of federal subsidy programs: the subsidy feedback loop. Federal research subsidies have motivated graduate schools to overproduce, which, in turn, leads to more demand for research subsidies to employ the ever-growing surplus. Universities have then taken advantage of the burgeoning supply of graduate students to relieve professors of their teaching duties. While major universities boast of the prominence of their "faculty," the truth is that many of them seldom set foot in a classroom. Instead, classes are taught frequently by teaching assistants, federally subsidized graduate students. Data from the 1980s showed that teaching assistants made up over half of the faculties at universities.[272] It has been estimated that some professors at the University of Michigan spent so little time teaching that they were making nearly $1,000 an hour for their actual contact time with students.[273] Federal research dollars have funded what almost amounts to early retirement for tens of thousands of "professors."

Universities, like virtually all subsidy interests, know well how to play the subsidy game. Some pay Washington lobbyists as much as $30,000 a month to keep the gravy train running.[274] The research-subsidy interest group, primarily universities, businesses, and researchers, argues that the continued success of the nation's economy depends on lavish federal subsidies for research. Typical is this statement by Ohio State University President E. Gordon Gee,

> *The future of this country is not going to be in our ability to produce cars or steel. We've already lost that . . . our ability to produce new ideas will produce jobs. The idea factories in this country are not steel mills. The idea factories are universities.*[275]

While Gee might be a little premature in writing off the automotive industry, where the combined 1998 revenues of General Motors, Ford, and Chrysler exceeded $400 billion, there is no question that university research has played an important role in advancing U.S. technology. But the proper role of the government is to fund basic research, not the applied research that gets the lion's share of federal funding. Businesses and foundations spent over $154 billion on research and development in 1998, almost five times federal nondefense research expenditures.[276] Federally funded applied research is simply a taxpayer subsidy to industries that can well afford to do their own research. Even with government funded basic research, there are serious doubts about how much of it is worthwhile. A 1990 study by the Institute for Scientific Information suggests that about half of it is useless. The study counted how often research papers published in the top 4,500 science journals, the cream of the crop, between 1981 and 1985 had been referred to in later papers. It found that 45 percent of them were not cited even once in the five years after publication.[277] Penn State University's Professor Roy Rustium summed it up when he said that researchers are little more than "welfare queens in white coats."[278] If half of university research is worthless and another substantial percentage is done on behalf of large and very profitable industries such as agriculture, automobiles, telecommunications, energy, and a host of others, then clearly most of the tens of billions of dollars of federally-funded research is nothing more than just another wasteful, special-interest subsidy.

9

A FEW MORE NOTABLE SUBSIDIES

There are more minor federal subsidies that have the same character-istics, but involve relatively small amounts of money. The largest programs—those accounting for more than 95 percent of federal subsidy spending—have already been covered, but there are a few additional programs that warrant mention.

The federal government owns almost 650 million acres of land or about 30 percent of the surface area of the United States.[1] National Parks cover nearly 77 million acres, the U.S. Fish and Wildlife Service manages 87 million acres, and the U.S. Forest Service and Bureau of Land Management manage 191 million acres and 267 million acres, respectively.[2] At an annual cost to the Treasury of less than $5 billion, federal subsidies to commercial operations on public lands seem like relatively small potatoes, but the price tag is much higher when externalities are considered. The destruction of tens of millions of acres of natural habitat, presided over by the Forest Service and BLM in their efforts to produce subsidies, is far more important than most Americans real-ize. Stanford University biologist Gretchen Daily cautions, "One in every three mouthfuls of food we eat in the United States comes from a plant that is polli-nated by a wasp, bee, bat, or bird that needs natural habitat to complete its life cycle."[3] In addition, public lands subsidies are perhaps the clearest case of politicians and federal bureaucracies going to extremes—some illegal—to maintain themselves and their subsidized interest groups with full knowledge that their actions are detrimental to the public interest.

The U.S. Forest Service

It would be most interesting to hear what Mark Twain, who called Congress the "native American criminal class," would say about the U.S. For-est Service, an agency of the U.S. Department of Agriculture. He would surely recognize a bureaucracy created by Congress in its own image; in service to itself, subsidized public-lands timber and grazing interests, and their politi-cians. It would be wrong to characterize all Forest Service employees as criminals, but the record of the agency's criminal actions is astounding. The record on its legal actions is hardly much better. Consider the following comments from GAO Congressional testimony in July of 1997,

> *Our report on the Forest Service's decision-making identifies an organizational culture of indifference toward accountability . . . inefficiency and waste have cost taxpayers hundreds of millions of dollars . . . Past efforts by the Forest Service to change its behavior have not been successful. Decision-making within the agency is broken and in need of repair.*[4]

The agency's record reveals relentless and shameless efforts to serve its vested interests at the expense of the American public. This is, of course, in sharp contrast to the agency's "Smoky the Bear" image. Many people find Smoky among their earliest childhood memories. He was the symbol of a Forest Service that stood for the protection and wise use of our national forests and the wildlife that lived there. Before World War II, that was indeed the primary role of the Forest Service, but during the 1950s, the stewardship role gradually gave way to exploitation. Powerful timber interests and their politicians passed legislation that removed forest protections and heavily subsidized timber companies to log public forests. The politicians appointed timber industry executives to top Forest Service positions, who implemented self-serving policies that funneled billions of taxpayer dollars to the industry and left much of the nation's best forest land decimated.

The beginnings of federal forest management date back to 1891 when President Benjamin Harrison created fifteen forest reserves in the western states in an attempt to protect watersheds by stopping the illegal and rapid destruction of public forests by timber companies, railroads, livestock interests, and settlers.[5] Due to lack of enforcement, little changed until President Theodore Roosevelt began a program of strict law enforcement on public lands and started the Bureau of Forestry, which would later become the U.S. Forest Service in 1905.[6] The Organic Act of 1897 authorized the sale of specifically marked "dead, mature, and large-growth trees" from public forests, allowing for timber production while protecting the watershed, wildlife, and recreational values of the forests. The Forest Service managed the national forests in conformity with this law until its transformation into an agent of the timber industry after World War II.

The building boom of the 1950s saw increased demand for lumber and greatly increased lobbying by the timber industry for the government to provide it with large volumes of national forest logs. Moreover, it wanted those logs to be heavily subsidized. The extent of the influence and agenda of the timber industry is revealed in a report, *Determination of Allowable Annual Timber Cut on Forty-Two Western National Forests*, issued in September 1962 by a board appointed by Forest Service Chief Edward P. Cliff.[7] Those consulted by the board in preparation of the report were several government employees, primarily from the Forest Service, and the four principal timber industry lobbyists.[8] Among the recommendations were: the government should pay for the construction of logging roads (a massive subsidy program); the government should manage the timber program for "community stability" (providing an excuse to subsidize timber sales); national forests should be managed for the needs of the timber industry; areas designated for scenic or landscape purposes should be logged; and strong career path ladders should be provided for Forest Service employees engaged in timber management (tying advancement to subsidized logging).[9] Over the next few years, the recommendations of that report became the guiding principles of the Forest Service.

By the late 1960s, logging on the national forests was on such a massive scale that it was not possible to comply with the provisions of the Organic Act of 1897, particularly the provision that required marking each tree to be cut. In response, the Forest Service began a practice that became routine: it simply violated the laws that interfered with the its logging plans and its timber industry partners. In some national forests, loggers were allowed to cut trees whether they were marked or not, while on others, forest rangers simply began marking all the trees. Frequently, loggers were allowed to simply leave trees they had cut but later decided were unmerchantable. By ignoring the law, timber companies were allowed to enter a forest and pretty much cut all the trees, taking just the trees they wanted; they were essentially clear-cutting the national forests illegally. Finally, faced with widespread disregard of the Organic Act requirements, several conservation organizations sued the Forest Service in 1973 to stop illegal clear-cutting on the Monongahela National Forest in West Virginia.

The Federal District Court ordered the Forest Service to comply with all the provisions of the Organic Act, and the ruling was upheld on appeal by the Fourth Circuit Court.[10] The Forest Service and timber industry knew that it would not be long before they faced similar suits all over the country; that threatened to dramatically reduce the supply of subsidized timber. The law had to be changed. In 1976, Congress passed the National Forest Management Act that superseded the Organic Act and essentially legalized what the Forest Service was already doing. But the Forest Service continued to violate another law, the Multiple Use-Sustained Yield Act of 1960, which required the agency to manage national forests for five balanced uses: watershed, recreation, timber, grazing, and wildlife. Instead, the agency consistently implemented policies to maximize its own benefits. That meant timber production at the expense of the other four uses. The timber industry and their politicians had shrewdly insured that Forest Service funding and staff promotions were closely tied to the production of subsidized federal timber. The transformation of one of America's most respected agencies to one of its most notorious was complete.

By making timber subsidies the driving force behind the Forest Service budget and promotional opportunities, Congress produced a case study in the incredible distortion that takes place in a subsidy-codependent federal agency. The intent of the politicians was to subsidize the timber industry and they were certainly successful at that. However, the Forest Service became more dependent on the subsidies it delivered than did the timber industry, and the agency was willing to lie, cheat, or steal to protect those subsidies. Virtually every action, report, calculation, as well as its entire accounting system were contrived to protect timber subsidies. Federal law requires that public timber be sold at not less than appraised value, which the Forest Service interprets to mean fair market value.[11] Yet, the pricing system used by the agency calculates a price that assures that the timber company purchasing the logs will make a profit, a system that most often results in a loss to the taxpayers.[12] The agency has a very distorted view of fair market value, but it is rock solid compared to its accounting practices.

As the GAO has concluded, "Generating revenue and reducing costs are not mission priorities for the Forest Service."[13] Therefore, it is not surprising that by 1996, the Forest Service was still spending about $3 billion annually,[14] but was unable to return anything to the Treasury from its timber sales.[15] According to the Forest Service, however, its timber sales generated just over a $3 billion return to the U.S. Treasury between 1989 and 1994.[16] But a cash flow analysis by forest economist Randal O'Toole found that rather than making money, the taxpayers actually lost $1.7 billion during that period.[17] An analysis by the GAO found that between 1992 and 1994, the Forest Service returned $300 million to the Treasury but spent $1.3 billion in the process, for a net one billion dollar loss.[18] (In contrast, ten western states run public timber programs on similar, state-owned lands and generate an average of $5.58 in revenue for each dollar spent.[19]) How can the Forest Service claim to be very profitable while all other analyses show huge losses? The answer lies in the Forest Service accounting system known as the "Timber Sale Program Information Reporting System," (TSPIRS).

TSPIRS was carefully contrived to produce very favorable results for Forest Service timber sales, thereby disguising the heavily subsidized nature of the great majority of sales. It simply and obviously overstates revenues and understates costs. For instance, frequently the largest cost of a sale is basic road construction to access the timber. Constructing these dirt roads through rugged, steep terrain can cost as much as one million dollars per mile, but the Forest Service largely ignores these costs. To make them all but disappear, the agency amortizes the costs over absurdly long periods. In 1990, the costs of logging roads constructed on the Colorado National Forest in Arizona were amortized over 2,818 years while those on the Chugach National Forest in Alaska were spread over 2,014 years.[20] Thus, for a timber sale that required a million dollar logging road on the Colorado National Forest, the Forest Service would count only $354.86 of that cost in any year. That same year, thirty national forests used amortization periods longer than two hundred years.[21] While an argument exists for amortizing the cost of logging roads, it is overwhelmed by the preposterous amortization periods, which can only have been designed to camouflage timber subsidies. After all, our reinforced concrete interstate highways are crumbling after thirty years, yet the Forest Service maintains that its dirt roads will last for hundreds or even thousands of years. Those who have traveled the national forests know that some logging roads do not last a single year.

So determined is the Forest Service to preserve its timber subsidy program that it persecutes its own employees who reduce logging when necessary to comply with federal law, while refusing to act against employees who knowingly break the law in the process of producing subsidized timber. Often at the suggestion of members of Congress, the agency has conducted intensive investigations of employees found to put the law above timber subsidies, looking for any minor violation of procedure, which is then used to force the employee into a choice between a transfer to a safe job or retirement. In 1992, a federal judge ruled that the agency's internal investigation of one long-time employee bordered on a "vendetta;" a year later, another federal judge ordered the Forest Service to reinstate another high-level employee whose only problem had been his policy of complying with federal law which limited subsidized timber production on his forest.[22] Meanwhile, several Forest Service managers on the Eldorado National Forest in California, who illegally attempted to increase production of subsidized timber and ended up costing the taxpayers millions of dollars, were rewarded.[23] Ignoring a referral for criminal prosecution, the Forest Service promoted the individuals involved.[24] That was not an isolated event. After an investigation of the Forest Service, the GAO concluded,

> . . . *numerous criminal investigators and other law enforcement employees of the Forest Service—as well as some federal prosecuters—have voiced what they perceive as interference in the Forest Service's investigative efforts. They have alleged that the nonlaw-enforcement Forest Service officials who supervise or influence the investigative process have often impeded, or interfered with investigations . . . many Forest Service law enforcement employees perceive that they are vulnerable to management retaliation for doing their job, that is investigating violations of federal statutes . . .*[25]

It is difficult to overstate the extent to which timber subsidies have thoroughly corrupted a once-model federal agency. Even more distressing is the fact that timber industry politicians in Congress actively support the agency's tactics, and have ignored reports exposing criminal activity. Indeed, the GAO has reported that the key to the Forest Service's continuing status as an agency that performs poorly and routinely ignores the law is that Congress will not hold it accountable for its actions.[26] That is no accident. In 1989, the USDA Office of the Inspector General (OIG) issued a report indicating that the Pacific Northwest Region was experiencing millions of dollars in losses due to timber theft, largely because it used a method of measuring timber volume (scaling), which is custom made for fraud.[27] Two years later, the OIG found that no attempt had been made to correct the situation.[28] All other regions had abandoned the scaling method, but, as it turned out, Senator Mark Hatfield intervened to keep the agency from abandoning the measuring practice in the Pacific Northwest. It was enabling timber purchasers to receive tens of millions of dollars of free timber, in addition to tens of millions in subsidized timber.[29] Unfortunately, such "constituent service" on the part of politicians is not at all uncommon. In 1991, U.S. District Attorney Jeffrey Kent estimated that scaling fraud may have cost the taxpayers $36 million in the Pacific Northwest between 1985 and 1991.[30] More recently, the Forest Service itself has admitted that timber theft and fraud may be costing taxpayers as much as $100 million per year, yet, in 1995, it abolished its Timber Theft Investigation Branch.[31]

The Forest Service is required by law to " . . . limit the sale of timber from each national forest to a quantity equal to or less than a quantity that can be removed from such forest annually in perpetuity on a sustained-yield basis."[32] While the law does allow temporary deviations from this rule, it is nonetheless illegal for the Forest Service to sell timber from the national forests faster than it is being replaced. Of course, it has become abundantly clear that the law is little more than an inconvenience to the agency and its politicians. A June 1992 report by the staff of the House Committee on Interior and Insular Affairs, noted that contrary to the testimony of the Forest Service Chief, Dale Robertson, forest regrowth was considerably less than the volume of timber being sold.[33] In a 1994 report, the Wilderness Society calculated that the amount of softwood (pines, firs, and spruces) declined 11 percent between 1977 and 1993.[34] The Forest Service has long gotten around that little legal problem by simply lying about the amount of timber in the national forests. The agency uses a model called FORPLAN to determine the amount of available timber in a national forest. However, K. Norman Johnson, the designer of the model, admitted in testimony before the House Agriculture Committee that the model overstated the amount of timber by as much as 20 percent.[35] Naturally, the model overstated timber yields rather than understating them. As with the agency's accounting system, TSPIRS, the "error" had enabled the Forest Service to produce more subsidized timber. Yet another Forest Service computer model, Prognosis, predicts how fast trees grow. The faster they grow, the more subsidized timber can be produced. Not surprisingly, Prognosis greatly overstates tree growth. It predicted trees growing to more than six hundred feet, twice the height of the tallest trees in the world.[36] Finally, the agency was forced to admit that the model can lead to predictions "that are not biologically reasonable."[37]

Forest Service systems never err on the side of reduced subsidies. With so many contrived systems, the agency's records and accounts could not possibly balance, and, predictably, they do not. The GAO found that in an attempt to prepare financial statements for 1988, the Forest Service had made adjustments exceeding $10 billion "to eliminate redundancies, correct errors, and conform information to accrual based reporting requirements."[38] That is a staggering fudge factor, but it is all the more alarming when you consider that it is about three times the size of the agency's annual budget.

For years, the Forest Service has attempted to justify its unabashed effort to preserve and expand timber subsidies by claiming that its timber sale program was vital for the home-building industry and the stability of rural logging communities. Neither claim is true. As University of Montana Economics Professor Thomas Michael Power points out,

> *For instance, in Montana and Oregon* [two of the largest national forest timber states] *the more important the wood products industry is as a source of income in a county, the lower the average income is . . . . The vast majority of available studies show that . . . community specialization in wood products either has no positive impact or a negative impact on a broad variety of indicators of local well-being.*[39]

In truth, it is the economic well being of timber companies and the Forest Service itself that benefits from subsidized timber programs—at the expense of rural communities. It is true that national forest timber is used in the home-building industry, but to a much smaller degree than the Forest Service and timber politicians would have the public believe. Only about 14 percent of the nation's annual forest fiber growth takes place in the national forests, and even that overstates their contribution to America's lumber supply.[40] The vast majority of timber in the U.S. comes from commercial and private forests. According to Thomas Power, the impact of cutting Forest Service harvests in half would be to reduce national timber supplies by only 5 percent.[41] In addition, the most accurate indicator of supply sufficiency, price, indicates that the total supply of lumber has been more than ample for decades. Real lumber prices barely rose at all between 1950 and 1986.[42]

This brief analysis of the Forest Service timber program has focused on the subsidy and economic aspects only. Perhaps of even greater importance are the extraordinarily detrimental environmental consequences of the agency's policies. It is noteworthy that while the Forest Service is selling trees for as little as a few dollars each—and losing hundreds of millions of dollars in the process—one of its own publications quantifies the environmental value of a tree. It states, "In fifty years, one tree generates $30,000 in oxygen, recycles $35,000 of water, and removes $60,000 of air pollution."[43] That alone comes to about $2,500 per tree, per year lost every time the Forest Service sells a tree, which would bring Forest Service losses into the hundreds of billions of dollars annually. Unfortunately for Americans, in a 1998 report, the GAO concluded, ". . . the Forest Service is still years away from achieving financial accountability and possibly a decade or more away from being accountable for its performance."[44]

The Federal Grazing Program

The other significant special interest subsidy program run by the Forest Service is livestock grazing on national forest lands. It is a sister program to that run by the Department of Interior's Bureau of Land Management on the 267 million acres of land that it manages. Virtually all of the public land managed for grazing is in the western states. Together, the Forest Service and BLM grazing programs barely show up on the federal subsidy radar screen, but public lands livestock grazing is interesting from several perspectives. First, it is arguably the most environmentally devastating practice in the nation's history. Second, it is a federal subsidy program that produces absolutely nothing. Most programs produce a loss for the taxpayers, but they have at least some minimal economic benefit; federal grazing yields nothing. Third, this program best exposes the true colors of those politicians who claim to be stalwarts of fiscal conservatism. There is no purer or more generous form of welfare in this country than public lands grazing. Yet, no group of Americans purports to be more conservative than public lands ranchers and their politicians. Perhaps more than any other federal program, public lands grazing proves that there are no fiscal conservatives in Congress; there are only unabashed free spenders and those without the courage to admit that they are.

Livestock grazing on the vast western public lands began in earnest in the mid-1800s. The range was open to all those wishing to use it, and use it they did. By the mid-1880s, there were an estimated 40 million cattle and 53 million sheep, far more than the land could support.[45] Albert Potter, head of the Grazing Section of the Forest Service at the time, described conditions as the 19th century drew to a close,

The grazing lands were stocked far beyond their capacity; vegetation was cropped by hungry animals before it had opportunity to reproduce; valuable forage plants gave way to worthless weeds and the productive capacity of the lands rapidly diminished. Class was arrayed against class—the cowman against the sheepman, the big owner against the little one—and might ruled more often than right. Deadlines stretched their threatening lengths across the country, jealously guarded by armed men; battles were fought and lives sacrificed; untold thousands of animals were slaughtered in the fight for the range. . . . The mountains were denuded of their vegetative cover, forest reproduction was damaged or destroyed, the slopes were seamed with deep erosion gullies, and the water-conserving power of the drainage basins became seriously impaired. Flocks passed each other on the trails, one rushing in to secure what the other had just abandoned as worthless . . . .[46]

In just a few decades, over seven hundred million acres of mixed grassland, an area equal to about 36 percent of the contiguous forty-eight states, were depleted, degraded, or destroyed.[47] The endless sagebrush desert so commonly depicted in the typical Hollywood western movie, and which is now a prominent feature throughout the west, is mostly the result of the devastation of the natural range by livestock. Even in arid New Mexico, studies have concluded that the area predominantly grew grass, not sagebrush, before it was overgrazed.[48] BLM range expert Roger Rosentreter notes that much of the western range before the introduction of livestock was typically 25 percent sage and 75 percent grass and forbs; today it is exactly the opposite.[49] Forest

Service plant ecologist Alma Winward, an authority on sagebrush-grass eco-systems, estimates that over 80 percent of the sagebrush-grass ecosystem has an imbalance in favor of sagebrush over the natural understory of grass and forbs. She states, "There is essentially no way to reestablish a native or intro-duced herbaceous cover without first removing some of the dense sagebrush canopy."[50] So rapid and severe was the destruction of the western range that the great era of cattlemen lasted only from about 1867 to 1887.[51] Unfortu-nately, much of the damage was permanent.

One of the primary results of denuding vast areas of public land has been the greatly diminished capability of the land to hold water. Not only did that permanently reduce the productivity of the land by lowering the water ta-ble, it also caused rain water to runoff quickly, producing serious flooding. The federal government has spent billions of dollars on flood control projects, in many cases primarily to mitigate flood threats due to overgrazing. However, the grazing legacy even adversely impacts the flood control structures because the floodwaters running off denuded watersheds carry large amounts of silt, which fills in the reservoirs. Eventually, the taxpayers will pay again to remedy that situation. Nonetheless, the overgrazing continues.

In the early 1900s, Congress finally passed legislation, most notably the Taylor Grazing Act, aimed at curtailing grazing abuses. While there has been some improvement in the condition of the public range since the turn of the century, much of that improvement was due simply to the collapse of in-tensive public lands ranching because the range was exhausted. The primary effect of federal grazing legislation has been to sustain a segment of that in-dustry almost entirely through federal subsidies and at the expense of continu-ing the damage to hundreds of millions of acres of public land. Assessments in 1988 and 1989 by the GAO, BLM, and the National Resources Defense Coun-cil (NRDC) all concluded that only about 30 percent of the public range ad-ministered by the BLM could be classified as in good or excellent condition.[52] The remaining 70 percent continues to be abused by a grazing program entirely supported by federal subsidies. As range ecologist, Karl Hess, Jr. has noted,

> . . . the effectiveness of legislatively controlling the open range
> has itself been so compromised by subsequent subsidies and poli-
> cies that pay and mandate overgrazing that it is a wonder that
> rangeland conditions have improved at all.[53]

Whether the condition of national rangelands has actually improved is really just a guess. The GAO has found that the Department of the Interior, which includes the BLM, still in 1999 had so little data about the resources that it manages that, ". . . it is difficult, at best, to determine whether the condition of key resources under Interior's stewardship is deteriorating, stabilizing, or im-proving."[54]

Given that the federal grazing program covers nearly 14 percent of the land area of the lower 48 states,[55] one might expect that a large percentage of the nation's livestock operations would be involved. Hardly. According to the

Commerce Department, there were 842,000 cattle and 92,000 sheep operations in the U.S. in 1987.[56] Only 27,000 of these operations, a mere four percent, used federal range lands.[57] The numbers have declined since then. But even four percent overstates the economic significance of the federal grazing program. Virtually all federal range lands are in the western part of the country, but in no western region does the number of jobs or income related to federal grazing account for more than one-tenth of one percent of employment.[58] Nationally, federal land provides only two percent of the feed consumed by beef cattle, and consequently two percent of beef production.[59] Because beef production in the U.S. is constrained by a perpetual state of excess supply, the total elimination of the federal grazing program would have no effect on beef supplies. In early 1997, beef was in such oversupply that real prices were the lowest since the mid-1930s.[60] Low-cost, unsubsidized producers would quickly and easily make up for the loss of the paltry production from federal lands. In addition, Thomas Power estimates that it would take only a week and a half of normal economic growth to make up for all the lost jobs.[61]

The fact that public lands ranching is of no economic value to the nation has not deterred the federal government from coming up with one subsidy program after another to assure its continuation. For starters, the grazing fee charged by the government is, and always has been, absurdly low by design. According to the GAO, the formula that determines the grazing fee the government charges double counts rancher costs and,

> . . . has the added effect of insulating public lands ranchers from the fairly steady increases in market prices for forage paid by ranchers leasing private grazing lands. [62]

The fee is structured such that when beef prices drop due to oversupply, the grazing fee drops, thereby encouraging additional subsidized production and putting more pressure on already low prices. When the GAO issued that report in 1991, the government charged ranchers $1.97 per month to graze a cow and a calf on federal land.[63] Thanks to the concerted efforts of about twenty Senators from western states—the self-proclaimed most "conservative" members of the Senate—the grazing fee dropped 31 percent to $1.35 in 1996.[64] However, as with many government fees, there is less than meets the eye. The government refunds half of all grazing fees back to the ranchers through their grazing associations for "range improvements," the definition of which is largely up to the ranchers themselves. One grazing group in Nevada used some of their range improvement funds for lobbying trips to Washington, D.C., another $40,000 was spent for legal fees, and $32,000 for payments to a pro-public lands ranching magazine.[65] The bottom line is that in 1996 the federal government's grazing fee was effectively 68 cents per Animal Unit Month or AUM (one AUM equals one cow and one calf or five sheep grazing for one month), which generated less than $12 million in revenue[66] for the grazing privileges on one-seventh of the continental U.S. The cost to graze private lands was at least ten times that much, but that comparison greatly understates the federal subsidy to public lands ranching.

The federal government provides a wide range of services to sustain senseless public lands ranching, including killing large numbers of wildlife, rehabilitating livestock-depleted range, range-fire fighting, water projects, soil management projects, road construction and maintenance, flood control, weed control, and disaster relief. These services are almost entirely necessitated because of livestock grazing, and those few services that might be needed in the absence of grazing would be funded at only a fraction of their current levels. A couple of these programs are so absurd that they merit a brief description. Under the Animal Damage Control Act of 1931,[67] the Department of Agriculture has spent hundreds of millions of dollars killing wild animals for the benefit of ranchers and farmers. Seventy-one percent of the 2.2 million animals killed by federal "biological science technicians," in 1992 were blackbirds, grackles, and starlings accused of eating farmers' grain.[68] Why this is a federal responsibility is very unclear. The remaining 638,000 animals included coyotes, foxes, bears, bobcats, beavers, and mountain lions that were found guilty of living on public lands, the fiefdom of public lands ranchers. In one case, federal trappers spent five hundred hours killing 56 animals, including 28 coyotes, a deer, several skunks, badgers, porcupines, and foxes in response to a claim by a public lands rancher that a coyote had killed a lamb valued at $83.[69] In 1994, the federal government spent $36 million on animal damage control.[70] The portion of that amount spent to benefit ranchers on public lands easily exceeded the total revenue from all grazing fees.

Virtually all public lands ranching is nonviable; that is, raising livestock adapted to wet European climates on the public lands in the arid areas of the western United States cannot be done without substantial government subsidies. But even with multiple subsidy programs, public lands ranchers frequently cannot make it. That situation demanded another subsidy program: the emergency feed program. Under this program, the government pays for half the cost of the feed ranchers buy during a drought, thus relieving the ranchers of any responsibility for maintaining their herds at sustainable levels. The incentive is to stock as many head as possible and let the taxpayers cover any shortfall. And in the western U.S., drought is not an "emergency" but a routine occurrence. Routine enough that ranchers have qualified for the emergency subsidy in four out of every ten years on average.[71] The cost of this subsidy program ranges from $100 million to $500 million annually,[72] mostly to support an interest group that contributes nothing to the economy and about $12 million annually to the U.S. Treasury. But regardless of how many subsidy programs there are, it is never enough. In April 1996, President Clinton ordered the Agriculture Department to buy an extra $50 million worth of beef to bolster low prices due to overproduction.[73] Most of that was to be used to add more fat to the school lunch program. Clinton also ordered that 36 million acres of Conservation Reserve farm land—land that the taxpayers had paid farmers and ranchers to take out of production—be opened for grazing,[74] thereby doubling the subsidy on those lands. Continuing to sustain the over-production of beef, of course, will necessitate further subsidies.

It is difficult to determine the total subsidy that public lands ranchers receive because they benefit from so many different programs. Estimates range as high as one billion dollars per year.[75] A conservative calculation by the author came to $397 million for 1991, almost $15,000 per public lands ranching operation. Based on seventeen million AUM's, that places the taxpayer cost at $23.35 per AUM. The Treasury received 99 cents per AUM from ranchers that year, or about $16.8 million dollars. That would mean that 96 percent of the cost of the federal grazing program was paid by taxpayers. Four hundred million dollars is just a drop in the federal subsidy bucket, but the real tragedy is that the extensive and frequently irreparable damage taking place on hundreds of millions of acres of public land is not only at public expense, but is only possible because of preposterous federal subsidies.

Mining on Federal Lands

Mining is the third major activity on public land, and, as we saw in Chapter 2, federal law allows tens of billions of dollars worth of valuable minerals to be removed from public lands without the taxpayers receiving a cent. Just between 1993 and 1995, an estimated $40 billion worth of federal minerals was given away.[76] Moreover, miners can obtain title to the land containing these minerals for a few dollars per acre. Since the Mining Law was passed in 1872, some 3.2 million acres of federal land containing more than $200 billion in minerals have been essentially given away.[77] In 1993, 23 of the 40 largest gold mines were foreign owned and extracted $2 billion worth of bullion.[78] However, U.S. taxpayers got nothing. The Mining law of 1872 is essentially a license to steal and everyone in Congress knows it.

It would be bad enough if Congress was simply presiding over the squandering of federal resources, but is much worse than that. Mining is a very messy business, and Congress has deliberately subsidized the creation of an environmental mess estimated to be in the tens of billions of dollars. All mining activity in the U.S. generates two billion tons of solid waste each year, about 40 percent of the nation's total solid waste.[79] That is about eight times as much hazardous waste as is generated by all non-mining activities combined.[80] Hardrock mining operations have deposited billions of pounds of highly toxic heavy metals and acids into rivers, streams, and lakes throughout the west. On a single day in February 1996, U.S. Geological Survey engineers estimated that one million pounds of lead from abandoned mine sites washed into Lake Coeur d'Alene in northern Idaho during a flood.[81] That added to the 140 billion pounds of toxic mining sediment already on the bottom of the lake.[82] From there, heavy metals flow down the Spokane River and into Lake Spokane in Washington state. Every day the Iron Mountain Mine in California delivers 4,800 pounds of iron, 1,466 pounds of zinc, 423 pounds of copper, and 10 pounds of cadmium into the Keswick Reservoir, the source of drinking water for the City of Redding.[83] A five-mile stretch of a tributary of the Arkansas River in Colorado was found to be devoid of life due to toxic mining waste.[84]

In all, about 12,000 miles of American rivers and streams are contaminated with mining caused pollution.[85]

Unfortunately, the problems do not stop when the mining stops. Long after they have been abandoned, many mines continue to leach toxic wastes into water supplies. Over 140 miles of the Clark Fork River in Montana, which feeds into the Columbia River, have been polluted by heavy metals and other toxic mining waste from seventy years of operations at the Anaconda Copper Mine.[86] The company that obtained the land for a few dollars per acre from the federal government went out of business in 1982, but as of 1990 the Environmental Protection Agency (EPA) had spent more than $20 million just studying the Clark Fork problem. The cleanup itself could cost up to $1.5 billion.[87]

In 1993, based on data obtained from the Western Governors' Association, the Mineral Policy Center concluded that there were 560,000 inactive or abandoned mines in the western U.S.[88] By far most of those are on public lands, and like the Anaconda Copper Company, the miners simply walked away from their environmental mess, leaving the cleanup to the taxpayers. The Bureau of Mines has estimated that the cleanup of mining sites on federal lands could cost as much as $35.3 billion.[89]

In 1976, Congress passed the Resource Conservation and Recovery Act (RCRA) and followed it in 1980 with the Comprehensive Environmental Response, Compensation and Liability Act, commonly known as Superfund, to address the growing problem of toxic waste. The stated intention of these laws was to make the parties responsible for pollution pay for remediation.[90] It has not worked out that way, partly because the legislation set up a tortuous process for determining liability and partly because Congress really does not want to penalize its subsidy recipients. The Superfund legislation requires the EPA to identify existing hazardous sites and to ensure proper remediation. (Unfortunately, the law also dispensed with many common law civil protections and gave extraordinary power, which is regularly abused, to EPA bureaucrats.) The cleanup bill is turning out to be far more expensive than the politicians anticipated, and fully 40 percent of all funds expended on Superfund sites have gone for legal fees.[91] In 1996, just $696 million of the $1.4 billion in Superfund spending went to actual cleanup work.[92] Because the process is so inefficient, the average time to clean up hazardous sites is 15 years,[93] and the government's attempt to obtain reimbursement from those deemed responsible for the pollution has not gone well. Through the end of 1995, the EPA had collected just 14 percent of the funds it had spent from responsible parties.[94] By 1996, just outstanding unrecovered, indirect (not associated with actual cleanup work) costs were nearly $4 billion.[95] The EPA predicted that the number of Superfund sites will increase to 2,000 by the year 2000, and further growth is a virtual certainty.[96] The CBO estimates that the final number of sites will be between 2,300 and 7,800.[97] Considering that a University of Tennessee study estimated that the cleanup costs for 3,000 sites could amount to $150 billion, not including legal fees,[98] and that the EPA is recovering about 10 percent of the costs, the taxpayers could be on the hook for well over $200 billion. Not all of these problem sites are associated with mining, but a large majority are. In 1998, 61 mining sites were being cleaned up under Superfund at a projected cost of $20 billion.[99]

Remarkably, despite the enormous costs that have been passed on to the taxpayers, mining extraction and benefication wastes are still not regulated by the federal government. The EPA decided in 1991 that these wastes would be regulated under Subtitle D of RCRA, but the act does not give EPA the necessary statutory authority under that Subtitle![100] Congress has again succeeded in its primary objective: preserving the status quo. Senators from western states, the ones who claim to be conservatives, have blocked all attempts to stop the giveaway of tens of billions of dollars of federal minerals. At the same time, effective legislation has not been passed to stop mining subsidy recipients from passing on billions of dollars of pollution to the taxpayers. That is the real work of Congress.

The Small Business Administration

Since small business is, by definition, a local issue, it is very difficult to conceive of why the federal government should be concerned with it. Nevertheless, it certainly is. The Small Business Administration (SBA) was created in 1954 to "assist, counsel, and advocate the interests of small business."[101] That, of course, means subsidies. The agency's primary subsidy mechanisms are the Guaranteed Business Loan program (Section 7(a)) and the Disaster Loan program. In addition, there are several smaller loan programs aimed at minorities, veterans, and the handicapped. The SBA's subsidized loan portfolio for all its programs was estimated at $42 billion as of the end of 1997.[102]

Under the guaranteed loan program, the government guarantees between 75 and 80 percent of the principal of loans made by commercial banks to small businesses. In 1996, the SBA guaranteed $5.8 billion in loans, putting the taxpayers at risk for $4.7 billion. That same year it had to pay $1.5 billion to banks to make good on guaranteed loans that defaulted.[103] However, according to an SBA report, The Bank Holding Company Study, just 27 large bank holding companies made $48.8 billion in loans to small businesses in 1996 without government assistance.[104] Clearly, the private sector is providing plenty of credit to small businesses—of the 780,000 new businesses started in 1995, less than two percent utilized SBA guaranteed loans.[105] Commenting on the Bank Holding Company Study, SBA chief counsel for advocacy, Jere W. Glover, noted, "We're also finding that small business-friendly banks are more profitable than banks making few small-business loans."[106] That raises the obvious question: If commercial banks are providing nearly all the credit to small businesses already, and doing so at higher profits than they earn on the rest of their portfolio, why is the federal government involved at all, and why is it losing money doing so? The answer to the first question is that federal subsidies are unrelated to need, and the answer to the second is that the SBA guarantees many loans for people who have no business being in business. Then, too, there is a high level of fraud, abuse, and mismanagement in SBA programs. The GAO and the SBA's own inspector general have issued numerous reports detailing these problems.

The SBA Section 8(a) program is considered one of the federal government's primary vehicles for developing small business that are owned by minorities and other economically disadvantaged individuals. Under this program, federal contracts are directed to participating firms, usually on a non-competitive basis. The program is a classic federal subsidy disaster as the GAO and SBA Inspector General have repeatedly documented. Due to numerous problems with the program, Congress has passed legislation on three separate occasions to improve SBA's administration of the program. However, despite all the effort and money channeled into the program over many years, it had just 5,155 firms in the entire nation enrolled in 1994.[107] That amounts to just 0.03 percent of the 17,253,000 businesses in America, and only 0.24 percent of the 2,149,000 minority-owned enterprises.[108] For a handful of companies, however, the 8(a) program is a taxpayer-financed bonanza. In 1994, a typical year, 50 companies, or one percent of those in the program, received 25 percent of the $4.37 billion in 8(a) contracts.[109] Nearly 88 percent of the contracts, about $4 billion, were awarded non-competitively, assuring that the taxpayers took a beating.[110] At the same time, 2,855 firms, or about 65 percent, received no contracts at all, meaning that only 2,300 companies actually participated in the program.[111] Aside from the fraud and abuse in the program, with so few participants it is obviously not capable of achieving any national objective. Yet, it lives on, consuming a preposterously high share of Congressional time and attention while a select few companies get fat at taxpayer expense.

About half of the SBA's outlays are for the Disaster Loan Program, which lends money to homeowners and businesses to repair uninsured property damage caused by a natural disaster.[112] Between 1977 and 1993, disaster loans amounted to $55.3 billion.[113] According to the SBA, loans can only be made to disaster victims who have a reasonable ability to make repayment of principal and interest. Loan terms are tailored to each borrower's financial capability, and each borrower is required to maintain appropriate hazard and flood insurance to reduce the need for future disaster loans. For 1998, those disaster victims who were deemed not to have other credit availability were charged between 3.625 and 4.0 percent interest, while those with other credit availability were charged between 7.125 and 8.0 percent interest.[114]

Obviously, those loans made at or below 4.0 percent are subsidized, and most of the higher rate loans are likely subsidized as well. The default rate on disaster loans has ranged between 10 and 13 percent,[115] meaning that in addition to the interest subsidy, the taxpayers will lose between $110 and $150 million on the $1.138 billion in disaster loans that the SBA made in 1997.[116] The annual subsidy cost, excluding program administration, therefore, totals approximately $200 million. That is certainly not much money by federal standards and beyond the subsidy aspect, the basic program sounds reasonable. However, a closer examination shows that in combination with several other federal programs, the true cost of the disaster loan program is much higher due to unintended consequences and moral hazard. Moral hazard is the tendency of insurance to increase risk taking. For example, the owner of an expensive car is less likely to lock the car if it is fully insured.

Federal Emergency Management Agency

Adding to the problems caused by subsidized disaster loans is the subsidized flood insurance provided through the Federal Emergency Management Agency. The federal flood insurance program was enacted in 1968 and provides unsubsidized insurance for structures that meet the program's building standards and subsidized insurance for structures that predate the standards. In 1994, the average premium for a subsidized policy was $401 while the average unsubsidized premium was $247.[117] The higher average rate for subsidized policies, however, does not reflect the considerably higher actuarial risk associated with those structures that do not meet the program standards. On average, nonconforming structures are four and one-half times more likely to suffer a flood loss and when a loss occurs, they suffer one-third more damage than structures that meet program standards.[118] Without the subsidy, the average premium for nonconforming structures would have been $1,100 or 274 percent more than the government charged. In 1998, 37 percent of the 2.7 million policies in effect were subsidized.[119]

In a flyer entitled, *Myths and Facts about the National Flood Insurance Program*, FEMA proudly points out, "It doesn't matter how many times your home, apartment, or business has flooded. You are still eligible for flood insurance . . ."[120] Loss data confirms the absurdity of that policy: While repetitive losses account for only three percent of flood insurance claims, they account for a third of total payouts.[121] And for those few policyholders who keep collecting repeatedly, there is even better news: their premiums do not go up. Given that they have been relieved of the risk of living in very flood-prone areas, it is not surprising that they just keep rebuilding in the exact same spots. As long as the government is willing to pay them to stay there, why should they move out of harm's way? Nor is it surprising that since 1968, the number of households located in flood hazard areas has grown by 40 percent.[122]

The real risk to federal taxpayers lies in the fact that the National Flood Insurance Program has no reserves to pay claims. In 1993, it had $229 billion in outstanding policies[123] but had to borrow $100 million from the U.S. Treasury to remain solvent.[124] By 1997, the value of outstanding policies had risen to $325 billion, and the program had borrowed over a billion dollars from the Treasury.[125] As the GAO has warned, "The flood insurance program is intentionally not actuarially sound . . . it is inevitable that claim losses and program expenses will exceed the programs funds in some years."[126]

Magnifying the negative effects of SBA's subsidized disaster loans and FEMA's subsidized flood insurance is the 1988 Robert T. Stafford Disaster Relief and Emergency Assistance Act, which provides that many disaster relief costs be picked up by the federal government.[127] Under the Act, once the president declares a region a disaster area, the federal government becomes liable for at least 75 percent of the costs for removal of debris, emergency protective measures, and rebuilding public and certain nonprofit facilities including roads, buildings, and utilities. Congress frequently increases eligibility and expands the categories of assistance, including grants to homeowners. And Congress can be very generous. The City of San Francisco got a $400,000 footbridge on a golf course that was destroyed by flooding rebuilt by federal taxpayers.[128] And one Los Angeles theater received $1.5 million to repair earthquake damage because it offered discount tickets to senior citizens and provided acting workshops for youth and seniors.[129]

After the January 1994 Los Angeles (Northridge) earthquake, the federal government picked up 90 percent of the costs and provided $7.0 billion in aid.[130] That same year, an additional $685 million was appropriated for the Midwestern states hit by floods in 1993.[131] In June of 1997, Congress passed another flood relief bill that delivered $5.6 billion to the upper Midwest.[132] Moreover, billions of dollars in hurricane relief aid are regularly sent to Florida. In all, the federal government provided $87 billion in relief aid to states, businesses, and individuals between 1977 and 1993.[133] A significant portion of that was nominally loans to the states, but neither the states nor the federal government seriously consider any of the funds repayable. Nine out of ten federal disaster relief loans are forgiven.[134]

Federal disaster aid, SBA disaster loans, and FEMA flood insurance all act in concert to raise the costs of each program. The subsidized SBA loans and flood insurance have enabled individuals to build homes in areas with high probabilities of floods, hurricanes, and earthquakes without assuming the associated risks. Much of the risk is passed on to federal taxpayers. Many do not even purchase subsidized flood insurance because they expect the federal government to cover them with disaster aid in the event of a problem as it almost always does. Even in earthquake-prone areas such as Los Angeles and San Francisco, less than a third of those at risk purchase earthquake insurance.[135] Despite living in a very high-risk area, only about 10 percent of affected homeowners had flood insurance during the 1993 Midwest flooding.[136] The basis of any insurance program is spreading the risk among a large number of insureds, and the generosity and certainty of federal disaster aid seriously undermine the viability of the federal flood insurance program, while raising demand for subsidized SBA loans. The GAO has cautioned,

> As long as people expect federal disaster assistance, they will be reluctant to purchase insurance. And when a disaster occurs, the federal government generally feels compelled to provide assistance to uninsured people who are financially harmed, perpetuating the cycle.[137]

Similarly, the CBO has reported, "In general, federal assistance to disaster victims can cause businesses and homeowners to underinsure against future disaster risks."[138]

In the absence of these subsidy programs, commercial insurers would charge actuarially sound rates for some types of coverage, and would likely offer no coverage for very high risks. Frank Reilly, Chief Actuary for the Federal Insurance Administration, stated that if the National Flood Insurance Program set rates to cover true risks, policies would be "totally unaffordable," with premiums exceeding $12,000 annually, for houses in high-risk coastal zones.[139] He calls those structures "uninsurable."[140] If the only recourse in the event of a disaster was very expensive homeowner's insurance—if it was available at all—few people would elect to buy homes on Florida beaches, along river banks, or on top of earthquake faults. Similarly, if state and local governments had to pay to rebuild roads, bridges, and public buildings destroyed in disasters, they would be far more careful about where they built them. The GAO has reported on the state and local government moral hazard problem,

> *Effective emergency preparedness can reduce the cost of disasters and minimize the long-term social, economic, and environmental damage they cause . . . . However, . . . state and local governments often do not treat disaster preparedness as a high priority . . . state and/or local governments may be reluctant to take actions to mitigate natural hazards: Hazard mitigation can conflict with development goals.* [141]

Had their unwillingness to accept an uninsurable risk caused consumers to forgo buying homes and governments to refuse to build infrastructure in high risk areas, a substantial portion of the hundreds of billions of dollars in losses that has occurred in the last thirty years during natural disasters would never have occurred, because there would have been few roads, bridges, homes, and stores to destroy. Moreover, homeowner's insurance would be far cheaper because the losses sustained by commercial insurers would have been considerably lower. Predictably, the effect of federal disaster subsidies has been a dramatic increase in the cost of disasters for all Americans—except the subsidy recipients.

Perhaps the worst aspect of federal disaster assistance is that in many cases it facilitates rebuilding in the same location where a hurricane, flood, or earthquake destroyed the original structure. Nowhere is the lunacy more apparent than in Florida and California. Understandably, since the federal government routinely pours billions of dollars into California earthquake and flood relief, *The Los Angeles Times* has repeatedly editorialized that disaster assistance requires a "national solution."[142] However, George Skelton also writing in the *LA Times* hit the nail on the head when he wrote,

> *There's a familiar pattern: The governor declares a disaster area and the president follows suit. Then billions of tax dollars are poured into helping victims rebuild where nature has just proved it dangerous to live. All too often—as along the Russian River— disaster strikes again even before the previous rebuilding loan is repaid. What kind of societal idiocy is this?*[143]

Idiocy indeed. Obviously, California should severely restrict new construction and certainly rebuilding in its many high-risk areas. However, the California Association of Realtors, an interest group with great power in the California legislature, has warned lawmakers that it would find "restrictions on rebuilding and resale repugnant."[144] Very few legislators even think of crossing the real estate lobby, so restrictions are not going to happen. But one state Senator, Tom Haden, asked,

> *Does everybody in California think that the American taxpayers are going to subsidize our lifestyle forever, that we can just present them a blank check every time we have a mudslide or flood?*[145]

An excellent question, but unfortunately the answer is yes. The California legislature and the residents of California have a great thing going and there is no reason in the world to change it. Taxpayers from all over America pay Californians to live in some of the nation's most beautiful—and disaster-prone—areas of the country. That is the definition of "a national solution:" the nation subsidizes California.

The other absurdly disaster-prone state, Florida, also strongly supports a national solution. U.S. Senator and former Florida governor, Bob Graham, again writing in the *Los Angeles Times* (a preferred forum for espousing multi-billion dollar federal disaster subsidies) stated,

> *Since the founding of the nation, we have understood that major challenges require a national response . . . Washington must ensure a reasonable safety net to assist states after unforeseen emergencies.*[146]

What Senator Graham does not acknowledge is that the "major challenges" have been deliberately created by Floridians and that hurricanes in Florida are anything but "unforeseen emergencies." There has never been a doubt; hurricanes always have and will continue to hit Florida regularly. Indeed, the insurance industry anticipates the next major hurricane will do $50 billion in damage.[147] But whether it be a major one, or just a run-of-the-mill $10 billion hurricane, poor and middle class Americans will be there to subsidize the well-off as they rebuild their beach-front retirement and vacation homes, as well as the roads and bridges to access them. Secure in that knowledge, the Florida Building Commission, at the behest of builders and developers, drafted a new statewide building code in 1999 that would *lower* many construction standards.[148] Florida builders do not see the need for strict building standards, which increase the cost of new construction. After all, if a house blows down in a hurricane, they will get to rebuild it at the expense of federal taxpayers.

Federal Deposit Insurance

While at $325 billion, federal flood insurance represents a significant liability for American taxpayers, it comprises only a small fraction of the nearly $5 trillion in outstanding federal insurance.[149] The federal government insures against a wide variety of risks, including war-related risks, but by far the largest program is deposit insurance for banks, savings associations, and credit unions, which added up to $2.9 trillion as of September 1995.[150] Against that liability, the government had $32 billion in reserves or 1.1 percent of the face value of its insured deposits.[151] By 1997, total reserves were expected to be very close to the 1.25 percent of insured deposits required by federal law, but that small increase is hardly comforting.[152] And of course, the government does not actually have any funds; they have been spent just as all trust fund and reserve funds are spent. The reserves consist of Treasury obligations, which would have to be redeemed to pay claims.

Federal deposit insurance was established during the 1930s to deal with bank and thrift closings on a massive scale and to protect small savers. Premiums are paid by the depository institutions based on their total deposits. Through the 1970s, the system worked well. As with many subsidy programs, the initial years went without significant problems, leading lawmakers to assume foolishly that such would always be the case. Deposit insurance was expanded far beyond its intended purpose, with the maximum insured deposit increased from $40,000 to $100,000 in 1980.[153] Small savers had nowhere near $100,000 in deposits and anyone who did was certainly not in need of subsidized government insurance. Shortly thereafter, American taxpayers were dealt a moral hazard body blow. The CBO explained the problem,

> In the case of deposit insurance, financial institutions have an incentive to undertake riskier investments with depositors' funds because those funds are insured. Indeed, with insurance, depository institutions can engage in risky practices without much concern that depositors will withdraw their funds or that their cost of funds will sharply increase . . . Because insurance premiums have traditionally been the same regardless of the riskiness of the institutions' investments, the system has tended to subsidize risk taking.[154]

During the 1980s, savings and loans throughout the country binged on government subsidized risk taking. At the same time, Congress and federal regulators exacerbated the situation by lowering capital requirements and easing oversight.[155] By the end of the decade, bad investments, encouraged by federal policies and overbuilt real estate markets partly resulting from those same policies, brought the house of cards crashing down: 747 S&Ls failed.[156] The cost of cleaning up the mess totaled $160 billion of which federal taxpayers paid $132 billion.[157] The government's deposit insurance fund proved woefully inadequate. While publicly calling for heads to roll, federal politicians were not at all anxious to have the extent of the debacle exposed, because it was almost entirely their doing. Accordingly, the National Commission on Financial Institution Reform, Recovery, and Enforcement, which Congress created in 1989 to report on the S&L problem, did not have its first meeting for almost three and a half years.[158] By delaying the resolution of the S&L mess to mask its true size, the politicians increased the losses taxpayers incurred by more than $50 billion.[159]

While the hard lessons learned from the S&L debacle have resulted in some reforms, fundamental problems remain and there has certainly been no change in the self-serving optimism and poor judgment of politicians. Indeed, an ill-conceived regulatory about-face by Congress in 1989 resulted in dozens of breach of contract lawsuits from owners of S&L's who were harmed by the action. A U.S. Supreme Court ruling in 1996 and a subsequent 1997 U.S. Court of Claims ruling in favor of the plaintiffs will likely add another $20 to $50 billion to the $132 billion the taxpayers have already paid for federal foolishness.[160]

The idea that another deposit insurance debacle could not happen is wishful thinking for several reasons. First, the moral hazard problem still exists, as do the inclinations to overbuild real estate developments in good economic times. Second, the deposit insurance-driven incentive for risk-taking increases as the financial condition of a depository institution deteriorates. The less equity the owners of an institution have, the more incentive they have to take bigger risks to improve their position; they have much to gain and little to lose. Finally, the check against that behavior is the examinations of savings and loans performed by the Office of Thrift Supervision (OTS) and of banks performed by the Federal Deposit Insurance Corporation (FDIC). The GAO has found that neither the OTS nor the FDIC examinations accurately assess the safety and soundness of depository institutions.[161] Further, the banking crisis in New England in the early 1990s (159 banks failed or required regulatory intervention) demonstrated that the Federal Deposit Insurance Improvement Act of 1991 did not assure the soundness of federally insured depository institutions.[162] Eighty percent of the banks that failed had been classified as "well-capitalized," the best of five categories, two years or less before they failed.[163]

The government has no idea what its subsidy costs are for deposit insurance because it operates on a cash basis. The GAO has cautioned,

The cash-based budget, which focuses on annual cash flows, does not adequately reflect the government's cost or the economic impact of federal insurance programs because generally costs are recognized when claims are paid rather than when the commitment is made.[164]

As such, the only time the extent of the subsidy becomes apparent is when the taxpayers are handed a huge bill for something like the S&L disaster. But the subsidy and the perverse incentives are always there. As University of Chicago law professor Geoffrey Miller observed, "The excesses of the 1980s would not have happened without the federal deposit insurance system."[165]

Federal Pension Insurance

The other major insurance liability of the federal government is private pension insurance, which amounted to more than $1 trillion in 1998.[166]

The Employee Retirement Income Security Act of 1974 created the Pension Benefit Guaranty Corporation (PBGC) to insure the benefits of corporate pensions. The federal agency charges premiums based on the funding level of each pension plan, and when an underfunded insured plan terminates—usually because of the bankruptcy of the corporate sponsor—PBGC becomes responsible for paying the plan's benefits. At the end of 1995, insured corporate funds were underfunded by $64 billion with General Motors having the largest shortfall at $6.45 billion.[167] By the end of 1997, the PBGC reported assets in excess of liabilities of nearly $4 billion, but it also noted that "reasonably possible" future losses—which were not yet classified as liabilities—were in the range of $21 billion to $23 billion.[168] While legislative reforms have improved the PBGC's financial condition, it still has very little capital to cover a trillion dollars worth of insured benefits, and the GAO continues to warn of risks to the taxpayers.

Government Sponsored Enterprises

One of the approaches taken by Congress to hide the true size of the S&L crisis was to create the Resolution Funding Corporation (REFCORP) for the sole purpose of borrowing funds to close failed thrifts. This sleight-of-hand allowed the politicians to borrow $30 billion of the initial $50 billion appropriated for the S&L cleanup, thereby reducing to $20 billion the apparent expenditure of tax dollars.[169] As noted in the section on deposit insurance, this approach ended up costing the taxpayers an extra $50 billion. Of course, borrowing is one thing, paying the money back is another. Since REFCORP was little more than a shell with no resources, Congress had to devise another gimmick to pay the interest on all those bonds. The interest bill was simply too large to pass off, so most of it is paid with tax dollars. However the politicians did find a way to bury $300 million annually—The Federal Home Loan Bank system (FHLBank).[170]

The FHLBank system consists of twelve regional Federal Home Loan Banks that were created by federal legislation in 1932 to lend money at below-market rates to the thrift industry during the Great Depression. The system is one of several Government Sponsored Enterprises (GSEs)—enterprises, created by the federal government, but owned by private investors. In the case of the FHLBanks, they are owned by their member institutions: thrifts, local banks, and some insurance companies. GSE federal charters grant some benefits such as exemption from state and local taxes, but by far the biggest benefit is that they can issue debt with an implicit guarantee from the federal government. That amounts to a multi-billion dollar annual subsidy because they can borrow money at nearly the same rate as the U.S. Treasury. While the federal government has no legal obligation to protect GSE creditors, federal ties with GSEs have contributed to the perception by investors that the federal government would not allow any of the GSEs to default on their obligations.[171] The federal government has fostered that perception. Indeed, when another GSE, the Farm Credit System, ran into trouble in the mid-1980s, Congress came to the rescue with $4 billion.[172]

Before 1991, the Federal Home Loan Bank Board, three federal employees appointed by the president, had the responsibility of overseeing the privately owned FHLBanks and the savings and loan industry. According to the CBO, "The Bank Board was responsible for the inappropriate and inadequate regulatory reaction to the massive thrift failures that constituted the thrift crisis."[173] The FHLBanks were not the cause of the crisis, but, in its effort to disguise the taxpayer cost, Congress saddled them with $300 million in annual interest payment on REFCORP bonds. If it were simply a matter of intentionally punishing the wrong party, it would be a case of federal abuse of power, but not an issue affecting federal taxpayers. However, there is no free lunch, and in an effort to achieve sufficient returns to make the mandated interest payments and remain profitable, the FHLBanks are increasing the risk of their investments. With an investment portfolio of $114 billion, essentially for the sole purpose of paying REFCORP interest and backed by an implicit federal guarantee, the increased risks taken to pay for the Congressional sleight-of-hand have come right back to the taxpayers.[174]

Perhaps the most galling part of the politicians' shell game is that the FHLBank system has outlived its initial purpose. If it were not for the REFCORP interest millstone, the federal government could sever all ties, explicit and implicit, thereby eliminating a subsidy and a contingent taxpayer liability. The once vital role that the FHLBanks played in providing liquidity to thrifts for home mortgages has been taken over by the secondary mortgage market. The $1.5 trillion secondary mortgage market[175] dwarfed the $120 billion in subsidized funding that these banks had outstanding in 1995.[176] There is simply no longer any need for the FHLBanks to have any affiliation with the federal government—except to cover for Congress.

Part of the reason that the FHLBanks are unneeded is that two other GSE's have largely taken over their function in providing liquidity to the mortgage market. The Federal National Mortgage Association (FNMA or Fannie Mae), a federal agency until 1968, and the Federal Home Loan Mortgage Association (FHLMC or Freddie Mac), federally chartered in 1970, are investor-owned GSE's that are heavily subsidized by taxpayers. While the Federal Housing Administration (FHA) and Veterans Administration (VA) provide liquidity to the lower end of the market, generally under $86,000 (1998 limit), through subsidized federal mortgage insurance, Fannie Mae and Freddie Mac provide nearly all the funding for mortgages between about $86,000 and $207,000 (1998 limits).[177] They do so by using funds obtained from the bond markets to acquire mortgages from local lenders.

In addition to being exempt from state and local taxes, Freddie Mac and Fannie Mae have the same implicit federal guaranty on their debt as the FHLBanks as the CBO confirms,

The financial markets are persuaded that the government stands behind the obligations of Fannie Mae and Freddie Mac. The markets take as evidence the special privileges the government grants to the GSE's as well as other actions that federal officials

have taken during times of financial stress at the housing GSE's.[178]

The ability of Freddie and Fannie to borrow at near U.S. Treasury rates provided them with a $6.5 billion federal subsidy in 1995 according to the CBO, of which $4.4 billion was passed on to mortgage borrowers and $2.1 billion was retained.[179] Because they provide mortgages between $86,000 and $207,00, the $4.4 billion in interest subsidies went to middle and upper class homeowners—in addition to the substantial subsidies they were already receiving. The remaining $2.1 billion subsidy was kept by Fannie and Freddie and enabled them to be among the most profitable privately owned institutions in the country, thanks to U.S. taxpayers. Indeed, according to the CBO, 40 percent of these two GSE's profits are due to taxpayer subsidies.[180] The following table for the period 1990-1995 tells the story.[181]

	Average Annual Rate of Return
Freddie Mac	40.3
Fannie Mae	31.6
Dow Jones Banks	30.0
Standard and Poor's Financials	24.0
Dow Jones Savings and Loans	18.6

While the private owners of Fannie Mae and Freddie Mac enjoy extraordinary returns, the U.S. taxpayers implicitly stand behind the nearly $1.8 trillion in mortgages that they had financed as of the end of 1998.[182]

As with the FHLBanks, the purpose for which Fannie Mae and Freddie Mac were established has been accomplished, and there is no longer any need for any federal involvement with either of the institutions. The CBO has concluded that the well-established secondary mortgage market would continue to function very well without federal subsidies for the two giant GSE's,

> *If the government eliminated the subsidy to Fannie Mae and Freddie Mac, the mortgage markets would not retrogress to pre-GSE condition. Rather, fully private intermediaries, probably including Fannie Mae and Freddie Mac, would provide the funding links between the markets.*[183]

Even those who support federal subsidies for housing (generally beneficiaries of the subsidies in one form or another) should have a tough time defending using the GSE's as a subsidy conduit because they retain $1 of subsidy for every $2 they pass on. As we have seen time and time again, there is no justification for continuing GSE subsidies except that they are in the best interest of the beneficiaries and their politicians.

International Affairs

One other area where the federal government has significant exposure for loans and guarantees is in its international affairs programs. A broad collection of over seventy programs fall under the international affairs budget, function 150 of the federal budget, which was funded at $18.1 billion in 1997.[184] As one might expect, funding for the U.S. State Department and international peacekeeping missions are included in this budget. Also included are such programs as U.S. Agency for International Development (USAID), the World Bank, and the Export-Import Bank (Eximbank), which are federal subsidy programs. While the function 150 budget is supposed to be the nation's international affairs budget, the GAO has identified dozens of additional programs outside that budget that are clearly international-related and which were funded at $7.6 billion in 1997.[185]

Because function 150 subsidy programs frequently have foreign policy as well as economic objectives, they are beyond the scope of this book. Nevertheless, the programs are plagued by some of the worst aspects of other federal subsidy programs and are clearly funded well beyond any level that could be justified by foreign policy objectives. For example, in 1997, U.S. taxpayers incurred $772.6 million in costs while providing $16.5 billion in subsidized financing to companies that included very profitable giant corporations such as Boeing, Raytheon, General Electric, McDonnell Douglas, Westinghouse, and AT&T.[186] In addition, the risk of default lies not with them, but with the U.S. Treasury. The World Bank and USAID have invested tens of billions of dollars with little positive, and frequently negative, results. A 1993 Clinton Administration task force concluded that "despite decades of foreign assistance, most of Africa, and parts of Latin America, Asia, and the Middle East are economically worse off today than they were twenty years ago."[187] Indeed, assistance frequently allows countries to avoid the legal and market reforms that are essential to economic growth, and in doing so, perpetuates the problems it is supposed to alleviate. Foreign assistance subsidy programs have developed a constituency, especially their own bureaucracies, that keeps them funded despite their complete failure to achieve their objectives. In that respect, there is no difference between foreign and domestic subsidy programs.

Research and Development

The federal government spends about $70 billion each year on research and development (R&D) about half of which is for military programs.[188] As we have already seen, a significant portion of most military programs is simply pork, which politicians dole out on the theory that their district is getting something at the expense of everyone else, and military research is certainly no exception. The other $34 billion[189] is spent on a broad array of nonmilitary programs at hundreds of university labs and some seven hundred government laboratories.[190] Many are nothing more than subsidy programs of one sort or another. Article 1, Section 8 of the Constitution gives Congress the power to "promote the progress of science and the useful arts, by securing, for limited times, to authors and inventions the exclusive rights to their respective writings and discoveries." In other words, Congress was empowered to promote art and science by granting copyrights and patents; there is no mention of subsidies. The Founders would be flabbergasted if they could see the extent to which Congress is now "promoting" science.

Much of the nation's early support for science was for military reasons. In 1863, shortly after the naval battle between the Monitor and the Merrimack, Congress established the National Academy of Sciences and one of its first tasks was to figure out how to operate a magnetic compass on an iron ship. Each successive war has seen the creation of more federal science agencies and ever-increasing funding. World War II prompted the establishment of numerous national laboratories, officially called Federally Funded Research and Development Centers (FFRDCS), many of which were dedicated to the development of the atomic bomb. The cold war accelerated nuclear weapons R&D and by 1969, there were 74 FFRDCS.[191] Today there are still 39 FFRDCs and many of them have had no mission since the nuclear race ended. However, with billions of dollars in funding—the Energy Department's ten largest labs had a budget in 1995 of $6 billion[192]—both the employees and the politicians are scrambling to find some nonmilitary function for the labs.

The problem is that the national labs have no expertise in commercial or industrial R&D, nor are they well structured to handle non-weapons work. Hirsch Cohen, who chaired a government panel that studied the labs in 1987, acknowledged their nuclear weapons expertise but added, "what is still to be proven is their ability to do anything else."[193] The record certainly bears that out. The GAO reported that the Energy Department—which operates a large percentage of the labs and spent over $50 billion on R&D between 1978 and 1995[194]—terminated 31 out of 80 major projects after investing over $10 billion between 1980 and 1996.[195] It only completed 15 projects, and most of those were behind schedule and over budget.[196] Here is how, according to the GAO, such stellar performance is achieved:

> *Contractors, such as those operating the large national laboratories, receive program guidance from many different program offices but are managed and evaluated by field offices that are not accountable to the program offices. Several program (and staff) offices can direct a single contractor, bypassing the field office and the other program offices.*[197]

The labs are drowning in bureaucracy. A study of the ten biggest labs found that their budgets could be cut in half without touching actual R&D at all.[198] Nonetheless, Congress would rather the labs just come up with schemes to justify their existence rather than stop the gravy train. Thus, the labs are embarking on all sorts of commercial R&D projects from automobiles to semiconductors—despite the dismal results of the labs' previous efforts. Billions of dollars spent during the 1970s to come up with alternative energy sources produced almost nothing.

As part of their new commercial mission, the labs are engaging in hundreds of cooperative R&D agreements with private companies who, not surprisingly, are only too happy to have the government subsidizing them. Moreover, the government generally does not require repayment of its investment in cost-shared technology development projects.[199] That, however, distorts the industrial picture because some firms are subsidized while others are harmed. Dupont found that the government's Wright Patterson lab was making—at taxpayer expense—a virtually identical polymer to one it developed with its own funds.[200] Furthermore, taxpayer-funded government labs compete directly with private research labs and universities for commercial research contracts. Then too, some of the R&D that American taxpayers subsidize goes to benefit foreign companies. The primary beneficiary of Extreme Ultraviolet Lithography technology for making advanced semiconductors developed by the Lawrence Livermore National Laboratory has been the Japanese company Nikon.[201]

A major impetus for the infusion of tens of billions of federal dollars into research every year is the premise that scientific research leads to technological development, which is crucial to the economic health of America. This theory became widely accepted during the 1980s when market share losses to the Japanese in some U.S. industries, such as automobiles and semiconductors, led many politicians to pronounce that America had lost its technological edge and its ability to compete in world markets. They predicted the demise of American industry and catastrophic trade deficits unless massive government funding for R&D reversed the trend. The scientific community, already heavily dependent on federal funding to support a subsidy-induced, ever-expanding surplus of PhDs, eagerly jumped on the band wagon. The problem is that there is little evidence to support that theory. Indeed, its proponents lack a basic understanding of trade economics.

Perennial trade deficits are not good. A nation that maintains substantial trade deficits for an extended period must eventually reduce its standard of living to repay the foreign loans used to finance those deficits.[202] But trade deficits are not a function of the quality of a nation's products, but a reflection of the difference between national savings and investment. The savings of American households as a percentage of gross national product declined from almost 20 percent in 1948 to less than 13 percent in 1993,[203] and the rate turned negative in late 1998.[204] If we save less than we invest, we must borrow surplus savings from other nations. To generate those surplus savings, we must buy more goods and services than we sell. New products or processes have nothing to do with it. In a 1989 report, the CBO tried to make this clear to Congress,

> Increasing the innovativeness of domestic industry would make the United States more competitive. But even if Congress established programs that successfully stimulated the development of new commercial products and processes, these programs would have little near-term impact on the trade deficit, which is largely a macro-economic phenomenon.[205]

Another aspect of the trade deficit that is frequently ignored is that foreign affiliates of U.S. firms account for a substantial portion (almost 20 percent in 1995) of U.S. merchandise imports.[206] This reflects American competitive strength, not weakness.

It is also a fallacy that government R&D leads to new products and processes. Given the enormous amount of tax dollars spent on R&D, it does occasionally happen, but it is clearly the exception, not the rule. In a detailed examination of the development of critical new technologies throughout history, Terence Kealey documents in his book *The Economic Laws of Scientific Research* that invariably scientists were nowhere to be found. There has always been plenty of research all the way back to the ancient Greeks. But the products and inventions were the result of tradesmen and engineers working to solve practical problems, not the result of scientific research. Kealey concludes that one of the great lessons of history is that technology came first and science followed.[207] The situation is no different with modern technology. Studies by Professor Don E. Kash of George Mason University show that new complex devices such as advanced computer chips are the result of better engineering, not new discoveries.[208] This is exactly the opposite of the view widely held by politicians that has resulted in hundreds of billions of tax dollars being channeled into research.

Interestingly, the one thing cited more than any other by politicians to justify massive government spending on R&D is Japan's economic power. If Japan were truly threatening the U.S. economy (it is not), the lesson would be to take the opposite course from the one Congress has chosen. R&D in Japan is overwhelmingly an undertaking of private industry, not the government. Professor Paul M. Kennedy of Yale notes,

> *Japan's second strength is that a far higher proportion of Japanese R&D is paid for and done by industry itself than in Europe and the United States where so much is done by governments and universities.*[209]

The investments that the Japanese government did make in R&D had a terrible record. A study by Richard Beason of Alberta University and David Weinterin of Harvard showed that the Japanese government consistently invested in the sectors of the economy that proved to be losers.[210] No government has proved adept at picking economic winners primarily because a profit motive, which governments lack, is an essential element. The CBO very succinctly stated why the U.S. government should avoid funding commercial R&D,

> *... further government assistance might not be appropriate for a number of reasons. To begin, the government has little experience in making commercial decisions; consequently, its efforts may lead to a misallocation of resources. Moreover, even if the federal government successfully stimulated new technologies, the advantage to the United States might be transitory. A domestic*

firm may decide to use the innovation in another country, or a foreign firm may be able to copy it quickly. Finally, private firms are responding to the greater competitive challenges in a variety of ways, one of which has been to increase R&D expenditures. Consequently the Congress may have more success in improving industry competitiveness by other means. These might include programs to increase savings and investment or to improve educational quality.[211]

Congress has not been lacking for proper guidance on this issue. In 1998, the GAO reported:

More than 150 panels, commissions, task forces, and GAO reports have cited excess capacity, poor maintenance, duplicative activities, and the failure of the federal Research, Development, Test, and Evaluation establishment to adapt missions and programs to the changing world environment.[212]

Unfortunately, the power of hard facts is feeble compared to that of a large and very influential subsidy interest group. Even with American industry and the economy in perhaps its best shape ever, federal politicians are attempting to increase rather than slash R&D subsidies. Senators Phil Gramm of Texas and Joe Lieberman of Connecticut introduced the National Research Investment Act of 1998, which would have doubled the nonmilitary R&D budget from $34 billion to $68 billion over nine years.[213] It makes no sense to further tax corporations to generate additional revenues to inefficiently undertake government-directed research, which has mostly proven to be useless. Far better to let industry keep the money and do its own research. However, subsidies are the primary source of political power and, not surprisingly, Texas and Connecticut institutions will see plenty of additional subsidy dollars if Senators Gramm and Lieberman have their way.

National Aeronautics and Space Administration (NASA)

About two-thirds of NASA's $14 billion annual budget is consumed by its eight laboratories.[214] And much of that is for one program: the International Space Station (ISS), which has never been anything other than an aerospace subsidy program supporting over seventy thousand workers in forty states.[215] Originally envisioned by Ronald Reagan, NASA claimed in 1983 that it could build a huge permanent space station for $8 billion and have it in operation by 1994.[216] When the Senate approved funding for the space station, Senator Bumpers lamented, "Not one Senator could say what it was for."[217] Fourteen years later, the taxpayers had shelled out $18 billion, the design was not even finalized, and the GAO was projecting that it would require an additional $78 billion to launch the ISS and operate it for ten years.[218] An investigation by *Business Week* found that half of the first $12 billion spent on the ISS, fully 75 percent of what NASA claimed the entire project would cost, bought nothing at all; it was "frittered away on a series of wheel-spinning re-designs . . . more than $5 billion has gone toward needless salaries, equipment, and blueprints."[219] In other words, it was pure scientific pork.[220]

As originally envisioned, the space station Freedom was essentially an American program. However, as costs skyrocketed, NASA internationalized the project to keep it alive, and finally, in an act of desperation, brought in the Russians for a major role despite a very slim chance that they could keep their commitments. Senator Bumpers characterized the strategy,

> *Everyone knew that Russia could not hold up its part of the bargain and the result was predictable . . . It was a cynical ploy to gin up political support for a project that was heading toward a richly deserved cancellation.*[221]

Russia has not kept its part of the bargain, and the project is falling further behind schedule and becoming ever more expensive. Further delays could push the price tag up by billions of dollars more and such delays are a virtual certainty. Indeed, there is a good chance that the station will never be completed. Despite the infusion of $662 million American taxpayer dollars through 1997,[222] Russia has had one delay after another. In September 1998, NASA advised Congress that it would need at least another $660 million to keep Russia's space agency afloat.[223] At the same time, the agency began implementing plans to build backups for the space station modules that the Russians were supposed to supply. But NASA is also counting on forty Russian rockets to launch hardware into space and to reboost the station's orbit. That is a very risky strategy at best. It is almost certain that the Russians will not come through, and the slack will have to be taken up by American space shuttles. Unfortunately, that is another very dubious strategy.

The U.S. currently has four space shuttles: Columbia, Discovery, Atlantis, and Endeavor. The primary purpose of twenty-seven of the thirty-four scheduled missions between 1997 and 2002 is to transport ISS components into orbit.[224] Columbia cannot provide adequate lift so it cannot be used for ISS transport and one other shuttle will undergo scheduled maintenance during the ISS transport period, meaning, at times, only two shuttles will be available.[225] Moreover, numerous modifications are required on the three transport shuttles to increase their lift capability. The GAO concluded, "NASA's schedule for meeting space station launch requirements appears questionable . . . . The remaining launch schedule is compressed and will be difficult to achieve . . . ."[226] That is if everything goes well.

The last shuttle, Endeavor, was completed in 1992, and NASA has no contingency plan to replace a shuttle in the event of a catastrophic accident. Nor could one seriously damaged in an accident be repaired because there are no structural spare parts available. Congress eliminated funding for structural spare parts for the only means of getting the space station into orbit.[227] Completing the 27 scheduled ISS transport flights anywhere near on schedule would be a miracle. If a shuttle were lost or seriously damaged, the ISS program would be delayed for years at a cost of many billions of additional dollars. It would take six to seven years if a decision were made to build another shuttle.[228] Unlikely to meet their own schedule, U.S. space shuttles are in no position to take on any of the transport load presently scheduled for Russian rockets. Yet Congress and NASA have committed nearly $100 billion taxpayer dollars to the ISS when even getting the components into space is a very tenuous proposition.

Then there is the question of the purpose of the space station. As Senator Bumpers pointed out, Congress has no idea, but it knows that the ISS is one hell of a subsidy program. Only an infinitesimal amount of the $94 billion cost will go for actual science experiments; nearly all the money is going to the companies supplying parts and the more than 70,000 people employed by the project. NASA claims that a primary space station mission is biological research. However, as ISS costs kept ballooning, NASA steadily downsized the station and stripped down its lab facilities. Very little science will be done on the ISS and nearly all of that could have been accomplished on earth or on unmanned spacecraft for a tiny fraction of the cost of the ISS. The head of NASA's Space Biomedical Research Institute, Lawrence Young, complained that NASA would "build a house, but not have any furniture."[229] Physicist Robert Park, director of public information for the American Physical Society, predicted that "the only thing [space station] Freedom might discover is a bag of human waste tossed overboard" by the Russian space station.[230] *Business Week* noted, "The space station has a better chance of finding Klingons than finding cures."[231]

With 40 states receiving contracts for ISS components, the space station is a near-perfect pork program from the Congressional viewpoint. For NASA, the ISS means survival. There never has been much of a point to the manned space program other than as a massive aerospace subsidy mechanism. While a maximum effort, costing an extraordinary amount of money, was mounted to achieve John F. Kennedy's goal of putting a man on the moon by 1969, it remains unclear why this was done. In 1994, 25 years after we reached the moon, less than 10 percent of the material brought back had been analyzed.[232] The supposed fruits of a major national effort sit untouched. What was the hurry and what was the point? There is simply very little space research that unmanned spacecraft cannot accomplish. Robert Park notes, "There no longer seems to be any need to expose humans to the space environment."[233] Using manned spacecraft dramatically increases the cost because of life support systems and numerous safety features not needed on unmanned spacecraft. However, NASA's budget and aerospace industry subsidies would decline dramatically in the absence of a manned space program.

The space shuttle was developed in the 1970s after the manned lunar program ended. Much like its later promise that the space station would cost $8 billion, NASA promised that the shuttle would make space flight routine and inexpensive, and it planned to make up to 60 flights per year.[234] Instead, the four shuttles make about eight flights per year combined and they are anything but inexpensive. NASA has worked diligently to hide the true cost of the shuttle program. In 1991, when the agency upped its construction estimate for the space station to $30 billion, it included in that figure the cost of the shuttle flights to transport the station components at $44 million each.[235] NASA arrived at this "marginal cost per flight" not by calculating all the costs of flying an average mission, but by calculating what it saved when it canceled a mission—basically, the costs of launch operations, fuel, and the boosters.[236] At the same time, the agency claimed that the average cost per flight was $413.5 million.[237] But the figure it presented to Congress for 28 transport flights for the space station was $1.2 billion, not the $11.6 billion that 28 flights at its stated average cost would run. But even if NASA had used the higher figure, it would have still dramatically understated the true cost.

In calculating the $413.5 million average cost per flight, NASA only included operating costs, ignoring the $30 billion spent to build the shuttles and the $1 billion that it spends annually to improve them.[238] Including all those costs and amortizing them over the expected life of the shuttle program, including ten years of ISS operation, brings the actual cost per flight to $718 million and the true cost of the 28 ISS transport flights to $20.1 billion.[239] (Based on the average shuttle payload of 26,000 pounds over the first 78 shuttle flights,[240] NASA's publicity stunt of sending 77 year old Senator John Glenn for a shuttle ride in 1998 cost the taxpayers about $5 million.) NASA surely knew that letting the taxpayers know how much the shuttle flights were really costing would jeopardize the program. Especially since virtually nothing done on shuttle missions needs to be done on manned spacecraft. Thus, when President Reagan proposed the space station, NASA saw the one thing that could save its shuttle program. Indeed, NASA Administrator Daniel Goldin admitted that without the space station, there would be no need for shuttles.[241] As is standard practice at NASA, it lowballed the space station cost to insure funding for the program to keep the shuttle program alive. Ever since, the agency has regularly told Congress that it must have more money or the program will be terminated. However, with NASA's gravy train running through 40 states, continued funding is assured. Ultimately, the primary purpose of the space station is to justify the shuttle program and the primary purpose of the shuttle program is to build the space station. Most of NASA's budget is dependent on the two programs, but neither program serves any significant purpose for science, the U.S. taxpayers, or the economy. The are simply subsidy programs. As the CBO concluded,

The balance of the evidence does not support higher levels of funding for NASA as a means to increase economywide productivity. In the short term, NASA's spending affects the economy in the same way that other government spending does—and is properly viewed as a cost rather than a benefit of the program. Over the longer term, NASA's contribution to the economy does not appear to be large when measured by the most objective standard.[242]

Davis-Bacon and AmeriCorps

Finally, before looking at how we might get out of this federal morass, we will briefly look at two subsidy programs that serve to recap the primary faults of virtually all federal subsidy programs. The Davis-Bacon Act was enacted in 1931 when Congress was desperately trying to protect wages and jobs in the face of the Great Depression. (Failing to allow wages to decline along with falling prices actually exacerbated the depression.) The Act required that "prevailing wages" be paid on all federally funded or federally assisted construction projects, which now total about $40 billion each year.[243] The problem at the time was that blacks and immigrants were taking the jobs of native-born white construction workers and Congress acted to reverse that trend. A study by Jennifer Morse of George Mason University concludes that the Act was racist in its intent.[244] Essentially, it required contractors to pay union-scale wages, thereby assuring that white union workers would be hired over less costly minority workers.

The Heritage Foundation estimates that Davis-Bacon still costs American taxpayers $1 billion annually in inflated construction costs.[245] For example, in Oakland, California in 1997, carpenters on private construction projects earned about $15 per hour; but, thanks to Davis-Bacon, carpenters on federal projects earned about $28 per hour.[246] Since the Act almost assures that union construction workers are employed on federal jobs, it essentially amounts to a billion-dollar subsidy program for union workers. The Act serves no other purpose because numerous other laws cover every aspect of worker health and safety as well as construction quality. Supporters of Davis-Bacon claim that repeal of the Act could jeopardize the quality of federal projects,[247] but this claim is preposterous. Thousands of commercial buildings, many far larger than federal buildings, have been built without Davis-Bacon restrictions with no quality problems. Indeed, the weakness of the claim only serves to highlight the fact that there is no legitimate reason for the Act. It is a pure subsidy program, with racist origins, that produces no benefits for the taxpayers funding it. Yet Congress refuses to repeal it because it benefits a powerful and generous interest group.

Despite budgetary constraints and mountains of evidence from both government and non-government sources that federal subsidy programs are, by far, the single biggest problem facing the American people, Congress passed Bill Clinton's National Community Service Trust Act, better known as AmeriCorps, in 1993. AmeriCorps allows participants who are at least 16 years old to earn education awards to help pay for postsecondary education in exchange for performing community service. Just based on its intent, the program is preposterous. The federal government already had a jumble of 154 overlapping job-training programs and was spending tens of billions of dollars annually subsidizing postsecondary education. Indeed, much of the rampant inflation in the cost of a college education is directly traceable to too much federal money being pumped into the system. The last thing the nation needed was another subsidy program for training or postsecondary education. Similarly, there were dozens of inefficient federal community assistance programs; we certainly did not need another one. The AmeriCorps statute created a new federal corporation, the Corporation for National and Community Service, to administer the program. To receive grants from the national corporation, the states must establish commissions on national service. All of this costly overhead to help local communities with local problems.

The GAO reported on three typical AmeriCorps projects in 1995.[248] The first was the renovation of a multifamily house and another was the building of a community farm market. The federal government already had programs through the Housing and Urban Development and Agriculture Departments that addressed both of those "needs." The third project was the renovation of a municipal stadium, and it is just possible that there was no federal subsidy program that addresses municipal stadiums—unless it was damaged by a natural disaster. AmeriCorps rose to the occasion. On average, the program consumes nearly $27,000 in resources to pay AmeriCorps "volunteers" about $13,000 in benefits.[249] That raises the question: Why didn't the federal government just let the local community keep the taxes it paid for the AmeriCorps program, use half the money to pay for the stadium renovation and keep the rest? Or use all the money locally to achieve twice as much?

The answer is that subsidies are the business of the federal government. They are the source of its power and the primary source of the hundreds of millions of dollars in campaign contributions that are little more than commissions paid by subsidy recipients. Congress is unconcerned with whether a subsidy program is in the national interest or whether it achieves its stated objective. Nor does it make any difference if a subsidy program spends ten dollars to achieve one dollar's worth of result. Subsidies are the business of the federal government and that must be changed.

10

THERE IS REALLY ONLY ONE PARTY: THE SUBSIDY PARTY

Without a doubt, a federal government that is involved in virtually all aspects of the lives of individual Americans is a far cry from what the founders envisioned. In the Kentucky Resolutions of 1798, Thomas Jefferson wrote,

> *The several states composing the United States of America . . . by compact . . . constituted a general government for specific purposes . . . reserving, each state to itself, the residual mass of right to their own self-government.*

In 1792, James Madison warned that if the Constitution was interpreted as empowering the national government to pursue whatever goals the people deemed appropriate as some "Nationalists" argued, "Everything from the highest object of state legislation to the most minute object of police would be thrown under the power of Congress."[1] Even the vision for the federal government of the Nationalists was nowhere near as pervasive as what we have today. One of them, Judge Alexander Addison, termed the warnings of Jefferson and Madison of a federal government deeply involved in all aspects of the affairs of the states "a supposition so extravagant, that I cannot persuade myself it will ever be honestly and seriously urged."[2] Time has proven Judge Addison very wrong.

One of the concerns of the Founders was factions, or what we now call special interests. But they were convinced that the many varied interests operating within the system of checks and balances they had devised would offset each other as Madison indicated in Federalist Paper Number 51,

> *Whilst all authority in it will be derived from and dependent on the society, the society itself will be broken into so many parts, interests, and classes of citizens that the rights of individuals, or of the minority, will be in little danger from interested combinations of the majority.*

Madison was clearly mistaken. As University of California Professor Donald Wittman has concluded, Madison overestimated the transaction costs in creating an extensive political coalition.[3] Of course, we did monkey with one of the primary mechanisms set up by the Founders to insure dynamic tension.

The Constitution provided that the president, members of the Senate, and members of the House of Representatives all be elected by different groups. House members were to be elected directly by the people, Senators were to be appointed by state legislatures, and the president was elected by the Electoral College, which was supposed to be composed of the most eminent individuals from each state. Thus, each body would have a separate electorate, and it was hoped that a variety of interests would be represented and a balancing of interests would result. All that was changed by the Twelfth and Seventeenth Amendments, which provided for direct election of the president and senators respectively. There is no way to know where we would be today had the original system been left intact; we might be in even worse shape. Nevertheless, the situation we have now has all federal politicians elected by the same electorate, and that has accorded special interests an unobstructed path to power.

Given the distaste that the Founders had for political factions, it is not surprising that the Constitution contains no provision for political parties. Nonetheless, they sprang up rather quickly and today we commonly speak of having a two-party system. However, there is really only one party: the Subsidy party, which has a right and left wing. Democrats, the left wing of the Subsidy party, tend to favor handouts for certain interest groups, while on the right, Republicans generally favor subsidies for others. That is essentially the difference between the two. There is a great deal of rhetoric for show, but year in and year out the two wings of the Subsidy party demonstrate unanimity in preserving each other's subsidy programs. Between 1992 and 1997, despite the Republican takeover of both houses of Congress and all the bluster about cutting spending, less than 4 percent of industry subsidies were phased out according to the Progressive Policy Institute.[4] Overall, subsidy spending increased. Indeed, there may be greater party unity today than at any time in history.

The distressing consequence of all this is that it really makes no difference who you vote for in a federal election, and Americans have figured that out. A 1996 poll conducted by the *Washington Post*, the Kaiser Foundation, and Harvard University found that half of the adults interviewed did not know whether their representative was a Republican or a Democrat.[5] Perhaps even more distressing is that even the brightest of our young people are tuning out. A 1993 University of Pennsylvania survey of Ivy League students, who have traditionally made up a very disproportionate percentage of federal officials, found that only half could name both their U.S. Senators.[6] As more and more Americans effectively withdraw from the democratic process, the power of subsidized interests is further entrenched.

Consistently working on behalf of subsidized interests now passes for public service. As University of Chicago Professor Cass Sunstein has observed, "If protection of the class of statutory beneficiaries is itself seen as a public value, many exercises of raw political power—even if in the service of faction—become automatically justifiable."[7] Federal politicians unabashedly go about the business of preserving existing subsidy programs and seeking to institute new ones while collecting commissions from the interest groups they represent. Not surprisingly, there is a strong correlation between the level of government subsidies and the amount recycled back to the politicians. A study by John R. Lott Jr., of the University of Chicago found that the most convincing explanation of rising campaign expenditures is rising government expenditures.[8] The level of commissions paid gives some insight into the value of the subsidies at stake: one billion dollars was spent on the 1996 Presidential and Congressional elections,[9] most of which came from subsidized interests. In their book *Dirty Little Secrets*, University of Virginia professor Larry Sabato and *Wall Street Journal* reporter Glenn Simpson conclude that corruption is not just a danger of political life, it is an unavoidable component of fundraising, political horsetrading, and campaigning.[10] Such has been the corrosive effect of pervasive federal subsidies.

As it becomes apparent that there is really only one party, special interests are increasingly ignoring the party and just dealing with their politicians by recycling a portion of their subsidies to them directly, and often, another portion on "independent expenditures." The politicians are acutely aware of who their contributions come from. According to UCLA Professor of Political Science Susanne Lohmann,

> Now we can see why political competition is impotent. The general public cannot effectively monitor whether a political candidate who promises to eliminate the policy bias toward special interests will keep his promise. Once elected, he shares the electoral incentives of his predecessors to favor special interests who are better able to monitor his performance.[11]

With the beneficiary groups providing hundreds of millions of dollars in campaign financing, the individual voter has become increasingly irrelevant. Unfortunately, as the late Senator Paul Tsongas observed, "What's good for America is not good for our candidates."[12] Too bad for America. Incumbents use the huge subsidy commissions they collect to roll over their opposition with meaningless but overpowering media campaigns. In 1995, political action committee (PAC) contributions to incumbents outnumbered those to challengers sixteen to one.[13] In Congress, extensive logrolling (you vote for my subsidy program and I will vote for yours) guarantees that everyone's programs are assured of continued funding while minimizing accountability. Lloyd Cutler, who served as White House Counsel to both Presidents Carter and Clinton, concluded that, "Neither party nor any individual we elect can fairly be held accountable for the hodgepodge of unwanted outcomes such as huge budget and trade deficits."[14] The Founders would be stunned at what has become of their carefully crafted institution.

The actual goings on in the halls of Congress are simply shameful. Seldom does a senator or representative read the bills they vote on, and floor debates are usually very poorly attended. Claremont McKenna College Professor John Pitney gives this disturbing insight into the legislative process,

> . . . the best you can say is that some of the lawmakers read some of the bills some of the time. The rest rely on staff-written summaries and word-of-mouth descriptions from colleagues and lobbyists. They often don't know what they're doing and then can't remember why they did it.[15]

Regarding the committee reports on which most legislation is based, Supreme Court Justice Antonin Scalia has observed, "It is not even certain that members of the issuing committees have found time to read them."[16] Who does know what is in the Committee reports and legislation passed by Congress? Why the people who write them, of course: staff members—especially the powerful committee staffs—and special interest lobbyists. Justice Scalia writes that,

> One of the routine tasks of the Washington lawyer-lobbyist is to draft language that sympathetic legislators can recite in a pre-written "floor debate"—or even better, insert in a committee report.[17]

Most often, the only ones who know what is actually in a piece of legislation are behind-the-scenes staffers and lobbyists whom the public knows nothing about. Congressmen and senators come and go, but powerful staff members are permanent—until they transition to direct, special-interest employment by becoming lobbyists themselves. They owe nothing to the voters and everything to the special interests that are the true base of power in Washington. Hundreds of them go about the daily business of preserving and expanding subsidy programs for thousands of special interest groups with whom they work closely. Harvard University professor Don Price concludes,

> The degree of independence of Congressional committees and their staffs and the related independence of specialized executive bureaus and agencies make it impossible to plan and carry out a coherent program. There is no clear center of authority in either the Congress or the executive that the voters can hold responsible.[18]

The loss of voter accountability has evolved along with the growth in federal subsidies as a necessary condition for maintaining and expanding those subsidies. There is no way to reestablish meaningful elections as long as subsidies are the primary focus of the federal government, but neither can the pervasive subsidy programs that grow larger every year be curtailed or eliminated without meaningful elections. It is a conundrum that none of the commonly proposed reforms will solve.

Some, primarily Republicans, have claimed that term limits would reduce the influence of special interests, but it is far more likely that the reverse would occur. Congressional staffers and bureaucrats already have enormous power in Washington, and limiting the terms of elected officials would do nothing but increase that power. It takes years to begin to understand the immensely complex money machine that is the federal government, and during their first few years in office, members of Congress are almost completely dependent on personal, agency, and committee staff. Term limits would insure that just as they became knowledgeable enough to direct staff rather than being dependent on them, he or she would have to leave to be replaced by another neophyte. The effect would be to hand over the government to the professional bureaucracy and Congressional staffers. There is probably nothing the subsidy interests would rather see.

Another solution often proposed is a balanced budget amendment. But that mechanism does not address the real problem: federal spending. In January 1999, the CBO projected that 1999 federal spending would grow from $1.7 trillion in 1999 to $2.3 trillion in 2009,[17] based on the fanciful assumption that Congress would make drastic cuts in spending over the next few years. That represents a 35.3 percent increase in ten years—after all the supposed budget tightening and cutting of the last few years—assuming that Congress complies with the spending caps dictated through the year 2002 by the Balanced Budget Act of 1997.[18] But those caps had already been broken even as the CBO was writing its report and federal politicians were diligently working on dozens of new and expanded subsidy programs, so the actual increase in spending will likely approach 50 percent. Caps or no caps, federal spending is slated to continue to increase substantially, and a balanced budget amendment, even one that required a supermajority to raise taxes, would not prevent that. It would simply require that Congress raise taxes as fast as it raises spending. Indeed, a balanced budget amendment could cause spending to balloon, because it would provide Congress with constitutional cover for raising taxes. The politicians could increase spending, and then claim that they were legally obligated to raise taxes to balance the budget. The problem is not deficit spending; it is too much spending. Way too much. A balanced budget amendment will not solve that problem.

Another idea that has received far more attention than it deserves is campaign finance reform. Why too much attention? Because as almost every politician and lobbyist knows, there is no plan that will have any significant impact on the recycling of subsidy dollars back to politicians that will also be acceptable to the U.S. Supreme Court. The Court has ruled that laws limiting campaign spending are a violation of a candidate's First Amendment rights and are, therefore, unconstitutional. Moreover, the very aspects of the present campaign laws that reformers cite as problems—PACs and "soft money" contributions—were enacted as reforms of previous "flawed" campaign finance laws. Any reform legislation that will pass Congress will be designed with sufficient loopholes and vehicles to insure that the flow of recycled subsides continues unabated. After all, the politicians who are the recipients of hundreds of millions of dollars in commissions are the same ones that must approve campaign finance reforms.

Nor will sending new people to Congress solve the problem. The reform fervor of newly elected members of Congress dies quickly. What happened to the 75 House Democrats who were swept into office in 1974 by their strong reform positions in the wake of the Nixon campaign finance scandals? Many of them are at the core of today's problems. As *Business Week* columnist Howard Gleckman observed, they failed to fundamentally change politics because they were co-opted by the system.[19] Who we elect literally makes no difference because the problem is not the people, it is the system. Efforts to reform campaign finance laws are misguided because their objective is to change the faces in Congress. That was largely accomplished in 1974 and again in 1994, but the avid reformers quickly settled into business as usual. It is the subsidy engine driving campaign finances that has to be addressed. In the words of Nobel laureate Gary Becker,

> . . . *the source of official corruption is the same everywhere; large governments with the power to dispense many goodies to different groups . . . instituting large cuts in the scope of government is the only surefire way to reduce corruption.*[20]

On the other hand, perhaps the problem has already been solved. President Clinton tells us that the federal civilian work force is the smallest it has been since the Kennedy Administration. In addition, federal politicians of all stripes have been boasting about budget surpluses. It is true that the civilian work force has declined in recent years, but that is largely because of huge reductions in the Defense Department after the end of the cold war. Non-defense civilian employment, the segment where you will find those who administer federal subsidy programs, is up 40 percent from 1963, when John F. Kennedy died.[21] JFK was primarily defending the country; the Clinton Administration is primarily defending subsidy interests.

And what about the much-publicized federal budget surpluses? Certainly, a budget slated to increase more than a half a trillion dollars between 1999 and 2009 shows that federal spending is scheduled to continue its rapid growth. As such, revenues must be rising rapidly as well, and indeed they are. Federal taxes have risen from 17.8 percent of GDP in 1992 to over 20 percent in 1999, the largest tax bite since World War II.[22] In 1999, the federal government consumed about 20 percent of the entire U.S. economy without a war and while the military was being down-sized.[23] But even with all the extra taxes, the federal budget is assuredly not balanced, as the politicians well know.

The CBO's January 1999 report, *The Economic and Budget Outlook: Fiscal Years 2000-2009*, tells the real story. Since the CBO answers to Congress, it has to pay lip service to the politicians' budget semantics, but its report clearly shows that gross federal debt will continue its inexorable climb, increasing from $5.48 trillion in 1998 to $5.8 trillion in 2006.[24] Given that, how can President Clinton claim that the federal budget is in surplus "as far as the eye can see?"[25] Accounting gimmickry. Consider the following excerpt from *Analytical Perspectives: Budget of the United States Government, Fiscal Year 1999* issued by the U.S. Office of Management and Budget:

> *Off-budget Federal entities are federally owned and controlled, but their transactions are excluded form the budget totals by law. When a federal entity is off-budget, its receipts, outlays, and deficit or surplus are not included in budget receipts, budget outlays, or the budget deficit or surplus; and its budget authority is not included in the budget authority for the total budget.*

Social Security was made an off-budget program in 1985, and the law clearly states that it is separate from the federal budget. For 1999, the CBO projected a Social Security surplus of $127 billion and a $19 billion deficit for the federal budget.[26] Yet all you hear from federal politicians is that the federal budget is running a $107 billion surplus. They have been doing the same thing since 1985: borrowing from Social Security and other trust funds to pay federal bills and publicly treating the loans as if they were general revenue. The name given to the result of this sleight-of-hand is the "unified budget," which serves no other purpose than to hide the deficit in the real budget. The GAO stated as much in 1989:

> *As the unified budget is presently structured, the surpluses in the trust funds are merged with the rest of the budget, effectively masking the magnitude of those surpluses and the size of the deficit in the rest of the government . . . Because the trust fund surpluses—especially those in Social Security—are growing so rapidly, the merger of trust and nontrust funds creates the erroneous impression that the deficit is under control and declining.[27]*

That erroneous impression is exactly what the politicians are after. And as such, while they pushed for more new subsidy programs, none of them mentioned that the 1999 gross federal debt increased by nearly $100 billion at the same time that the government was running a "surplus".

However, even the projected unified budget surpluses will prove elusive. You will recall that the CBO advised that its projections assumed Congress would adhere to the budget caps agreed to in 1997. The Balanced Budget Act was a classic example of Washington smoke and mirrors. The president and members of Congress indulged in an orgy of public self-congratulation because the Act provided for a balanced budget by the year 2002. While it increased discretionary spending by $96 billion over five years,[28] the Act did not make the necessary, tough spending decisions to achieve a balanced budget. The decisions on what spending to cut were pushed out into future years. In addition, the balanced budget calculation made very optimistic assumptions about huge Medicare cost savings—mostly by again cutting payments to doctors and hospitals—which are unlikely to materialize. The politicians took credit for balancing the budget when in fact they significantly increased spending while only agreeing to take steps over the following four years to meet broad spending caps.

According to former CBO director Robert Reischauer, those caps require Congress to vote to reduce discretionary spending by 12 percent between 1998 and 2002.[29] However, Congress has not been willing to make tough spending decisions. Indeed, the 1993 budget agreement required similar cuts in 1998, but Congress and the president refused to make them. Ironically, they used the 1997 Balanced Budget Act to increase the 1998 spending cap (set in the 1993 budget agreement) by $8.5 billion thereby avoiding the required spending cuts.[30] Then in 1998, unwilling to make the spending cuts required for 1999, Congress passed an omnibus spending bill that exceeded the now higher cap by $21 billion.[31] Through 1999, the required spending cuts were modest, but the politicians still could not make them. The deep cuts come in 2000, 2001, and 2002. Reischauer suggests "a bit of skepticism about the political system's ability to mete out such sacrifice."[32] Perhaps more than a bit. The politicians will not abide by the Balanced Budget Act of 1997 and they never intended to. The budget proposed by President Clinton for 2000 exceeded the caps by $30 billion while the 2000 budget resolution approved by Congressional Republicans was $15 billion over the limit.[33] Actual spending will be even higher. Perhaps that is what led Washington Post Columnist Robert J. Samuelson to opine, "The whole exercise exhibits an enormous contempt for the public's intelligence and integrity."[34]

It is a certainty then, that the forecasted surpluses will not be achieved, because they are based on the assumption that the budget caps will be met, and that assumption has already proved invalid. Fully 75 percent of the projected $1 trillion "on-budget" surplus is predicated on that assumption.[35] Indeed, when the additional spending that Congress has been approving is factored into the equation, it becomes clear that the entire $1 trillion is an illusion. In addition, according to Reischauer, virtually the entire unified budget surplus has been provided by increased tax revenue from the richest one percent of Americans.[36] That makes the projected surpluses largely dependent on a sky-high stock market. Then, too, there is the inherent unreliability of budget forecasts. The CBO added the following caution for those using its 1998 surplus projections,

> . . . the economic and other assumptions underlying CBO's baseline could prove to be too optimistic . . . if a recession similar to the one that struck in 1990 was to begin next year or the year after, the nearly balanced budgets anticipated for the next few years could turn into $100 billion deficits.[37]

Annual deficit projections since 1980 have been off by an average 21 percent.[38] And those were short term, not ten-year projections. In January 1999, Federal Reserve Chairman Alan Greenspan cautioned the Senate Budget Committee,

> *We cannot confidently project large surpluses in our unified budget over the next 15 years, given the inherent uncertainties of budget forecasting. . . . How can we ignore the fact that virtually all forecasts of the budget balance have been wide of the mark in recent years?*[39]

Perhaps *The Economist* said it most clearly, " . . . these forecasts of budget surpluses, particularly the ones spread over a decade or more, are barely worth the paper they are written on."[40]

In 1966, the economy grew at 5.9 percent, the third year in a row that growth topped 5 percent.[41] President Lyndon Johnson, much like today's politicians, made the convenient assumption that the boom would last indefinitely and provide plenty of additional tax revenues for subsidy programs. We have not seen such growth since, and the Great Society programs that resulted from his rose-colored-glasses economic view are at the core of our budget problems today. Another recession will come; it's just a matter of time. Of greater and more immediate concern is that, just as they did thirty years earlier under the cover of yet-to-be-achieved budget surpluses, federal politicians from both the right and the left are pushing hundreds of billions of dollars in *new* subsidy programs. This, while they are supposed to be reducing discretionary spending by 12 percent. It is a foregone conclusion that the very prospect of budget surpluses will insure that they are never achieved. The money will be spent long before it is ever collected. As Gary Becker notes, "Budget surpluses generate higher spending, which often becomes permanent, even after the budget goes from surplus to deficit." [42]

Contrary to its rhetoric, the right wing of the Subsidy party will not restrain spending. The "conservative" revolution of 1994—which was almost entirely rhetorical—is officially over, or more precisely, it never really began. That Congress achieved so little that Daniel Schorr characterized it as setting "some new records in non-governing."[43] Moreover, spending on the 38 largest programs slated for elimination in the "Contract with America" budget actually grew by 1.3 percent between 1995 and 1997.[44] In 1998, the Republican-controlled Congress failed for the first time in 24 years to pass a budget resolution as required by law;[45] but it did approve spending that exceeded the budget caps by tens of billions of dollars. And in June of 1998, the right-wing controlled House found a way to do less than nothing—negative work. It passed a bill to eliminate the federal tax code by January 1, 2002, without providing a replacement source of funding. The bill was completely meaningless because it would only go into effect if Congress passed a new funding mechanism for the federal government before the effective date. Of course, when and if Congress devises a replacement taxing mechanism, the old tax code would, by definition, be eliminated. The complete waste of time and money, which the

Washington Post termed, "arguably the least responsible idea in American politics,"[46] was further evidence that Congress is simply dysfunctional.

On the other hand, America might have been better off if the House had stuck to meaningless legislation through the entire 1998 session. As House Budget Committee Chairman John Kasich, one of the very few true fiscal conservatives, lamented, "The jig is up around here when it comes to cutting the budget."[47] In the spring of 1998, the House enthusiastically did its part to help Congress pass the largest single pork bill in history. It was a $217 billion highway bill that exceeded the Balanced Budget Act of 1997 cap, passed only a year earlier, by $33 billion.[48] Included in the package were critical highway projects like $1.6 million for a botanical garden, almost $3 million to build an access road to a baseball stadium, and another $3 million to produce a television documentary.[49]

Again, at a time when the Congress was supposed to be cutting, it was working on a bill that contained, according to the *Washington Post,* "Twice as much pork as all the other highway bills of modern times put together."[50] In a true display of Subsidy party cooperation, the House version contained earmarked pork projects spread over 80 percent of all Congressional districts.[51] Demonstrating its party unity, the House Transportation Committee approved the bill by a vote of 69 to zero, and the full House approved it by a vote of 337 to 80. House leaders promised to honor the 1997 budget deal by making offsetting spending cuts elsewhere, but they and everyone else knew that they would not. Former CBO Director Rudolph G. Penner's comment? "They're going to bust the caps either explicitly or by subterfuge."[52] Of course they are; there is no shame in Washington.

The last decade has provided us with an opportunity to study the responses of federal politicians in a time of recession with large budget deficits and in a period of extended non-inflationary growth that substantially reduced deficits. There was no discernible difference. In good times as well as bad, they increased spending. And they have proved beyond a shadow of a doubt that they will not keep their word on any budget agreement that controls spending. Indeed, the budget agreements are little more than political propaganda largely intended to deceive the public while the politicians go about the business of subsidy interests. We have also seen that there is really only one party. Republicans claim to be against big government, but under Ronald Reagan, federal subsidies to farmers and ranchers climbed from $8.8 billion in 1980 to $31 billion seven years later.[53] As David Stockman, President Reagan's Budget Director, concluded, "The Reaganites were, in the final analysis, just plain welfare state politicians like everybody else."[54] Then Republicans regained control of both houses in 1994 after decades out of power . . . and nothing happened. Indeed, in 1997, the Republicans submitted a budget to President Clinton that called for $4 billion more spending than the president requested.[55] In 1986, David Stockman called it,

. . . the modern dirty little secret of the Republican Party: The
conservative opposition helped build the American welfare state
brick by brick during the three decades prior to 1980.[56]

All the rhetoric notwithstanding, the right and left have stood shoulder to shoulder in supporting each other's subsidy programs to the clear detriment of the nation. Regardless of who goes to Washington, spending goes up. What Americans must face up to is that we have truly entered a period of one-party rule, and the ship of state it is piloting is the Titanic.

Perhaps the more difficult reality is that the federal government cannot be reformed within the framework of presently available options. All attempts to restrain the federal subsidy beast have totally failed. Sending different people to Washington has been tried repeatedly. That has failed every time. Sending reformers to Washington has been tried. That too has failed. Reforms to reduce the influence of special interests have actually increased their influence. The problem is the system itself and those entering the system are co-opted by it. In a relatively short time, reformers end up defending the system against reform. In his 1995 testimony before the Senate Committee on Government Affairs, Jeffrey Eisenach, President of the Progress and Freedom Foundation, spoke of what he described as two unavoidable conclusions:

> *1. A very significant portion of the Federal government we have*
> *today is obsolete. The challenge for this generation of policy-*
> *makers is no less than remaking much, probably most, of what it*
> *does.*
> *2. Everything we know about how to create and run Federal pro-*
> *grams is questionable, and most of it is wrong.*[57]

The Founders, never dreaming that the federal government could become a giant subsidy dispensary, did not provide safeguards against such a possibility. As presently constituted, the system provides copious incentives for the federal government to grow indefinitely in its primary role as a tax and subsidy authority. Theoretically, the check against that growth is the power vested in the voters. However, much like bacteria that develop antibiotic resistance, the federal system has adapted mechanisms that effectively negate the power of the vote. Perhaps the most effective mechanism is simply the size and complexity of the federal government. It defies comprehension by all but the most dedicated citizens. Unfortunately, that only reinforces the widespread civic disinterest that is prevalent today, thereby paving the way for even more growth. In addition, it is abundantly clear that an uninformed majority is no match for a well-financed and highly motivated subsidy interest group that can use mass media to misinform any members of the electorate who might be paying attention. The noise level alone of numerous such simultaneous efforts is an effective tool against any concerted effort by the public to stem the money flow. Numerous surveys have found that Americans believe they are powerless to influence their government[58] with the result that voters are increasingly abandoning the democratic process. Voter turnout continues to decline and reached a modern low of 36 percent in 1998.[59] It is unlikely that the steady decline over the past four decades in the opinion that Americans have of their government[60] is unrelated to the fundamental shift in the role of the federal government, from governing to subsidizing, that has taken place during the same period.

With so few eligible voters choosing to participate in the political process, power is now vested in a minority which, not surprisingly, is heavily made up of subsidy interests. The only answer is a fundamental change in the system that minimizes the incentives of the special interests to influence the federal government. Virtually all the reforms proposed or tried thus far have focused on attempting to regulate the behavior of special interests and politicians while leaving the incentives in place. That is why they cannot succeed. Unless the incentives are substantially reduced or eliminated, the subsidy interests will not relinquish control of the federal government, no matter what other measures are taken. Former Congressman Tim Penny and Carlton College's Steven E. Schier write,

> *Taxing and spending are major duties of our nation's trustees. Never before in American history has our government abused these duties so much for so long. Sweeping changes are in order.*[61]

The fundamental change I propose is a State Based Subsidy Plan (SBSP) that would strip the federal government of its authority to subsidize any entity, except for federal retirement programs including Social Security; a limited, basic science program; and as specifically required for national security. This is a radical solution requiring a constitutional amendment, but the problem demands resolution very soon and nothing less will succeed. In addition, it is a single step, which solves a host of problems all at once. We do not have the luxury of decades to effect reform; without radical surgery very soon, the nation is assuredly headed for an inter-generational war.

Initially, the concept of a nearly subsidy-free federal government might seem to be beyond the realm of possibility, but it is achievable and would greatly improve the economy, the environment, and social conditions in the United States. The end of federal subsidies does not mean the end of subsidy programs. While many subsidy programs should simply be terminated, there are programs that must be continued. Certainly, there has to be a safety net for the truly unfortunate. Education and health care will always require some level of subsidy. However, none of these can or should be administered by the federal government; they must become exclusively state programs. Not because state government is somehow more efficient or less subject to subsidy interest influence than the federal government, but because abuses, extravagances, and incompetence by state governments can be very effectively checked by individual citizens. The fundamental problem with the federal government, complete loss of accountability to individual Americans, is solved.

By restoring accountability, democratic government, with all its potential, is restored and an era of more efficient democratic government is begun.

The SBSP would greatly restrict federal subsidies, but would empower the states to implement any subsidy programs they choose. The dramatic decrease in federal spending would be accompanied by a similar decrease in federal taxation. The federal income tax and all federal payroll taxes could be abolished and replaced with a 16.5 percent national retail sales tax. In addition, certain federal excise taxes, such as the gasoline tax, would be retained. In the absence of a federal income tax, the states would be free to utilize income taxes to generate the additional revenues they would need to support the subsidy programs that they choose to implement. A state could simply elect to replace every discontinued federal subsidy program and replicate the same combined federal and state tax burden, thereby making the change almost transparent to its residents. On the other hand, another state might choose to pare back federal programs dramatically, thus giving its residents fewer handouts, but also rewarding them with a substantial reduction in their total tax burden. However, unlike the federal government, the states could not institute programs that they refused to pay for. They could not run up huge debts, passing their expenses on to their grandchildren as federal politicians do, nor could they print money to monatize their debt. States can institute all the subsidy programs that they are willing to pay for. That is the first of the two pillars of efficient democracy.

The game played by subsidy interests and their politicians at the federal level is to let the cost of their programs get lost in a colossal and incomprehensible $1.7 trillion budget, or better yet, get the people from other states to foot a disproportionate share of the cost. However, faced with the prospect of actually having to raise the taxes to pay for all their subsidy programs, states would be forced to tell their residents just how much all their programs were costing. And there would be no question about who was footing the bill. That would most certainly result in lively debate. The more programs a state instituted, the livelier the debate would get. No doubt, subsidy interests would be just as charming and generous with state legislators as they are with members of Congress. Indeed, it is likely that in at least some states, they would pay politicians much higher commissions then they paid at the federal level. But there would be no way to hide the cost of subsidy programs or escape raising the taxes necessary to pay for them, and that is more than half the battle. There is absolutely nothing wrong with a state having many generous subsidy programs if that is what its residents want and are willing to pay for.

It is entirely possible—indeed, very likely—that a state legislature with a broad social agenda might enact generous and expensive subsidy programs along with a very progressive tax structure, with the objective that a small minority of high-income residents would shoulder nearly all of the resulting heavy tax burden. That has been a constant theme of the left wing in Congress since the Johnson Administration, and it will likely prove irresistible to a least a few states given their newfound powers. But they will very quickly come face to face with the renewed power of the individual taxpayer because, as opposed to the present system, individual taxpayers have veto power in a SBSP. They can vote with their feet by moving to a state that has policies more to their liking.

The power of individual taxpayers to vote with their feet as an absolute check on state spending and taxes cannot be overstated. In a democracy, it is the only power greater than that of subsidy interests. The inability of Americans to escape the jurisdiction of the Internal Revenue Service is precisely why subsidy programs have to be stripped from the federal government and transferred to the states. While citizens of high-tax states and cities have shown a reluctance to move over modestly higher taxes, it is clear that a tax burden deemed unreasonable has caused some to move. And that is under a system where federal taxes comprise the lion's share of the total tax burden and are consequently unavoidable. With that situation reversed, states will pay a heavy penalty in *taxpayers* if they become too extravagant, too inefficient, or they try to make their tax system too progressive. Individual taxpayers can reject a state's tax-benefit ratio and a relatively small number of those most heavily taxed can force a change in its structure. No amount of collusion between legislators and subsidy interests can trump that power. That is the second pillar of efficient democracy.

Implementing the SBSP puts the two pillars of efficient democracy in place and brings to government the same remarkable benefits that free-market competition brings to an economy. States are forced to compete with each other for residents and taxpayers. The competition for residents will determine what kind of a culture a state has, and cultural subsidies will undoubtedly make a state more attractive. It is a matter of fact that some desirable cultural activities have seldom, if ever, been self-sustaining. Similarly, the quality of health care and educational institutions are a major factor in a state's quality of life. Those, too, require subsidies. However, under SBSP, residents become consumers who are both quality and price conscious. States will have to balance quality and cost. If they get out of balance one way, they become less attractive places to live; the other way, they price themselves out of the market and lose the revenue necessary to support their programs. Under the SBSP, Americans will become very informed "state consumers" with the same result that we see in the marketplace. State governments and their employees will find it necessary to compete to stay in business. While a state cannot disappear from the map, it most certainly can drive away its tax base, thereby forcing it to terminate programs and employees. Quality and price consciousness replace complacency, and acting out of self-interest, the states would produce efficient democracy.

The benefits arising from forcing the states to compete with each other are far greater than the simple elimination of some subsidy programs. While that alone would produce dramatic savings for taxpayers and provide a huge boost to the economy, the improvement in government efficiency would magnify that effect. State and local governments treat subsidies they receive just like any other beneficiary group; they are far less efficient with them than they are with their own money. That was confirmed by a National Bureau of Economic Research study by Allison F. DelRossi of the University of Wyoming and Robert P. Inman of the University of Pennsylvania. They found that when a 1986 law forced local governments to pay for a larger share of big water projects, overall spending fell by 35 percent.[62] They concluded that requiring local governments to use more of their own money resulted in "a more efficient balancing of budgetary costs and benefits."[63]

Contrary to their popular image, government workers are generally capable people. On average, they are not any more inefficient than anyone else, except that they are employed by a monopoly. Unfortunately, human beings in secure, noncompetitive positions are usually not very productive. Even worse, government managers are often people who obtained their jobs through political patronage and who are often incompetent. The result is frequently too many people being paid too much to do too little. Because government is a monopoly, its employees are better able to press for wages and benefits that simply would not be possible in a competitive environment. Employee compensation data demonstrate that government employees are overcompensated. In 1991, state and local government employees earned 10 percent more than private sector employees, while federal nonmilitary compensation was 47 percent higher.[64] Total excess government employee compensation in the U.S. during 1991 was estimated at $240 billion.[65] Under the SBSP, most federal jobs would be eliminated entirely, and much of the excess compensation at the state and local level would be squeezed out of the system by competitive pressures. A substantial portion of the hundreds of billions in excess compensation would be returned to the taxpayers with no loss of government services. That would result in additional economic growth and more taxable income, which, in turn, would allow for either more government programs or reduced taxes.

Local government experience demonstrates the substantial gains in productivity and reductions in cost that come from introducing competition into government functions. The City of Indianapolis found that requiring its own transportation department to bid against private contractors resulted in an immediate 27 percent decrease in street repair costs as well as a 68 percent increase in productivity.[66] All the work was performed by the low bidder—the Indianapolis Department of Transportation, which has continued to be the low bidder 80 percent of the time.[67] Introducing competition to its vehicle maintenance and sanitation departments also produced dramatic improvements in both costs and productivity from existing city employees. The key difference was that they were forced to compete and given the flexibility to become competitive. City departments did not fare so well in Philadelphia where 33 of 37 city services subjected to competitive bidding were contracted out.[68] But the city, previously on the verge of bankruptcy, and its residents have reaped huge benefits in a revitalized community with better services at lower costs. Competition was the key.

Another multi-billion dollar savings with no loss of services would result from eliminating all the duplication at the federal and state level. A wide variety of subsidy programs including agriculture, education, housing, welfare, health care, transportation, and labor have both state and federal agencies pursuing the same objectives. Often the job of the federal agency is to administer programs through a similar state agency. Ostensibly, the reason for the federal agency is that there are federal subsidies to be dispensed and administered. But why should the federal government collect taxes from residents of the states, pass them through large bureaucracies in Washington who consume a significant portion of the funds supporting themselves, and then return a diminished amount back to the states with pages and pages of regulations on precisely what they may and may not do with what is left of their own money?

Though politicians sometimes seem to imply otherwise, about 97 percent of federal tax revenues come from citizens and businesses that are domiciled in states.[69] There is no magic formula that allows the federal government to collect more revenue with lower taxation than the states can. In this case, the whole is not greater than the sum of its parts. What, then, is the point of sending one dollar to Washington in order to receive 75 cents and a long list of regulations back? The previous chapters of this book have demonstrated conclusively that there is not only no unique wisdom in federal programs, but that they are very inefficient and frequently counterproductive. As such, why not leave the tax revenue in the states, eliminate the duplicative federal agencies that administer federal subsidy programs, and let the states administer their own programs with their own money? Eliminating the funds lost to federal bureaucracies would effectively give state agencies a significant budget increase or enable taxes to be reduced.

Aside from the additional cost of having the federal government administer subsidy programs, the programs, with rare exceptions, end up with a one-size-fits-all approach. Thus, the federal regulations that apply in Florida also largely apply in Alaska. Obviously those two states are very different and certainly have different needs and problems, but federal programs are ill suited to flexibility. Even where programs have some flexibility, the starting point is the baseline set of federal regulations. Clearly, a far better approach is to design the program from the bottom up, around the needs and circumstances of the specific group that it is intended to benefit. Federal programs are necessarily designed from the top down. That approach means that the core elements of a program are generally the same throughout the country, which minimizes innovation and insures that programs that fail do so on a grand scale.

On the other hand, if the states were freed of federal funding and all the strings attached, they would each set out to meet the needs of their residents in the manner they deemed most appropriate. The result would certainly be a variety of approaches to similar problems that would allow for real-world analysis of the costs and effectiveness of each. Programs that proved more effective could be adopted by other states, and failures would be limited in scope and duration. The competition for residents would drive innovation and insure the timely demise of ineffective programs. Under our present system, federal programs are frequently based on an idea from academia or an interest group looking for a federal handout. With little more than that to go on, it is implemented nationally at a cost of billions of dollars. Programs that fail to deliver the promised benefits continue, because it is claimed that they need more time to work. With no competing programs for comparison, the funding just keeps coming, entrenching the subsidy beneficiaries and program bureaucracy ever deeper. There is no competition to force innovation and performance and, of course, no way to terminate the program. The problem that the program was intended to remedy, if there ever really was one, remains unsolved. Under the SBSP, each state would become a laboratory where new ideas could be realistically tested. When a successful program was adopted in other states, additional innovation would further improve it, and effective elements from various programs could be joined together to produce a single program that was superior to those from which it was derived. In short, all the forces that make competitive markets produce ever-better products at the same or lower cost, would be brought to bear on government programs.

Wisconsin's very successful welfare innovations provide a hint of what could be achieved under SBSP. The state began implementing bold reforms to the federal-state welfare program in 1987. Over the next ten years, while the nation's welfare caseloads increased substantially, Wisconsin's dropped by 50 percent, the only state to show a sharp departure from the trend.[70] The drop was not accomplished simply by slashing spending; on the contrary, the state increased its spending per family on welfare.[71] Rather, the reforms were centered around responsibility codes, training, and work requirements. The accomplishments might even have been greater, except that every deviation from federal welfare regulations required a federal waiver. Wisconsin Governor Tommy Thompson complained that the waiver process is cumbersome and does not allow sufficient freedom for real change.[72] Nonetheless, most of the other states also obtained federal waivers, and many began successfully implementing some of the ideas proven in Wisconsin. Much more could have been achieved if the states did not have to go to Washington "on bended knee" asking for permission to improve their welfare systems, as Michigan Governor John Engler put it.[73]

With programs such as welfare and health services completely under state control, it might not be as easy to move from state to state and maintain benefits as it is under federal programs. However, that should not present a major problem. While the Supreme Court ruled that states cannot base welfare benefits on how long a resident had been in the state (*Saenz v. Roe*), that was with welfare still predominantly a federal program. Moreover, the court did not preclude states from charging different fees to in-state and out-of-state students at their public universities, which, as we have seen, receive billions of dollars in federal funding. While some initial problems could be expected and some residency requirements would almost certainly be enacted, it is also likely that states would rather quickly develop reciprocity agreements that would minimize such problems.

For the great majority of subsidies, transferring full authority for a program from the federal government to the states should prove considerably easier than terminating the federal program. As we have seen, terminating a federal subsidy program is all but impossible, but under the SBSP, the programs are not necessarily being terminated, just transferred. The subsidy beneficiaries will not only have the opportunity to convince state governments to continue supporting them with tax dollars, but also to increase the subsidy level. That should diminish—but certainly not eliminate—their opposition to SBSP. Some will undoubtedly see that once they lose federal control, their program is doomed and they will vigorously oppose SBSP, but they are precisely the reason we need the program in the first place. Indeed, the process of implementing SBSP will very quickly expose unjustifiable subsidies—their beneficiaries will be the ones hollering the loudest in opposition.

While federal subsidy programs will be relatively easy to transfer to the states, many federal subsidies are not accomplished through programs, but through taxes, services, and regulation. Those present a more difficult problem, but one that is no less urgent. The foundation of the SBSP is that nearly all non-defense federal subsidies be eliminated, but some services, such as air traffic control and food inspection, are more efficient at the federal level. The costs associated with these services should be recouped through user fees. The elimination of the federal income tax, by itself, would abolish a very long list of tax subsidies, but excise taxes are another matter. As we have seen, the military cost of protecting our dependence on foreign oil comes to about $50 billion each year, and the users of petroleum products do not pick up the tab. Revenues from the federal motor fuel taxes are used largely for highway programs, while the costs of the Department of Defense are paid from general revenues. To remedy that situation, federal taxes on petroleum products should be set at rates that will generate the revenue necessary to pay all the public costs associated with the use of those products. That would include, at a minimum, military and environmental costs. The objective would be to collect taxes from the users of oil products such that the public cost, and, therefore, the federal subsidy, would be zero.

It is one thing to decide that the federal subsidy for some service will be zero; it is quite another to determine what the real level of the subsidy associated with federal services is so that appropriate user fees can be charged. The federal government had 546 separate user fees in 1996,[74] but few if any of those were fully costed. If left to Congress, politics would insure that the user fees established would reflect only a small portion of the actual government cost. The best answer to this problem is to give the job of determining the cost of government programs to the GAO, the federal accounting agency least susceptible to Congressional pressure. Its charge would be to determine total program costs, including operating and capital costs, as well as charges for future liabilities and externalities. That cost would then have to be recovered from the beneficiaries of the service. If the cost of a service was determined to be exorbitant, as some surely will be, Congress could act to modify the program to reduce costs to a reasonable level. That is what it should have been doing already. However, it would be precluded from charging beneficiaries less than the full cost of the program.

The benefits from this approach would be numerous. Returning to federal motor fuel taxes, we can reasonably expect fuel consumption to drop significantly once it is fully costed, but there are less apparent benefits as well.

The states would become fully responsible for funding all road maintenance and construction. Shutting down the federal highway subsidy machine would instantly shift the focus to road maintenance and away from new construction. Aside from the obvious benefit of finally putting the road spending emphasis where it belongs, the major factor in destroying our central cities, new subsidized highways to an ever-expanding suburbia, would be sharply curtailed. No other single measure would have nearly as beneficial an effect on our cities. At the same time, removing the federal gasoline subsidy would give another huge boost to cities by increasing demand for urban housing and far more efficient use of automobiles would result in a substantial decline in traffic congestion. Nearly 30 years of federal efforts to achieve those objectives through regulations such as CAFE mileage requirements have not only failed, but have actually increased traffic congestion and the usage of motor fuels because they remained heavily subsidized. Fully priced, motor fuel usage would decline and would become a more valued, and consequently more efficiently used, commodity. Our dangerous dependence on foreign oil and the negative environmental impacts of internal combustion engines would both be reduced. Last, but certainly not least, fully pricing petroleum products would insure that those who benefit from their usage also pay the cost.

Any other necessary federal service associated with a specific beneficiary group should also be fully priced to bring the public cost to zero. That would include agencies such as the Federal Aviation Administration, most agencies of the Department of Agriculture, Bureau of Land Management, Bureau of Reclamation, Army Corps of Engineers, and the Federal Communications Commission, to name a few. These agencies would become essentially self-sufficient, supported entirely by user fees. Initially, imposing the costs of agency operations on users might result in relatively high user fees because most of the agencies have large bureaucracies and are not very efficient. They are what the incentives in the present system have made them. However, cut off from general revenues, market forces would be brought to bear on them. High user fees would discourage the use of agency services, thereby reducing its revenues. With no other source of revenue, the agencies would be forced to slash overhead and "reinvent" themselves in a hurry. We have seen repeatedly that government agencies are very much like living organisms in their determination to survive. Faced with the prospect of becoming extinct, and with no possibility of additional funding from general revenues, they will respond positively. Service will improve, costs will drop dramatically, and users will return, willing to pay a reasonable price.

Excise taxes and user fees are not always the solution, however. Take tobacco. In 1998, the Senate nearly passed a bill that would have imposed very high taxes on cigarettes. The hundreds of billions of dollars generated were, in part, supposed to reimburse the government for the costs of treating smoking-related illnesses. However, the mechanism had two major flaws. First, the government is still willing to extensively subsidize individuals who develop smoking-related illnesses through medical treatment that can cost hundreds of thousands of dollars. Few smokers are likely to pay anywhere near that much in cigarette taxes. As such, a serious moral hazard problem still exists. Second, the attempt to raise as much cigarette tax revenue as possible establishes a scenario that we have seen many times: very high punitive taxes inevitably result in an extensive black market and the crime that comes with it. Canada imposed large tax increases on cigarettes in the early 1990s. Consequently, in 1993 alone it is estimated that 100 million cartons of cigarettes were smuggled into the country, and the Canadian government lost $2 billion in tax revenue.[75] Punitive taxes only result in increased crime.

Again, a far better approach is to end the federal subsidy. Because the SBSP would get the federal government out of all health care programs, that problem is solved. With a national retail sales tax as the federal government's primary revenue source, cigarettes, like all other products would be taxed at the federal level, and given that taxing an activity leads to a reduction in that activity, states might want to add a moderate cigarette tax as well. However, states could also decide not to subsidize lifestyle-related illnesses including smoking. Senators J. Robert Kerry and John C. Danforth, who headed the Bipartisan Commission on Entitlement and Tax Reform in 1995, proposed addressing " . . . rising health care costs by emphasizing market incentives and personal responsibility."[76] The simplest way to achieve that would be to limit public health care funding for individuals with specific lifestyle-related illnesses. Everyone would be free to smoke, but they would have to pay for any resulting medical care themselves. Similar restrictions could apply to illnesses resulting from certain dietary habits, overly sedentary lifestyles, and long-term alcohol or drug abuse.

There is an enormous body of medical evidence that has positively correlated certain lifestyle problems with serious illnesses, which would allow public health benefits for highly-correlated illnesses to be restricted. Since most such illnesses take years to develop, every effort could be made to help individuals who desired to affect lifestyle changes. Those who either had no desire to change or refused to complete programs aimed at either changing their negative behavior or controlling the effects of that behavior could be denied publicly-funded medical care for those specific conditions. Medical tests have already been devised that can detect gene damage due to cigarette smoke as opposed to other pollutants, and such tests will make it very feasible to deny treatment for certain lifestyle-related conditions.[77] There is no reason why the public should go to great expense to care for someone who knowingly and intentionally contracts a serious disease. Nor is there any reason why society should have to suffer the crime that inevitably results from attempts to heavily tax such behavior.

The SBSP will not eliminate national defense subsidies. That is most unfortunate because defense programs are loaded with pork, but some defense subsidies are necessary. Being the "last refuge of scoundrels," defense is also where huge subsidies are most easily hidden. However, in a new era where all other federal subsidies are illegal and with a policy that defense spending may only contain subsidies that are essential for national security, it is highly likely that the amount of subsidy dollars in the defense budget would fall significantly. It would be naive to believe that Congress will not attempt to make maximum use of its only remaining vehicle for delivering pork, but with so many fewer issues to deal with, the defense budget would be subjected to greater scrutiny by both the press and the public. Moreover, without a myriad of other subsidy programs to trade for, legislators from states that derive little benefit from military spending are unlikely to go along with pork programs that their residents pay for but do not benefit from. The net result is that while SBSP would not directly eliminate defense pork, it would indirectly cause a substantial reduction, and that is probably as good as it gets.

As we have seen, the federal government spends tens of billions of dollars annually on science and technology subsidies. Most of these should be terminated, but it does make sense to have a small national program—funded at perhaps one-third of present levels—to support basic health and science research. To keep the budget from ballooning, funding could be tied to GDP. All applied science and industrial research programs would be terminated, as would all manned space flight programs. States with special interests in specific areas—agriculture or metallurgy, for example—might fund their own applied research programs, but mostly it would be left to the private sector. Our science and technology will progress faster if we let industry do their own applied research, rather than taxing corporations to pay for pork-laden federal research programs.

The large, unfunded federal retirement programs, civil service and railroad retirement, would certainly have to be left with the federal government. The seriously flawed Disability Insurance and Supplemental Security Income programs administered by the Social Security Administration would be turned over to the states. Then there is Social Security, the giant federal Ponzi scheme. It is unlikely that the staggering unfunded retirement liability could be transferred before massive reform based on personal retirement accounts. Even then, the unfunded liability would still present a staggering problem. Social Security must be privatized. As Gary Becker has observed, "there is no more reason for the federal government to be running a massive pension system than for it to run steel or life insurance companies."[78]

Since President Franklin Roosevelt first decided to misrepresent Social Security as an insurance program in order to con a very skeptical public into accepting his pyramid scheme, Social Security deception has been standard political practice. Repeated program expansions and massive increases in unearned benefits were portrayed as non-threatening to the viability of the system. Then, hefty tax increases supposedly insured the long-term viability of the system. Now, faced with an impending multi-trillion dollar shortfall, we are being assured that simply investing a portion of Social Security taxes in the stock market will, like magic, make the system whole. Somehow, several years of rapid rises in equities seems to have erased the real history of the stock market. Instead, we are told that high returns from the market will enable everyone to live happily ever after. What proponents of such plans are not talking much about is where the money to invest in the market would come from. All the Social Security taxes presently collected are used either to pay beneficiaries or to pay regular operating expenses of the federal government. Indeed, the claimed budget surpluses are a direct result of treating Social Security taxes as general revenue. Therefore, funds invested in the market would mostly come from new taxes. While there are sound reasons to privatize Social Security to allow individuals to take advantage of equity markets, allowing the federal government to invest retirement funds in the stock market is not only unlikely to miraculously rescue the system, it could very well make a bad situation worse.

Perhaps the first rule of investing is that past performance does not predict future results. The performance of the stock market during the last few years, though spectacular, does not portend similar future results. A more sober analysis reveals that since 1900, the stock market has posted annual declines about a third of the time, including the extended periods from 1901 to 1921, 1928 to 1948, and 1962 to 1982.[79] If anything, the present very lofty level of stock prices makes a significant decline as likely as further gains. If Social Security taxes were invested in the stock market, any significant market decline would result in tremendous pressure for the federal government to make up the losses to prevent the retirement funds from being wiped out. The politicians would almost certainly respond, thereby making the federal government the insurer of the stock market and increasing its existing trillions of dollars of liabilities by trillions more. Whatever measures are taken in an attempt to repair the damage to Social Security from decades of political fraud, solutions that simply perpetuate the fraud or expose the federal government to additional trillions of dollars of liabilities must be rejected.

There are, of course, those who claim that we are in a "new economy" and that the market declines of the past will not be repeated. That is a particularly interesting viewpoint because very similar predictions have preceded some of the worst market declines. Just days before the crash of 1929, Yale Economics Professor Irving Fisher commented, "Stocks have reached what looks like a permanently high plateau." Not quite. The truth is that the economy is constantly becoming a new economy, but there are no "new" human beings. The same emotions, excesses, and wild optimism that existed then also exists now. Neither the "new economy" nor the stock market provide a magic solution to the Social Security problem. It is a matter of mathematics and the numbers can only be fudged until the time when the checks have to be written on an overdrawn account.

Although unlikely, it is possible that the states might let Uncle Sam off the hook on Social Security. In 1997, the state of Oregon asked Congress to allow it to opt out of the Social Security system and set up its own plan for Oregon residents.[80] Colorado followed suit in 1998, and the states of Arizona, Georgia, Indiana, New Hampshire, South Carolina, Utah, and Washington were all considering similar legislation.[81] It is unclear whether these states have fully evaluated the ramifications of such a move, but state control would certainly result in a more honest and actuarially sound system.

To see how federal and state finances would change under the SBSP, the $1.66 trillion 1998 federal budget can be broken down into items that would remain in the federal budget, those potentially transferred to the states, and those that would necessarily be eliminated. In this analysis, about $14 billion of federal spending is eliminated due to the reduction in the federal work force and the elimination of the Energy Department and most of the Commerce Department. The Departments of Education, Housing and Urban Development and Health and Human Services, as well as nearly all of the Agriculture Department, would also be eliminated, but the analysis assumes that their administrative expenditures would be replicated at the state level. That certainly would not happen, but it is the most conservative approach. The resulting federal budget totals just over $1.03 trillion of which defense, Social Security and interest on the national debt make up over 82 percent. Net spending is reduced to $924 billion by $107 billion in offsetting receipts consisting largely of customs fees, excise taxes and an estimated $25 billion in new user fees.

To generate $924 billion in revenues from a national retail sales tax would have required a tax rate of 16.5 percent based on personal consumption expenditures of $5.62 trillion in 1998.[82] While that is a significant sales tax, it would replace individual and corporate federal income taxes, as well as Social Security and Medicare payroll taxes. As such, only state imposed income or payroll taxes, if any, would be deducted from paychecks. In addition, there would be no federal income tax returns to file. Only about 23 million retailers, a small fraction of the number of individuals and businesses that file income tax returns, would need to file sales tax reports.[83] Alternatively, a national Value Added Tax (VAT) would raise the same amount of revenue from the same tax rate and would appear identical to final consumers.[84] The choice of which system to use essentially comes down to which one is easier to administer. Either way, a national consumption tax would be far simpler and much less costly to administer than the federal income tax and would replace all federal taxes except excise taxes and user fees. If the states assumed liability for retirement benefits, and the Social Security system were ended, the national sales tax would drop to only 10.4 percent. Of course, state taxes would have to increase to provide funds for the new state retirement programs.

In addition to simplicity, there are a number of other advantages to a national consumption tax. Perhaps the most notable is that it is considerably more difficult to hide than payroll taxes. As we saw in Chapter 3, to mask the size of Social Security and Medicare taxes, the federal government requires employers to "match" the taxes withheld from an employee's paycheck. However, employees pay the full tax, the "employer's share" is just part of their wages that they never see. With a consumption tax, consumers would know how much extra they are paying to support the federal government. In addition, a study by the National Association of Manufacturers found that replacing payroll taxes with a consumption tax would result in the creation of as many as 2.4 million new jobs due to reduced labor costs.[85]

The consumption tax also solves a problem that will become very large in the future: how to tax Internet sales. The Internet Tax Freedom Act prohibits taxes on Internet sales through 2001, but the states are clamoring for a sales tax thereafter. Presently, most states have sales taxes, but they are ill equipped to tax Internet sales and catalog sales that very often take place across state lines. In the future, a much larger percentage of retail sales will take place on the Internet, which will deprive states of part of their traditional sales tax revenue and present them with a very complex and difficult tax situation. In addition, their inability to tax catalog and Internet sales puts in-state retail merchants at a price disadvantage since they do pay state sales taxes. This problem is largely solved by making the income tax exclusively available to states and having the federal government rely on a consumption tax that would include Internet and catalog sales.

Another highly desirable aspect of the consumption tax is that, to the extent that taxing an activity discourages that activity, it discourages something that we could do with less of: consumption. The present federal system heavily taxes income, something that we surely do not want to discourage. And payroll taxes increase the cost of labor, which reduces the demand for low-skilled workers. On the other hand, we have a dangerously low savings rate, which requires us to import huge amounts of capital. For the year ending March 31, 1998, net capital inflows to the U.S. totaled a record $264 billion.[86] In mid-1997, U.S. net investment income, the income earned by American investors overseas, less that earned by foreign investors in the U.S., turned negative for the first time since World War II.[87] While our heavy reliance on foreign capital has not been much of a problem thus far, we cannot get away with it indefinitely. Then there is the new single currency of the European monetary union, the Euro. For years, we have benefited from having the dollar as the world reserve currency, but the Euro could become a serious competitor and make satisfying our capital requirements more difficult and expensive. To the extent that a consumption tax discourages consumption and increases our savings rate, it would help solve a serious national problem.

In 1998, the 50 states spent about $950 billion.[88] Under the SBSP, $702 billion—not including Social Security—would be eliminated from the federal budget and some percentage of that would be picked up by the states. While there is no way to know how much, it is not unreasonable to assume that 25 percent of that spending would either not be picked up or would be eliminated through consolidation. That would leave the states with an additional $525 billion in expenditures which they would have to finance through some combination of taxes. Thirty-eight billion dollars in spending transferred from the federal government would be for transportation costs, which most states would likely generate from additional fuel taxes. That would leave about $487 billion to be raised primarily from sales and income taxes. As we have just seen, state sales taxes are becoming increasingly problematic, so most states would likely look to the income tax.

While state general revenues would have to increase a substantial 51 percent, that is not as great a problem as it might seem because state sales taxes and income taxes have relatively low rates. Sales taxes range from three to seven percent,[89] while income taxes range from zero in states such as Nevada, Florida and Washington to 9.3 percent in California. A 50 percent increase in a three or four percent tax rate is still a very modest tax. Even if California chose to increase its 9.3 percent income tax rate 50 percent to 13.95 percent, it would still not be catastrophic considering that federal income and payroll taxes would be simultaneously eliminated. The bottom line is that no matter how the states decided to raise additional revenue, the combined state and federal tax burden would be significantly lower initially and would drop even further as market forces went to work on the states.

One of the claimed advantages of the income tax is that it is progressive, that is, those who earn more pay disproportionately higher taxes. The federal income tax is structured such that those with low incomes pay no taxes at all. While there is merit to the idea that those better able to shoulder the tax burden should pay more, it is questionable whether it is healthy for a democracy to have a significant number of citizens who pay no taxes. Nonetheless, that supposedly demonstrates that we are a compassionate society. However, it is largely a ruse because non-progressive federal payroll taxes start with the first dollar of income, thereby offsetting the progressive nature of the income tax. As we have seen, payroll taxes are just general revenues in disguise and about three-quarters of all Americans pay more in non-progressive payroll taxes than they do in progressive federal income tax. So much for the progressive nature of the current system.

A broadly based national sales tax would not be progressive; although, because those with more wealth buy more, they would certainly pay more taxes. In order to avoid falling into the same tax-subsidy pit that we just came out of, it would be essential that a national sales tax be broadly based with very few, if any, exemptions. While arguments are made for exempting items such as food and medical services, over half of Americans, including the poor, are seriously overweight and we are greatly over-consuming medical services. To avoid continuing to provide subsidy incentives for over-consumption, all retail goods and services should be taxed. And all Americans should contribute to the essential national services provided by the subsidy-free federal government. When U.S. fighting forces defend the nation, those who die do so for all Americans, rich and poor alike.

Requiring Americans to pay a national sales tax on all goods and services would not mean that the poor need be more heavily taxed than they are now. Indeed, most would likely see their tax burden decline. The states would also be free to structure their taxes to minimize or even offset the effect of the national sales tax on the poor or they could structure social programs to provide services to effectively achieve the same thing. But after spending trillions of dollars on failed antipoverty programs, we would do well to recognize that the one antipoverty program that has proved remarkably effective has been a strong economy. The booming economy of the 1990s has achieved more than decades of government programs for the poor and it cost the taxpayers nothing. Clearly, the best thing we can do for the poor is to maintain a strong, growing economy. Even liberal economist Barry Bluestone of the University of Massachusetts states, "It is precisely by arguing for policies that will assure faster growth that we can encourage our redistributionist agenda."[90]

The greatest impediment to economic growth is government. The Clinton Administration estimated in 1995 that the cost of complying with federal regulations absorbed almost 10 percent of gross domestic product (GDP), or nearly $725 billion.[91] And a study by economists Richard W. Rahn, Harrison W. Fox and Lynn H. Fox found that economic growth suffers once government expenditures exceed 10% to 15% of GDP.[92] Total government expenditures in the U.S. exceed 30 percent of GDP. Substantially reducing the size and cost of government is by far the most beneficial action we can take on behalf of the poor, the rich, and everyone in between.

At one time, many people believed that subsidy programs were the answer to most economic and social problems, but time has clearly proven otherwise. Charles L. Shultze who served as chairman of the Council of Economic Advisors under President Carter, notes,

> *When it comes to things like long-term growth of the economy, the distribution of income or the quality of education in our schools, the truth is, government has got to work like hell to make a difference of even a couple of tenths of a percentage-point.*[93]

The realization that government is not the answer has proven such a disappointment for some that they simply refuse to acknowledge the obvious. Far too many have simply figured out how to benefit from programs that have failed miserably in achieving their intended objective. The programs live on to feed the unintended beneficiaries. And, of course, the political establishment benefits from all subsidy programs, whether they work as intended or not, because some group will make the program work for them and pay commissions to insure its immortality.

Clearly, a dramatic cut in subsidies is required and only by transferring subsidy authority to the states can that be accomplished. But that stirs fears of a "race to the bottom" by states as they try to streamline their subsidy programs or refuse to pick up discontinued federal programs. Fears that the social safety net could be dismantled are not unreasonable, but recent experience indicates that it is unlikely. Gary Becker points out that Western European countries, in many ways similar to the states under the SBSP, have not cut taxes or regulations excessively.[94] He further suggests that the U.S. would be better off with more competition between the states.[95]

A report issued by the Health and Human Services Department after the first full year under the 1996 welfare reform law that gave the states relatively broad flexibility in setting their benefit levels and requirements, found that, on average, the states spent more per welfare recipient after welfare reform than they did before.[96] Another report from the National Governor's Association indicated that between 1996 and 1998, states increased their spending on child care by 55 percent.[97] There is no race to the bottom by states, nor do welfare recipients race to the top. A study by the National Bureau of Economic Research of interstate welfare migration from 1979 to 1992 found no evidence that welfare recipients relocated to other states to take advantage of higher welfare benefits.[98] Another study published by the Federal Reserve Bank of Dallas found that immigrants do not chase welfare benefits either.[99] Rather, they settle in areas with large immigrant populations. These studies show that states need not fear becoming a "welfare magnet" if they choose to implement generous social programs, just as the poor need not fear that the social safety net will disappear under the SBSP.

Another area that would be a cause for concern under the SBSP is disaster aid because the federal program would be terminated. For many years, federal disaster aid has shielded the states from the consequences of their poor planning and irrational development. No more. Federal disaster aid could be replaced by a program whereby the federal government would make disaster loans to states that met certain conditions. States would have to build and maintain disaster reserves, perhaps equal to 200 percent of the average amount of their disaster expenditures—in inflation adjusted dollars—during the previous 10 years. If a state had proper reserves and a disaster event wiped out those reserves, it could borrow funds from the federal government, which would have to be repaid with interest over five years. The federal government could be authorized to raise the retail sales tax by two percentage points in any state that failed to make the required payments on its loan until such time as all amounts owing had been recouped. Such a program would allow the states to provide aid to victims of disasters much sooner, but would put the cost of irresponsible planning and development where it belongs—on the shoulders of those responsible for those actions. It would also have those who choose to live in disaster-prone areas bear the associated risk. It is almost a certainty that this program would result in significantly reduced disaster losses.

Not the least of the benefits of the SBSP would be the liberation of Congress and the president to do the jobs that only the federal government can do, and to do them properly. A review of our elected leaders' performance in managing the affairs of state since World War II is a primer on how not to do the job. In his first two years in office, President Clinton spent a total of two hours with his Director of Central Intelligence, James Woolsey.[100] We won the cold war partly because our economy was strong enough to withstand the heavy burden of extraordinarily wasteful and unnecessary weapons programs while the Soviet economy was not. Our leaders had no idea that they spent $5.5 trillion on our nuclear weapons programs. In addition, more than two decades after OPEC exposed our dangerous dependence on oil from the very unstable Middle East, the oil weapon could still be used against us today with disastrous economic effects. Our elected leaders must do better.

We also might expect members of Congress to study issues themselves rather than relying on staff and lobbyists. Under the SBSP, there would be no need for large staffs and most lobbyists would have no further interest in Washington, D.C. Without subsidy programs consuming nearly all their time, politicians could actually read the bills they vote on. And they might begin to pass thoughtful legislation. Much of what Congress has done in recent decades is typified by the Americans With Disabilities Act (ADA), a law so vague that it is essentially meaningless—except to the Supreme Court. To the Court, it has meant the opportunity to sculpt the law the way it sees fit, and it has extended ADA benefits to over 20 percent of the population of the U.S., about 50 million people.[101] Yet, the GAO found that only about 2.3 million Americans have severe disabilities.[102] As we have seen time and time again, the judiciary will legislate when Congress provides it with vague legislation. While judicial activism is a matter of concern, the courts are not the primary problem; Congress has been too busy passing out subsidies to do its legislative job properly.

Many of the federal subsidy programs that have become a critical problem for Americans trace their origins to President Franklin D. Roosevelt. However, in fairness to FDR, he did not intend the federal government to become a giant cash dispensary any more than the Founders did. He believed in experimenting with innovate approaches to problems. In 1932 he stated, "The country needs, and, less I mistake, demands, bold persistent experimentation."[103] I believe that FDR was correct, but true experimentation is virtually impossible at the federal level. All programs become permanent whether they work or not. FDR provided the answer to the problems created by his own experiments gone haywire: experimentation. Transferring subsidy programs to the states is the only way to accomplish that.

> *The remedy is simple. The Government must get out of the 'protective' business and the 'subsidy' business and the 'improvement' business. It must let trade and commerce and manufactures, and steamboats, and railroads, and telegraphs alone. It cannot touch them without breeding corruption.*
>
> —Edwin Lawrence Godkin
> Editor of *The Nation*, 1873

NOTES

1
ICEBERG, DEAD AHEAD

[1] Congressional Budget Office (CBO), *The Economic and Budget Outlook: Fiscal Years 1999-2008*, January 1998, p. 64.

[2] "A Much Bigger Federal Work Force," *Washington Post*, December 28, 1998.

[3] *The 1998 World Almanac and Book of Facts*, (Mahwah, NJ, World Almanac Books, 1997), pp. 108, 112.

[4] *The Right Data*, Edwin S. Rubenstein, (New York, National Review, 1994), p. 389.

[5] Ibid.

[6] U.S. General Accounting Office (GAO), *High-Risk Program, Information on Selected High Risk Areas*, May 1997, p. 4.

[7] Ibid., p. 17.

[8] GAO, *Medicare Automated Systems: Weakness in Managing Information Technology Hinder Fight Against Fraud and Abuse*, September 29, 1997, p. 1.

[9] GAO, *High-Risk Program, Information on Selected High Risk Areas*, May 1997, p. 32.

[10] Ibid., p. 111.

[11] Ibid.

[12] GAO, *Major Management Challenges and Program Risks: Department of Transportation*, January 1999, p. 7.

[13] GAO, *High-Risk Program, Information on Selected High Risk Areas*, May 1997, p. 79.

[14] Ibid.

[15] GAO, *Government Management: Status of Progress in Correcting Selected igh-Risk Areas*, February 3, 1993.

[16] GAO, *Government Management—Report on 17 High-Risk Areas*, January 8, 1993.

[17] David Gergen, "Headline Happy in D.C.," *U.S. News & World Report*, July 20, 1998.

[18] "Al Gore's Biggest Fix," *U.S. News & World Report*, September 13, 1993.

[19] Walter Mears, "The Politics of Reinvention," Associated Press, September 9, 1993.

[20] James Bovard, *The Farm Fiasco* (San Francisco, ICS Press 1989), p.10.

[21] CBO, *The Economic and Budget Outlook: Fiscal Years 1999-2008*, January 1998, p. 70.

[22] *The 1994 World Almanac and Book of Facts* (New Jersey, Funk &Wagnalls, 1994), p.101.

[23] Peter G. Peterson, "Remember Cost Control," *Newsweek*, July 25, 1994.

[24] Gloria Borger, "The Lame-Duck Book of Virtues," *U.S. News & World Report*, July 25, 1994.

[25] George F. Will, "R=C2," *Newsweek*, July 11, 1994.

[26] Lawrence Kudlow, "Chaos Comes to Congress," *National Review*, July 11, 1994.

[27] "Continuing State of Emergency," *Reason*, January, 1999.

[28] GAO, *Addressing the Deficit*, March 1994.

[29] Reuters, June 10, 1991.

[30] Jonathan Rauch, "Suckers!" *Reason*, May 1994.

[31] "House Seats: $1 million each," *Business Week*, December 9, 1996.

[32] Jack Anderson and Dale Van Atta, "Congress's Big Spenders," *Washington Post*, December 8, 1991.

[33] Congressional Budget Office, *The Economic and Budget Outlook: Fiscal Years 1999-2008*, January 1998, pp. 70, 78.

[34] Statement of Robert Reischauer on National Saving and the Role Played by the Baby Boomers before the Senate Finance Committee, June 17, 1994.

[35] "A Course Toward National Bankruptcy," *U.S. News & World Report*, August 22, 1994.

[36] Ibid.

[37] Ibid.

[38] CBO, *An Economic and Budget Outlook Update*, August 1998, p. 37.

[39] CBO, *The Economic and Budget Outlook: Fiscal Years 2000 - 2009, January 1999*, p.44.

[40] GAO, *Social Security And Surpluses: GAO's Perspective on the President's Proposals*, February 23, 1999, p. 22.

2
THE BEST OF INTENTIONS

[1] James Bovard, *The Farm Fiasco*, (San Francisco, ICS Press, 1989) p. 10.

[2] GAO, *Cargo Preference Requirements*, September 1994, p.3.

[3] GAO, *Value of Hardrock Minerals Extracted From, and Remaining on Federal Lands*, August 1992, p.2.

[4] GAO, *Testimony of Clarence C. Crawford before the House Subcommittee on Employment, Housing and Aviation*, August 4, 1994.

[5] Letter from Senator John McCain to President Clinton, dated May 4, 1998.

[6] Bovard, *The Farm Fiasco*, p. 62.

[7] GAO, *Commodity Programs: Impact of Support Provisions on Selected Commodity Programs*, February 1997, p. 18.

[8] *Journal of Commerce*, May 17, 1988.

[9] GAO, *Sugar Program*, April 1993, p.10.

[10] GAO, *Sugar Program: Impact on Sweetener Users and Producers*, May 24, 1995.

[11] Ibid., p. 28.

[12] Ibid., p. 38.

[13] "Preliminary Marketing Allotments Established," *Idaho Farmer*, February 1995.

[14] Walter Williams, Creators Syndicate Inc., October 23, 1997.

[15] GAO, *Cargo Preference Requirements*, September 1994, p.16.

[16] Ibid., p.2.

[17] GAO, *Maritime Industry: Cargo Preference Laws—Estimated Costs and Effects*, November 1994, p. 3.

[18] GAO, *Cargo Preference Requirements*, September 1994, p. 4.

[19] Ibid., p. 6.

[20] GAO, *Maritime Industry: Cargo Preference Laws—Estimated Costs and Effects*, November 1994, p. 21.

[21] "Trade Barriers Force Americans to Pay More," Associated Press, November 27, 1994.

[22] Ibid.

[23] GAO, *Testimony of James Duffus III before the House Subcommittee on Energy and Mineral Resources*, August 5, 1993.

[24] GAO, *Value of Hardrock Minerals Extracted From, and Remaining on Federal Lands*, August 1992, p. 2.

[25] Tom Kenworthy, "Negotiators Admit Defeat Over Mining Law," *Washington Post*, September 30, 1994.

[26] Tom Kenworthy, "For $5 an acre, $8 billion in gold," *Washington Post*, April 17, 1994.

[27] Ibid.

[28] Sharon Begley and Daniel Glick, "The Last Great Giveaway," *Newsweek*, May 30, 1994.

[29] Ibid.

[30] Ibid.

[31] GAO, *Value of Hardrock Minerals Extracted From, and Remaining on Federal Lands*, August 1992, p. 2.

[32] GAO, *Testimony of James Duffus III before the House Subcommittee on Energy and Mineral Resources*, August 5, 1993.

[33] Begley and Glick, "The Last Great Giveaway."

[34] Christina Del Valle, "Doing a Job on the Job Corps," *Business Week*, January 16, 1995.

[35] Ibid.

[36] GAO, *Testimony of Clarence C. Crawford before the Senate Committee on Labor and Human Resources*, September 28, 1994.

[37] GAO, *Testimony of Clarence C. Crawford before the Senate Subcommittee on Education, Labor and Health and Human Services*, June 18, 1993.

[38] Ibid.

[39] GAO, *Multiple Employment Training Programs*, March 1994, p. 3.

[40] GAO, *Testimony of Clarence C. Crawford before the House Subcommittee on Employment, Housing and Aviation*, August 4, 1994.

[41] GAO, *Dislocated Workers*, November 21, 1989.

[42] GAO, *Integrating Human Services*, September 24, 1992.

[43] Pembroke Rathbone,"Guest Opinion," *Boise Statesman*, December 1992.

[44] House Ways and Means Committee, *1994 Green Book*, p. 325.

[45] Gene Koretz, "Economic Trends," *Business Week*, January 23, 1995.

[46] *Congressional Quarterly Almanac, 1973*, (Washington, D.C., Congressional Quarterly, Inc., 1974) pp. 316-17.

[47] Dennis S. Ippolito, *Hidden Spending*, (Chapel Hill, University of North Carolina Press, 1984) p. 36.

[48] CBO, *Reducing the Deficit: Spending and Revenue Options*, March 1994, p.119.

[49] Howard Gleckman et. al., "Downsizing," *Business Week*, January 25, 1995.

[50] Peter G. Peterson and Neil Howe, *On Borrowed Time* (San Francisco, ICS Press, 1988) p. 157.

[51] CBO, *The Economic and Budget Outlook*, August 1998, p. 43.

[52] GAO, *Sugar Program*, April 1993, p. 11.

[53] Peter F. Drucker, *The New Realities*, (New York, Harper & Row, 1989) p. 99.

[54] Ippolito, *Hidden Spending*, p. 36.

[55] GAO, *Multiple Employment Training Programs*, July 1994, p. 4.

[56] GAO, *Testimony of Clarence C. Crawford before the Senate Committee on Labor and Human Resources*, September 28, 1994.

[57] GAO, *Budget Issues: Fiscal Year 1996 Agency Spending by Budget Function*, May 1997, p. 16.

[58] www.usda.gov, February 22, 1999.

[59] GAO, *USDA: Revitalizing Structure, Systems and Strategies*, September 1991, p. 2.

[60] GAO, *Addressing the Deficit*, March 1994, p. 60.

[61] USDA, *Agriculture Fact Book* 1996, p. 70.

[62] Dorcas R. Hardy and C. Colburn Hardy, *Social Insecurity*, (New York, Villard Books, 1991) p. 40.

[63] Begley and Glick, "The Last Great Giveaway."

[64] Dixy Lee Ray, *Environmental Overkill*, (Washington, D.C., Regnery Gateway, 1993) p. 141.

[65] GAO, *Federal Land Management: Information to Inventory Abandoned Hard Rock Mines*, February 23, 1996.

[66] Dr. Glen Miller, "Molding the Landscape," *Clementine*, Journal of the Mineral Policy Center, Winter 1990, p. 6.

[67] Daniel M. Horowitz, "Mining and Right-to-Know," *Clementine,* Journal of the Mineral Policy Center, Winter 1990, p. 10.

[68] Ibid.

[69] Tom Knudson, "Mining's Grim Ecology," *Clementine,* Journal of the Mineral Policy Center, Spring/ Summer 1990.

[70] John B. Wright, "The Real River that Runs Through it: Montana Imperiled," *Focus,* Spring 1993.

[71] Richard Manning, "Going For the Gold," *Audubon,* Jan-Feb 1994.

[72] James S. Lyon et al., *Burden of Gilt,* Mineral Policy Center, Washington, D.C., June 1993.

[73] GAO, *Mortgage Financing,* October 1994, p. 2.

[74] Ippolito, *Hidden Spending,* p. 28.

[75] Thomas A. Stanton, *A State of Risk,* (New York, Harper Collins, 1991) p. 26.

[76] GAO, *Mortgage Financing,* October 1994, p. 15.

[77] "The New America," *Business Week,* September 25, 1989.

[78] "Homeownership Rates," a chart in the 1994 Time Almanac, Reference Edition CDROM.

[79] "The New America," *Business Week,* September 25, 1989.

[80] Walter Shapiro, "The Ghetto: From Bad to Worse," *Time,* August 24, 1987.

[81] Stanton, *A State of Risk,* p. 26.

[82] Ibid.

[83] Joseph A. Pechman, *Tax Reform,* (Washington, D.C., Brookings Institution, 1989) p. 80.

[84] Paul Zane Pilzer, *Other People's Money,* (New York, Simon & Shuster, 1989) p. 73.

[85] Jack E. White, "Bright City Lights," *Time,* November 1, 1993.

[86] Kevin Fedarko, "The Other America," *Time,* January 20, 1992.

[87] Walter Shapiro, "The Ghetto: From Bad to Worse," *Time,* August 24, 1987.

[88] "Poverty's Foundation: Housing," *The Economist,* April 11, 1992.

[89] "The New America," *Business Week,* September 25, 1989.

[90] Ibid.

[91] Richard Woodbury, "Down in the Big Queasy," *Time,* February 28, 1994.

[92] Peter Weber, "Scenes from the Squatting Life," *National Review,* February 27, 1987.

[93] "Anybody Home?" *Time,* August 21, 1989.

[94] Ibid.

[95] Fedarko, "The Other America."

[96] "The New America," *Business Week,* September 25, 1989.

[97] John C. Weicher, *Maintaining the Safety Net,* (Washington, D.C., American Enterprise Institute, 1984) p. 95.

[98] Scott Minerbrook, "The Big-City Push to Fill the Housing Gap for the Poor," *U.S. News & World Report,* August 28, 1989.

[99] Robert Woodson, "Poverty: Why Politics Can't Cure it," *Imprimis,* Hillsdale College, July 1988.

[100] Paul Zane Pilzer, *Other People's Money*, (New York, Simon & Shuster, 1989) p. 81.

[101] Ibid. pp. 69-70, 73-74.

[102] CBO, *The Economic Effects of the Savings and Loan Crisis*, January 1992, p. ix.

[103] Ibid. p. 82.

[104] Richard Behar, "The Great Office Giveaway," *Time*, March 4, 1991.

[105] GAO, *Budget Issues: Budgeting for Federal Insurance Programs*, September 1997, p.154.

[106] CBO, *Resolving the Thrift Crisis*, April 1993, p. ix.

[107] Michael Waldman, *Who Robbed America*, (New York, Random House, 1990) p. 230.

[108] "FDIC Cuts Deposit Insurance Rate; Annual Savings Put at $4 Billion," *Minneapolis Star Tribune*, August 9, 1995.

[109] GAO, *Deposit Insurance Funds*, August 1994, p. 2.

[110] "FDIC Cuts Deposit Insurance Rate; Annual Savings Put at $4 Billion," *Minneapolis Star Tribune*, August 9, 1995.

3
A NATIONAL DISGRACE

[1] Marlys Harris, "Money Helps," *Money*, July, 1993.

[2] 26 USC Sec. 3121

[3] Dorcas R. Hardy and Colburn Hardy, *Social Insecurity*, (New York, Villard Books, 1991), p .5.

[4] George G. Kaufman, *The U.S. Financial System*, (Englewood Cliffs, Prentice Hall, 1989) p. 238.

[5] "Rebuilding Retirement," *U.S. News & World Report*, April 20, 1998.

[6] Calculations by author; data: GAO, *The Economic and Budget Outlook, August 1994*. pp. 29, 31.

[7] CBO, *The Economic and Budget Outlook: Fiscal Years1 999-2008, January, 1998*, p. 70;

[8] GAO, *Social Security Financing: Implications of Government Stock Investing for the Trust Fund, the Federal Budget, and the Economy*, April 1998, p. 29.

[9] "If It's On Paper; It Must Be Real—Or Is It?" *Washington Post National Weekly Edition*, December 21, 1998.

[10] U.S. Senator Kent Conrad speaking on the Senate floor, February 9, 1995.

[11] GAO, *Social Security Financing: Implications of Government Stock Investing for the Trust Fund, the Federal Budget, and the Economy*, April 1998, p. 2.

[12] Peter G. Peterson speaking to the Bipartisan Commission on Entitlement and Tax Reform, CSPAN, December 14, 1994.

[13] John Wood, "Social Security: Invaluable or Outmoded?" *Modern Maturity*, April-May 1992.

[14] Howard Gleckman, et.al., "Social Security's Dirty Little Secret," *Business Week*, January 29, 1990.

[15] GAO, *Social Security Financing: Implications of Government Stock Investing for the Trust Fund, the Federal Budget, and the Economy*, April 1998, p. 29.

[16] Ibid.

[17] Spencer Rich, "Tax Cut Plan Could Bankrupt Social Security, Study Says," *Washington Post*, February 22, 1991.

[18] Ibid.

[19] Spencer Rich, "Social Security and Fairness: Should Tax Rate Be Cut?" *Washington Post*, February 18, 1991.

[20] CBO, *The Economic and Budget Outlook: Fiscal Years 1999-2008, January, 1998*, p. 48.

[21] Ibid.

[22] James Bennet, "The W-2 Step," *Washington Monthly*, June 1991.

[23] Internal Revenue Service, *Employer's 1995 Tax Guide*, p. 9.

[24] William J. Baumol and Alan S. Blinder, *Economics, Principles and Policy*, (San Diego, Harcourt, Brace, Jovanovich, 1988), p. 732.

[25] Hardy and Hardy, *Social Insecurity*, p. 26.

[26] GAO, *Social Security: Restoring Long-Term Solvency Will Require Difficult Choices*, February 10, 1998, p. 9.

[27] Hardy and Hardy, *Social Insecurity*, p. 20.

[28] William J. Baumol & Alan S. Blinder, *Economics, Principles and Policy*, (San Diego, Harcourt, Brace, Jovanovich, 1988), p. 722.

[29] Hardy and Hardy, *Social Insecurity*, p .20.

[30] Ibid.

[31] Lawrence B. Lindsey, "The Big Black Hole," *Forbes*, November 21, 1994.

[32] Hardy and Hardy, *Social Insecurity*, pp. 27-28.

[33] GAO, *Social Security: Different Approaches for Addressing Program Solvency*, July 1998, p. 12.

[34] *The World Almanac, 1994*, (Mahwah, Funk &Wagnalls, 1993), p. 361.

[35] GAO, *Social Security Trends, Demographic Trends Underlie Long-Term Financing Shortage*, November 20, 1997, p. 5.

[36] Baumol and Blinder, *Economics, Principles and Policy*, p. 723.

[37] Hardy and Hardy, *Social Insecurity*, pp.12; GAO, *Social Security Financing: Implications of Government Stock Investing for the Trust Fund, the Federal Budget, and the Economy*, April 1998, p. 2.

[38] Hardy and Hardy, *Social Insecurity*, pp. 23.

[39] Walter Williams, "Our Fun, Disaster for Our Children," *Washington Times*, February 26, 1994.

[40] Lawrence B. Lindsey, "The Big Black Hole," *Forbes*, November 21, 1994.

[41] Lucy Howard and Ned Zeman, "Generational War," *Newsweek*, February 10, 1992.

[42] James K. Glassman, "The Budget with the Hidden Generation Gap," *Washington Post*, February 15, 1995.

[43] Lewellyn Rockwell, "Nation's Youth Pay High Price For Social Security Scam," *Insight on the News*, October 31, 1994.

[44] Hardy and Hardy, *Social Insecurity*, pp. xxiii-xxiv.

[45] John Attarian, "No Time For Gimmicks," *National Review*, May 10, 1993.

[46] David Hage and Robert F. Black, "A Hardheaded Budget Play," *U.S. News & World Report*, January 23, 1995.

[47] House Committee on Ways and Means, *1994 Green Book*, p. 49.

[48] Ibid., p. 48.

[49] OASDI Tax Rate Table, Office of the Chief Actuary, Social Security Administration, October 23, 1997.

[50] "Disability Insurance Trust Fund," *Annual Statistical Supplement to the Social Security Bulletin*, Office of the Chief Actuary, Social Security Administration, July 24, 1998.

[51] Ibid.

[52] GAO, *Testimony of Jane L. Ross before the Subcommittee on Social Security*, House Ways and Means Committee, April 22, 1993.

[53] GAO, *Social Security: Disability Programs Lag in Promoting Return to Work*, March 1997, p. 1.

[54] GAO, *Testimony of Joseph F. Delfico before the Subcommittee on Social Security and Family Policy, Senate Finance Committee*, April 27, 1992.

[55] GAO, *Social Security Disability: SSA Making Progress in Conducting Continuing Disability Reviews*, September 1998, p. 1.

[56] Ibid.

[57] GAO, *Testimony of Joseph F. Delfico before the Subcommittee on Social Security and Family Policy, Senate Finance Committee*, April 27, 1992.

[58] GAO, *Supplemental Security Income: Opportunities Exist for Improving Payment Accuracy*, March 1998, p. 1.

[59] House Committee on Ways and Means, *1994 Green Book*, p. 207.

[60] GAO, *Supplemental Security Income: Action Needed on Long-Standing Problems Affecting program Security*, September 1998, p. 2.

[61] CBO, *The Economic and Budget Outlook: Fiscal Years 1999-2008, January, 1998*, p. 70.

[62] Hobart Rowen, "What Your Taxes Actually Buy," *Washington Post*, December 29, 1994.

[63] CBO, *The Economic and Budget Outlook: Fiscal Years 1999-2008, January, 1998*, pp. 64, 70.

[64] House Committee on Ways and Means, *1994 Green Book*, p. 326.

[65] "Intricate New System," *Newsday*, August 2, 1996.

[66] GAO, *Testimony of Jane L. Ross before the Subcommittee on Human Resources, House Ways and Means Committee*, January 27, 1995.

[67] Ibid.

[68] Ibid.

[69] GAO, *Supplemental Security Income: Organizational Culture and Management Inattention Place Program at Continued Risk*, April 21, 1998, p. 2.

[70] GAO, *Supplemental Security Income: Long-Standing Problems Put Program at Risk for Fraud, Waste and Abuse*, March 4, 1997, p. 7.

[71] Hardy and Hardy, *Social Insecurity*, p. 33.

[72] 42 USC Sec 402.

[73] GAO, *Social Security Reform: Demographic Trends Underlie Long-Term Financing Shortage*, November 20, 1997, p. 5.

[74] (Five years older than the average life expectancy which in 1992 was 75.7 years.) *The World Almanac, 1994*, (Mahwah, Funk &Wagnalls, 1993), p. 972.

[75] Hardy and Hardy, *Social Insecurity*, p .33.

[76] Robert J. Barro, "Don't Dicker With Social Security, Reinvent It," *Business Week*, June 8, 1998.

[77] "Social Security Reform: Ready For Prime Time?" *Business Week*, January 19, 1998.

[78] Warren Rudman, "Social Security's Fund Cannot Be Trusted," *Washington Times*, May 2, 1994.

[79] Thomas Paine, *Common Sense*, (Philadelphia, 1776).

[80] Walter Williams, "Our Fun, Disaster for Our Children," *Washington Times*, February 26, 1994.

[81] Social Security Administration, Office of Research, Evaluation and Statistics, "Current Operating Statement," October 1998.

[82] CBO, *Reducing Entitlement Spending*, September 1994, p. 7.

[83] Peter G. Peterson and Neil Howe, *On Borrowed Time* (San Francisco, ICs Press, 1988), p. 157.

[84] Ibid.

[85] GAO, *High Risk Series: Medicare*, February 1997, p. 14.

[86] House Committee on Ways and Means, *1994 Green Book*, p. 76.

[87] CBO, *The Economic and Budget Outlook: Fiscal Years 1999-2008, January 1998*, p. 133.

[88] Ibid.

[89] House Committee on Ways and Means, *1994 Green Book*, p. 175.

[90] CBO, *The Economic and Budget Outlook: Fiscal Years 1999-2008, January 1998*, p. 133.

[91] Robert J. Samuelson, "A Nation in Denial," *Washington Post*, March 5, 1995.

[92] Calculations by author; data: CBO, *The Economic and Budget Outlook: Fiscal Years 1999-2008*, January 1998, p. 133.

[93] Ibid.

[94] "Health Care: Prognosis 1999," *Business Week*, January 11, 1999.

[95] "HMOs Take a Hike from Medicare," *Investors Business Daily*, October 28, 1998.

[96] Ibid.

[97] House Committee on Ways and Means, *1994 Green Book*, p. 180.

[98] Ibid.

[99] "Economic Trends: It's Not Just Social Security," *Business Week*, October 26, 1998.

[100] Dr. Timothy Flaherty, testimony on behalf of the American Medical Association before the National Bipartisan Commission on the future of Medicare on September 8, 1998.

[101] "Panel May Urge Medicare Overhaul," *U.S. News & World Report*, January 18, 1999.

[102] Paul Starr, *The Social Transformation of American Medicine*, (New York, Basic Books, 1982), p. 180.

[103] Terree P. Wasley, *What Has Government Done to Our Health Care?*, (Washington, D.C., Cato Institute, 1994), pp. 56-57.

[104] Ibid., p. 60.

[105] Peter J. Ferrara, "Medical Savings Accounts: A Solution to Financing Health Care?" *USA Today Magazine*, May 1, 1996.

[106] Ibid.

[107] CBO, *The Economic and Budget Outlook: Fiscal Years 1999-2008, January 1998*, p. 135.

[108] Dan Morgan, "A Mixed Blessing of Bureaucracy," *Washington Post*, February 2, 1994.

[109] CBO, *The Economic and Budget Outlook: Fiscal Years 1999-2008, January 1998*, p. 135.

[110] Ibid.

[111] Susan Dentzer, Untangling Universal Coverage, *U.S. News & World Report*, July 11, 1994

[112] GAO, *Medicaid: Demographics of Nonenrolled Children Suggest State Outreach Strategies*, March 1998, p. 1.

[113] GAO, *Testimony of Jane L. Ross before the Subcommittee on Human Resources, House Ways and Means Committee*, January 27, 1995.

[114] Dan Morgan, "A Mixed Blessing of Bureaucracy," *Washington Post*, February 2, 1994; and "Medicaid Grows into Budgetary Time Bomb," *Washington Post*, January 30, 1994.

[115] Cheryl Wetzstein, "High Cost of Aliens in U.S. Tallied," *Washington Times*, June 28, 1994.

[116] Dan Morgan, "Nursing Home Costs Lead Middle-Class Elderly to Shield Assets," *Washington Post*, February 1, 1994.

[117] GAO, *Long-Term Care Insurance, High Percentage of Policy Holders Drop Policies*, August 1993, p. 2.

[118] Dan Morgan, "Medicaid Bills Come Home to Roost," *Washington Post National Weekly Edition*, February 6-12, 1995.

[119] Judi Hasson, "States' Medicaid Funding Loophole Called A 'Scam'," *USA Today*, November 20, 1991.

[120] Joseph A. Califano Jr., "The Last Time We Reinvented Health Care," *Washington Post*, April 1, 1993.

[121] Ibid.

[122] Steven Hayward and Erik Peterson, "The Medicare Monster," *Reason*, January 1993.

[123] Terree P. Wasley, *What Has Government Done To Our Health Care?*, (Washington, D.C., Cato Institute, 1994), p. 63.

[124] Joseph A. Califano Jr., "The Last Time We Reinvented Health Care," *Washington Post*, April 1, 1993.

[125] Joseph A. Califano Jr., America's Health Care Revolution, (New York, Random House, 1986), p. 54.

[126] GAO, *Medicare: HCFA Faces Multiple Challenges to Prepare for the 21st Century*, January 29, 1998, p. 3.

[127] Hayward and Peterson, "The Medicare Monster."

[128] Califano, "The Last Time We Reinvented Health Care."

[129] Peter J. Levin, "The Ripple of the Unintended Consequences of Health Care," *Insight on the News*, June 28, 1994.

[130] CBO, *The Economic and Budget Outlook: Fiscal Years 1999-2008, January 1998*, pp. 123, 135.

[131] "Insiders," *Money*, November 13, 1991.

[132] "The World's Forgotten Danger," *The Economist*, November 14, 1998.

[133] "Labor Pains," *U.S. News & World Report*, March 13, 1995.

[134] Aaron Bernstein et al., "What Happened to the American Dream?," *Business Week*, August 19, 1991.

[135] James K. Glassman, "Unemployment's Gray Zone," *U.S. News & World Report*, March 17, 1997.

[136] John Wood, "Social Security: Invaluable or Outmoded?" *Modern Maturity*, April-May 1992.

[137] "These Taxing Times," *Washington Post National Weekly Edition*, January 25, 1999.

[138] Ibid., p. 23.

[139] John Wood, "Social Security: Invaluable or Outmoded?" *Modern Maturity*, April-May 1992.

[140] Lani Luciano, "Eight Myths of Retirement, " *Money*, February 1990.

[141] Ed Carson, "Market Approval," *Reason*, February, 1995.

[142] Ibid.

[143] Christopher Farrell et al., "The Economics of Aging," *Business Week*, September 12, 1994.

[144] Albert B. Crenshaw, "Social Security Sending a Message About Benefits, *Washington Post*, July 17, 1994.

[145] Christopher Farrell et al., "The Economics of Aging," *Business Week*, September 12, 1994.

[146] Elizabeth Larson, "Retiring Plans," *Reason*, June 1993.

[147] Albert B. Crenshaw, "Social Security Sending a Message About Benefits, *Washington Post*, July 17, 1994.

[148] Ibid.

[149] Aaron Bernstein et al., "What happened to the American Dream?," *Business Week*, August 19, 1991.

[150] Ibid.

[151] Robert J. Samuelson, "Redefining Elderly," *The Washington Post National Weekly Edition*, November 9, 1998.

[152] Jerry Adler with Shawn D. Lewis, "The Joys of Living Large," *Newsweek*, May 17, 1993.

[153] "Highlights of the National Health Expenditure Projections, 1997-2007," Health Care Financing Administration, www.hcfa.gov/stats/nhe-proj/hilites.htm, January 1999.

[154] Aetna Insurance Company, *The Managed Care Solution*, 1992, p. 2.

[155] CBO, *Projections of National Health Expenditures*, October 1992, p. 40.

[156] Robert J. Samuelson, "Health Care," *Newsweek*, October 4, 1993.

[157] GAO, *Testimony of Janet L. Shikles before the Subcommittee on Health, House Ways and Means Committee*, March 8, 1993.

[158] Ibid.

4
THE FEDERAL TAX SYSTEM

[1] Peter F. Drucker, *The New Realities*, (New York, Harper & Row, 1990), p. 65.

[2] GAO, *Tax Policy and Administration: 1996 Annual Report of GAO's Tax-Related Work*, July 1997, p. 8.

[3] Michael Ruby, "Three Cheers For a Flat Tax," *U.S. News & World Report*, February 20,1995.

[4] Rob Norton, "Our Screwed-up Tax Code," *Fortune*, September 6, 1993.

[5] Charles Adams, *For Good and Evil*, (Lanham, Madison Books, 1993), p. 302.

[6] Ibid.

[7] Ibid., p. 303.

[8] Edwin S. Rubenstein, *The Right Data*, (New York, National Review, 1994), p. 324.

[9] Data: Edwin S. Rubenstein, *The Right Data*, (New York, National Review, 1994), p. 326, calculations by author.

[10] Ibid.

[11] House Ways and Means Committee, *Green Book*, p. 675.

[12] GAO, *Tax Expenditures Deserve More Scrutiny*, June 1994, p 3.

[13] Ibid.

[14] CBO, *The Economic and Budget Outlook: Fiscal Years 1999-2008*, January 1998, p. 48.

[15] Ibid.

[16] "Mortgage Tax Break Increases in Value," *Washington Times*, February 26, 1993.

[17] Miles Maguire, "Home Buyers, Developers May Get Tax Benefits," *Washington Times*, January 27, 1992.

[18] Michael Wolff et al., *Where We Stand*, (New York, Bantam Books, 1992), pp. 16-17.

[19] Ibid.

[20] Ibid.

[21] Dan Goodgame, "Welfare for the Well-off," *Time*, February 22, 1993.

[22] Wolff et al., *Where We Stand*, pp. 16-17.

[23] CBO, *Reducing the Deficit: Spending and Revenue Options, February 1995*, p. 342.

[24] "Reinstated Tax Credit Fuels Rise in Housing," *Washington Times*, October 20, 1993.

[25] Vicki Kemper, "Home Inequity," *Common Cause*, Summer 1994.

[26] David Hage, David Fisher and Robert F. Black, "America's Other Welfare State," *U.S. News & World Report*, April 10, 1995.

[27] Ibid.

[28] Ibid.

[29] CBO, *Reducing the Deficit: Spending and Revenue Options*, February 1995, p. 343.

[30] David Hage, David Fisher and Robert F. Black, "America's Other Welfare State," *U. S. News & World Report*, April 10, 1995.

[31] GAO, *Reducing the Deficit: Spending and Revenue Options*, March 1997, p. 370.

[32] Ibid., pp. 370, 372.

[33] CBO, *Reducing the Deficit: Spending and Revenue Options*, February 1995, p. 342.

[34] GAO, *Reducing the Deficit: Spending and Revenue Options*, March 1997, p.348.

[35] CBO, *The Tax Treatment of Employment-Based Health Insurance*, March 1994, p. xii.

[36] CBO, *An Analysis of the Managed Competition Act*, April 1994, pp. 10-11.

[37] Senator Phil Gramm, "Health Benefits Tax Threat," *Washington Times*, June 30, 1994.

[38] CBO, *The Tax Treatment of Employment-Based Health Insurance*, March 1994, p. xi.

[39] Ibid., pp. 30-31.

[40] Dan Goodgame, "This May Hurt a Bit," *Time*, May 16, 1994.

[41] GAO, *Effects of Changing the Tax treatment of Fringe Benefits*, April 1992, p. 58.

[42] CBO, *The Tax Treatment of Employment-Based Health Insurance*, March 1994, p. 22.

[43] Ibid., p11.

[44] GAO, *Tax Expenditures Deserve More Scrutiny*, June 1994, p. 50.

[45] House Ways and Means Committee, *Green Book*, p. 682.

[46] Calculation by author; Data: Pension Benefit Guaranty Corp., www.pbgc.gov, December 1998; GAO, *Pension Guaranty Benefit Corporation: Financial Condition Improving but Long Term Risks Remain*, October 6, 1998.

[47] House Ways and Means Committee, *Green Book*, p. 683.

[48] Ibid., p. 684.

[49] CBO, *Controlling Losses of the Pension Benefit Guarantee Corporation*, January 1993, p. 1.

[50] Ibid., p5.

[51] Ibid., p1,3.

[52] bid.

[53] Ibid., p16.

[54] Pension Benefit Guaranty Corporation, www.pbgc.gov, January 1999.

[55] GAO, *Pension Guaranty Benefit Corporation: Financial Condition Improving but Long Term Risks Remain*, October 6, 1998.

[56] CBO, *Reducing the Deficit: Spending and Revenue Options*, February 1995, p. 344.

[57] CBO, *The Economic and Budget Outlook: Fiscal Years 1999-2008*, January 1998, p. 340.

[58] Donald L. Barlett and James B. Steele, America: Who Really Pays the Taxes? (New York, Touchstone, 1994), p. 258.

[59] CBO, *Reducing the Deficit: Spending and Revenue Options*, February 1995, p. 344.

[60] CBO, *The Economic and Budget Outlook: Fiscal Years 1999-2008*, January 1998, p. 355.

[61] Ibid.

[62] Calculations by Thomas W. Shumate, CPA, San Jose, CA.

[63] Social Security Administration, "Current Operating Statistics," January 1999.

[64] Barlett and Steele, America: Who Really Pays the Taxes? p. 124.

[65] CBO, *The Economic and Budget Outlook: Fiscal Years 1999-2008, January 1998*, p.342.

[66] Barlett and Steele, *America: Who Really Pays the Taxes?* p. 133.

[67] Adam Zagorin, "Remember the Greedy," *Time*, August 16, 1993.

[68] "Average Americans, Not the Super-rich Are the Real Givers," *U.S. News & World Report*, December 22, 1997.

[69] Zagorin, "Remember the Greedy."

[70] Larry Witham, "Donors, Volunteers, Fewer But More Avid," *Washington Times*, October 19, 1994.

[71] "Average Americans, Not the Super-rich Are the Real Givers."

[72] Ibid.

[73] Caroline Pesce, "Holding the 'Radical Line'; Animal Group Shocks Even its Supporters," *USA Today*, September 3, 1991.

[74] William Tucker, "Sweet Charity," *The American Spectator*, February 1995.

[75] CBO, *The Economic and Budget Outlook: Fiscal Years 1999-2008, January 1998*, p. 342.

[76] Scott Shepard, "'Grass Roots ' or 'Astroturf'?" *Washington Times*, December 20, 1994.

[77] "Taxpayers Pick Up Large Part of Tab for America's Political Partyers," *Washington Post*, July 4, 1995.

[78] Ibid.

[79] Ibid.

[80] William Tucker, "Sweet Charity," *The American Spectator*, February 1995.

[81] Ibid.

[82] Ibid.

[83] Ibid.

[84] Bill McAllister, "Nonprofit Mail Discounts on Route to Cancellation," *Washington Post*, May 11, 1993.

[85] Bill McAllister, "Postal Panel Backs Across the Board Hike," *Washington Post*, March 8, 1994.

[86] "Charity Head's Salaries Increased 5 Times Rate of Inflation," *Washington Post,* July 5, 1998.

[87] Cynthia Grenier, "Many Happy (tax) Returns; Hillary's Creative Calculator," *Washington Times,* July 19, 1993.

[88] Joint Committee on Taxation, Estimates of Federal Tax Expenditures for Fiscal Years *1993-1997,* August 24, 1992.

[89] *Cato Handbook for Congress,* 105th Congress, Cato Institute, Washington, D.C.

[90] Barlett and Steele, *America: Who Really Pays the Taxes?* pp. 143-144.

[91] Ibid., p. 246.

[92] Ibid.

[93] Joseph A. Pechman, *Tax Reform, the Rich and the Poor,* (Washington D.C., The Brookings Institution, 1989), p. 191.

[94] Barlett and Steele, *America: Who Really Pays the Taxes?* p. 149.

[95] Calculations by author. Corporate revenues exceed 87 percent of GNP: Baumol and Blinder, *Economics, Principles and Policy,* p. 653. GNP data: *1994 World Almanac and Book of Facts,* p. 104.

[96] Calculations by author. Data: Edwin S. Rubenstein, *The Right Data,* (New York, National Review, 1994), p. 30.

[97] David Craig and Beth Belton, "The Debt Bomb," *USA Today,* April 12, 1990.

[98] Ibid.

[99] William McWhirter, "The Profits of Doom," *Time,* March 19, 1990.

[100] Craig and Belton, "The Debt Bomb."

[101] Larry Light, "Corporate Finance," *Business Week,* April 3, 1995.

[102] 138 revisions between 1976 and 1989: David Burnham, *A Law Unto Itself; Power, Politics and the IRS,* (New York, Random House, 1989), p. 303; plus the 1990 and 1993 tax acts.

[103] Adams, *For Good and Evil, the Impact of Taxes on the Course of Civilization,* p. 454.

[104] James L. Payne, *Costly Burdens: The Burdens of the U.S. Tax System,* (San Francisco, ICS Press, 1993), p. 4.

[105] GAO, *Serious Problems Exist in the quality of IRS Communications with Taxpayers, Testimony before the House Committee on Government Operations,* July 13, 1988, pp. 11-12.

[106] Dan Pilla, CSPAN2, April 14, 1995.

[107] Mortimer B. Zuckerman, "No Taxation Without Simplification," *U.S. News & World Report,* August 15, 1988.

[108] Ibid.

[109] "Complexity Theory," *Reason,* December 1997.

[110] Statement on the floor of the US Senate, October 6, 1994.

[111] GAO, *Tax Administration, Tax Compliance Initiatives and Delinquent Taxes,* February 1, 1995, p. 2.

[112] GAO, *Internal Revenue Service: Composition and Collectibility of Unpaid Assessments,* October 29, 1998.

[113] Ibid., p. 1.

[114] GAO, *Tax Systems Modernization, Comment's on IRS' Fiscal Year 1994 Budget Request*, April 27, 1993, p. 4.

[115] GAO, *Tax Policy and Administration, 1994 Annual Report on GAO's Tax-Related Work*, February 1995, p. 4.

[116] "Money's Sixth Annual Tax Preparers' Test," *Money*, March 1993.

[117] Adams, *For Good and Evil, the Impact of Taxes on the Course of Civilization*, p. 451.

[118] Ibid.

[119] GAO, *Internal Revenue Service Receivables*, February 1995, p. 7; GAO, *Internal Revenue Service: Composition and Collectibility of Unpaid Assessments*, October 29, 1998.

[120] Payne, *Costly Burdens: The Burdens of the U.S. Tax System*, p..4.

[121] GAO, *Tax Gap: Many Actions Taken, But a Cohesive Compliance Strategy Needed*, May 1994, p. 4.

[122] David Burnham, *A Law Unto Itself; Power, Politics and the IRS*, (New York, Random House, 1989), p. 304.

[123] Ibid., p. 303.

[124] GAO, *Tax Gap: Many Actions Taken, But a Cohesive Compliance Strategy Needed*, May 1994, p. 4.

[125] Payne, *Costly Burdens: The Burdens of the U.S. Tax System*, (San Francisco, ICS Press, 1993), p. 150.

[126] Ibid., p. 17.

[127] Ibid., p150.

[128] Ibid.

5

DEFENSE SPENDING

[1] Stated in conversations with the author.

[2] Pratt and Whitney Corporation "Pricing Basis" document for TF33 engine.

[3] Kenneth L. Adelman and Norman R. Augustine, *The Defense Revolution*, (San Francisco, ICS Press, 1990), pp.136-137.

[4] J. Ronald Fox with James L. Field, *The Defense Management Challenge*, (Boston, Harvard Business School Press, 1988), p. 41.

[5] President's Blue Ribbon Commission on Defense Management, *A Quest for Excellence*, June 1986.

[6] A. Earnest Fitzgerald, *The Pentagonists*, (Boston, Houghton Mifflin, 1989), p. 211.

[7] Robert Wrubel, "Addicted to Fraud?" *Financial World*, June 27, 1989.

[8] Ibid.

[9] Peter Cary and Paul Glastris, "Charge of the Fix-It Brigade," *U.S. News & World Report, August 15, 1988*.

[10] Fox, *The Defense Management Challenge*, p. 310.

[11] Steven Pearlstein, "Navy Plane Controversy Continues; Committees Probe Aftermath of A-12," *Washington Post*, July 25, 1991.

[12] Bruce B. Auster, "Air Defense," *U.S. News & World Report*, January 21, 1991.

[13] "The Cost of Embarrassing the Boss," *Newsweek*, December 19, 1990.

[14] "The Devil and Mr. Jones," *Common Cause Magazine*, November-December 1990.

[15] Ibid.

[16] Richard A. Stubbing and Richard A. Mendel, "How to Save $50 billion a Year," *The Atlantic*, June 1989.

[17] Testimony of Ralph C. Nash, Jr., Professor of Law, George Washington University, before the Senate Subcommittee on Defense Acquisition Policy, February 20, 1985, "Defense Procurement Process," p. 21.

[18] Cary and Glastris, "Charge of the Fix-It Brigade."

[19] Eliot A. Cohen, "Missions, Structures and Weapons: What to do about National Defense?" *Current*, February 1995.

[20] Ibid.

[21] Fox, *The Defense Management Challenge*, p. 92.

[22] David Segal, "The Shell Game," *Washington Monthly*, July-August, 1993.

[23] "Proud Russia on Its Knees," *U.S. News & World Report*, February 8, 1999.

[24] "Russia's Problem—and Ours," *Washington Post National Weekly Edition*, November 30, 1998.

[25] Cohen, "Missions, Structures and Weapons: What to do about National Defense?"

[26] GAO, *National Security: Impact of China's Military Modernization in the Pacific Region*, June 1995, p. 29.

[27] Michael D. Swaine, "Fear of the Dragon," *Washington Post National Weekly Edition*, May 26, 1997.

[28] "China's Arms Buildup: Is the Paper Tiger Growing Claws?" *Business Week*, March 1, 1999.

[29] "Russia and China, Allies Once Again?" *Washington Post National Weekly Edition*, November 30, 1998.

[30] Eliot A. Cohen, "Missions, Structures and Weapons: What to do about National Defense?" *Current*, February 1995.

[31] Franklin C. Spinney, *Quadrennial Defense Review: What Went Wrong? How to Fix It*, www.infowar.com/mil_c4i/qdrup/qdrup.html-ssi, June 20, 1997.

[32] Jerome B. Wiesner, Philip Morrison and Kosta Tsipis, "Ending Overkill," *Bulletin of the Atomic Scientists*, March 1993.

[33] GAO, *F-15 Replacement is Premature as Currently Planned*, March 1994, p. 2.

[34] GAO, *Tactical Aircraft: Restructuring of the Air force F-22 Program*, June 1997, p. 11.

[35] GAO, *F-15 Replacement is Premature as Currently Planned, March 1994*, p. 4.

[36] Nick Kotz, *Wild Blue Yonder*, (Princeton, Princeton University Press, 1988), p.112.

[37] Calculation by author; sources: "Rockwell's B-1 Bomber Attacked in Congress," *Reuters*, March 5, 1991, and GAO, *Embedded Computers: B-1B Computers Must Be Upgraded To Support Conventional Requirements*, February 1996, p. 1.

[38] GAO, *Future Years Defense Programs: Optimistic Estimates Lead to Billions in Overprogramming*, January 1995, p. 1.

[39] *Washington Post*, March 15, 1971.

[40] David Segal, "The Shell Game," *Washington Monthly*, July-August 1993.

[41] Fox, *The Defense Management Challenge*, p. 317.

[42] Kotz, *Wild Blue Yonder*, p. 128.

[43] Ibid., p. 129.

[44] Ibid., p. 133.

[45] Ibid., p. 134.

[46] GAO, *Strategic Bombers: Issues Related to the B-1B Aircraft Program*, March 6, 1991, p. 11.

[47] GAO, *Strategic Bomber: Issues relating to the B-1B's Availability and Ability to Perform Conventional Missions*, January 1994, p. 10.

[48] "B-1 Repairs May Require $1 Billion: 3 Big Flaws Persist," *Washington Post*, March 7, 1991.

[49] Ibid.

[50] GAO, *Air Force Bombers: Conventional Capabilities of the B-1B Bomber*, May 4, 1994, p. 4.

[51] GAO, *Strategic Bombers, Need to Redefine Requirements for B-1B Defensive Avionics Systems*, July 1992, p. 2.

[52] GAO, *Strategic Bombers: Issues Related to the B-1B Aircraft Program*, March 6, 1991, pp. 8-9.

[53] Ibid.

[54] "B-1 Repairs May Require $1 Billion: 3 Big Flaws Persist," *Washington Post*.

[55] "The Might and Myth of the B-52," *Newsweek*, February 18, 1991.

[56] GAO, *Operation Desert Storm: Evaluation of the Air Campaign*, June 1997, p. 16.

[57] "Rockwell's B-1 Bomber Attacked in Congress," *Reuters*, March 5, 1991.

[58] "B-1 Bomber Grounded for Gulf War Due to Testing," *Reuters*, March 6, 1991.

[59] Kotz, *Wild Blue Yonder*, p. 99.

[60] "Air Force Activates B1-B Bomber Unit," *Washington Post*, October 2, 1986.

[61] GAO, *Strategic Bomber: Issues Relating to the B-1B's Availability and Ability to Perform Conventional Missions*, January, 1994, p. 2.

[62] "U.S Bombs Missed 70 Percent of the Time," *Washington Post*, March 16, 1991.

[63] GAO, *Weapons Acquisition, Precision Guided Munitions in Inventory, Production and Development*, June 1995, p. 14.

[64] GAO, *B1-B Bomber: Evaluation of Air Force Report on B-1B Operational Readiness Assessment*, July 1995, p. 6.

[65] GAO, *U.S. Combat Air Power: Reassessing Plans to Modernize Interdiction Capabilities Could Save Billions*, May 1996, p. 5.

[66] GAO, *Air Force, Assessment of DOD's Report on Plan and Capabilities for Evaluating Heavy Bombers,* January 1994, p. 4.

[67] GAO, *Operation Desert Storm: Limits on the Role and Performance of B-52 Bombers in Conventional Conflicts,* May 1993, p. 4.

[68] "Rockwell's B-1 Bomber Attacked in Congress," *Reuters,* March 5, 1991.

[69] "Rain of Terror Awaits Iraq," *Washington Times,* October 12, 1994.

[70] Kotz, *Wild Blue Yonder,* p.154.

[71] "The Might and Myth of the B52," *Newsweek.*

[72] GAO, *U.S. Combat Air Power: Reassessing Plans to Modernize Interdiction Capabilities Could Save Billions,* May 1996, p. 7.

[73] "America's Arms Race With Itself," *America's Defense Monitor,* Center For Defense Information, October 16, 1994.

[74] Kotz, *Wild Blue Yonder,* p. 210.

[75] Ibid.,p. 216.

[76] GAO, *Defense Weapons System Acquisition,* February 1997, p. 10.

[77] Kotz, *Wild Blue Yonder,* pp. 163-164.

[78] GAO, *Cruise Missile Defense: Progress Made but Significant Challenges Remain,* March 1999, p. 3.

[79] Ibid.

[80] Stephen Budiansky, "Good Ideas that Never Fly," *U.S. News & World Report,* July 10, 1989.

[81] Kotz, *Wild Blue Yonder,* p.164.

[82] "War's New Science," *Newsweek,* February 18, 1991.

[83] "U.S. Coverting Air-Launched Cruise Missiles," *Reuters,* April 21, 1999.

[84] GAO, *Cruise Missiles: Proven Capability Should Affect Aircraft and Force Structure Requirements,* April 1995, p.3.

[85] GAO, *Missile Development: Status and Issues at the Time of the TSSAM Termination Decision,* January 1995, p. 2-3.

[86] Ibid., p. 3-4,6,10-12.

[87] Cohen, "Missions, Structures and Weapons: What to do about National Defense?"

[88] Neville Brown, *The Future of Air Power,* (New York, Holmes & Meier, 1986), p. 269.

[89] GAO, *Cruise Missiles: Proven Capability Should Affect Aircraft and Force Structure Requirements,* April 1995, p. 7.

[90] Ibid., p. 9.

[91] GAO, *Operation Desert Storm: Limits on the Role and Performance of B-52 Bombers in Conventional Conflicts,* May 1993, p. 4.

[92] David Corn, "Flacks, Hacks and Iraq," *The Nation,* April 29, 1991.

[93] Tom Wicker, "Gulf War Gores Press Freedom," *Boise Statesman,* March 24, 1991.

[94] "Journalists Call Military Briefings Incomplete, Restrictions Too Tight," *USA Today,* January 22, 1991.

[95] David H. Hackworth, "The Lessons of the Gulf War," *Newsweek*, June 24, 1991.

[96] "Operation Highlights Weakness of U.S. Forces," *Washington Post*, February 10, 1992.

[97] Trevor N. Dupuy, "How the War was Won," *National Review*, April 1, 1991.

[98] Bruce W. Nelan, "Could Saddam Have Done Better?" *Time*, March 11, 1991.

[99] Ibid.

[100] "Gulf War," *USA Today*, April 24, 1992.

[101] Hackworth, "The Lessons of the Gulf War."

[102] "The Secret History of the War," *Newsweek*, March 18, 1991.

[103] Bruce B. Auster, "The Myth of the Lone Gunslinger," *U.S. News & World Report*, November 18, 1991.

[104] Ibid.

[105] Ibid.

[106] Ibid.

[107] "Stars Brought out for Stealth," *Washington Post*, May 1, 1991.

[108] Evan Thomas and John Barry, "War's New Science," *Newsweek*, February 19, 1991.

[109] "The Secret History of the War," *Newsweek*.

[110] U.S. News & World Report Staff, *Triumph Without Victory*, (New York, Random House, 1992) pp. 223-224.

[111] Ibid., pp. 219-221.

[112] "The Secret History of the War," *Newsweek*.

[113] Time-Life Editors, *Air Strike*, (New York, Time-Life Books, 1991), p. 93.

[114] Ibid., p. 152.

[115] GAO, *Operation Desert Storm: Evaluation of the Air Campaign*, June 1997, p. 101.

[116] "Air Force Head Flies to Defense of Increasingly Embattled B-2," *Washington Post*, September 14, 1991.

[117] Ibid.

[118] Hackworth, "The Lessons of the Gulf War."

[119] GAO, *Operation Desert Storm: Evaluation of the Air Campaign*, June 1997, p. 101.

[120] Hackworth, "The Lessons of the Gulf War."

[121] Jeffrey Record, *Hollow Victory*, (McLean, VA, Brassey's, 1993), p. 109.

[122] "A-10 Team Knocks Out 23 Tanks," *USA Today*, February 27, 1991.

[123] "The Day We Stopped the War," *Newsweek*, January 20, 1992.

[124] Col. David H. Hackworth, "The Lessons of the Gulf War," *Newsweek*, June 24, 1991.

[125] GAO, *Operation Desert Storm: Evaluation of the Air Campaign*, June 1997, p. 106.

[126] Ibid.

[127] Time-Life Editors, *Air Strike*, (New York, Time-Life Books, 1991), pp. 151-152.

[128] "U.S. Bombs Missed 70 percent of the Time," *Washington Post*, March 16, 1991.

[129] GAO, *Operation Desert Storm: Evaluation of the Air Campaign*, June 1997, p. 124.

[130] "U.S. Bombs Missed 70 percent of the Time," *Washington Post.*

[131] Richard Zoglin, "Assessing the War Damage," *Time*, March 18, 1991.

[132] "Patriot Power KOs the Scuds," *USA Today*, January 21, 1991.

[133] "Scud Record," *USA Today*, February 8, 1991.

[134] "Effectiveness of Patriot Missile Questioned," *Washington Post*, April 17, 1991.

[135] Ibid.

[136] Ibid.

[137] Ibid.

[138] David Brock, "Patriot Games," *Insight*, September 21, 1991.

[139] GAO, *Operation Desert Storm: Project Manager's Assessment of Patriot Missile's Overall Performance is not Supported*, April 7, 1992, p. 1.

[140] Ibid., pp. 3-4.

[141] GAO, *Operation Desert Storm, Data Does Not Exist to Conclusively Say How Well Patriot Performed*, September 1992, pp. 1,3.

[142] Ibid.

[143] David Holzman, "Scud-buster Perks Up 'Star Wars'," *Insight*, February 25, 1991.

[144] "Zeroing in on a Missile Shield," *Washington Post*, May 25, 1998.

[145] Ibid.

[146] David Brock, "Patriot Games."

[147] Bruce Van Voorst, "Setback for Star Wars," *Time*, August 13, 1990.

[148] Public Law 102-190, div. A, title II, part c, Dec. 5, 1991.

[149] Ibid.

[150] "Star Wars Under Fire," *Time*, June 15, 1992.

[151] The CBO reported in March 1997 that total funding for 1998 through 2002 was $15.5 billion, (CBO, *Reducing the Deficit: Spending and Revenue Options*, March 1997, p. 23), but Congress subsequently added additional funding.

[152] CBO, *Reducing the Deficit: Spending and Revenue Options, March 1997*, p. 23.

[153] Ibid.

[154] GAO, *Ballistic Missile Defense: Improvements Needed in THAAD Acquisition Planning*, September 1997, p. 1.

[155] "Pentagon Gives THAAD a Boost; $15.4 Billion Weapon to Forgo More Prototype Testing," *Washington Post*, August 20, 1999.

[156] GAO, *National Missile Defense: Even With Increased Funding, Technical and Schedule Risks Are High*, June 1998, p. 5.

[157] Ibid., p. 18.

[158] "Zeroing In on a Missile Shield," *Washington Post National Weekly Edition*, May 25, 1998.

[159] "Combat in the Sand," *Time*, February 11, 1991.

[160] U.S. News & World Report Staff, *Triumph Without Victory*, (New York, Random House, 1992) p. 222.

[161] Kenneth L. Adelman and Norman R. Augustine, *The Defense Revolution*, (San Francisco, ICS Press, 1990), p. 66.

[162] Christopher A. Preble, "Shrink, Shrink, Shrink the Navy," *USA Today Magazine*, May 1994.

[163] Ibid.

[164] GAO, *Navy's Aircraft Carrier Program: Investment Strategy Options*, January 1995, p.1.

[165] "New U.S. Strategy Called Mutual Assured Safety," *Washington Times*, September 23, 1994.

[166] Wiesner, Morrison, and Tsipis, "Ending Overkill."

[167] U.S. Navy Captain Bill DuBois, "Carrier Aviation Roadmap," wdubois@opnav-emh.navy.mil.

[168] Kenneth L. Adelman and Norman R. Augustine, *The Defense Revolution,* (San Francisco, ICS Press, 1990), pp. 55-56.

[169] "To Dissolve, To Disappear," *The Economist*, June 10, 1995.

[170] GAO, *Naval Aviation: F-14 Upgrades Are Not Adequately Justified*, October 1994, p. 6.

[171] Jeffrey Record, *Hollow Victory*, (McLean, VA, Brassey's, 1993), p. 131.

[172] GAO, *Naval Aviation: The Navy is Taking Actions to Improve the Combat Capabilities of Its Tactical Aircraft*, July 1993, p. 15.

[173] Phillip Gold, "Anchors Away," *Insight*, October 7, 1991.

[174] DuBois, "Carrier Aviation Roadmap."

[175] Christopher Bowie, Fred Frostic, Kevin Lewis, John Lund, David Ochmanek, and Phillip Propper, *The New Calculus: Analyzing Airpower's Changing Role in Joint Theatre Campaigns*, (Santa Monica, Rand Corporation, 1993), p. 82.

[176] Barry M. Blechman, William J. Durch, David R. Graham, John H. Henshaw, Pamela L. Reed, Victor A. Utgoff, and Steven A. Wolfe, *Key West Revisited: Roles and Missions of the U.S. Armed Forces in the Twenty-First Century*, (Washington, D.C., Henry L. Stimson Center, 1993), p. 22.

[177] GAO, *Navy Modernization: Alternatives for Achieving a More Affordable Force*, April 26, 1994, pp. 6-7.

[178] GAO, *Navy Shipbuilding Programs: Nuclear Attack Submarine Requirements*, March 16, 1995, p 2.

[179] Department of the Navy white paper, "Forward From the Sea," November 9, 1994.

[180] Gregory L. Vistica, *Fall From Glory*, (New York, Touchstone, 1997), p. 309

[181] "Working with Gulf Allies to Contain Iraq and Iran," Remarks of Defense Secretary William Perry to the Council on Foreign Relations, New York, May 18, 1995.

[182] "Defense Leaders Say Middle East Threats Rising," *American Forces Press Service*, June 20, 1997.

[183] Ibid.

[184] "Is the Right Stuff in the Wrong Hands?," *U.S. News & World Report*, March 11, 1999.

[185] Ibid.

[186] William E. Burrows and Robert Windrem, *Critical Mass,* (New York, Simon & Schuster, 1994), pp. 507, 508.

[187] Ibid., p.508.

[188] Gold, "Anchors Away."

[189] Kenneth L. Adelman and Norman R. Augustine, *The Defense Revolution* (San Francisco, ICS Press, 1990) p. 55.

[190] GAO, *Undersea Surveillance: Navy Continues to Build Ships Designed for Soviet Threat,* December 1992, p. 6.

[191] "Navy Prepares to Deal With North Korea's Submarines," *Washington Times,* June 16, 1994.

[192] GAO, *Undersea Surveillance: Navy Continues to Build Ships Designed for Soviet Threat,* December 1992, pp. 5,8.

[193] GAO, *Navy Mine Warfare: Budget Realignment Can Help Improve Countermine Capabilities,* March 1996, p. 3; Navy Mine Warfare: Plans to Improve Countermeasures Capabilities Unclear, June 1998, pp. 1, 3.

[194] Adelman and Augustine, *The Defense Revolution,* pp. 72-73.

[195] David Isenberg, "The Pentagon's Fraudulent Bottom-Up Review," Policy Analysis No. 206, Cato Institute, April 21, 1994, p. 7.

[196] "NATO Survey: Armies and Arms," *The Economist,* April 24-30, 1999.

[197] GAO, *Navy Modernization: Alternatives for Achieving a More Affordable Force,* April 26, 1994, p. 7-8.

[198] Ibid., p. 8.

[199] Ibid.

[200] GAO, *Cruise Missiles: Proven Capability Should Affect Aircraft and Force Structure Requirements,* April 1995, p. 4, 16.

[201] Ibid., p. 35.

[202] GAO, *Naval Aviation: Consider All Alternatives Before Proceeding With the F/A-18E/F,* August 1993, p. 3.

[203] GAO, *Suppression of Enemy Air Defenses,* September 1993, p. 4-5.

[204] Adelman and Augustine, *The Defense Revolution,* p. 98.

[205] Mark Thompson, "Why the Pentagon Gets A Free Ride," *Time,* June 5, 1995.

[206] Eugene J. Carroll, "Pentagon Pursues Implausible Scenario," *Newsday,* May 22, 1997.

[207] Marcus Corbin, "President Clinton's First Military Budget: Billions for Cold War Weapons," *Defense Monitor* 22, No.4, 1993, p. 3.

[208] GAO, *Strategic Mobility: Serious Problems Remain in U.S. Deployment Capabilities,* April 1994, p. 1.

[209] Howard Banks, "Parkinson's Law Revisited," *Forbes,* August 15, 1994.

[210] GAO, *Bottom-Up Review: Analysis of Key DOD Assumptions,* January 1995.

[211] GAO, *Bottom-Up Review: Analysis of DOD War Game to Test Key Assumptions,* June 1996, p. 2-3.

[212] Office of the Assistant Secretary of Defense (Public Affairs), News Release Number 250-97.

[213] Ann Markusen, "An Economist Examines the QDR," www.comw.org/qdr/amarkus.htm, May 27, 1997.

[214] CBO, *A Look at Tomorrow's Tactical Air Forces*, January 1997, p. 6.

[215] Ibid.

[216] GAO, *Combat Air Power: Joint Mission Assessments Needed Before Making Program and Budget Decisions*, July 27, 1996, p. 12.

[217] GAO, *Navy Aviation: F/A-18E/F Development and Production Issues*, March 1998, p. 2.

[218] CBO, *A Look at Tomorrow's Tactical Air Forces*, January 1997, p. xii.

[219] GAO, *Combat Air Power: Joint Mission Assessments Needed before Making Program and Budget Decisions*, July 27, 1996, p. 12.

[220] GAO, *Combat Air Power: Joint Mission Assessments Needed Before Making Program and Budget Decisions*, June 27, 1996, p. 12; GAO, *Aircraft Acquisition: Affordability of DOD's Investment Strategy*, September 1997, p. 5.

[221] GAO, *Combat Air Power: Joint Mission Assessments Needed Before Making Program and Budget Decisions*, June 27, 1996, p. 12.

[222] Ibid., p. 11.

[223] CBO, *A Look at Tomorrow's Tactical Air Forces*, January 1997, p. xiii.

[224] "The Pentagon Dodges Another Budget Bullet, *U.S. News & World Report*, December 7, 1998.

[225] Ibid., p. xv.

[226] Ibid.

[227] GAO, *Combat Air Power: Joint Assessment of Air Superiority Can Be Improved*, February 1997, p. 9.

[228] GAO, *New Attack Submarine: Program Status*, December 1996, p. 3.

[229] Congress Defies Navy; Forces Upgrade of Unneeded Subs," *The Wastebasket*, March 1, 1999.

[230] "Can Peacekeepers Make War," *U.S. News & World Report*, January 19, 1998.

[231] GAO, *Bottom-Up Review: Analysis of Key DOD Assumptions*, January 1995.

[232] GAO, *Peacetime Operations: Heavy Use of Key Capabilities May Affect Response to Regional Conflicts*, March 1995, pp. 5-6.

[233] GAO, *Army Training: One-third of 1993 and 1994 Budgeted Funds Were Used for Other Purposes*, April 1995, p. 1.

[234] Bruce B. Auster, "Running on Empty at the Pentagon, *U.S. News & World Report*, October 10, 1994.

[235] Ibid.

[236] GAO, *Army National Guard: Combat Brigade's Ability to Be Ready for War in 90 Days Is Uncertain*, June 1995, p. 3.

[237] Michael O'Hanlon, "Putting America's Military in Jeopardy," *Washington Post National Weekly Edition*, August 17, 1998.

[238] "U.S. Troops Struggle Amid Serious Equipment Shortages," Gannett News Service, February 28, 1999.

[239] "Can Peacekeepers Make War," *U.S. News & World Report*, January 19, 1998.

[240] Mark Thompson, "Why the Pentagon Gets A Free Ride," *Time*, June 5, 1995.

[241] GAO, *DOD Budget: Evaluation of Defense Science Board Report on Funding Shortfalls*, April 1994, p. 3.

[242] GAO, *F-15 Replacement is Premature as Currently Planned*, March 1994, p. 2.

[243] William S. Cohen, "Defense: Getting Down to Basics," *Washington Post National Weekly Edition*, April 27, 1998.

[244] "The Chiefs New Tune on Troop Readiness," *U. S. News & World Report*, October 12, 1998.

[245] "Senate Passes Massive Budget Package," Associated Press, October 21, 1998.

[246] "Experience Shows Base Closing Costs Outweigh Savings," *Washington Times*, March 20, 1995.

[247] William V. Kennedy, "A Study in Redundancy," *Washington Post National Weekly Edition*, March 17, 1997.

[248] GAO, *Military Bases: Analysis of DOD's 1995 Process and Recommendations for Closure and Realignment*, April 1995, p. 3.

[249] Stan Crock, "The Real Math of Military Shutdowns," *Business Week*, March 29, 1999.

[250] Banks, "Parkinson's Law Revisited."

[251] "Operation Fix-My-Bifocals," *U.S. News & World Report*, March 17, 1997.

[252] Mark Thompson, "Why the Pentagon Gets A Free ride," *Time*, June 5, 1995.

[253] "Everyone Gets Into the Terrorism Game," *U.S. News & World Report*.

[254] "Leaderless Terror War," *U.S. News & World Report*, November 2, 1998.

[255] Ibid.

6

FARM SUBSIDIES

[1] GAO, *Federal Dairy Programs: Insights Into Their Past Provide Perspectives on their Future*, February 1990, p. 2.

[2] James Bovard, "Kill Farm Subsidies Now," *Washington Post*, October 13, 1995.

[3] Edwin Feulner, "Entitlement Pie: Slice for Everyone?" *Washington Times*, December 7, 1993.

[4] "The Subsidy That's Taken on a Life of Its Own," *Washington Post National Weekly Edition*, September 4-10, 1995.

[5] James Bovard, *The Farm Fiasco*, (San Francisco, ICS Press, 1991), p. 30.

[6] GAO, *U.S. Agriculture: Status of the Farm Sector*, March 1995, p. 9.

[7] "Farm Numbers," Associated Press, July 31, 1992.

[8] James Bovard, *The Farm Fiasco*, (San Francisco, ICS Press, 1991), p. 44.

[9] Stephen Budiansky et al., "Eating into the Deficit, " *U.S. News & World Report*, March 6, 1995.

[10] USDA Economic Research Service, "Agricultural Income and Finance," M2 PressWIRE, January 15, 1998.

[11] Ibid.

[12] "Farm Subsidy Ax May Fall," *Idaho Farmer*, January 1995.

[13] "Farm Subsidies: Who Really Benefits," *Farm Aid News*, May 23, 1995.

[14] "U.S. Food and Agricultural Policies Report," University of Missouri, www.ssu.missouri.edu/ssu/AgEc/Cite/policy/cite3.htm, January 1999.

[15] Joseph S. Davis, *On Agricultural Policy*, (Palo Alto, Stanford University, 1938), p. 435.

[16] Bovard, "Kill Farm Subsidies Now."

[17] USDA Economic Research Service, *U.S. Farm Programs and Agricultural Resources*, Agricultural Information Bulletin No. 614, 1990.

[18] USDA Economic Research Service, "Agricultural Income and Finance," M2 PressWIRE, January 15, 1998.

[19] Environmental Working Group, "City Slickers," (www.ewg.org/Slickers, 1995), Executive Summary p. 1.

[20] GAO, *Hired Farmworkers: Health and Well-Being at Risk*, February 1992, p. 3.

[21] U.S. Department of Commerce, Bureau of Economic Analysis, *National Income and Product Accounts, Year Ending 1991.*

[22] "Hired Workers Down 3 Percent, Wages Up 4 Percent From a Year Ago," National Agricultural Statistics Service, M2 PressWIRE, November 23, 1998.

[23] USDA, Farm Service Agency Mission Statement, (www.usda.gov/mission/miss-m2.html), 1995.

[24] Ibid.

[25] "Database," *U.S. News & World Report*, November 27, 1995.

[26] "USDA to Issue More Than $1.3 Billion in CRP Payments," USDA News Release No. 01413.98, October 13, 1998.

[27] "Track Record: U.S. Crop Production," Report 96120, USDA National Agriculture Statistics Service.

[28] CBO, *The Outlook for Farm Commodity Program Spending, Fiscal Years 1992-1997*, June 1992, p. 19.

[29] Production data: "Track Record: U.S. Crop Production," Report 96120, USDA National Agriculture Statistics Service. Usage data: CBO, *The Outlook for Farm Commodity Program Spending, Fiscal Years 1992-1997*, June 1992, pp. 23, 35.

[30] GAO, *U.S. Agricultural Exports, Strong Growth Likely but U.S. Export Assistance Programs' Contribution Uncertain*, September 1997, p. 1.

[31] Ibid.

[32] "Excess of Grain Harvest Expected to Make Farmers Scramble to Find Storage," Gannett News Service, August 22, 1998.

[33] "As Harvests Drop, Farm Income Rises," *U.S. News & World Report*, November 1, 1993.

[34] David Greising, "For Farmers Devastation—and Bumper Crops," *Business Week*, October 11, 1993.

[35] James Bovard, *Policy Analysis No. 241*, Cato Institute, September 26, 1995, p. 12.

[36] "Farmers Plan Less Grain, Slightly More Hay," *Idaho Farmer-Stockman*, May-June 1993.

[37] "The Cash Croppers: Corn," Environmental Working Group, (www.ewg.org/Croppers/Chapter_5.html), 1995.

[38] Bovard, *The Farm Fiasco* p. 3.

[39] "Commodities," USDA Farm Service Agency, 1996.

[40] Richard T. Clark, James B. Johnson, and Stephen H. Amosson, "A Brief History of the CRP," *Idaho Farmer*, August 1994.

[41] "Grain Boom May Lure Long-Idle Land into Crops," Reuters, November 21, 1995.

[42] GAO, *Conservation Reserve Program: Alternatives are Available for Managing Environmentally Sensitive Croplands*, February 1995, p. 3.

[43] "Tax Dollars at Work: Old MacDonald Had a Boondoggle," *Business Week*, March 18, 1996.

[44] GAO, *Conservation Reserve Program: Alternatives are Available for Managing Environmentally Sensitive Croplands*, February 1995, p. 2.

[45] GAO, *Sugar Program: Changing Domestic and International Conditions Require Program Changes*, April 1993, p. 4.

[46] Ibid.

[47] James Bovard, *Policy Analysis No. 241*, Cato Institute, September 26, 1995, p. 7.

[48] Ibid.

[49] Dan Carney, "Dwayne's World," *Mother Jones*, July-August 1995.

[50] Ethanol—"A Natural Alternative," South Dakota Corn Utilization Council (ta.net/~schnaidt/vanguard1.html#About-Ethanol).

[51] "Clinton Administration Opposes Limits on Ethanol," *Environmental News Network*, September 27, 1995.

[52] GAO, *Gasohol: Federal Agencies' Use of Gasohol Limited by High Prices and Other Factors*, December 1994, p. 5.

[53] Ibid.

[54] Greg Clock, "Gasohol: Is it a Plus or Minus in the U.S.?" *Oil & Gas Journal*, March 3, 1980.

[55] Claudia Winkler, "Green Giveaway Rooted in Cornpower," *Washington Times*, March 21, 1994.

[56] Carney, "Dwayne's World."

[57] Ibid.

[58] "Clinton Administration Opposes Limits on Ethanol," *Environmental News Network*.

[59] Peter Stone, "The Big Harvest," *National Journal*, July 30, 1994.

[60] Rick Henderson, "Dirty Driving: Donald Stedman and the EPA's Sins of Emission," *Policy Review*, April 1992.

[61] "Ethanol," Associated Press, April 29, 1992.

[62] Jonathan Adler, "Alternative Fuel Follies with Ethanol Vapors," *Washington Times*, May 3, 1995.

[63] "Ethanol Tax Break Fight Cost Millions, But Farmers' Clout Decisive," *AP Online*, November 16, 1998.

[64] USDA Office of Energy, Fuel Ethanol and Agriculture: An Economic Assessment, USDA Agricultural Economic Report No. 562, p. 38.

[65] James Bovard, "Dairy Program Just Milks the Taxpayers," *USA Today*, July 11, 1990.

[66] Title 1, P.L. 73-10.

[67] GAO, *Dairy Programs: Effects of the Dairy Termination Program and Support Price Reductions*, June 1993, p. 2.

[68] GAO, *Federal Dairy Programs: Information on Inventory Management Activities*, March 1990, p. 1.

[69] House Ways and Means Committee, *1994 Green Book*, p. 827.

[70] GAO, *Food Assistance: Information on WIC Sole-Source Rebates and Infant Formula Prices*, May 1998, p. 4.

[71] Ibid., p. 1.

[72] Peter H. Rossi, *Feeding the Poor: Assessing Federal Food Aid*, (Washington, D.C., AEI Press, 1998), pp. 61, 64.

[73] Ibid., pp. 47, 61.

[74] GAO, *Federal Dairy Programs: Insights into Their Past Provide Perspectives on Their Future*, February 1990, p. 25.

[75] *Washington Post*, June 18, 1985.

[76] GAO, *Dairy Programs: Effects of the Dairy Termination Program and Support Price Reductions*, June 1993, pp. 4, 30.

[77] Ibid., p.30.

[78] Bovard, *The Farm Fiasco*, p. 108.

[79] GAO, *Dairy Programs: Effects of the Dairy Termination Program and Support Price Reductions*, June 1993, p 2.

[80] GAO, *Federal Dairy Programs: Insights into Their Past Provide Perspectives on Their Future*, February 1990, p. 21.

[81] James Bovard, "Washington's Iron Curtain Against East European Imports," *USA Today Magazine*, March 1993.

[82] Ibid.

[83] Testimony of John E. Frydenlund, Citizens Against Government Waste, submitted to the House Agricultural Subcommittee on Livestock, Dairy, and Poultry, March 26, 1998.

[84] Ibid.

[85] GAO, *Dairy Industry: Potential for and Barriers to Market Development*, December 1993, p. 6.

[86] U.S. Department of State Dispatch, "Agriculture in U.S. Foreign Policy," August 1992.

[87] GAO, *Addressing the Deficit: Budgetary Implications of Selected GAO Work for Fiscal Year 1996*, March 1995, p. 143.

[88] "Weekly Farm: Dairy Processors, Farmers Square Off Over Butter," *AP Online*, July 5, 1998.

[89] Ibid.

[90] Ibid.

[91] "U.S. Farm Aid Hits $6 billion, but Joy is Limited," Reuters, October 14, 1998.

[92] "The Cash Croppers: Wheat," Environmental Working Group, (www.ewg.org/Croppers/Chapter_6.html) 1995.

[93] "Commodities," USDA Farm Service Agency, 1996.

[94] Ibid.

[95] GAO, *Wheat Commodity Program: Impact on Producers' Income*, September 1993, p. 2.

[96] GAO, *U.S. Agricultural Exports: Strong Growth Likely but U.S. Export Assistance Programs' Contribution Uncertain*, September 1997, p. 39

[97] "Policy Tools for U.S. Agriculture," Agricultural and Food Policy Center, Department of Agricultural Economics, Texas A&M University, January 1993.

[98] GAO, *The Impact of Target Prices Versus Export Subsidies*, June 1994, p.1.

[99] Ibid.

[100] "Farm Subsidies: Who Really Benefits," *Farm Aid News*, May 23, 1995.

[101] GAO, *USDA: Foreign Owned Exporter's Participation in the Export Enhancement Program*, May 1995, p. 7.

[102] GAO, *Cotton Program: Costly and Complex Government Program Needs to be Reassessed*, June 1995, p. 6.

[103] Production data: "Track Record: U.S. Crop Production," Report 96120, USDA National Agriculture Statistics Service; Usage data: "U.S. Cotton Crop to be Smaller," Associated Press, November 24, 1995.

[104] GAO, *Cotton Program: Costly and Complex Government Program Needs to be Reassessed*, June 1995, p. 22.

[105] Ibid., pp. 27, 37.

[106] Ibid., p. 47.

[107] Ibid., p. 27.

[108] GAO, *Commodity Programs: Impact of Support Provisions on Selected Commodity Prices*, February 1997, p. 10.

[109] Ibid., p. 11.

[110] "Commodities," USDA Farm Service Agency, 1996.

[111] GAO, *Commodity Programs: Impact of Support Provisions on Selected Commodity Prices*, February 1997, p. 4.

[112] GAO, *Rice Program: Government Support Needs to Be Reassessed*, May 1994, p. 2.

[113] Ibid., p. 4.

[114] "Commodities," USDA Farm Service Agency, 1996.

[115] GAO, *Rice Program: Government Support Needs to Be Reassessed*, May 1994, p. 4.

[116] "The Cash Croppers: Rice," Environmental Working Group, (www.ewg.org/Croppers/Chapter_4.html) 1995.

[117] GAO, *Rice Program: Government Support Needs to Be Reassessed*, May 1994, p. 4.

[118] GAO, *Commodity Programs: Impact of Support Provisions on Selected Commodity Prices*, February 1997, p. 10.

[119] Calculations by author; data: GAO, *Commodity Programs: Impact of Support Provisions on Selected Commodity Prices*, February 1997, p. 18.

[120] Ibid.

[121] GAO, *Sugar Program: Changing Domestic and International Conditions Require Program Changes*, April 1993, p. 3.

[122] Jack Egan, "A New Battle for the Sultans of Sugar," *U.S. News & World Report*, July 17, 1995.

[123] GAO, *Sugar Program: Changing Domestic and International Conditions Require Program Changes*, April 1993, p. 3.

[124] "ASA Chairman Hails USDA Endorsement of Sugar Policy," PR Newswire, May 25, 1995.

[125] Ibid.

[126] GAO, *Peanut Program: Changes Are Needed to Make the Program Responsive to Market Forces*, February 1993, p 3.

[127] GAO, *Peanut Program: Impact on Peanut Producers, Users, and the Government*, June 8, 1995, p. 3.

[128] Ibid., p. 2.

[129] GAO, *Commodity Programs: Impact of Support Provisions on Selected Commodity Prices*, February 1997, p. 15.

[130] GAO, *Peanut Program: Changes Are Needed to Make the Program Responsive to Market Forces*, February 1993, p 17.

[131] Ibid., p.4.

[132] GAO, *Commodity Programs: Impact of Support Provisions on Selected Commodity Prices*, February 1997, p. 15.

[133] GAO, U.S. *Department of Agriculture: Issues Related to Export Credit Guarantee Programs*, May 6, 1993, p. 1.

[134] Ibid., p. 2.

[135] Ibid., p. 1.

[136] GAO, *Export Promotion: Rationales For and Against Government Programs and Expenditures*, May 23, 1995, p. 10.

[137] GAO, *USDA: Improvements needed in Foreign Agricultural Service Management*, November 10, 1993, p. 1.

[138] "Russia Skips Loan Payment," Reuters, September 2, 1998.

[139] "U.S. Pays $360 million to Cover Iraq's Default," *Houston Chronicle*, March 29, 1992.

[140] Ibid.

[141] GAO: *Agricultural Loan Guarantees: National Advisory Council's Critical Views on Loans to Iraq Withheld*, October 1993, p. 2.

[142] Ibid., p. 4.

[143] GAO, *ADP Modernization: Half-Billion Dollar FmHA Effort Lacks Adequate Planning and Oversight*, October 1991, p. 2.

[144] GAO, *High Risk Series: Farm Loan Programs*, February 1995, p. 6.

[145] Ibid., pp. 6-7.

[146] GAO, *Farmers Home Administration: Farm Loans to Delinquent Borrowers*, February 1994, p. 8.

[147] Ibid., pp. 10-11.

[148] "Owed Billions of Dollars, Farmer's Loan Office is Noted for Forgiveness," *Washington Post*, January 28, 1994.

[149] GAO, *ADP Modernization: Half-Billion Dollar FmHA Effort Lacks Adequate Planning and Oversight*, October 1991, p. 2.

[150] GAO, *High Risk Series: Farm Loan Programs*, February 1995, p. 10.

[151] GAO, *Consolidated Farm Service Agency: Update on the Farm Loan Portfolio*, July 1995, p. 10.

[152] GAO, *Rural Credit: Availability of Credit for Agriculture, Rural Development, and Infrastructure*, November 1992, p. 3.

[153] "Farm Credit," Associated Press, February 13, 1994.

[154] "Farm Credit System Reports 1995 Third Quarter and Nine-Month Net Income," Business Wire, November 9, 1995.

[155] Ibid.

[156] GAO, *Consolidated Farm Service Agency: Update on the Farm Loan Portfolio*, July 1995, p. 3.

[157] GAO, *Crop Insurance: Federal Program Faces Insurability and Design Problems*, p. 10.

[158] Ibid.

[159] 7 USC Sec. 1508(e)(3).

[160] GAO, *Crop Insurance: Federal Program Faces Insurability and Design Problems*, p. 12.

[161] GAO, *Crop Insurance: Additional Actions Could Further Improve Program's Financial Condition*, September 1995, p. 18.

[162] "New Rules," *Idaho Farmer*, January 1995.

[163] Ibid.

[164] "U.S. Farm Aid Hits $6 Billion but Joy is Limited," Reuters, October 14, 1998.

[165] "Crop Insurance," All Things Considered, National Public Radio, December 14, 1997.

[166] GAO, *Crop Revenue Insurance: Problems With New Plans Need to Be Addressed, April 1998*, p. 15.

[167] GAO, *USDA: Improvements Needed in Market Promotion Program*, March 25, 1993, p. 1.

[168] Calculation by author; data: GAO, *USDA: Improvements Needed in Market Promotion Program*, March 25, 1993, p. 1, USDA, *Agriculture Fact Book 1996*, p. 98.

[169] GAO, *Agricultural Trade: Five Countries Foreign Market Development for High-Value Products*, December 1994, p. 5.

[170] Ibid., p. 17-18.

[171] GAO, *Agricultural Trade: Changes Made to Market Access Program but Questions Remain on Economic Impact*, April 1999, p. 11.

[172] Peter H. Rossi, *Feeding the Poor: Assessing Federal Food Aid*, (Washington, D.C., AEI Press, 1998), p. 26.

[173] Ibid.

[174] House Ways and Means Committee, *Green Book*, July 15, 1994, p. 757.

[175] The Heritage Foundation, *Issues '94*, 1994, p. 127.

[176] Ibid., pp. 126-127.

[177] Ibid., p. 124.

[178] Ibid., p. 126.

[179] Rossi, *Feeding the Poor: Assessing Federal Food Aid*, p. 28.

[180] Charles D. Hobbs, "Working on Welfare; How to Reform the System," *Reason*, April 1994.

[181] Rossi, *Feeding the Poor: Assessing Federal Food Aid*, p. 36.

[182] Ibid., p. 28.

[183] GAO, *Food Assistance: Reducing Fraud and Abuse in the Food Stamp Program with Electronic Benefit Transfer Technologies*, February 2, 1994, p. 4.

[184] Ibid., p. 3.

[185] Ibid.

[186] House Ways and Means Committee, *Green Book*, July 15, 1994, p. 774.

[187] GAO, *Food Assistance: Reducing Benefit Overpayments in the Food Stamp Program*, February 1, 1995, p. 3.

[188] "Up Front: Who Said the Poor Don't Have Lobbyists?" *Business Week*, June 12, 1995.

[189] Ibid.

[190] GAO, *Food Assistance: Reducing Fraud and Abuse in the Food Stamp Program with Electronic Benefit Transfer Technologies*, February 2, 1994, p. 2.

[191] "Now on the GOP's Plate: School Lunches," *U.S. News & World Report*, March 6, 1995.

[192] Ibid.

[193] GAO, *Food Assistance: USDA's Multiprogram Approach*, November 1993, p. 25.

[194] "A Lot of Bologna About School Lunches," *Washington Times*, March 18, 1995.

[195] Ibid.

[196] "The New Free Lunch," *Washington Post*, September 24, 1994.

[197] Ibid.

[198] 42 U.S.C. Sec. 1758(a)(2).

[199] 42 U.S.C. Sec. 1755(e)(1)(D).

[200] 42 U.S.C. Sec. 1762(b).

[201] 42 U.S.C. Sec. 1755(a)(3).

[202] GAO, *Food Assistance: Processing of USDA Commodities Donated to the National School Lunch Program*, December 1991, p. 12.

[203] "School Lunches High on Fat, Salt," Associated Press, October 26, 1993.

[204] CSPAN2, September 7, 1994.

[205] Ibid.

[206] "Anti-Fat Advocate Targets 2% Milk," *USA Today*, April 17, 1995.

[207] Mark Belinger, Julie Rabinovitz, and Tricia Obester, *Making Room on the Tray: Fruits and Vegetables in the School Lunch Program*, (Washington, D.C., Public Voice for Food and Health Policy, 1993), p. 17.

[208] Ibid., p. 18.

[209] "Clinton OKs Relief Options for Stricken Beef Industry," *Minneapolis Star Tribune*, May 1, 1996.

[210] Ibid.

[211] "Glickman Announces Steps to Help Pork Producers, " USDA press release, December 17, 1998.

[212] 42 U.S.C. Sec. 1758(a)(1).

[213] 42 U.S.C. Sec. 1769e(a), (c).

[214] GAO, *Food Nutrition: Better Guidance Needed to Improve Reliability of USDA's Food Composition Data*, October 1993, p. 1.

[215] Ibid.

[216] Ibid., p. 2.

[217] Ibid.

[218] Ibid., p. 3.

[219] 42 U.S.C. Sec. 1758(a)(4).

[220] USDA, "Dietary Guidelines For Americans," (http://www.nalusda.gov/fnic/dga/dga95.html), 1995.

[221] "Healthy Heart Tips For Children," Johns Hopkins Bayview Medical Center, (http://www.jhu.edu/cardiology/parnership/kids/jcr95.txt), 1995.

[222] Traci Watson with Corina Wu, "Are You Too Fat?" *U.S. News & World Report*, January 8, 1996.

[223] Kathy S. Feld, "Are Our Children Well-Nourished?," *American Health*, May 1989.

[224] Elizabeth M. Whelan and Fredrick J. Stare, "Nutrition," *JAMA*, May 16, 1990.

[225] Bernard Gutin, et. al., "Blood Pressure, Fitness and Fatness in 5- and 6- Year-Old Children, *JAMA*, September 5, 1990.

[226] Kerry J. Stewart, et. al., "Results From the FRESH Study," *Journal of Cardio pulmonary Rehabilitation*, 15:122-129, 1995.

[227] David Blumenthal, "Making Sense of the Cholesterol Controversy," *FDA Consumer*, June 1990.

[228] N.D. Wong, S.L. Bassin, and R. Deitrick, "Relationship of Blood Lipids to Anthropometric Measures and Family Medical History in an Ethnically Diverse School-Aged Population," *Ethnicity and Disease*, Fall 1991.

[229] Ibid.

[230] Ibid.

[231] David Blumenthal, "Making Sense of the Cholesterol Controversy," *FDA Consumer*, June 1990.

[232] Barbara Buell, "An Arsenal of New Weapons Against Stroke," *Business Week*, September 11, 1995.

[233] Ibid.

[234] Geoffrey Cowley with Karen Springen, "Critical Mass," *Newsweek*, September 25, 1995.

[235] GAO, *Cholesterol Measurement, Test Accuracy and Factors that Influence Cholesterol Levels,* December 1994, p. 2.

[236] Dr. Barbara Levine, "Fighting Cancer With Your Fork," *Newsweek*, Health & Fitness Winter Edition, 1995.

[237] "Feds Endorse Vegetarian Diet for the First Time," *ENN Daily News*, (http://www.enn.com/news/010396/01039606.htm), January 3, 1996.

[238] Rossi, *Feeding the Poor: Assessing Federal Food Aid*, p. 22.

[239] USDA, *Agriculture Fact Book 1996*, p. 100.

[240] GAO, *Food Assistance: Alternatives for Delivering Benefits*, May 23, 1995, p. 7.

[241] USDA, *Agriculture Fact Book 1996*, p. 100.

[242] GAO, *Food Assistance: USDA's Multiprogram Approach*, November 1993, p. 1.

[243] Ibid., p. 8.

[244] "To Russia With Love," *National Review*, September 20, 1993.

[245] Brian Duffy, "The Old Guard Feeds at the Aid Trough," *U.S. News & World Report*, August 23, 1993.

[246] Ibid.

[247] GAO, Public Law 480 Title 1: Economic and Market Development Objectives Not Met, August 3, 1994, p.1.

[248] "U.S. Offers Tons of Food to Russians," *Washington Post*, November 5, 1998.

[249] "Russia Exporting Grain Despite Getting U.S. Food Aid," *The Idaho Statesman*, November 15, 1998.

[250] "Russian Deal Limits Exports of Cheap Steel," *The New York Times*, February 23, 1999.

[251] Ibid.

[252] www.usda.gov, February 22, 1999.

[253] USDA, *Agriculture Fact Book 1996*, p. 70.

[254] Donald Lambro, "No Shortage of Pork in the Diet," *Washington Times*, August 23, 1993.

[255] www.usda.gov, February 22, 1999.

[256] Terry Day, Washington State University, "Should the Public Invest in Agricultural Science and Technology?" *Idaho-Farmer Stockman*, April 1993.

7
NATURAL RESOURCES AND INFRASTRUCTURE

[1] "Japan to Press Its Trade Demands With U.S.," *Associated Press Online*, April 13, 1998.

[2] "Trade Deficit Tops $113B," *Newsday*, February 20, 1998.

[3] D. Koplow, *Federal Energy Subsidies: Energy, Environmental and Fiscal Impacts*, The Alliance to Save Energy, April 1993.

[4] Thomas H. Lee, Ben C. Ball Jr., Richard D. Tabors, *Energy Aftermath*, (Boston, Harvard Business School Press, 1990), p. 57.

[5] Ibid.

[6] William J. Baumol and Alan S. Blinder, *Economics: Principles and Policy*, (Orlando, Harcourt Brace Jovanovich, 1988), p. 701.

[7] Ibid.

[8] Paul Stevens, "Understanding the Oil Industry: Economics as a Help or a Hindrance," *Energy Journal*, January 1, 1995.

[9] Lee, Ball, and Tabors, *Energy Aftermath*, p. 56.

[10] Jerry Taylor, "Energy Conservation and Efficiency: the Case Against Coercion," *CATO Institute*, March 1993.

[11] Ibid.

[12] "Faisal and Oil: Driving Toward a New World Order," *Time*, January 6, 1975.

[13] Kenneth Nowotny and James Peach, "Changes in Energy Consumption, 1970-1989, and Energy Policy in the United States," *Journal of Economic Issues*, March 1, 1992.

[14] U.S. Department of Energy, *Monthly Energy Review*, June 1993.

[15] "Faisal and Oil: Driving Toward a New World Order," *Time*.

[16] Ibid.

[17] Lee, Ball, and Tabors, *Energy Aftermath*, p. 38.

[18] "Faisal and Oil: Driving Toward a New World Order," *Time*.

[19] Terrence R. Fehner and Jack M. Hall, "The United States Department of Energy 1977-1994," US Department of Energy, Energy History Series.

[20] Ibid.

[21] "Carter at the Crossroads," *Time*, June 23, 1979.

[22] Paul W. MacAvoy, *Energy Policy: An Economic Analysis,* (New York, W.W. Norton & Co., 1983), p. 63.

[23] National Energy Plan, Office of the President, Energy, Policy and Planning, 1977.

[24] Lee, Ball, and Tabors, *Energy Aftermath*, p. 24.

[25] John Tatom, "Are There Useful Lessons From the 1990-1991 Oil Price Shock?" *Energy Journal*, January 1, 1993.

[26] Lee, Ball, and Tabors, *Energy Aftermath*, p. 24.

[27] Fehner and Hall, "The United States Department of Energy 1977-1994."

[28] Roland Hwang, "Money Down the Pipeline: Uncovering the Hidden Subsidies to the Oil Industry," Union of Concerned Scientists, September 12, 1995.

[29] Howard Glickman, et. al., "Gas Pump Politics," *Business Week,* May 13, 1996.

[30] "Petroleum Subsidies," Domestic Fuels Alliance, March 13, 1995.

[31] Deborah Gordon, *Steering a New Course: Transportation, Energy and the Environment*, (Washington D.C., Island Press, 1991), p. 15.

[32] Leonard Ellerbrock, "Cars and Nature: A Case Study in Environmental Economics for Educational Programs," *Environmental Education Research,* October 1, 1995.

[33] Pietro Nivola and Robert Crandall, "The Extra Mile," *Brookings Review*, January 1, 1995.

[34] "Carter at the Crossroads," *Time*.

[35] Fehner and Hall, "The United States Department of Energy 1977-1994."

[36] Ibid.

[37] Pietro Nivola, "Gridlocked or Gaining Ground? U.S. Regulatory Reform in the Energy Sector," *Brookings Review*, June 1, 1993.

[38] Stevens, "Understanding the Oil Industry: Economics as a Help or a Hindrance."

[39] "The New Economics of Oil, " *Business Week*, November 3, 1997.

[40] Ibid.

[41] MacAvoy, *Energy Policy: An Economic Analysis*, p. 40.

[42] Tatom, "Are There Useful Lessons From the 1990-1991 Oil Price Shock?"

[43] MacAvoy, *Energy Policy: An Economic Analysis*, p. 29.

[44] William Beaver, "The U.S. Failure to Develop Synthetic Fuels in the 1920s," *Historian*, January 1, 1991.

[45] "Synthetic Fuels," *Grolier Multimedia Encyclopedia*, Release 6, 1993.

[46] Beaver, "The U.S. Failure to Develop Synthetic Fuels in the 1920s."

[47] Lee, Ball, and Tabors, *Energy Aftermath*, p. 69.

[48] "A History of the Synfuels Plant," Basin Electric Corp., January 1996.

[49] Linda Cohen and Roger Noll, "The Technology Pork Barrel," The Brookings Institution, 1991.

[50] "Carter at the Crossroads," *Time*.

[51] *The World Almanac and Book of Facts*, 1993, p. 151.

[52] Calculations by Author, data: *The World Almanac and Book of Facts*, 1993, p 151; Lee, Ball, and Tabors, *Energy Aftermath*, p. 45.

[53] *The World Almanac and Book of Facts*, 1993, p 151.

[54] "Cheap Gasoline," *Washington Post National Weekly Edition*, November 20-26, 1995.

[55] "Southland Gas Prices Fall to Lowest Level in Years," *Los Angeles Times*, February 13, 1998.

[56] Daniel Yergen, "How to Design a New Energy Strategy," *Newsweek*, February 11, 1991.

[57] Pietro S. Nivola, Deja Vu All Over Again," *Brookings Review*, January 1, 1991.

[58] " U.S. Oil Imports Surge to Record, *USA Today*, August 19, 1994.

[59] "Experts See World Dependent on Oil 50 More Years," Environmental News Network, May 13, 1996.

[60] Nivola, "Gridlocked or Gaining Ground? U.S. Regulatory Reform in the Energy Sector."

[61] David Feldman, "How Far Have We Come?" *Environment*, May 1, 1995.

[62] Ibid.

[63] Lee, Ball, and Tabors, *Energy Aftermath*, p. 81.

[64] Ibid.

[65] "Closing Bell: Cooking With Natural Gas," *Business Week*, February 7, 1994.

[66] "Restructuring May Lead to Decrease in Gas Consumption," *Energy Online*, September 1995.

[67] Alexander Melamid, "International Trade in Natural Gas," *Geographical Review*, April 1, 1994.

[68] The Electronic Universe project, University of Oregon, (http://zebu.uoregon.edu/ph162).

[69] Kip Viscusi et. al., "Environmentally Responsible Energy Pricing," *Energy Journal,* January 1, 1994.

[70] CBO, *Federal Financial Support of Business,* July 1995, p. 24.

[71] "Air Pollution Control Efforts Still Leave 2/3 of Americans at Risk," *Journal of Environmental Health,* September 1, 1993.

[72] "Outlook: Our Breath-Taking Air," *U.S. News & World Report,* May 20, 1996.

[73] "Air Quality," *Earth Explorer,* February 1, 1995.

[74] Brian Doherty, "Selling Air Pollution," *Reason,* May 1996.

[75] "Environmentalists Chalk Up Pollution for Clean Air," *Los Angeles Times,* October 10, 1993.

[76] Ibid.

[77] "Pollution Credits Stir Controversy," Environmental News Network, May 3, 1996.

[78] GAO, *Air Pollution: Overview and Issues on Emissions Allowance Trading Programs,* July 9, 1997, p. 1.

[79] Doherty, "Selling Air Pollution.".

[80] Robert Samuelson, "The Rise of 'Ecorealism'," *Newsweek,* April 10, 1995.

[81] "EPA Sees Huge Health Benefits in Curbing Acid Rain," Reuters, December 15, 1995.

[82] *Policy Implications of Greenhouse Warming,* National Academy of Sciences, 1991, p. 73.

[83] Energy Information Administration, U.S. Department of Energy, "Annual Energy Outlook 1995."

[84] David Isenberg, Desert Storm II: Is a New Persian Gulf War on the Horizon? *USA Today Magazine,* September 1, 1994.

[85] "Uncle Sam Bulks Up in the Persian Gulf," *Washington Post National Weekly Edition,* November 27-December 3, 1995.

[86] Ibid.

[87] "Perry 'Grudgingly' Approves Gulf Plan, *Washington Times,* January 8, 1996.

[88] Michael J. Ellerbrock and Leonard A. Shabman, "Cars and Nature: A Case Study in Environmental Economics for Educational Programs, *Environmental Education Research,* January 1, 1995.

[89] David Isenberg, *Desert Storm II: Is a New Persian Gulf War on the Horizon? USA Today Magazine,* September 1, 1994.

[90] "Washington Report," *Farmer-Stockman,* November 1996.

[91] "The Newest Pollution Target: Motorboats," *U.S. News & World Report,* November 14, 1994.

[92] Ibid.

[93] M.A. Delucchi, *Summary of Nonmonetary Externalities of Motor Vehicle Use,* Union of Concerned Scientists, October 1995.

[94] Ibid.

[95] "Smog causes Increase in Hospital Visits, Study Says," Environmental News Network, June 21, 1996.

[96] CNN Headline News, May 23, 1996.

[97] Jack Doyle, "Oil Slick: Profits Abroad and Poison at Home; Big Petroleum Ships Out, Leaving Behind a Big Mess," *Washington Post*, July 31, 1994.

[98] Ibid.

[99] U.S. Energy Information Administration, *Monthly Energy Review*, February 1991.

[100] John A. Tatom, *Paved With Good Intentions: The Mythical National Infrastructure Crisis*, Policy Analysis No. 196, Cato Institute, August 12, 1993.

[101] Washington Department of Transportation Newsletter, Volume 95, Number 44, November 3, 1995.

[102] Ibid.

[103] Eric Cooper, "Bridge Research: Leading the Way to the future," *Public Roads*, Federal Highway Administration, June 1, 1995.

[104] Ibid.

[105] "Highway Trust Fund Primer," U.S. Department of Transportation Federal Highway Administration, July 24, 1997.

[106] Gabriel Roth, "How to Improve America's Highways," *Consumers' Research*, February 1, 1991.

[107] Ibid.

[108] GAO, *Department of Transportation: Issues Related to Transportation Funding*, January 11, 1995, p 1.

[109] Bruce Van Voorst, "Why America Has So Many Potholes," *Time*, May 4, 1992.

[110] GAO, *Surface Transportation: Funding Limitations and Barriers to Cross-Modal Decision Making*, March 31, 1993, p. 5.

[111] "Piling Up Pork," *Washington Post National Weekly Edition*, April 6, 1998.

[112] Ibid., p. 6.

[113] GAO, *Surface Transportation: Tight Budget Environment Requires Sound Investment Strategy*, March 8, 1994, p. 7.

[114] GAO, *Surface Infrastructure: Costs, Financing and Schedules for Large-Dollar Transportation Projects*, February 1998, p. 5.

[115] GAO, *Highway Demonstration Projects: Improved Selection and Funding Controls Are Needed*, May 1991, p. 1.

[116] Van Voorst, "Why America Has So Many Potholes."

[117] GAO, *Surface Transportation: Funding Limitations and Barriers to Cross-Modal Decision Making*, March 31, 1993, p. 4.

[118] GAO, *Surface Transportation: Tight Budget Environment Requires Sound Investment Strategy*, March 8, 1994, p. 2.

[119] Washington Department of Transportation Newsletter, Volume 95, Number 44, November 3, 1995.

[120] GAO, *Transportation Infrastructure: Preserving the Nation's Investment in the Interstate Highway System*, August 1991, p. 16.

[121] GAO, *Transportation Financing: Challenges in Meeting Long-Term Funding Needs for FAA, Amtrak, and the Nation's Highways*, May 7, 1997, p. 10.

[122] CBO, *Paying For Highways, Airways and Waterways: How Can User's Be Charged?* May 1992, p. 11.

[123] GAO, *Transportation Infrastructure: Preserving the Nation's Investment in the Interstate Highway System*, August 1991, pp. 15, 19.

[124] Ibid., p. 3.

[125] Ibid., p. 23.

[126] "Bridging Politics and Practicality Over the Highway Bill," *Washington Post National Weekly Edition*, March 2, 1998.

[127] Sheldon Strickland, "Congestion Control and Demand Management," *Public Roads*, January 1, 1995.

[128] "Outlook 1997," *Business Week*, January 6, 1997.

[129] Gabriel Roth, "How to Improve America's Highways," *Consumer's Research Magazine*, February 1, 1991.

[130] GAO, *Transportation Infrastructure: Panelists' Remarks at New Directions in Surface Transportation Seminar*, December 1989, p. 23.

[131] GAO, *Reshaping the Federal Role Poses Significant Challenges for Policy Makers*, December 1989, p. 4.

[132] GAO, *National Highway System: Refinements would Strengthen the System*, March 1, 1994, p. 4.

[133] Tatom, *Paved With Good Intentions: The Mythical National Infrastructure Crisis*.

[134] Ibid., p. 6.

[135] Ibid.

[136] Ibid., p. 2.

[137] GAO, *Amtrak: Deteriorated Financial and Operating Conditions*, January 26, 1995, p. 1.

[138] "Paving Pasadena," Friends of the Earth, (www.essential.org/orgs/FOE/greenpart21.html).

[139] "Waste Virginia Highway," Friends of the Earth, (www.essential.org/orgs/FOE/greenpart20.html).

[140] "Road to Nowhere," Friends of the Earth, (www.essential.org/orgs/FOE/greenpart8.html).

[141] James J. Flink, *The Automobile Age*, (Cambridge, MIT Press, 1988).

[142] Deborah Gordon, The Union of Concerned Scientists, *Steering a New Course: Transportation, Energy and the Environment*, (Washington D.C., Island Press, 1991), p. 4.

[143] "A Dream that Clinton and Gingrich Agree On," *U.S. News & World Report*, April 8, 1996.

[144] Ibid.

[145] GAO, *Mass Transit Systems: Significant Federal Investment is not Adequately Protected*, June 12, 1991, p. 5.

[146] Lee, Ball, and Tabors, *Energy Aftermath*, p. 65.

[147] Ibid.

[148] GAO, *Los Angeles Red Line: Financing Decisions Could Affect This and Other Los Angeles County Rail Capital Projects*, May 1996, p. 1.

[149] "Imagine London Without the Tube—Imagine L.A. With It," *Washington Post National Weekly Edition*, March 3, 1997.

[150] "L.A. Subway Tests Mass Transit Limits," *Washington Post*, June 10, 1998.

[151] Ibid.

[152] Revenue data: American Public Transit Association, http://www.apta.com, January 31, 1996.

[153] GAO, *Mass Transit: Issues Related to Fiscal Year 1995 Appropriations*, April 13, 1994, p. 1.

[154] "L.A. Subway Tests Mass Transit Limits," *Washington Post*.

[155] GAO, *Mass Transit: Issues Related to Fiscal Year 1995 Appropriations*, April 13, 1994, p. 8.

[156] Ibid.

[157] *The Public Purpose Urban Transport Fact Book*, Wendell Cox Consultancy.

[158] GAO, *Major Management Challenges and Program Risks: Department of Transportation*, January 1999, p. 11.

[159] GAO, *Intercity Passenger Rail: Financial Performance of Amtrak's Routes*, May 1998, p. 7.

[160] Ibid.

[161] James K. Glassman, "A Failing Train of Thought," *U.S. News & World Report*, March 31, 1997.

[162] "Intercity Transport Fact Book: Amtrak 6 Year Severance Repealed," *The Public Purpose*, Wendell Cox Consultancy, December 3, 1997.

[163] GAO, *Traffic Congestion: Trends, Measures and Effects*, November 1989, p. 15.

[164] "Broken Cities," *Policy Review*, March-April 1998.

[165] Ibid.

[166] "Throwing Money at the Problem," *Washington Post National Weekly Edition*, April 20, 1998.

[167] Ibid.

[168] GAO, *Traffic Congestion: Trends, Measures and Effects*, November 1989, p. 16.

[169] Malcolm Gladwell, "The New York Story," *Washington Post National Weekly Edition*, March 18-24, 1996.

[170] Richard Rudolph and Scott Ridley, *Power Struggle*, (New York, Harper and Row, 1986), p. 46.

[171] Ibid., p. 67.

[172] Joan Biskupic, "Taking the States' Side," *Washington Post National Weekly Edition*, April 8-14, 1996.

[173] Ibid.

[174] Rudolph and Ridley, *Power Struggle*, p. 73.

[175] "Tennessee Valley Authority," *Hoover's Handbook Database*, (Austin, TX, The Reference Press, 1995)

[176] GAO, *Tennessee Valley Authority: Financial Problems Raise Questions About Long-term Viability*, August 1995, pp. 3, 14.

[177] Stephen Moore, *Government: America's No. 1 Growth Industry*, (Lewisville, TX, Institute for Policy Innovation, 1995), p. 9.

[178] GAO, *Tennessee Valley Authority: Financial Problems Raise Questions About Long-term Viability*, August 1995, p. 17.

[179] Ibid.

[180] Ibid., p. 65.

[181] Ibid., p. 69.

[182] Ibid., p. 67.

[183] Rudolph and Ridley, *Power Struggle* p. 80.

[184] GAO, *Rural Utilities Service: Opportunities to Operate Electricity and Telecommunications Loan Programs More Effectively*, January 1998, p. 2.

[185] Ibid., p. 3.

[186] GAO, *Rural Utilities Service: Risk Assessment for the Electric Loan Portfolio*, March 30, 1998, pp. 3, 4.

[187] Joseph Graves, "The $8.4 Billion Drain," *Electric Perspectives*, May 1, 1995.

[188] Marc Reisner, *Cadillac Desert*, (New York, Penguin Books, 1986), p. 121.

[189] Ibid.

[190] GAO, *Central Arizona Project: Costs and Benefits of Acquiring the Harquahala Water Entitlement*, May 1995, p. 7.

[191] GAO, *Water Transfers: More Efficient Water Use Possible, If Problems Are Addressed*, May 1994, p. 23.

[192] Reisner, *Cadillac Desert*, p. 172.

[193] Ibid., p. 149.

[194] Ibid., p. 147.

[195] "Water World," *Reason*, June 1997.

[196] Ibid., p. 193

[197] David Campbell, "The Pick-Sloan Program: A Case of Bureaucratic Economic Power," *Journal of Economic Issues*, June 1984.

[198] GAO, *Federal Power: Recovery of Federal Investment In Hydropower Facilities in the Pick-Sloan Program*, May 2, 1996, p. 11.

[199] Ibid.

[200] Doug Hawes-Davis, "Managing the Missouri River Basin: The Failure of the Pick-Sloan Program," *Focus*, December 1, 1991.

[201] GAO: *Federal Power: Recovery of Federal Investment In Hydropower Facilities in the Pick-Sloan Program*, May 2, 1996, p. 5.

[202] Hawes-Davis, "Managing the Missouri River Basin: The Failure of the Pick-Sloan Program."

[203] Reisner, *Cadillac Desert*, p. 199.

[204] "Bargeload of Subsidy," Friends of the Earth, http://www.essential.org/orgs/FOE, January 15, 1996.

[205] "Midwesterners Fear a Repeat of Catastrophic Flooding," Morning Edition, National Public Radio, April 13, 1994.

[206] Larry Larson, "Tough Lessons From Recent Floods," *USA Today Magazine*, July 1, 1994.

[207] Sharon Begley, "Lessons From the Flood Plain," *National Wildlife*, April 1, 1994.

[208] "Hundreds Flee Rising Rivers in Missouri, Illinois," *Los Angeles Times*, May 19, 1995.

[209] "What's Left From the Great Flood Of '93," *New York Times*, August 10, 1993.

[210] James Tripp, "Flooding: Who's to Blame?" *USA Today Magazine*, July 1, 1994.

[211] Larson, "Tough Lessons From Recent Floods."

[212] "Midwesterners Bailing Out of Flood-Prone Plains," *Los Angeles Times*, July 9, 1995.

[213] Begley, "Lessons From the Flood Plain."

[214] GAO, *Animas-La Plata Project: Status and Legislative Framework*, November 1995, p. 8.

[215] Michael Satchell, "The Last Water Fight," *U.S. News & World Report*, October 23, 1995.

[216] GAO, *Animas-La Plata Project: Status and Legislative Framework*, November 1995, p. 11.

[217] "Natural Resources: GOP Victory Proves a Watershed for Controversial Reservoir Project," *Los Angeles Times*, December 27, 1994.

[218] Ibid.

[219] Satchell, "The Last Water Fight."

[220] GAO, *Federal Electric Power: Operating and Financial Status of DOE's Power Marketing Administrations*, October 1995, p. 2.

[221] Ibid., pp. 1-2, 7-8, 13.

[222] Ibid., p. 13.

[223] Ibid., p. 14.

[224] Ibid., p. 13.

[225] GAO, *Bonneville Power Administration: Borrowing Practices and Financial Condition*, April 1994, p. 3.

[226] GAO, *Federal Power: Issues Related to the Divestiture of Federal Hydropower Resources*, March 1997, p. 5.

[227] GAO, *Federal Electric Power: Operating and Financial Status of DOE's Power Marketing Administrations*, October 1995, p. 14.

[228] GAO, *Bonneville Power Administration: Borrowing Practices and Financial Condition*, April 1994, p. 3.

[229] Ibid., p. 2.

[230] GAO, *Federal Electric Power: Operating and Financial Status of DOE's Power Marketing Administrations*, October 1995, p. 5.

[231] GAO, *Federal Power: Options for Selected Power Marketing Administration's Role in a Changing Electricity Industry*, March 1998, p. 4.

[232] GAO, *Bonneville Power Administration: Borrowing Practices and Financial Condition*, April 1994, p. 3.

[233] "Bonneville Power Administration Forced to Continue Providing Cheap Power," *Energy Online*, November 1, 1995.

[234] Residential Electric Rates as compiled by Jacksonville Electric Authority for May 1995.

[235] Ibid.

[236] Reisner, *Cadillac Desert*, p. 173.
[237] GAO, *Bonneville Power Administration: Borrowing Practices and Financial Condition*, April 1994, p. 4.
[238] "Hydroelectric at Capacity; Northwest is Seeking Alternatives," *Los Angeles Times*, August 8, 1993.
[239] "DOE Pushes For Energy-Efficiency Standard," Environmental News Network, May 8, 1996.
[240] Graves, "The $8.4 billion Drain."
[241] "Government Urged to Privatize Federal Electric Utilities," *Business Wire*, March 14, 1996.
[242] "Power Politics," *Reason*, April 1997.
[243] Rudolph and Ridley, *Power Struggle*, p. 92.
[244] Ibid., p. 109.
[245] 42 USC Sec. 2210
[246] Ibid., p. 171, 222.
[247] Arthur Gottschalk, "LILCO Debacle Sheds Light on Global Power Woes," Electronic News Network, January 25, 1996.
[248] GAO, *Tennessee Valley Authority: Financial Problems Raise Questions About Long-Term Viability*, August 1995, p. 20.
[249] Ibid., p. 21.
[250] Ibid.
[251] GAO, *Federal Electric Power: Operating and Financial Status of DOE's Power Marketing Administrations*, October 1995, p. 30.
[252] *The World Almanac and Book of Facts*, (Mahwah, Funk & Wagnalls, 1993), p. 156.
[253] Robert Perry et al., *Development and Commercialization of the Light Water Reactor, 1946-1976*, (Santa Monica, California, Rand Corporation, 1977), p. 13.
[254] Rudolph and Ridley, *Power Struggle*, p. 106.
[255] "Fusion Confusion," Friends of the Earth, www.essential.org/orgs/FOE, January 15, 1996.
[256] *The Fusion Energy Program*, Office of Technology Assessment, February 1995.
[257] Ibid.
[258] GAO, *Energy R&D: Observations on DOE's Success Stories Report*, April 17, 1996, p. 2.
[259] "Prognosis 1999: Utilities," *Business Week*, January 11, 1999.

8
GOOD INTENTIONS

[1] *IPI Insights*, Institute for Policy Innovation, First Quarter 1998.
[2] Ibid.

[3] CBO, *The Economic and Budget Outlook: Fiscal Years 2000-2009*, January 1999, p. 70.

[4] GAO, *Housing and Urban Development: Major Management and Budget Issues*, January 19, 1995, p. 2.

[5] Nabeel Hamdi, *Housing Without Houses*, (New York, Van Nostrand Reinhold, 1991), pp. 12-13.

[6] Elizabeth Shogren, "Destroying Pockets of Despair," *Los Angeles Times*, June 5, 1995.

[7] Ibid.

[8] William Raspberry, "At HUD, Reinvention by Necessity," *Washington Post*, January 4, 1995.

[9] Marshall Kaplan, "Urban Policy," *Urban Affairs Review*, May 1, 1995.

[10] Ibid.

[11] "The HUD Chief Finds His Own Pulpit," *The Washington Post National Weekly Edition*, June 7, 1999.

[12] Peter Montgomery, "Inside Job," *Common Cause Magazine*, July-August, 1989.

[13] Kaplan, "Urban Policy."

[14] Montgomery, "Inside Job."

[15] Ibid.

[16] Jennifer E. Firstin, "An Oversight by HUD Overseers," *Insight*, January 28, 1991.

[17] Ibid.

[18] Ibid.

[19] Ibid.

[20] "Senate Report Cites Reagan in HUD Mess," *USA Today*, November 14, 1990.

[21] "Panel: HUD Ex-boss 'Was Less Than Honest'," *USA Today*, November 2, 1996.

[22] Quoted in "Oversight by HUD Overseers," *Insight*, January 28, 1991.

[23] GAO, *Housing and Urban Development: Reforms at HUD and Issues for Its Future*, February 22, 1995, p. 1.

[24] Ibid., p. 3.

[25] GAO, *Housing and Urban Development: Reform and Reinvention Issues*, March 14, 1995, p. 1.

[26] GAO, *Housing and Urban Development: Limited Progress Made on HUD Reforms*, March 27, 1996, p. 1.

[27] GAO, *High Risk: Department of Housing and Urban Development*, February 1997, GAO, *Major Management Challenges and Program Risks: Department of Housing and Urban Development*, January, 1999, p. 10.

[28] U.S. Department of Housing and Urban Development Audit of Fiscal Year 1997 Financial Statements, Office of Audit, Office of Inspector General, March 20, 1998.

[29] GAO, *Major Management Challenges and Program Risks: Department of Housing and Urban Development*, January, 1999, p. 25.

[30] GAO, *Section 8 Tenant-Based Housing Assistance: Opportunities to Improve HUD's Financial Management,* February 1998, p. 5.

[31] GAO, *Single Family Housing: Improvement Needed in HUD's Oversight of Property Management Contractors,* March 1998, p. 3.

[32] "Cisneros is Shrinking HUD to Save It," *Business Week,* August 7, 1995.

[33] Ibid.

[34] "Housing Assistance," National Association of Home Builders, http://www.nahb.com/low2.html.

[35] Peter D. Salins, "Housing," *The Fortune Encyclopedia of Economics,* (New York, Warner Books, 1993), p. 690.

[36] Ibid.

[37] "Housing Project a Costly Lesson for Taxpayers," *Los Angeles Times,* May 16, 1994.

[38] "Low-Income Housing: Is There a Better Way?" *Business Week,* June 22, 1992.

[39] GAO, *Public Housing: Status of HUD's Takeover of the Chicago Housing Authority,* September 5, 1995, p. 2.

[40] GAO, *Housing and Urban Development: Major Management and Budget Issues,* January 19,1995, p. 6.

[41] Howard Husock, "Humble Homes," *Reason,* April 1993.

[42] Ibid.

[43] Ibid.

[44] "The Lord of 84 Lumber Co. is Back Behind the Counter," *Business Week,* June 22, 1992.

[45] 1990 Census data, Database C90STF1C.

[46] GAO, *Housing and Urban Development: Major Management and Budget Issues,* January 19,1995, p. 7.

[47] Shogren, "Destroying Pockets of Despair."

[48] CBO, *The Challenge Facing Federal Rental Assistance Programs,* December 1994, p. xiii.

[49] Ibid., p. 3.

[50] Ronald D. Utt, *Time for a Bipartisan Reform of Public Housing,* The Heritage Foundation, May 6, 1996.

[51] Kaplan, "Urban Policy."

[52] GAO, *Housing and Urban Development: Major Management and Budget Issues,* January 19,1995, p. 4.

[53] "Outlook: Attracting Workers to Public Housing," *U.S. News & World Report,* October 19, 1998.

[54] GAO, *Public Housing: Converting to Housing Certificates Raises Major Questions About Cost,* June 1995, p. 3.

[55] Ibid., p. 4.

[56] Utt, *Time for a Bipartisan Reform of Public Housing.*

[57] Ibid.

[58] GAO, *Multifamily Housing: HUD's Mark-to-Market Proposal,* June 15, 1995, p. 3.

[59] Amy Barrett, "Uncle Sam May Raise the Rent," *Business Week*, September 11, 1995.

[60] GAO: *Multifamily Housing: Progress Made In Establishing HUD's Office of Multifamily Housing Assistance Restructuring*, October 1998, p. 3.

[61] GAO, *Multifamily Housing: HUD's Mark-to-Market Proposal*, June 15, 1995, p. 4.

[62] "Low Income Subsidies in a Bind," *Los Angeles Times*, May 16, 1996.

[63] GAO: *Multifamily Housing: Progress Made In Establishing HUD's Office of Multifamily Housing Assistance Restructuring*, October 1998, p. 4.

[64] "Low Income Subsidies in a Bind," *Los Angeles Times*.

[65] GAO, *Multifamily Housing: HUD's Mark-to-Market Proposal*, June 15, 1995, p. 8.

[66] Barrett, "Uncle Sam May Raise the Rent."

[67] P.L. 105-65.

[68] GAO, *Property Disposition: Information on HUD's Acquisition and Disposition of Single-Family Properties*, July 1995, p. 1.

[69] GAO, *Homeownership: Management Challenges Facing FHA's Single-Family Housing Operations*, April 1, 1998, p. 1.

[70] GAO, *Mortgage Financing: Financial Health of FHA's Home Mortgage Insurance Program Has Improved*, October 1994, pp. 15, 3.

[71] GAO, *High Risk Programs*, GAO/AIMD-94-72R, January 27, 1994, p. 6.

[72] GAO, *Multifamily Housing: HUD's Proposal to Restructure Its Portfolio*, June 13, 1995, p. 3.

[73] Ibid.

[74] GAO, *Housing and Urban Development: Major Management and Budget Issues*, January 19, 1995, p. 1.

[75] GAO, *HUD Management: Greater Oversight Needed of FHA's Nursing Home Insurance Program*, August 1995, pp. 9, 10, 11.

[76] GAO, *HUD Management: Information and Issues Concerning HUD's Management Reform Efforts*, May 7, 1998, p. 3.

[77] "GNMA I Mortgage-Backed Securities," HUD Home Page, http://hud.gov.gnma1.html.

[78] GAO, *Rural Housing Programs: Opportunities Exist for Cost Savings and Management Improvement*, November 1995, p. 4.

[79] Ibid., p. 10.

[80] Ibid.

[81] Ibid.

[82] House Ways and Means Committee, *1994 Green Book*, p. 814.

[83] CBO, *The Challenge Facing Federal Rental Assistance Programs*, December 1994, p. xv.

[84] Calculations by author; data: GAO, *Urban Poor: Tenant Income Misreporting Deprives Other Families of HUD-Subsidized Housing*, July 1992, p. 3.

[85] CBO, *The Challenge Facing Federal Rental Assistance Programs*, December 1994, p. xiii.

[86] GAO, *Homeownership: Potential Effects of Reducing FHA's Insurance Coverage for Home Mortgages*, May 1997, p. 4.

[87] Ibid., p. 5.

[88] GAO, *HUD Management: Information and Issues Concerning HUD's Management Reform Efforts*, May 7, 1998, p. 3.

[89] Marvin Olansky, "The Right Way to Replace Welfare," *Policy Review*, March-April 1996.

[90] "A Letter from Lyndon Johnson," *Public Welfare*, January 1, 1993.

[91] Lawrence M. Mead, *The New Politics of Poverty*, (New York, Basic Books, 1992), pp. 5, 6.

[92] Stuart M. Butler, *Privatizing Federal Spending*, (New York, Universe Books, 1985), p. 92.

[93] CBO, *The Economic and Budget Outlook: Fiscal Years 2000-2009*, January 1999, p. 70.

[94] *Poverty Rates Fall, but Remain High for a Period With Such Low Unemployment*, report by the Center on Budget and Policy Priorities, October 8, 1998.

[95] GAO, *Welfare Programs: Opportunities to Consolidate and Increase Program Efficiencies*, May 1995, p. 5.

[96] House Ways and Means Committee, *1994 Green Book*, p. 389.

[97] Ibid.

[98] Ibid., 324.

[99] Ibid.

[100] Eleanor Holmes Norton, "America's Welfare Wake-Up Call," *Washington Post*, April 3, 1994.

[101] Graham C. Kinloch, *Society As Power*, (Englewood Cliffs, NJ, Prentice Hall, 1989), p. 206.

[102] GAO, *Teen Mothers: Selected Socio-Demographic Characteristics and Risk Factors*, June 1998, p. 1.

[103] Ibid.

[104] Barbara Dafoe Whitehead, "Dan Quayle Was Right," *The Atlantic Monthly*, April 1993.

[105] Ibid.

[106] Ibid.

[107] James Q. Wilson, Independent Policy Forum Luncheon Speech, sponsored by the Independent Institute, Sheraton Palace Hotel, San Francisco, January 19, 1995.

[108] M. Anne Hill and June O'Neill, *Underclass Behaviors in the United States: Measurement and Analysis of Determinants*, (New York, City University of New York, August 1993).

[109] Wilson, Independent Policy Forum Luncheon Speech.

[110] Patrick Fagan, "Disintegration of the Family is the Real Root Cause of Violent Crime," *USA Today Magazine*, May 1, 1996.

[111] Whitehead, "Dan Quayle Was Right."

[112] Nicholas Eberstadt, "Prosperous Paupers and Affluent Savages," *Society*, January 1, 1996.

[113] House Ways and Means Committee, *1994 Green Book*, p. 324.

[114] Senator John Ashcroft, et. al., "Can Government Save the Family?," *Policy Review, September-October* 1996.

[115] Kay C. James, "Transforming America," *Vital Speeches*, Volume 62, April 15, 1996.

[116] Gary S. Becker, "What Makes the Welfare Bill a Winner," *Business Week*, September 23, 1996.

[117] Michael Tanner, Stephen Moore and David Hartman, *The Work vs. Welfare Trade-Off,* Policy Analysis No. 240, CATO Institute, September 19,1995, p. 1.

[118] Lawrence M. Mead, *The New Politics of Poverty*, (New York, Basic Books, 1992), p. 258.

[119] Ibid., p. 6.

[120] Tanner, Moore, and Hartman, *The Work vs. Welfare Trade-Off*, p. 3.

[121] Joe Klein, "There Are Jobs in Chicago," *Newsweek*, December 20, 1993.

[122] Lawrence M. Mead, *The New Politics of Poverty*, (New York, Basic Books, 1992), pp. 118-126.

[123] Ibid., p. 92.

[124] Gary S. Becker, "Illegal Immigration: How to Turn the Tide," *Business Week*, February 22, 1993.

[125] Rick Henderson, "Balance Sheet" *Reason*, July 1994.

[126] Edwin S. Rubenstein, *The Right Data*, (New York, National Review, 1994), p. 366.

[127] "Drawing the Poverty Line," *Washington Post,* May 10, 1993.

[128] David Whitman, "The Poor Aren't Poorer," *U.S. News & World Report*, July 25, 1994.

[129] "Drawing the Poverty Line," *Washington Post.*

[130] "Poor Numerology," *National Review*, November 1, 1993.

[131] Whitman, "The Poor Aren't Poorer."

[132] Peter J. Ferrara, *Issues '94*, (Washington, D.C., The Heritage Foundation, 1994), p. 126.

[133] Nicholas Eberstadt, "Prosperous Paupers and Affluent Savages," *Society*, January 1, 1996.

[134] Ferrara, *Issues '94*, p. 125.

[135] W. Michael Cox and Richard Alm, *Myths of Rich and Poor: Why We're Better off than We Think*, (New York, Basic Books, 1999), Table 1.2

[136] Rich Thomas, "A Rising Tide Lifts the Yachts," *Newsweek*, May 1, 1995.

[137] Ferrara, *Issues '94*, p. 126.

[138] Ibid.

[139] Constance F. Citro and Robert T. Michael, "Poor Excuse for a Yardstick; How to Fix Outdated Tool For Measuring Poverty," *Washington Post,* October 15, 1995.

[140] Eberstadt, "Prosperous Paupers and Affluent Savages."

[141] Ibid.

[142] Robert Woodson, "Poverty: Why Politics Can't Cure it," *Imprimis*, Hillsdale College, July 1988.

[143] Ibid.

[144] "Kassebaum Says States Should Regulate Welfare," *Washington Times*, March 8, 1994.

[145] Jacqueline J. Cissell, "This Conservative Tells Liberals 'Let My People Go'," *National Minority Politics*, February 28, 1995.

[146] GAO, *Community Development: Challenges Face Comprehensive Approaches to Address Needs of Distressed Neighborhoods*, August 3, 1995, p. 2.

[147] GAO, *Community Development: Comprehensive Approaches Address Multiple Needs but Are Challenging to Implement*, February, 1995, p. 5.

[148] Charles D. Hobbs, "Working on Welfare," *Reason*, April 1994.

[149] Mead, *The New Politics of Poverty*, p. 196.

[150] Ibid.

[151] Ibid., p. 200.

[152] "Unions Fear Job Losses in Welfare Reform: Public Employee Groups Intensify Efforts to Slow Plan to Require Community Service," *Washington Post*, January 1, 1994.

[153] Butler, *Privatizing Federal Spending: A Strategy to Eliminate the Deficit*, pp. 96-97.

[154] "Washington Washes Its Hands," *Newsweek*, August 12, 1996.

[155] "The Welfare Decision," *The Washington Post National Weekly Edition*, August 12-18, 1996.

[156] "Welfare Time Bomb," *Business Week*, August 19, 1996.

[157] "A Healthy Dose of Concern," *Washington Post National Weekly Edition*, September 2-8, 1996.

[158] "Stop Attacking Immigrants," *Business Week*, October 14, 1996.

[159] "Going Borderline Broke," *Government Waste Watch*, Citizens Against Government Waste, Summer 1996.

[160] "Capital Wrap-up: Welfare Loophole," *Business Week*, October 21, 1996.

[161] GAO, *Welfare Reform: State and Local Responses to Restricting Food Stamp Benefits*, December 1997, p. 4.

[162] Ibid.

[163] "The Crunch Comes for Welfare Reform," *The Economist*, March 20, 1999.

[164] *IPI Insights*, Institute for Policy Innovation, First Quarter 1998.

[165] "Washington Washes Its Hands," *Newsweek*.

[166] "Untouched by Reform," *Washington Post National Weekly Edition*, January 11, 1999.

[167] Mead, *The New Politics of Poverty*, p. 167.

[168] Mortimer B. Zuckerman, "Fixing the Welfare Mess," *U.S. News & World Report*, January 16, 1995.

[169] Judith M. Gueron, "A Way Out of the Welfare Bind," *Washington Post*, September 12, 1995.

[170] Jonathan Walter, "If We Use Block Grants, How Do We Track Them?, *Newsday*, March 27, 1996.

[171] GAO, *Welfare to Work: Participants' Characteristics and Services Provided in JOBS*, May 1995, p. 6.

[172] GAO, *Welfare to Work: Measuring Outcomes for JOBS Participants*, April 1995, p. 2.

[173] GAO, *Block Grants: Characteristics, Experience, and Lessons Learned*, February 1995, p. 2.

[174] Ibid., pp. 2-3.

[175] James L. Sundquist, "Jobs, Training and Welfare for the Underclass," *Agenda for the Nation*, (Washington, D.C., The Brookings Institution, 1968), p. 69.

[176] Milton Friedman, "Public Schools: Make Them Private," *Washington Post*, February 19, 1995.

[177] "Violence in Schools," *U.S. News & World Report*, November 8, 1993.

[178] "Trends: Voucher Venture," *Reason*, November 1992.

[179] GAO, *Department of Education: Challenges in Promoting Access and Excellence in Education*, March 20, 1997, p. 2.

[180] GAO, *School Finance: Trends in U.S. Education Spending*, September 1995, p. 2.

[181] "Reading, Writing and Enrichment," *The Economist*, January 16-22, 1999.

[182] Results published by the Education Excellence Partnership.

[183] John Leo, "Hey, We're No. 19," *U.S. News & World Report*, March 9, 1998.

[184] John E. Chubb and Terry M. Moe, *Politics, Markets and America's Schools*, (Washington, D.C., The Brookings Institution, 1990), p. 144.

[185] "Economic Trends: Is the Race Gap a Skills Gap?," *Business Week*, September 23, 1996.

[186] Howard Gardner, "Beyond the Walls of School," *Newsweek*, 1992.

[187] Nancy J. Perry, "What We Need to Fix U.S. Schools," *Fortune*, November 16, 1992.

[188] George Roche, *The Fall of the Ivory Tower*, (Washington, D.C., Regenery Publishing, 1994), p. 28.

[189] GAO, *Federal Education Funding: Multiple Programs and Lack of Data Raise Efficiency and Effectiveness Concerns*, November 6, 1997, p. 6.

[190] CBO, *The Federal Role in Improving Elementary and Secondary Education, May 1993*, p. 1

[191] GAO, *Federal Education Funding: Multiple Programs and Lack of Data Raise Efficiency and Effectiveness Concerns*, November 6, 1997, p. 1.

[192] Ibid., p. 9.

[193] Ibid., p. 2.

[194] GAO, *Head Start: Challenges in Monitoring Program Quality and Demonstrating Results*, June 1998, p. 1.

[195] Ibid.

[196] "No Longer A Sacred Cow," *Newsweek*, April 12, 1993.

[197] High/Scope Education Research Foundation study of the Perry Preschool program, 1980.

[198] *The Impact of Head Start on Children, Families and Communities: Head Start Synthesis Project*, U.S. Department of Health and Human Services, June 1985, p. 1.

[199] John Hood, *Caveat Emptor: The Head Start Scam*, Cato Institute Policy Analysis Number 187, December 18, 1992, p. 5.

[200] GAO, *Early Childhood Programs: Local Perspectives on Barriers to Providing Head Start Services*, December 1994, p. 4.

[201] GAO, *Head Start: Challenges in Monitoring Program Quality and Demonstrating Results*, June 1998, p. 3.

[202] GAO, *Federal Education Funding: Multiple Programs and Lack of Data Raise Efficiency and Effectiveness Concerns*, November 6, 1997, p. 13.

[203] CBO, *The Federal Role in Improving Elementary and Secondary Education*, May 1993, p. 2.

[204] U.S. Department of Education, *Reinventing Chapter 1*, February 1993, pp. 99-104.

[205] GAO, *Federal Education Funding: Multiple Programs and Lack of Data Raise Efficiency and Effectiveness Concerns*, November 6, 1997, p. 6.

[206] "Stupid Spending Tricks," *U.S. News & World Report*, July 18, 1994.

[207] Ibid.

[208] GAO, *Major Management Challenges and Program Risks: Department of Education*, January 1999, p. 9.

[209] CBO, *The Federal Role in Improving Elementary and Secondary Education*, May 1993, p. 1.

[210] John E. Berthound, *Who Got It Right?*, Study by the Alexis de Tocqueville Institution, Arlington, VA, January 18, 1996.

[211] "Bush and Clinton's Fat Cats," *Common Cause Magazine*, Fall 1992.

[212] "Teaching the Teachers a Lesson," *Washington Post National Weekly Edition*, June 10-16, 1996.

[213] "Washington Outlook: Empty War Chest," *Business Week*, March 14, 1994.

[214] "Parochial Concerns," *Newsweek*, September 2, 1996.

[215] Friedman, "Public Schools: Make Them Private."

[216] CBO, *The Federal Role in Improving Elementary and Secondary Education*, May 1993, p. 6.

[217] Chester E. Finn, "How Special is Special Education?," Education Excellence Network, http://www.edexcellence.net.

[218] Regina Lee Wood, "Our Golden Road to Illiteracy," *National Review*, October 18, 1993.

[219] Finn, "How Special is Special Education?"

[220] Wood, "Our Golden Road to Illiteracy."

[221] Finn, "How Special is Special Education?"

[222] "Will Schools Ever Get Better?," *Business Week*, April 17, 1995.

[223] Ibid.

[224] John E. Chubb, "Public Schools," *The Fortune Encyclopedia of Economics*, (New York, Warner Books, 1993), p. 705.

[225] U.S. Department of Education National Center for Education Statistics, "NCES Fast Facts," http://nces.ed.gov/fastfacts/482.asp?type=2.

[226] William J. Bennett, *The Index of Cultural Leading Indicators*, (New York, Simon & Schuster) p. 89.

[227] "Reading, Writing, and Enrichment," *The Economist*, January 16 - 22, 1999.

[228] Douglas D. Dewey, "An Echo, Not a Choice," *Policy Review*, Nov-Dec 1996.

[229] Leonard P. Liggio and Roger E. Meiners, "The Growth of Government Control of American Higher Education," *Federal Support of Higher Education*, (New York, Paragon House, 1987), p. 224.

[230] Dan Usher, "The Private Cost of Public Funds: Variations on Themes by Browning, Atkinson and Stern," *Economic Research*, Queen's University, 1982.

[231] David D. Henry, "A Program of Action for Higher Education," Higher Education and the Federal Government: Papers Presented at the 45th Annual Meeting of the American Council on Education, October 1962, p. 99.

[232] Public Law, 85-864, sec. 401.

[233] "Education Bill Advanced in Committees," *Congressional Quarterly Almanac*, 1991, p. 365

[234] GAO, *Student Financial Aid: Schools' Experiences Using the National Student Loan Data System*, September 1998, p. 5.

[235] GAO, *Higher Education: Selected Information on Student Financial Aid Received by Legal Immigrants*, November 1995, p. 1.

[236] GAO, *Guaranteed Student Loans: Actions to Ensure Continued Student Access to Subsidized Loans*, February 1995, p. 2.

[237] William F. Goodling and Howard McKeon, "Making College Loans Fair," *Washington Post*, April 21, 1995.

[238] GAO: *Stafford Student Loans: Lower Subsidy Payments Could Achieve Savings Without Affecting Access*, January 1992, p. 2.

[239] James K. Glassman, "Why Student Loans are Unfair," *Washington Post*, May 30, 1995.

[240] Ibid.

[241] GAO, *Financial Audit: Federal Family Education Loan Program's Financial Statements for Fiscal Years 1993 and 1992*, June 1994, p. 55.

[242] GAO, *Higher Education: Ensuring Quality Education from Proprietary Institutions*, June 6, 1996, p. 1.

[243] GAO, *Major Management Challenges and Program Risks: Department of Education*, January 1999, p. 14.

[244] GAO, *Debt Collection: Improved Reporting Needed on Billions of Dollars in Delinquent Debt and Agency Collection Performance*, June 1997, p. 1.

[245] GAO, *Financial Audit: Federal Family Education Loan Program's Financial Statements for Fiscal Years 1993 and 1992*, June 1994, p. 7.

[246] GAO, *Major Management Challenges and Program Risks: Department of Education*, January 1999, p. 6.

[247] GAO, *Higher Education: Ensuring Quality Education from Proprietary Institutions*, June 6, 1996, p. 1.

[248] Berthound, *Who Got It Right?*

[249] GAO, *Proprietary Schools: Poorer Student Outcomes at Schools that Rely More on Federal Student Aid,* June 1997, p. 4.

[250] GAO, *Higher Education: Ensuring Quality Education from Proprietary Institutions,* June 6, 1996, p. 3.

[251] "The Core of the Matter," *U.S. News & World Report,* March 25, 1996.

[252] John Leo, "Miss Piggy was a Smarter Choice," *U.S. News & World Report,* June 3, 1996.

[253] Kate Obensshain Griffin, "Job Prospects for College Grads: What's the Problem?" Young American's Foundation, September 7, 1995.

[254] "From the Lab to the Library," *Newsweek,* December 7, 1992.

[255] "Give Me an A or Give Me Death," *Newsweek,* June 13, 1994.

[256] "Stanford Faces Tightening of Grading Policy," *Los Angeles Times,* May 24, 1994.

[257] John Leo, "A for effort. Or for showing up," *U.S. News & World Report,* October 18, 1993.

[258] "Rethinking Failure," *U.S. News & World Report,* June 13, 1994.

[259] "Battle for Your Brain," *Newsweek,* October 11, 1993.

[260] "Just How Welcome is the Job Market to College Grads?," *Business Week,* November 9, 1992.

[261] "The Wage Increase Squeeze," *Business Week,* July 17, 1995.

[262] "Just How Welcome is the Job Market to College Grads?," *Business Week.*

[263] "C- For Cybereducation," *P C magazine,* June 22, 1999.

[264] "No Bachelor's Degree Needed," *U.S. News & World Report,* November 1, 1993.

[265] "R&D Continues to Rebound in U.S.," Newsbytes News Network, January 4, 1999.

[266] GAO, *University Research: U.S. Reimbursement of Tuition Costs for University Employee Family Members,* February 1995, p. 8.

[267] Carl Weiser, "Colleges May Feel Squeeze in Federal Science Funding," Gannett News Service, May 17, 1996.

[268] Kent John Chabotar and James P. Honan, "Coping with Retrenchment: Strategies and Tactics," *Change,* November-December 1990, p. 28.

[269] "Colleges May Feel Squeeze in Federal Science Funding," Gannett News Service.

[270] "Could America Afford the Transistor Today?," *Business Week,* March 7, 1994.

[271] Daniel S. Greenberg, "So Many PhDs," *Washington Post National Weekly Edition,* July 10-16, 1995.

[272] George Roche, *The Fall of the Ivory Tower,* (Washington, D.C., Regnery Publishing, 1994), p. 213.

[273] Ibid.

[274] "The Scientific Pork Barrel," *U.S. News & World Report,* March 1, 1993.

[275] "Lobbying for University Research," *USA Today,* April 25, 1996.

[276] "R&D Continues to Rebound in U.S.," Newsbytes News Network, January 4, 1999.

[277] "Gridlock in the Labs," *Newsweek*, January 14, 1991.

[278] Ibid.

9
A FEW MORE SUBSIDIES

[1] GAO, *Land Ownership: Information on the Acreage, Management, and Use of Federal and Other Lands*, March 1996, p. 2.

[2] Ibid., p. 6.

[3] "How Much is a Forest Worth?," *U.S. News & World Report*, May 26, 1997.

[4] GAO, *The Results Act: Observations on the Forest Service's May 1997 Draft Plan*, July 31, 1997.

[5] Duane A. Smith, *Rocky Mountain West*, (Albuquerque, N.M., University of New Mexico Press, 1992), p. 204.

[6] Gordon Robinson, *The Forest and the Trees*, (Washington, D.C., Island Press, 1988), p. 13.

[7] Ibid., p. 36.

[8] Ibid., p. 37.

[9] Ibid., pp. 43-45.

[10] 522 F. 2d 945 (1975).

[11] Forest Service Manual 2421.3.

[12] Randal O'Toole, *Reforming the Forest Service*, (Washington, D.C., Island Press, 1988), p. 33.

[13] GAO, *Forest Service: Barriers to Generating Revenue or Reducing Costs*, February 1998, p. 3.

[14] Ibid., p. 2.

[15] GAO, *Forest Service: Unauthorized Use of the National Forest Fund*, August 1997, p. 4.

[16] U.S. Forest Service, *Timber Sale Program Information Reporting System 1989-1994*.

[17] Randal O'Toole, "Timber Sale Subsidies, But Who Gets Them?," *Different Drummer*, Spring 1995.

[18] GAO, *Forest Service: Distribution of Timber Sale Receipts Fiscal Years 1992-94*, September 1995, p. 1.

[19] "Terry L. Anderson, "Make Forest Service Pay Its Own Way," *Rocky Mountain News*, June 7, 1998.

[20] Richard E. Rice, "Taxpayer Losses from National Forest Timber Sales, FY 1990," A Wilderness Society Forest Policy Update, May 1991.

[21] Ibid.

[22] "Forest Service Dunked by its Own Witch Hunt," *High Country News*, August 8, 1994.

[23] *Business as Usual: A Case Study of Environmental and Fiscal Malpractice on the Eldorado National Forest*, Public Employees for Environmental Responsibility, Washington D.C., February 27, 1996, p. 5.

[24] Ibid.

[25] GAO, *U.S. Forest Service: Independence Still Lacking in Law Enforcement Organization*, October 5, 1993, p. 2.

[26] GAO, *Forest Service: Barriers to Generating Revenue or Reducing Costs*, February 1998, p. 6.

[27] United States Department of Agriculture Office of Inspector General, *Forest Service Timber Theft Prevention Controls*, Audit Report No. 08601-8-SF, March 1996.

[28] Ibid.

[29] "Cutting Corners: Log Scaling Scam Bilks Feds Out of $36 Million," *Forest Watch*, November 1991.

[30] Ibid.

[31] "De-emphasis on Resource Crime at U.S.F.S.," *PEEReview*, Summer 1997.

[32] 16 U.S.C. 1611.

[33] Staff of the Committee on Interior and Insular Affairs, U.S. House of Representatives, Management of Federal Timber Resources: the Loss of Accountability, June 15, 1992.

[34] The Wilderness Society, *Shareholder's Report on National Forests*, September 1994, p. 7.

[35] Jeffrey St. Clair, "Cutting by Numbers," *Forest Watch*, October 1991.

[36] "Subsidies Anonymous No. 7," *Electronic Drummer*, www.teleport.com/rot/SA07, February 6, 1996.

[37] Ibid.

[38] GAO, *Financial Audit: Forest Services' Financial Statements for Fiscal Year 1988*, March 1991, p. 14.

[39] Thomas Michael Power, *Lost Landscapes and Failed Economies*, (Washington, D.C., Island Press, 1996), pp. 142, 143.

[40] Ibid., p. 155.

[41] Ibid., p. 157.

[42] Kenneth D. Fredrick and Roger A. Sedjo, *America's Renewable Resources*, (Washington, D.C., Resources for the Future, 1991), p. 102.

[43] U.S. Forest Service publication, "Why Plant Trees?," R1-92-100.

[44] GAO, *Forest Service: Lack of Financial and Performance Accountability Has Resulted in Inefficiency and Waste*, March 26, 1998, p. 1-2.

[45] Lynn Jacobs, *Waste of the West: Public Lands Ranching*, (Tucson, Arizona, Lynn Jacobs, 1991), pp. 11, 12.

[46] Albert Potter, "The National Forests and Livestock Industry," *Potter Papers*, 1912, cited by William D. Rowley, U.S. Forest Service Grazing and Rangelands, (College Station, Texas, Texas A&M University Press, 1985), pp. 16, 20-21.

[47] Denzel and Nancy Ferguson, *Sacred Cows at the Public Trough*, (Bend, Oregon, Maverick Publications, 1983).

[48] Fredrick and Sedjo, *America's Renewable Resources*, p 131.

[49] From a 1991 interview with the author.

[50] "Thinning Sagebrush*," Idaho Farmer-Stockman*, April 1997.

[51] William D. Rowley, *U.S. Forest Service Grazing and Rangelands*, (College Station, Texas, Texas A&M University Press, 1985), p. 8.

[52] GAO, *Rangeland Management: Comparison of Range Condition Reports*, July 1991, p. 3.

[53] Karl Hess, Jr., "Public Rangelands: Twenty-Five Years of Stalemate*," Different Drummer*, Summer 1996.

[54] GAO, *Major Management Challenges and Program Risks: Department of the Interior*, January 1999, p. 17.

[55] "Reforming the Western Range," *Different Drummer*, Spring 1994, p. 28.

[56] GAO, *Packers and Stockyards Administration: Oversight of Livestock Market Competitiveness Needs to be Enhanced*, October 1991, p.4.

[57] "Reforming the Western Range," *Different Drummer*, p. 28.

[58] "The Economic Importance of Federal Grazing to the Economies of the West," a presentation by University of Montana Economics Professor Thomas Michael Power, February 19, 1994.

[59] Thomas Michael Power, *Lost Landscapes and Failed Economies*, (Washington, D.C., Island Press, 1996), p. 182.

[60] "Starting to Expand," *Idaho Farmer-Stockman*, April 1997.

[61] Ibid., p. 186.

[62] GAO, *Rangeland Management: Current Formula Keeps Grazing Fees Low*, June 1991, p. 17.

[63] Ibid., p. 23.

[64] "Beef Oversupply Lowers Grazing Fees," Associated Press, January 25, 1996.

[65] "Western Roundup: Nevada," *New Voices*, January 1996.

[66] BLM lands provide 9.6 million AUMs and Forest Service lands another 7.7 million; "Reforming the Western Range," *Different Drummer*, Spring 1994, p.27.

[67] 7 U.S.C. 426-426c.

[68] Donald G. Schueler, "Contract Killers," *Sierra*, November-December 1993.

[69] Ibid.

[70] GAO, *Animal Damage Control Program: Efforts to Protect Livestock from Predators*, October 1995, p. 2.

[71] Karl Hess Jr., and Jerry L. Holechek, Babbitt Inherited a Mess, His Plan Will Make It Worse," *High Country News*, November 1, 1993.

[72] Karl Hess Jr., "Storm Over the Rockies," *Reason*, June 1995.

[73] "U.S. OKs Big Beef Buy to Help U.S. Cattlemen," Reuters, May 1, 1996.

[74] "NRA Criticizes Grazing Plan," Associated Press, May 10, 1996.

[75] Jacobs, *Waste of the West: Public Lands Ranching*, p. 402.

[76] Jessica Mathews, "Mining Law—The Billions We Give Away," *Washington Post National Weekly Edition*, October 16-22, 1995.

[77] Senator Dale Bumpers, "The Great Mining Giveaway," *Washington Post*, September 17, 1995.

[78] "Is This What U.S. Grant Had in Mind?" *U.S. News & World Report*, September 18, 1995.

[79] John E. Tilton, *Mining and the Environment*, (Washington, D.C., Resources for the Future, 1994), p. 76-77.

[80] Ibid.

[81] "Taking Back the Land that Once Was So Pure," *U.S. News & World Report*, May 4, 1998.

[82] Ibid.

[83] "Mining's Grim Ecology," *Clementine* (Mineral Policy Center), Spring/Summer 1990.

[84] Ibid.

[85] Mineral Policy Center.

[86] GAO, *Superfund: Progress, Problems and Reauthorization Issues*, April 21, 1993, p. 4.

[87] "Mining's Grim Ecology," *Clementine*.

[88] GAO, *Federal land Management: Information on Efforts to Inventory Abandoned Hard Rock Mines*, February, 1996, p. 6.

[89] Ibid., p. 10.

[90] Tilton, *Mining and the Environment*, p. 58.

[91] Ibid., p. 71.

[92] GAO, *Superfund: Trends in Spending for Site Cleanups*, September 1997, p. 1.

[93] Tilton, *Mining and the Environment*, p. 72.

[94] GAO, *High Risk Series: Superfund Program Management*, February 1997, p. 14.

[95] Ibid., p. 9.

[96] GAO, *Superfund: Progress, Problems and Reauthorization Issues*, April 21, 1993, p. 2.

[97] CBO, *The Total Costs of Cleaning Up Nonfederal Superfund Sites*, January 1994, p. xi.

[98] Ibid., p. x-xi.

[99] "Taking Back the Land that Once Was So Pure," *U.S. News & World Report*, May 4, 1998.

[100] Tilton, *Mining and the Environment*, p. 79.

[101] GAO, *Small Business: Losses on Individual SBA Programs Are Not Fully Disclosed*, April 1992, p. 2.

[102] SBA, Office of the Inspector General, Semiannual Report of the Inspector General, March 31, 1996, p. i.

[103] CBO, *Reducing the Deficit: Spending and Revenue Options*, March 1997, p. 136.

[104] Small Business Administration Office of Advocacy, Banking Study 1996, www.sba.gov/smallbusinesslending1996.

[105] Scott A. Hodge, *Balancing America's Budget*, (1997, Washington D.C., Heritage Foundation), p. 201.

[106] Small Business Administration Office of Advocacy, Banking Study 1996.

[107] GAO, *Small Business: Status of SBA's 8(a) Minority Business Development Program*, March 6, 1995, p. 2.

[108] U.S. Department of Commerce; www.census.gov/agfs/smoke/view/s_pr.txt.

[109] GAO, *Small Business: Status of SBA's 8(a) Minority Business Development Program*, March 6, 1995, p. 4.

[110] GAO, *Small Business Administration: 8(a) is vulnerable to Program and Contractor Abuse*, September 1995, p. 4.

[111] GAO, *Small Business: Status of SBA's 8(a) Minority Business Development Program*, March 6, 1995, p. 4.

[112] CBO, *Reducing the Deficit: Spending and Revenue Options, March 1997*, p. 135.

[113] GAO, *Disaster Assistance: Information on Federal Costs and Approaches for Reducing Them*, March 26, 1998, p. 3.

[114] SBA, "Fact Sheet about U.S. Small Business Administration Disaster Loans," http://www.sba.gov/gopher/Disaster? General-Information-And-Publications/dad2.txt.

[115] CBO, *Reducing the Deficit: Spending and Revenue Options, March 1997*, p. 135.

[116] SBA, "Fact Sheet about U.S. Small Business Administration Disaster Loans."

[117] GAO, *Flood Insurance: Financial Resources May Not Be Sufficient to Meet Future Expected Losses*, March 1994, p. 3.

[118] Ibid., p. 5.

[119] "Higher Ground," A Study by the National Wildlife Federation, 1998.

[120] FEMA 40-001-02(10/95)

[121] "On the Disaster Dole," *Newsweek*, August 2, 1993.

[122] "Savings and Loan of the Seas," Friends of the Earth, www.essential.org/orgs/FOE/greenpart28.html.

[123] "Beachfront Bailout," *Common Cause*, Summer 1993.

[124] GAO, *Flood Insurance: Financial Resources May Not Be Sufficient to Meet Future Expected Losses*, March 1994, p. 7.

[125] GAO, *Budget Issues: Budgeting for Federal Insurance Programs*, September 1997, p. 36.

[126] GAO, *Flood Insurance: Financial Resources May Not Be Sufficient to Meet Future Expected Losses*, March 1994, p. 2.

[127] 42 U.S.C. 5121.

[128] "$400K Bridge: Par for the Course," *Newsweek*, February 26, 1996.

[129] GAO, *Disaster Assistance: Improvements Needed in Determining Eligibility for Public Assistance*, May 1996, p. 4.

[130] GAO, *Disaster Assistance: Guidance Needed for FEMA's "Fast Track" Housing Assistance Process*, October 1997, p. 1.

[131] "Senate Panel Boosts Quake Relief to $9.5 Billion," Gannett News Service, February 8, 1994.

[132] "GOP Bows, Congress OKs $8.6 Billion Disaster Aid," *Newsday*, June 13, 1997.

[133] GAO, *Disaster Assistance: Information on Expenditures and Proposals to Improve Effectiveness and Reduce Future Costs*, March 16, 1995, p. 5.

[134] "Budget Passage Brings Hurricane Loan Money Closer to St. Thomas," Gannett News Service, April 25, 1996.

[135] GAO, *Federal Disaster Insurance: Goals are Good, but Insurance Programs Would Expose the Federal Government to Large Potential Losses*, May 26, 1994, p. 6.

[136] Ibid., p. 7.

[137] Ibid.

[138] CBO, *Reducing the Deficit: Spending and Revenue Options*, March 1997, p. 135.

[139] Peter Overby, "Beachfront Bailout," *Common Cause*, Summer 1993.

[140] Ibid.

[141] GAO, *Disaster Assistance: Information on Expenditures and Proposals to improve Effectiveness and Reduce Future Costs*, March 16, 1995, p. 3, 8.

[142] Editorial: "Disaster Insurance: The Job is Too Big For the States," *The Los Angeles Times*, October 14, 1996.

[143] George Skelton, "Little Incentive to Stay Out of Harm's Way," *Los Angeles Times*, January 27, 1997.

[144] Ibid.

[145] Ibid.

[146] Bob Graham, "Natural Calamities Need a National Response," *Los Angeles Times*, October 16, 1995.

[147] "Hurricane Andrew," National Public Radio, August 24, 1997.

[148] "Hurricane Warning," *U.S. News & World Report*, June 7, 1999.

[149] GAO, *Budget Issues: Budgeting for Federal Insurance Programs*, September 1997, p. 4.

[150] Ibid., p. 36.

[151] Ibid.

[152] Ibid.

[153] CBO, *The Economic Effects of the Savings and Loan Crisis*, January 1992, p. 2.

[154] Ibid., p. 3.

[155] Ibid., p. 9.

[156] GAO, *Resolution Trust Corporation: Management Improvements Reduce risks but Transition Challenges Remain*, June 20, 1995, p. i.

[157] GAO, *Budget Issues: Budgeting for Federal Insurance Programs*, September 1997, p. 154.

[158] "Volker Says Warnings Would Have Caused Panic," *Idaho Statesman*, January 16, 1993.

[159] Statement of Marvin Phaup, Deputy Assistant Director, Special Studies Division of the Congressional Budget Office, before the Task Force on Budget Process, Committee on the Budget, U.S. House of Representatives, April 23, 1998.

[160] "Taxpayers Keeping for Savings and Loan Scandal," Gannett News Service, December 31, 1997.

[161] GAO, *Thrift Examination Quality: OTS Examinations Do Not Fully Assess Thrift safety and Soundness*, February 1993, p. 3; GAO, Bank Examination Quality, FDIC Examinations Do Not Fully Assess Bank Safety and Soundness, February 1993, p. 3.

[162] Joe Peek and Eric Rosengren, "How Well-Capitalized are Well-Capitalized Banks?" *New England Economic Review*, September 19, 1997.

[163] Ibid.

[164] GAO, *Budget Issues: Budgeting for Federal Insurance Programs*, September 199, p. 4.

[165] Cornelius Chapman, "Banking on Markets," *Reason*, May 1994.

[166] Phaup, Special Studies Division of the Congressional Budget Office.

[167] "Private Pension Shortfalls Soared in '95, Agency Says," *Los Angeles Times*, December 13, 1996.

[168] Phaup, Special Studies Division of the Congressional Budget Office.

[169] CBO, *Resolving the Thrift Crisis*, April 1993, p. 77.

[170] Ibid.

[171] GAO, *Government Sponsored Enterprises: Advantages and Disadvantages of Creating a Single Housing GSE Regulator*, July 1997, p. 2.

[172] Ibid.

[173] CBO, *Resolving the Thrift Crisis*, April 1993, p. 75.

[174] GAO, *FHLBANK SYSTEM: Reforms Needed to Promote Its Safety, Soundness and Effectiveness*, September 27, 1995, p. 7.

[175] Amy Barrett, "Riskier and Riskier at the Home Loan Banks," *Business Week*, January 30, 1995.

[176] Ibid.

[177] CBO, *Assessing the Public Costs and Benefits of Fannie Mae and Freddie Mac*, May 1996, p. 3.

[178] Ibid., p. 7.

[179] Ibid., p. xi-xii.

[180] Ibid., p. x.

[181] Ibid., p. 7.

[182] Fannie Mae 1998 portfolio was $1 trillion, Source: http://fanniemae.com/company/history.html; Freddie Mac 1998 portfolio was $775 billion, Source: Freddie Mac 1998 Annual Report.

[183] CBO, *Assessing the Public Costs and Benefits of Fannie Mae and Freddie Mac*, May 1996, p. xii.

[184] GAO, *International Affairs Budget: Framework for Assessing Relevance, Priority, and Efficiency*, October 30, 1997, p. 2.

[185] Ibid., p. 6.

[186] GAO, *Export-Import Bank: Reauthorization Issues*, April 29, 1997, pp. 10, 12.

[187] *The Cato Handbook for Congress*, (Washington, D.C., Cato Institute, 1995), p. 320.

[188] "Report Urges New Approach for Government Science Funding," Reuters, December 1, 1995.

[189] "A Brawl is Brewing in the Laboratory," *Business Week*, January 22, 1996.

[190] "Firefight Over the Weapons Labs," *Business Week*, June 7, 1993.

[191] GAO, *Federally Funded R&D Centers: Information on the Size and Scope of DOD-Sponsored Centers*, April 1996, p. 1.

[192] "Firefight Over the Weapons Labs," *Business Week*, June 7, 1993.

[193] Ibid.

[194] GAO, *Energy R&D: Observations on DOE's Success Stories Report*, April 17, 1996, p. 2.

[195] GAO, *Major Management Challenges and Program Risks: Department of Energy*, January 1999, p. 6.

[196] Ibid.

[197] Ibid., pp. 19-20.

[198] John Carey, "Throwing Money at Science Just Creates a Monster," *Business Week*, June 19, 1995.

[199] GAO, *Energy Research: Recovery of Federal Investment in Technology Development Projects*, August 1, 1996, p. 1.

[200] "Firefight Over the Weapons Labs,"*Business Week*.

[201] "What's Good for Intel...," *U.S. News & World Report*, October 6, 1997.

[202] Alan S. Blinder, "Is the National Debt Really, I Mean Really, Really a Burden?" James M. Rock, *Debt and the Twin Deficits Debate*, (Mountain View, CA, Mayfield Publishing, 1991), p. 209.

[203] "Total U.S. Savings as a Percent of GDP," Institute for Policy Innovation, www.ipi.org, September 15, 1997.

[204] "Two Big Speed Bumps Are Coming Up in 1999," *Business Week*, December 21, 1998.

[205] CBO, *Using Federal R&D to Promote Commercial Innovation*, April 1988, p. ix.

[206] "The Trade Gap Won't Be All Bad," *Business Week*, March 30, 1998.

[207] Terence Kealey, *The Economic Laws of Scientific Research*, (New York, Saint Martin's Press, 1996), p. 24.

[208] "What Price Science," *Business Week*, May 26, 1997.

[209] Paul Kennedy, *Rise and Fall of Great Powers*, (New York, Random House, 1988), p. 241.

[210] Richard Beason and David Weinstein, *Growth, Economics of Scale and Targeting in Japan (1955 - 1990)*, (Boston, Harvard Institute of Economic Research, 1994).

[211] CBO, *Using Federal R&D to Promote Commercial Innovation*, p. xiii.

[212] GAO, *Best Practices: Elements Critical to Successfully Reducing Unneeded RDT&E Infrastructure*, January 1998, p. 4.

[213] "Building Bridges," *Reason*, February 1998.

[214] "Firefight Over the Weapons Labs," *Business Week.*

[215] "Is the Manned Space program Doomed?," *U.S. News & World Report*, April 19, 1993.

[216] Senator Dale Bumpers, "Bumpers Amendment Would Ground Space Station," Capitol Hill Press Releases, July 22, 1997; GAO, *Space Station: Estimated Total U.S. Funding Requirements*, June 1995, p. 2.

[217] Senator Dale Bumpers in a Senate floor speech on October 14, 1993.

[218] GAO, *International Space Station: U.S. Life-Cycle Funding Requirements*, May 1998, p. 2.

[219] Bumpers, "Bumpers Amendment Would Ground Space Station."

[220] "2002, A Space Odyssey—Or Just Pork in the Sky," *Business Week*, August 15, 1994.

[221] Bumpers, "Bumpers Amendment Would Ground Space Station."

[222] Ibid.

[223] "Bailout of Russian Space Station Hit; NASA Needs Cash for Orbital Station," *Washington Times*, October 8, 1998.

[224] GAO, *Space Shuttle: Declining Budget and Tight Schedule Could Jeopardize Space Station Support*, July 1995, p. 1.

[225] Ibid.

[226] Ibid., p. 2.

[227] GAO, *Space Shuttle: NASA's Plans for Repairing or Replacing a Damaged or Destroyed Orbiter*, July 1994, p. 1.

[228] Ibid., p. 4.

[229] Charles Arthur, "Science: 2003: A Space Odyssey," *Independent* (UK), February 23, 1998.

[230] "Should the Labs Get Hit," *U.S. News & World Report*, November 6, 1995.

[231] "Reality Check: The Space Station," *Business Week*, July 3, 1995.

[232] CNN Headline News, July 24, 1994.

[233] "Could Robots Man Space Station?," *Idaho Statesman*, April 19, 1997.

[234] GAO, Space Transportation: The Content and Uses of Shuttle Cost Estimates, January 1993, p. 2.

[235] Ibid., pp. 8, 9.

[236] Ibid., p. 8.

[237] Ibid.

[238] Ibid., p. 7.

[239] Calculation by author based on NASA's operating costs, capital costs and improvement costs as reported by the GAO amortized over 185 flights: 97 flights through 1998, 28 scheduled ISS transport flights and six flights annually to the ISS for 10 years thereafter.

[240] NASA, "Summary of Payload-Chargeable Cargo and Satellite Weights," http://shuttle.nasa.gov/reference/green/sumcarg.pdf, March 13, 1998.

[241] "Superpowers in the Sky," *U.S. News & World Report*, February 6, 1995.

[242] CBO, *Reinventing NASA*, March 1994, p. 2.

[243] GAO, *Davis Bacon Act: Labor's Actions Have Potential to Improve Wage Determinations*, May 1999, p. 1.

[244] Jennifer R. Morse, *Report Regarding the Davis-Bacon Act*, (Fairfax, VA, George Mason University, November 30, 1995).

[245] Scott A. Hodge, *Balancing America's Budget*, (Washington, D.C., The Heritage Foundation, 1997), p. 409.

[246] Ibid.

[247] CBO, *Reducing the Deficit: Spending and Revenue Options, March 1997*, p. 210.

[248] GAO, *National Service Programs: AmeriCorps USA—Early Program Resource and Benefit Information*, August 1995, p. 11.

[249] Hodge, *Balancing America's Budget*, p. 304.

10
THE SUBSIDY PARTY

[1] Burke Marshall, *A Workable Government: The Constitution After 200 Years*, (New York, W.W. Norton & Co., 1987), p. 38.

[2] Ibid., p. 39.

[3] Donald Wittman, et. al., *The Federalist Papers and the New Institutionalism*, (New York, Agathon Press, 1989) p. 76.

[4] "The End of Corporate Welfare As We Know It?," *Business Week*, February 10, 1997.

[5] "Tuned Out and Turned Off," *Washington Post National Weekly Edition*, February 5-11, 1996.

[6] "Inside the Ivy League," *U.S. News & World Report,* April 12, 1993.

[7] Cass R. Sunstein, *The Partial Constitution*, (Cambridge, Mass., Harvard University Press, 1993), p. 35.

[8] "Common Causes," *Reason*, April 1996.

[9] "A Deepening Cesspool of Politics and Cash," *Business Week*, July 22, 1996.

[10] Larry J. Sabato and Glenn R. Simpson, *Dirty Little Secrets*, (New York, Times Books, 1996).

[11] Susanne Lohmann, "Can Washington Change?," *Reason*, August/September 1996.

[12] Paul Tsongas, "The Taboo Topics in the Campaign," *Washington Post National Weekly Edition*, October 14-20, 1996.

[13] "A Deepening Cesspool of Politics and Cash," *Business Week.*

[14] Marshall, *A Workable Government: The Constitution After 200 Years*, p. 53.

[15] John J. Pitney, Jr., "Don't Vote For Me," *Reason*, June 1996.

[16] Antonin Scalia, *A Matter of Interpretation*, (Princeton, N.J., Princeton University Press, 1997), p. 32.

[17] Ibid., p. 34.

[18] Don K. Price, *America's Unwritten Constitution*, (Baton Rouge, LA, Louisiana, State University Press, 1983), p. 5.

[19] CBO, *The Economic and Budget Outlook: Fiscal Years 2000 - 2009*, January 1999, p. 61.

[20] Ibid.

[21] Howard Gleckman, "Lessons From the Class of '74," *Business Week*, January 29, 1996.

[22] Gary S. Becker, "If You Want to Cut Corruption, Cut Government," *Business Week*, December 11, 1995.

[23] Robert J. Samuelson, "Bumper-Sticker Politics," *Washington Post National Weekly Edition,* September 30-October 6, 1996.

[24] Institute for Policy Innovation, *Economic Scorecard*, Second Quarter 1997, First Quarter 1999.

[25] Ibid.

[26] CBO, *The Economic and Budget Outlook: Fiscal Years 2000 - 2009*, January 1999, p. 38.

[27] "Clinton Says U.S. Budget Can Be Balanced Long Term," Reuters, February 2, 1998.

[28] CBO, *The Economic and Budget Outlook: Fiscal Years 2000 - 2009*, January 1999, p. 31.

[29] GAO, *Managing the Cost of Government*, October 1989, p. 9.

[30] Scott A. Hodge, *The Heritage Foundation Backgrounder*, May 12, 1997.

[31] Robert D. Reischauer, "Those Surpluses: Proceed With Caution," *Washington Post National Weekly Edition*, September 29, 1997.

[32] Ibid.

[33] "Talking Peace, Preparing for War," *The Economist*, March 13, 1999.

[34] Reischauer, "Those Surpluses: Proceed With Caution."

[35] "Budgetary Follies," *The Economist*, June 5, 1999.

[36] Robert J. Samuelson, "Good Theater, Bad Policy," *Washington Post National Weekly Edition*, August 11, 1997.

[37] "A No on Taxes," *Washington Post National Weekly Edition*, July 19-26, 1999.

[38] "Counting Their Chickens," *The Economist*, February 16, 1999.

[39] CBO, *The Economic and Budget Outlook: Fiscal Years 1999 - 2008*, January 1998, p. *xv*.

[40] James K. Glassman, "Your Guess is as Good as Theirs," *U.S. News & World Report,* March 3, 1997.

[41] "A Surplus of Wishful Thinking?," *U.S. News & World Report*, February 8, 1999.

[42] "Dividing the Spoils," *The Economist*, July 3, 1999.

[43] Timothy J. Penny and Steven E. Schier, *Payment Due, A Nation in Debt, A Generation in Trouble*, (Boulder, Colorado, Westview Press, 1996), p. 27.

[44] Gary S. Becker, "Don't Look for Tax Cuts From this Budget Surplus," *Business Week*, September 14, 1998.

[45] Daniel Schorr, "Rhinos and Tigers and Pork, Oh My!" *Christian Science Monitor*, April 17, 1998.

[46] Stephen Moore, "Not-So-Radical-Republicans," *Reason,* July 1998.

[47] "Talking Peace, Preparing for War," *The Economist.*

[48] "Why Not Sunset the House," *Washington Post National Weekly Edition*, June 22, 1998.

[49] Moore, "Not-So-Radical-Republicans."

[50] "Will Tons of Highway Pork Flatten the Balanced Budget?," *Business Week*, April 13, 1998.

[51] "Piling Up the Pork," *Washington Post National Weekly Edition*, April 6, 1998.

[52] Ibid.

[53] "House Panel Approves Highway Bill," *Washington Post*, March 25, 1998.

[54] "Will Tons of Highway Pork Flatten the Balanced Budget?," *Business Week.*

[55] "Growth Without End, Amen?," *National Review*, March 7, 1994.

[56] David A. Stockman, *The Triumph of Politics*, (New York, Harper & Row, 1986), p. 385.

[57] Moore, "Not-So-Radical-Republicans."

[58] David A. Stockman, *The Triumph of Politics*, (New York, Harper & Row, 1986), p. 385.

[59] Senate Testimony May 18, 1995.

[60] "Have the People Lost Their Voice?," *Washington Post National Weekly Edition*, June 28, 1999.

[61] Robert J. Samuelson, "Freedom From Politics," *Washington Post National Weekly Edition,* December 7, 1998.

[62] "Politics Brief: Is There a Crisis?" *The Economist*, July 17, 1999.

[63] Penny and Schier, *Payment Due, A Nation in Debt, A Generation in Trouble*, p. 101.

[64] "A Case For Cutting Pork," *Business Week*, April 27, 1998.

[65] Ibid.

[66] "Government Cost Review," *The Public Purpose*, Wendell Cox Consultancy, April 1998.

[67] Ibid.

[68] Stephen Goldsmith, "Can-Do Unions," *Policy Review*, March - April 1998.

[69] Ibid.

[70] "Philadelphia Mayor Ed Rendell: 1996 Municipal Leader of the Year," *American City and County*, November 1, 1996.

[71] CBO, *The Economic and Budget Outlook: Fiscal Years 1999-2008*, January 1998, p. 48.

[72] "Wisconsin's Welfare Miracle," *Policy Review*, March - April 1997.

[73] Ibid.

[74] "Going Their Own Ways," *Washington Post national Weekly Edition*, February 12-18, 1996.

[75] Ibid.

[76] GAO, *Federal User Fees: Some Agencies Do Not Comply With Review Requirements*, June 1998, p. 7.

[77] "Firing Up a Black Market," *Business Week*, May 25, 1998.

[78] *Final Report to the President*, Bipartisan Commission on Entitlement and Tax Reform, January 1995, p. 7.

[79] "Shedding Light on Damaged DNA," *Business Week*, June 8, 1998.

[80] Gary S. Becker, "Uncle Sam Should Stay Away from Wall Street," *Business Week*, February 8, 1999.

[81] "How Not to Fix Social Security," *Business Week*, March 23, 1998.

[82] "State of the States: Social Security Opt-Out Update," *Policy Review*, July-August 1998.

[83] Ibid.

[84] Estimated 1998 personal consumption expenditures based on a four-percent growth rate over the $5.4 trillion reported for the first quarter of 1997.

[85] GAO, *Tax Administration: Potential Impact of Alternative Taxes on Taxpayers and Administrators*, January 1998, p. 112.

[86] Ibid., p 109.

[87] David S. Broder, "The Payroll Crunch, *Washington Post National Weekly Edition*, May 20-26, 1996.

[88] "The Dollar's Coming U-Turn," *Business Week*, July 6, 1998.

[89] Ibid.

[90] Estimated 1998 state expenditures based on four-percent annual growth from 1995 expenditures of $837 billion.

[91] GAO, *Tax Administration: Potential Impact of Alternative Taxes on Taxpayers and Administrators*, January 1998, p. 107.

[92] "Morning in America, 1998-Style," *Business Week*, May 4, 1998.

[93] Gary S. Becker, "Why the Dole Plan Will Work," *Business Week*, August 26, 1996.

[94] Paul Craig Roberts, "Time to Cut Government a Smaller Slice of the Pie, *Business Week*, October 14, 1996.

[95] "Yes, Stupid, It's the Economy—But Nobody Controls It," *Washington Post National Weekly Edition*, May 13-19, 1996.

[96] "Gary S. Becker, "What's Wrong With a Centralized Europe? Plenty," *Business Week*, June 29, 1998.

[97] Ibid.

[98] "Fewer Welfare Recipients, More Spending on Them," *Washington Post National Weekly Edition*, February 16, 1998.

[99] "States Ante Up for Workfare," *Business Week*, July 6, 1998.

[100] "Does Welfare Act As A Magnet?" *Business Week*, February 12, 1996.

[101] "Do Immigrants Chase Benefits?" *Business Week*, December 1, 1997.

[102] "Cox Reports," *Reason*, August/ September 1999.

[103] "The Americans with Minor Disabilities Act," *U.S. News and World Report*, July 6, 1998.

104 GAO, *Adults with Severe Disabilities: Federal and State Approaches for Personal Care and Other Services*, May 1999, p. 2.
105 "The Real Roosevelt Legacy," *Newsweek*, October 14, 1996.

INDEX